LIBRARY OF HEBREW BIBLE/
OLD TESTAMENT STUDIES

733

Formerly Journal for the Study of the Old Testament Supplement Series

Editors
Laura Quick, Oxford University, UK
Jacqueline Vayntrub, Yale University, USA

Founding Editors
David J. A. Clines, Philip R. Davies and David M. Gunn

Editorial Board
Sonja Ammann, Alan Cooper, Steed Davidson, Susan Gillingham,
Rachelle Gilmour, John Goldingay, Rhiannon Graybill, Anne Katrine
Gudme, Norman K. Gottwald, James E. Harding, John Jarick, Tracy Lemos,
Carol Meyers, Eva Mroczek, Daniel L. Smith-Christopher, Francesca
Stavrakopoulou, James W. Watts

THE ANIMALISING AFFLICTION OF NEBUCHADNEZZAR IN DANIEL 4

Reading Across the Human–Animal Boundary

Peter Joshua Atkins

LONDON • NEW YORK • OXFORD • NEW DELHI • SYDNEY

T&T CLARK
Bloomsbury Publishing Plc
50 Bedford Square, London, WC1B 3DP, UK
1385 Broadway, New York, NY 10018, USA
29 Earlsfort Terrace, Dublin 2, Ireland

BLOOMSBURY, T&T CLARK and the T&T Clark logo are trademarks of
Bloomsbury Publishing Plc

First published in Great Britain 2023

A catalogue record for this book is available from the British Library.

Library of Congress Control Number: 2022947481

ISBN: HB: 978-0-5677-0619-5
        ePDF: 978-0-5677-0620-1

Series: Library of Hebrew Bible/Old Testament Studies, volume 733
ISSN 2513-8758

Typeset by RefineCatch Limited, Bungay, Suffolk

To find out more about our authors and books visit www.bloomsbury.com
and sign up for our newsletters.

CONTENTS

ACKNOWLEDGEMENTS

The final stages of this book were written during several months of national lockdown restrictions in the UK enacted as a response to the COVID-19 pandemic in 2020. Aside from forcing me to work from home, this situation also meant many people experienced a prolonged period of social isolation, increased pressures upon their mental health, and began to appear progressively more unkempt due to the closure of barbers and hairdressers. It was impossible not to recognize the similarity between the effects of this contemporary situation and the affliction of Nebuchadnezzar described in Daniel 4. While it may have taken divine intervention for Nebuchadnezzar's life to be restored, I hope it will not be as difficult for people to begin returning to their normal lives in our current context.

My doctoral thesis, upon which this book is based, would not have been possible without the generous financial support I have received from both the Bible Society and the Theology and Religious Studies department at the University of Chester. I have benefitted in a variety of other ways from my time at Chester's TRS department and have appreciated sharing many encouraging academic conversations with both Liam Metcalf-White and Helen Thomas. I am also grateful for numerous valuable contributions and questions about my work from various members of staff at the department, particularly to Prof. David Clough whose theological work on animals has significantly affected my own thought. However, my work owes its biggest academic debt to the huge amount of tireless and generous support from my principal doctoral supervisor: Dr Matthew A. Collins. He has seemingly never been too busy to offer guidance and suggestions on the topic and thrust of my work, and such was his keen interest in supporting me throughout my doctoral journey that we would often spend several hours during our supervision meetings discussing the complexities and difficulties associated with my work. It was an absolute pleasure to have such a congenial supervisor throughout the process of writing and editing this work. The finished piece owes an immeasurable debt to his critical insight and suggestions.

Since completing the written doctoral thesis, this book has undergone various changes and significant improvements. My PhD examiners, Prof. Paul Middleton and Dr Casey Strine, proved to be valuable conversation partners who helped me to further refine and articulate my argument. I would also like to express my gratitude to Prof. Laura Quick and Prof. Jacqueline Vayntrub for accepting my book into this series, and for the anonymous peer-reviewers whose comments have improved the scope and presentation of this book. I am also grateful for the communication and work put in by the editorial staff at Bloomsbury, particularly Lucy Carroll, Lily McMahon, and Dominic Mattos. Despite all these positive influences upon my work, any errors are, of course, my own.

I would also like to thank my good friend Marco Condorelli, who has been a trusty companion throughout the process of completing our respective theses. I have also valued my time working at Chester Cathedral where the good humour of various colleagues was always a welcome distraction from my research. I extend particular thanks to James Gillespie who has steadfastly encouraged me over the past several years, especially during difficult patches along the way.

I am particularly grateful for the support of my parents, Terry and Nick Atkins. I have been fortunate to have parents who always encouraged my own curiosity about animals and fostered my interest and understanding of biblical texts. No doubt it is from them that I first heard the narrative in Daniel 4. I am also grateful for my brother and sister-in-law, Jon and Jo Atkins-Potts, who have both carefully proofread my work at various stages. However, my final expression of appreciation is reserved for my partner, Jenn Burlingame, who has seemingly made it their mission to support me as much as possible over the last four years. Whether it has been listening to my lectures rehearsed from behind a clothes drying rack, or participating in "covert" operations to identify and copy obscure journal articles before libraries were locked down, I could not have brought this book to completion without them. Such as it is, I dedicate this study to them.

ABBREVIATIONS

Θ	Theodotion
AB	Anchor Bible
ABAW	Abhandlungen der Bayerischen Akademie der Wissenschaften
AcOr	*Acta Orientalia*
ActAnt	*Acta Antiqua Academiae Scientiarum Hungaricae*
ACW	Ancient Christian Writers
AJSL	*American Journal of Semitic Languages and Literatures*
ANEM	Ancient Near East Monographs/Monografías sobre el Antiquo Cercano Oriente
ANET	Pritchard, James B., ed. *Ancient Near Eastern Texts Relating to the Old Testament*. 3rd ed. Princeton: Princeton University Press, 1969
ANF	*The Ante-Nicene Fathers*. Edited by Alexander Roberts and James Donaldson. 1885–1887. 10 vols. Repr., Peabody, MA: Hendrickson, 1994
AnSt	*Anatolian Studies*
AOAT	Alter Orient und Altes Testament
AOS	American Oriental Series
AOTC	Abingdon Old Testament Commentaries
ASJ	*Acta Sumerologica*
AUSS	*Andrews University Seminary Studies*
BASOR	*Bulletin of the American Schools of Oriental Research*
BCOTWP	Baker Commentary on the Old Testament Wisdom and Psalms
BDB	Brown, Francis, S. R. Driver, and Charles A. Briggs, *A Hebrew and English Lexicon of the Old Testament*. Oxford: Clarendon, 1907
BEATAJ	Beiträge zur Erforschung des Alten Testaments und des antiken Judentum
BETL	Bibliotheca Ephemeridum Theologicarum Lovaniensium
BGE	George, Andrew R. *The Babylonian Gilgamesh Epic: Introduction, Critical Edition and Cuneiform Texts*. 2 vols. Oxford: Oxford University Press, 2003
Bib	*Biblica*
BibS(F)	Biblische Studien (Freiburg, 1895–)
BIOSCS	*Bulletin of the International Organisation for Septuagint and Cognate Studies*
BKAT	Biblischer Kommentar, Altes Testament
BN	*Biblische Notizen*
BSOAS	*Bulletin of the School of Oriental and African Studies*
BZ	*Biblische Zeitschrift*
BZAW	Beihefte zur Zeitschrift für die alttestamentliche Wissenschaft
CAD	Gelb, Ignace J., et al., eds. *The Assyrian Dictionary of the Oriental Institute of the University of Chicago*. 21 vols. Chicago: The Oriental Institute of the University of Chicago, 1956–2010
CBQMS	The Catholic Biblical Quarterly Monograph Series

CDA	Black, Jeremy, Andrew George, and Nicholas Postgate, eds. *A Concise Dictionary of Akkadian.* 2nd ed. Santag Arbeiten und Untersuchungen zur Keilschriftkunde 5. Wiesbaden: Harrassowitz Verlag, 2000
CEJL	Commentaries on Early Jewish Literature
CHJ	*Cambridge History of Judaism* ed. William D. Davies and Louis Finkelstein. 4 vols. Cambridge: Cambridge University Press, 1984–2006
CM	Cuneiform Monographs
CMG	*Corpus Medicorum Graecorum.* 11 vols. (1908–). Cited according to volume, part, and page number
CO	*Ioannes Calvini, Opera Quae Supersunt Omnia* ed. Guilielmus Bum, Eduardus Cunitz and Eduardus Reuss. 59 vols. Vols 29–87 of *Corpus Reformatorum.* Brunswick: C.A. Schwetschke and Son, 1863–1900. Cited according to volume (CO 1 = CR 29) and column number
CSCO	*Corpus Scriptorum Christianorum Orientalium* ed. Jean Baptiste Chabot et al. Paris, 1903
CurBR	*Currents in Biblical Research*
DCB	*Dictionary of Christian Biography* ed. William Smith and Henry Wace. 4 vols. London: Murray, 1877–1887
DCH	*Dictionary of Classical Hebrew* ed. David J. A. Clines. 9 vols. Sheffield: Sheffield Phoenix, 1993–2016
DCLS	Deuterocanonical and Cognate Literature Studies
DJD	Discoveries in the Judaean Desert
EANEC	Explorations in Ancient Near Eastern Civilizations
EncJud	*Encyclopedia Judaica* ed. Fred Skolnik and Michael Berenbam. 2nd ed. 22 vols. Detroit: Macmillan Reference USA, 2007
ETCSL	*The Electronic Text Corpus of Sumerian Literature* ed. Jeremy A. Black, Graham Cunningham, Jarle Ebeling, Esther Flückiger-Hawker, Eleanor Robson, Jon Taylor and Gábor Zólyomi. Oxford 1998–2006 (http://etcsl. orinst.ox.ac.uk/)
FC	Fathers of the Church
FOTL	The Forms of the Old Testament Literature
GELS	*A Greek-English Lexicon of the Septuagint* by Takamitsu Muraoka. Leuven: Peeters, 2009
HDR	Harvard Dissertations in Religion
HSS	Harvard Semitic Studies
HUCA	*Hebrew Union College Annual*
ICC	International Critical Commentary
IDBSup	*The Interpreter's Dictionary of the Bible: Supplementary Volume* ed. Keith Crim. Nashville: Abingdon, 1962
IEJ	*Israel Exploration Journal*
ISBE	*International Standard Bible Encyclopedia* ed. Geoffrey W. Bromiley. Rev. ed. 4 vols. Grand Rapids: Eerdmans, 1979–1988
JAJSup	Journal of Ancient Judaism Supplements
JANES	*Journal of the Ancient Near Eastern Society of Columbia University*
JAOS	*Journal of the American Oriental Society*
Jastrow	Jastrow, Morris, comp. *A Dictionary of the Targumim, the Talmud Babli and Yerushalmi, and the Midrashic Literature with an Index of Scriptural Quotations.* London: Luzac: 1903

JBL	*Journal of Biblical Literature*
JCS	*Journal of Cuneiform Studies*
JETS	*Journal of the Evangelical Theological Society*
JHebS	*Journal of Hebrew Scriptures*
JNES	*Journal of Near Eastern Studies*
JNSL	*Journal of Northwest Semitic Languages*
JSJ	*Journal for the Study of Judaism in the Persian, Hellenistic, and Roman Periods*
JSJSup	Supplements to Journal for the Study of Judaism
JSOT	*Journal for the Study of the Old Testament*
JSOTSup	Journal for the Study of the Old Testament Supplement Series
JSP	*Journal for the Study of the Pseudepigrapha*
JSPSup	Journal for the Study of the Pseudepigrapha Supplement Series
JTS	*Journal of Theological Studies*
LEH	*Greek-English Lexicon of the Septuagint* ed. Johan Lust, Erik Eynikel and Katrin Hauspie. Rev. ed. Stuttgart: Deutsche Bibelgesellschaft, 2003
LHBOTS	The Library of Hebrew Bible/Old Testament Studies
Liv. Pro.	Lives of the Prophets
LSTS	The Library of Second Temple Studies
LXX	Septuagint
MC	Mesopotamian Civilizations
MDOG	*Mitteilungen der Deutschen Orient-Gesellschaft*
MSU	Mitteilungen des Septuaginta-Unternehmens
MT	Masoretic Text
NETS	New English Translation of the Septuagint
NIDNTT	*New International Dictionary of New Testament Theology* ed. Colin Brown. 4 vols. Grand Rapids: Zondervan, 1975–1978
NIDOTTE	*New International Dictionary of Old Testament Theology and Exegesis* ed. Willem A. VanGemeren. 5 vols. Grand Rapids: Zondervan, 1997
NPNF	*A Select Library of Nicene and Post-Nicene Fathers of the Christian Church* ed. Philip Schaff and Henry Wace. 28 vols. In 2 series. 1886–1889. Repr., Grand Rapids: Eerdmans, 1956
NRSV	New Revised Standard Version
OB	Old Babylonian
OBO	Orbis Biblicus et Orientalis
OG	Old Greek
OLP	*Orientalia Lovaniensia Periodica*
OrAnt	*Oriens Antiquus*
OTL	Old Testament Library
OTP	*Old Testament Pseudepigrapha* ed. James A. Charlesworth. 2 vols. New York: Doubleday, 1983/1985
OtSt	Oudtestamentische Studiën
PG	Patrologia Graeca [= Patrologiae Cursus Completus: Series Graeca] ed. Jacques-Paul Migne. 162 vols. Paris, 1857–1886
PL	Patrologia Latina [= Patrologiae Cursus Completus: Series Latina] ed. Jacques-Paul Migne. 217 vols. Paris, 1844–1864
PTMS	Pittsburgh Theological Monograph Series
RA	*Revue d'Assyriologie et d'archéologie orientale*

RB	*Revue biblique*
RevQ	*Revue de Qumran*
RIA	*Reallexikon der Assyriologie und Vorderasiatischen Archäologie* ed. Erich Ebeling et al. 15 vols. Berlin: De Gruyter, 1928–2018
SB	Standard Babylonian text of *The Gilgamesh Epic*
SBS	Stuttgarter Bibelstudien
SC	Sources chrétiennes. 600 vols. Paris: Cerf, 1943–
SCS	Septuagint and Cognate Studies
SFM	*The Sumerian Flood Myth*
SHR	Studies in the History of Religions
SJOT	*Scandinavian Journal of the Old Testament*
SPAW	*Sitzungsberichte der Preussischen Akademie der Wissenschaften*
STDJ	Studies on the Texts of the Desert of Judah
STVP	Studia in Veteris Testamenti Pseudepigrapha
TBC	Torch Bible Commentaries
TBN	Themes in Biblical Narrative
TCS	Texts from Cuneiform Sources
TDNT	*Theological Dictionary of the New Testament* ed. Gerhard Kittel and Gerhard Friedrich. Translated by Geoffrey W. Bromiley. 10 vols. Grand Rapids: Eerdmans, 1964–1976
TDOT	*Theological Dictionary of the Old Testament* ed. G. Johannes Botterweck, Helmer Ringgren and Heinz-Josef Fabry. Translated by John T. Willis et al. 16 vols. Grand Rapids: Eerdmans, 1974–2018
THB	*Textual History of the Bible* ed. Armin Lange and Emanuel Tov. 3 vols. Leiden: Brill, 2016–
ThH	Théologique Historique
TOTC	Tyndale Old Testament Commentaries
TS	*Theological Studies*
TSAJ	Texte und Studien zum antiken Judentum
TUGAL	Texte und Untersuchungen zur Geschichte der altchristlichen Literatur
UET	*Ur Excavation Texts*
UF	*Ugarit-Forschungen*
UUA	Uppsala Universitetsårsskrift
VT	*Vetus Testamentum*
VTSup	Supplements to Vetus Testamentum
WBC	Word Biblical Commentary
WO	*Die Welt des Orients*
WOO	Wiener Offene Orientalistik
WUNT	Wissenschaftliche Untersuchungen zum Neuen Testament
YNER	Yale Near Eastern Researches
YOSR	Yale Oriental Series, Researches
ZA	*Zeitschrift für Assyriologie*
ZAW	*Zeitschrift für die alttestamentliche Wissenschaft*

Chapter 1

INTRODUCTION

Animals pose a persistent threat to humans in the biblical book of Daniel. Within the various court narratives of Dan. 1–6, Daniel and his friends are troubled by the prospect of eating animals (Dan. 1:8–17), before Daniel himself braves an overnight stay in a den of lions (Dan. 6).[1] The apocalyptic visions in the second half of the book (Dan. 7–12) describe terrifying animals which appear to destroy and devour (Dan. 7), followed by a battling ram and goat (Dan. 8). Even the Additions to Daniel in the Greek versions portray Daniel's confrontation with a great dragon, and his second confinement in a lion's den (Bel and the Dragon [Dan. 14] 23–42). However, perhaps the most significant threat that animals pose to humanity in the book of Daniel is described in the fourth chapter.

1.1 The Animalising Affliction in Daniel 4

Daniel 4 contains a narrative about King Nebuchadnezzar of Babylon (seemingly meant to reflect the historical Nebuchadnezzar/Nebuchadrezzar II, who reigned 643–562 BCE), the second of his two dreams (cf. Dan. 2), and its subsequent enactment. One night, while sleeping in his palace, Nebuchadnezzar is troubled by a dream about a great tree that grows up over the whole world only to then be chopped down to a stump by order of 'a holy watcher' (Dan. 4:1–14 MT).[2]

---

1. There are a variety of ways to understand the genre of the Danielic tales (Dan. 1–6), though they are most commonly referred to as 'court tales'; for example, see John J. Collins, 'The Court-Tales in Daniel and the Development of Apocalyptic', *JBL* 94 (1975): 218–234; Susan Niditch and Robert Doran, 'The Success Story of the Wise Courtier: A Formal Approach', *JBL* 96 (1977): 179–193; Tawny L. Holm, *Of Courtiers and Kings: The Biblical Daniel Narratives and Ancient Story Collections*, EANEC 1 (Winona Lake, IN: Eisenbrauns, 2013).

2. The verse numberings of Dan. 4 here follow that of the Aramaic edition (MT), which noticeably varies from most English translations (e.g., NRSV) and from the Greek editions. For an overview of the different editions of Dan. 4, see Appendix A. For a presentation of the various comparative verse numberings of Dan. 4 in a textual synopsis, see Appendix B.

Nebuchadnezzar afterwards recounts his dream to Daniel, the only one of his wise courtiers who can interpret it, who reluctantly explains that the tree symbolizes the king himself who will leave the throne of Babylon for a period of seven years (Dan. 4:16–24 MT). A year passes until this dream is fulfilled and, after being announced by a heavenly voice, Nebuchadnezzar is driven out of his kingdom and into the wilderness (Dan. 4:25–30 MT). The narrative concludes at the end of a seemingly seven-year-long period after which Nebuchadnezzar acknowledges divine authority and is restored to his throne (Dan. 4:33–34 MT).

Perhaps the most remarkable aspect of the narrative is the exact imagery employed to describe the experience of the king when he is removed from his throne. During the period that he is absent from Babylon, Nebuchadnezzar is not merely exiled but also seems to experience a divinely appointed affliction. Over the course of the chapter, this affliction is described multiple times (Dan. 4:11–14; 20–23; 29; 30 MT) and is repeatedly expressed using animalising imagery. Within the dream itself, the watcher commands that Nebuchadnezzar's 'heart be changed from that of a human, and let the heart of an animal be given to it' (Dan. 4:13 MT).[3] The heavenly voice pronounces that 'from humanity you will be driven out, and with the animals of the field is your dwelling, they will feed you grass like animals' (Dan. 4:29 MT) and this is fulfilled in later events as the king 'was driven out and he was eating grass like oxen and his body was wet from the dew of the heavens, until when his hair grew long like that of eagles and his nails were like those of birds' (Dan. 4:30 MT). The experience of Nebuchadnezzar in exile thus seems to be described as a form of animalising affliction.

Nonetheless, while it is plain that the king's affliction will involve him resembling an animal in some way, the degree to which he actually *becomes* an animal is less clear. Nebuchadnezzar's unusual condition has intrigued numerous subsequent readers and, amongst the variety of explanations for the narrative events, has provoked two predominant lines of interpretation which attempt to clarify how best to understand it. First, there is a long interpretative history of commentators who understand this affliction as a physical metamorphosis whereby the king is considered to have actually changed shape into an animal and assumed bestial form. This has typically been countered by a second set of interpretations which explicitly deny a physical metamorphosis and consider the text in alternate ways which preclude any meaningful animal transformation of the king. These commentators tend to state that Nebuchadnezzar merely resembled or behaved *like* an animal, rather than transforming into one. The question of a physical

---

3. These quotations are all taken from the Aramaic edition (MT) of Dan. 4. All subsequent translations of Dan. 4 are my own unless otherwise specified. The texts and my translations of all the principal editions of Dan. 4 are provided in full in Appendix B and these various editions will be discussed at some length in chapters 3 and 5. English translations of non-Danielic biblical texts throughout this study are, unless otherwise specified, taken from the NRSV.

metamorphosis of Nebuchadnezzar into an animal has thus been a key interpretative struggle for those who seek to explicate the narrative of Dan. 4 and has never been satisfactorily resolved.

1.2 Note on Terminology

This struggle over understanding Nebuchadnezzar's animalising affliction constitutes the starting point for the present study. In what follows, I use particular phrases in an attempt to carefully distinguish between different understandings of Nebuchadnezzar's condition in Dan. 4. While 'animalising affliction' is used as a general term to refer to the condition experienced by Nebuchadnezzar as portrayed in the Danielic narrative, I use the phrase 'metamorphosis' to refer to a particular kind of animalising affliction, one which involves a person's change of *physical form* from one creature (i.e., human) into another (i.e., animal). In the context of Dan. 4, a metamorphosis would therefore indicate that Nebuchadnezzar somehow physically transforms into an animal, whether wholly or partially. This is the kind of change which characterises the first traditional interpretative trend about Nebuchadnezzar's exile in Dan. 4. Finally, I use the term 'animal transformation' more broadly to describe any form of animalising affliction which involves a change of *category* whereby an individual can be effectively referred to or reclassified as an animal and no longer as a human. This transformation may be understood in various ways and may or may not involve a physical change. In this context it should be noted that the second traditional interpretative trend about the king's affliction in Dan. 4 tends to deny *any* kind of animal transformation in the text.

1.3 Trajectory of this Study

A major aspect of the narrative in Dan. 4 is the animalising imagery employed to describe the affliction received by Nebuchadnezzar when he is driven from his throne, and this has spawned a division between two principal lines of interpretation which attempt to clarify how to understand this imagery. The first typically advocates reading the narrative so that Nebuchadnezzar undergoes a type of physical metamorphosis into an animal form; the second line of interpretation encompasses diverse ways of reading the text that specifically preclude or deny an animal transformation of the king. This study addresses such bifurcation of interpretative opinion about Nebuchadnezzar's affliction, examining why such interpretation is so divided and demonstrates ultimately how neither of these traditional interpretations best reflect the narrative events in Dan. 4.

First, in chapter 2, I survey the range of previous interpretations of Nebuchadnezzar's animalising affliction that are concerned with the question of a possible physical metamorphosis. I demonstrate how such interpretations can be grouped broadly into these two general tendencies: those which conclude the king physically metamorphosed into animal; as well as those seeking to preclude any animal transformation in the narrative. I will describe how these two main interpretative tendencies have varied over time and attempt to explain both how and why these different interpretations have developed at different time periods.

In chapter 3, I examine in detail the various texts and forms of the narrative to show how metamorphic interpretations of Dan. 4 are largely reliant upon later developments within the textual tradition and are not supported by the earliest edition of Nebuchadnezzar's animalising affliction. I investigate potential source material for the narrative and conclude there is no evidence that the king's affliction was portrayed as a physical metamorphosis in such documents. I then outline the principal textual editions of Dan. 4 and, while I propose an explanation for how the metamorphic line of interpretation may have developed, I argue that the primary edition of Nebuchadnezzar's animalising affliction contains no substantive reason to suggest the king underwent a physical metamorphosis here either.

However, while the various editions of Dan. 4 seem to contain no explicit evidence that a metamorphosis was ever intended, I go on to show that it is equally inadequate to state that the king does not undergo an animal transformation at all. Turning to the wider ancient Near Eastern context of the Danielic narrative, in chapter 4 I examine a range of ancient Mesopotamian texts which appear to conceive of specific divine–human–animal boundaries that are governed by the possession of certain divine characteristics (wisdom and immortality). Through this examination, I demonstrate how this example of a Mesopotamian conception of the human–animal boundary is indicated primarily in relation to the possession or lack of the divine characteristic of wisdom.

Finally, in chapter 5, I build a case that such divine–human–animal boundaries can also be detected within Dan. 4. Demonstrating how various Hebrew Bible and Second Temple Jewish texts appear to reflect the same conceptual boundaries, I argue that the narrative in Dan. 4, through the king's loss of reason, in fact represents a far more significant categorical change from human to animal than has hitherto been recognized. This study therefore demonstrates that both traditional readings of Nebuchadnezzar's animalising affliction are inadequate. Read instead in the context of this wider ancient Mesopotamian worldview, the narrative of Dan. 4 describes a more subtle yet much more profound crossing of the human–animal boundary, one which may further constitute an essential undoing and reversal of Genesis 3.

Chapter 2

THE ISSUE OF AN ANIMAL METAMORPHOSIS: INTERPRETATIONS OF DANIEL 4

As has been described previously, Daniel 4 has spawned a debate about how the narrative should be interpreted. The issue of a possible metamorphosis of King Nebuchadnezzar seems to have plagued Dan. 4 almost from the period of the first commentary on the book. This recurring understanding of the chapter has also caused issues for those commentators who seem to be significantly troubled by such interpretations. This chapter will survey the main interpretations that have fuelled the idea that Nebuchadnezzar metamorphosed, attempt to explain how and why these interpretations may have originated and developed, and examine the response these interpretations elicited among other commentators who argue against an animal transformation.

Notable previous work on the reception and interpretation of Dan. 4 has been carried out by both David Satran and Matthias Henze.[1] These studies focused on understanding different interpretations of Nebuchadnezzar's affliction at specific points (Satran analysed early Jewish and Christian interpretations, whereas Henze examined early Rabbinic and Syriac exegesis). However, these studies both focus on the reception of Dan. 4 more generally and neither explicitly focus on the question of Nebuchadnezzar's supposed metamorphosis. Additionally, neither of these surveys of interpretation continue into the medieval period or beyond. More recently Bernd Roling has examined interpretations of Nebuchadnezzar's transformation, though he focuses primarily on the early modern period and does not take note of Jewish or Syriac exegesis.[2] Thus, while portions of this chapter draw upon all their work, it will also expand upon their observations and

---

1. David Satran, 'Early Jewish and Christian Interpretation of the Fourth Chapter of the Book of Daniel' (PhD diss., Hebrew University, 1985); and Matthias Henze, *The Madness of King Nebuchadnezzar: The Ancient Near Eastern Origins and Early History of Interpretation of Daniel 4*, JSJSup 61 (Leiden: Brill, 1999), 101–202.

2. Bernd Roling, *Physica Sacra: Wunder, Naturwissenschaft und historischer Schriftsinn zwischen Mittelalter und Früher Neuzeit*, Mittellateinische Studien und Texte 45 (Leiden: Brill, 2013).

conclusions. This is therefore the first attempt to trace a supposed metamorphosis in interpretation of Dan. 4 from the early post-biblical period to modern scholarship.

This survey has restricted its scope to those interpreters who seem explicitly interested in the animalising affliction of Nebuchadnezzar himself. It is not an exhaustive survey of such interpretations; rather it serves to illustrate the general views, trends and opinions about Nebuchadnezzar's affliction in Dan. 4 and focuses particularly on comments that address whether or not this affliction is a form of metamorphosis.[3] This survey is not restricted in scope to those who have self-consciously attempted to write a commentary on Dan. 4. Instead, I have included a range of individuals who have commented upon this Danielic narrative and who have thereby addressed the nature of Nebuchadnezzar's affliction. This means there are a range of different people included as part of this survey, and quotes are taken from texts which are both intended as a commentary on the Bible and also texts which may generally be classified in a different genre and so only refer to Nebuchadnezzar's affliction secondarily. By nature of the discipline and the time period covered the commentators upon this passage are somewhat limited in terms of geographic and gender distribution, though I have endeavoured to maintain as much diversity as I can both in tradition and across time.

2.1 Penitential Metamorphosis (Second–Fourth Century CE)

One of the first trends in interpreting the affliction of Nebuchadnezzar can be found in comments offered by the early North African Christian author Tertullian (*ca.* 155–*ca.* 240 CE). While the first extant Christian commentary on Daniel was written by Hippolytus of Rome around 204 CE, Tertullian wrote two treatises which refer to Dan. 4 that are commonly dated 198–203 CE.[4] Entitled 'On Penitence' (*De paenitentia*) and 'On Patience' (*De patientia*), these treatises were written at a similar time and are linked in both their ecclesiastical content and their sermonic format.[5]

Tertullian remarked most expansively upon Nebuchadnezzar's affliction in *De paenitentia*. This treatise addressed an important issue for the early church: post-baptismal sin. Tertullian's solution was to allow for a single second repentance

---

3. Not all those who comment on Dan. 4 are expressly concerned with addressing the issue of whether Nebuchadnezzar underwent an animal metamorphosis. For instance, Salvian of Marseille makes no reference to Nebuchadnezzar's transformation in his comments on Dan. 4; see Salvian of Marseille, *Ad ecclesiam* 1.51–63 (SC 176:174–184).

4. Satran, 'Early Jewish and Christian Interpretation', 210. For more comments on Tertullian's interpretation of Dan. 4, see Henze, *Madness of King Nebuchadnezzar*, 183–90.

5. Timothy D. Barnes, *Tertullian: A Historical and Literary Study* (Oxford: Clarendon Press, 1971), 117.

(*paenitentia secunda*) after baptism.[6] This was enacted through a process which Tertullian called *exomologesis* (ἐξομολόγησις).[7] He carefully elucidated this penitential practice which involved various actions including wearing sackcloth and ashes, prayer, fasting, weeping, lying at the feet of priests, and an outward confession of guilt (Tertullian, *De paenitentia* 9.3–5). Once Tertullian had defined this process, he finished by reemphasizing its importance by using two biblical examples: Nebuchadnezzar and Pharaoh.

> Will the sinner knowingly spurn exomologesis, which has been instituted by God for his restoration? that (*sic*) exomologesis which restored the king of Babylon to his royal throne? Long did he offer the Lord a sacrifice of penance, performing his exomologesis for seven squalid years, his nails growing wild like the talons of an eagle, his hair unkempt like the shaggy mane of a lion. Oh the blessedness of this harsh treatment! One whom men shunned with horror, God received! The ruler of Egypt, who on the contrary, pursuing the people of God, whom he had persecuted for a long time and long kept back from their Lord, fell upon them in battle and, after all the warnings of the plagues, he perished in the parted sea, passable to none but the chosen people, when the waters rolled back upon him. For he had rejected penitence and its instrument, exomologesis. (Tertullian, *De paenitentia* 12.7–8)[8]

In contrasted with Pharaoh, who rejected penance, Nebuchadnezzar serves as the perfect model for Tertullian's proposal of the practice of *exomologesis*. The king underwent humiliation and harsh discipline followed by restoration from God, a pattern which mirrors the penance and forgiveness for the repentant, baptized sinner.

Tertullian returns to Dan. 4 in the treatise *De patientia* in which he dealt with 'bodily patience' (*patientia corporis*) involving askesis, continence and martyrdom. This led him to the example of Nebuchadnezzar once again:

> Thus that Babylonish king, after being exiled from human form in his seven years' squalor and neglect, because he had offended the Lord; by the bodily immolation of patience not only recovered his kingdom, but – what is more to be desired by man – made satisfaction to God. (Tertullian, *De patientia* 13.4)[9]

---

6. Barnes, *Tertullian*, 120.

7. For an assessment of *exomologesis*, see Eric Osborn, *Tertullian, First Theologian of the West* (Cambridge: Cambridge University Press, 1997), 172; William P. Le Saint, trans., *Tertullian: Treatises on Penance*, ACW 28 (London: Longmans, 1959), 171–2 n.151.

8. The English translation is taken from: Le Saint, trans., *Tertullian: Treatises on Penance*, 36.

9. The English translation is taken from *ANF* 3:715.

Here, Tertullian uses Nebuchadnezzar as a proof that penance can satisfy (*satisfactio*) God, by fulfilling a compensatory function.[10] So closely is Dan. 4 bound up with Tertullian's thought on the subject of penance that it is possible the chapter directly influenced the creation of this penitential doctrine.[11] Therefore, in Tertullian's interpretation of Dan. 4, the king's affliction is understood as the primary example of the *exomologesis* a penitent must participate in. The extraordinary bestial affliction of Nebuchadnezzar is the discipline he must undergo for his extraordinary hubristic sin.[12]

However, by creating a penitent Nebuchadnezzar, Tertullian is required to advocate that the king's transformation was purely a physical change – 'being exiled from human form'. A person is required to be of sound mind in order to repent and take actions to satisfy God, thus Tertullian's entire doctrine of penitence is bound up with rationality. If Nebuchadnezzar lost his mind, then he would be unable to satisfactorily fulfil the penitential discipline and would not function as an example penitent. Brennan Breed has well suggested that a physical affliction in Dan. 4 is critical for Tertullian 'because he reads this episode as highlighting Nebuchadnezzar's repentance, which requires his mental capacities'.[13] In order to maintain the efficacy of his repentance, Nebuchadnezzar's mind must remain intact throughout his ordeal, so therefore Tertullian must view the transformation in purely physical terms.

Nevertheless, it is clear from some of his later writings that he stopped short of describing Nebuchadnezzar's affliction as a complete metamorphosis. In his treatise 'On the Soul' (*De anima*), Tertullian thoroughly refuted the possibility that a human may become an animal through reincarnation (*metensomatosis*), stating 'it is impossible for the human soul to pass into beasts' (Tertullian, *An.* 32.2).[14] Through discussing the differences between different animals and humans, he stated that '[n]o matter what elements may make up the human soul, I maintain that it could never be reborn into animals so contrary to its original nature' (Tertullian, *An.* 32.4). While his own comments on Dan. 4 seem to indicate he was open to a bodily

10. He is the first Christian to speak of penance as achieving this result; see Henze, *Madness of King Nebuchadnezzar*, 188.

11. Satran, 'Early Jewish and Christian Interpretation', 214. The Old Greek version of Dan. 4 seems to have been particularly influential for penitential interpretations. For discussion of this edition of Dan. 4 and its influence on later interpretations, see the later section in this book: §3.3.2.

12. For further discussion, see David Satran, 'Fingernails and Hair: Anatomy and Exegesis in Tertullian', *JTS* 40 (1989): 116–120 (120).

13. Carol A. Newsom with Brennan W. Breed, *Daniel: A Commentary*, OTL (Louisville, KY: Westminster John Knox, 2014), 155.

14. English translations of this text are from: Rudolph Arbesmann, Emily Joseph Daly and Edwin A. Quain, eds and trans, *Tertullian, Apologetical Works and Minucius Felix, Octavius*, repr., FC 10 (Washington, DC: Catholic University of America Press: 1985).

transformation from human to animal, the soul of a human was, for Tertullian, too different to that of an animal to be able to adapt to life in an animal body.

As the writings of Tertullian eventually came to influence other commentators, the penitential interpretation of Nebuchadnezzar's affliction developed until it becomes appropriate to categorise it as a physical metamorphosis.[15] This development took shape most prominently in the fourth century.[16] Paulinus of Nola (*ca.* 353–431 CE) is one theologian who adopted Tertullian's penitential approach to Dan. 4, as he stated Nebuchadnezzar 'stands as an exemplar of faith to us, so that we may fear to lose the kingdom within us by sinning, and remember to seek it again by repentance' (Paulinus of Nola, *Epist.* 23.20).[17] Nebuchadnezzar's affliction in the wilderness is understood as a penance which he must undergo to return to his kingdom. Just like Tertullian, this interpretation requires Paulinus to view Nebuchadnezzar's affliction as a physical one because the king needs to retain his mental faculties in order to repent:

> When the Assyrian king was condemned to the exile of a wild animal, his unshorn hair grew grievously stiff and bristled like a lion's mane. As a result, even in physical appearance he was changed into a wild beast, exiled not only from his kingdom but also from human feelings. His dilapidated hair was a lion's, his hooked claws a vulture's, his sensations and his food made him an ox; for since he had resembled many beasts in character, he was compelled to resemble more than one in his punishment. (Paulinus of Nola, *Epist.* 23.19)

Paulinus' description of Nebuchadnezzar's physical transformation seems more extravagant than Tertullian's and these physical changes form the key part of Paulinus' description of the king's affliction.

Possibly the most significant writer for proposing a penitential metamorphosis of Nebuchadnezzar, in the fourth century CE, was Cyril of Jerusalem. In his second Catechetical sermon (*ca.* 350 CE), Cyril attempted to explain why Nebuchadnezzar was afflicted:

> You have seen the magnitude of his evil deeds – now attend to the loving-kindness of God. [Nebuchadnezzar] was turned into a wild beast, he dwelt in the

---

15. Not all those who adopted Tertullian's penitential understanding of Dan. 4 proposed a physical metamorphosis. Pacian of Barcelona's interpretation, while referring to Nebuchadnezzar's *exomologesis*, neglects any mention of a physical metamorphosis; for example, see Pacian of Barcelona, *Paraenesis ad paenitentiam* 9.

16. It is curious that it took a couple of centuries for other Christian writers to really adopt Tertullian's penitential interpretation of Dan. 4. For discussion of this, see Satran, 'Early Jewish and Christian Interpretation', 215–220.

17. English translations of Paulinus' letters are taken from P. G. Walsh, trans., *Letters of St. Paulinus of Nola*, 2 vols., ACW 35–36 (New York: Paulist, 1966).

wilderness, he was scourged in order that he might be saved. He had claws like a lion, for he was a plunderer of the Sanctuary. He had a lion's mane, for he was a ravaging, roaring lion. He ate grass like an ox, for he was a brute beast, not recognizing Him who had given him the kingdom. His body was drenched with dew, because, having seen the fire quenched by the dew, he did not believe. (Cyril of Jerusalem, *Catecheses* 2.18)[18]

The important difference in Cyril's treatment of Dan. 4 is that instead of being the penance itself (as per Tertullian), the transformation of the king was a punishment through which Nebuchadnezzar was ultimately brought to repentance (e.g., 'he was scourged in order that he might be saved'). This is made more explicit in a variant recension of the same passage: 'he was turned into a wild beast, not so that he might perish, but that by repentance he might be saved' (*Catecheses* 2.18 [recension altera]). For Cyril, the transformation of the king was not a forced penance he must undergo, but is the means by which he will realize that he needs to repent.[19] Thus only after undergoing the affliction for a time did Nebuchadnezzar make 'penitence for what he had done, and recognised his own weakness, then God gave back to him the honor of his kingdom' (Cyril of Jerusalem, *Catecheses* 2.18).[20] This punishment stems from the notion of God's loving-kindness (φιλανθρωπια) which Cyril adopted in his sermon. God's kindness to Nebuchadnezzar was demonstrated in that, through this affliction, he was able to repent and be saved. Nebuchadnezzar's affliction is described by Cyril in purely physical terms as he takes on characteristics, qualities and actions of different animals. For Cyril, who is an advocate of the literal truth of miraculous transformations in scripture, the king has miraculously turned into a beast.[21] This description of Nebuchadnezzar's affliction thus provides compelling evidence for a physical penitential metamorphosis of the king in such early Christian writings.

2.2 Hybrid Metamorphosis (ca. Fourth Century CE)

The second major metamorphic understanding of events in Dan. 4 may be found in the *Vita Danielis*.[22] This short text is, along with twenty-two other *vita*, part of

---

18. Unless otherwise specified, English translations of Cyril's *Catecheses* are taken from David Satran, *Biblical Prophets in Byzantine Palestine: Reassessing the Lives of the Prophets,* Studia in Veteris Testament Pseudepigrapha 11 (Leiden: Brill, 1995), 87.

19. See Satran, *Biblical Prophets in Byzantine Palestine,* 88.

20. This English translation is taken from Satran, 'Early Jewish and Christian Interpretation', 225.

21. Elsewhere, Cyril of Jerusalem adamantly defends the transformations of Lot's wife and of Moses' rod; for example, see Cyril of Jerusalem, *Catecheses* 18.12. For a longer study of Cyril's use of scripture in these sermons, see Pamela Jackson, 'Cyril of Jerusalem's Use of Scripture in Catechesis', *TS* 52 (1991): 431–450.

22. Though traditionally dated to the Second Temple period, the finished extant text should be dated to the fourth century CE.

the larger work *Vitae Prophetarum* or Lives of the Prophets.[23] The evidence for this text is diverse and extant versions of Liv. Pro. are found in Latin, Syriac, Ethiopic, Hebrew, Arabic and Armenian; yet it is the Greek versions which scholars primarily study.[24] The various Greek manuscripts of Liv. Pro. are commonly classified into six recensions:[25]

1 *Epiphanius Prior* [EP¹], whose principal witness is the Codex Parisinus Graecus 1115. This manuscript is dated to 1276, is ascribed to Epiphanius of Cyprus, and is the recension known chiefly by scholars in the sixteenth and seventeenth centuries.
2 *Epiphanius Alter* [EP²], a second, shorter recension explicitly attributed to Epiphanius of Cyprus.
3 *Dorotheus* [Dor.], attributed to the third-century figure Dorotheus of Tyre.
4 *Recensio Anonyma* [An.], known primarily from the uncial manuscript Codex Marchalianus (which is often referred to by its siglum 'Q'). This Codex is widely dated no later than the sixth century, though the leaves containing Liv. Pro. seem to be additions and may be dated slightly later.[26] It is this recension which has been most valued by researchers as it is regarded as representing the earliest extant version of Liv. Pro. in Greek.[27]
5 A shortened recension preserved in the *scholia* to Theodoret of Cyrrhus and in the writings of Theophylact. This is sometimes assigned to Hesychius of Jerusalem.

23. The oldest Greek manuscript, the Codex Marchalianus, provides accounts of the lives of twenty-three prophets in total: Isaiah, Jeremiah, Ezekiel, Daniel, Hosea, Micah, Amos, Joel, Obadiah, Jonah, Nahum, Habakkuk, Zephaniah, Haggai, Zechariah, Malachi, Nathan, Ahijah, Joad, Azariah, Elijah, Elisha, and Zechariah son of Jehoiada. The exact number and order vary depending on the textual witness.

24. For examples of this treatment, see Douglas R. A. Hare, 'The Lives of the Prophets', in *OTP* 2:379–400 (379); and Satran, *Biblical Prophets in Byzantine Palestine*, 9. Both these scholarly works also provide translations of the Greek text alone.

25. Theodor Schermann, *Propheten- und Apostellegenden nebst Jüngerkatalogen des Dorotheus und verwandter Texte*, TUGAL 31.3 (Leipzig: Hinrichs, 1907), 2–43. For a critical edition of these recensions, see Theodor Schermann, ed., *Prophetarum vitae fabulosae indices apostolorum discipulorumque Domini Dorotheo, Epiphanio, Hippolyto aliisque vindicate*, Bibliotheca Scriptorum Graecorum et Romanorum Teubneriana (Leipzig: Teubner, 1907).

26. Satran, *Biblical Prophets in Byzantine Palestine*, 11.

27. Hare, 'Lives of the Prophets', 379. For in depth discussion of which are the chief witnesses, see Schermann, *Propheten- und Apostellegenden*, 2–43; Albert-Marie Denis, *Introduction aux pseudépigraphes grecs d'Ancien Testament*, STVP 1 (Leiden: Brill, 1970), 85–90; Satran, *Biblical Prophets in Byzantine Palestine*, 9–16.

6 The final recension, found in the Greek church tradition of the *menologia* and
   synaxaria.

These varied ascriptions post-date the text itself and neither Epiphanius, Dorotheus,
nor Hesychius should be seen as the original author of the work. It is possible that
the reason for the attribution to both Epiphanius and Dorotheus is due to these
figures' supposed familiarity with the Hebrew language.[28] According to the
superscription attached to Q, these 'lives' consist of 'the names of the prophets, and
where they are from, and where they died and how, and where they lie' (Liv. Pro.
superscription).[29] While this is the content of most of the 'lives', some include
extended material about these prophetic figures which is both legendary and
biographical in nature. It is this type of material that we find in the *Vita Danielis*
and it offers information that has no parallel in the canonical accounts of Daniel.

   Along with the rest of Liv. Pro., the *Vita Danielis* describes the origins and
eventual death of the prophet. However, other than this, the *Vita* is surprisingly
uninterested in the general exploits of the prophet Daniel. There is no mention of or
reference to Daniel's assessment of the writing on the wall (Dan. 5) nor of Daniel's
time in the lion's den (Dan. 6). Instead the text is almost solely about Nebuchadnezzar's
affliction in Dan. 4, and the relevant passage is quoted here in full:

> He prayed much for Nebuchadnezzar, at the entreaty of his son Baltasar, when he
> became a wild animal and beast of the field, so that he might not perish. His fore
> parts with the head were like an ox, and the feet with the hind parts like a lion.
> Concerning this mystery it was revealed to the holy man that [Nebuchadnezzar]
> had become a beast of the field because he was fond of pleasure and stiff-necked,
> and because those who belong to Beliar become like an ox under yoke. Tyrants
> have these [vices] in their youth, and in the end they become monsters, seizing,
> destroying, killing, and smiting.
>
>   Through divine revelation the saint knew that he was eating grass like an ox
> and that it became human food. It was also for this reason that Nebuchadnezzar,
> recovering a human heart after digestion, used to weep and honor the LORD,
> praying forty times each day and night. Behemoth used to come upon him, and
> he would forget that he had been a man; his tongue was taken from him so that
> he might not speak, and perceiving [this] he immediately wept; his eyes were like
> raw flesh from crying. For many were going out of the city and gazing at him.
> Daniel alone did not wish to see him, because he was in prayer for him the whole
> time of his changed condition; and he kept saying, 'He will become a man again',
> and they did not believe him.

---

28. Charles C. Torrey, *The Lives of the Prophets: Greek Text and Translation,* Journal of
Biblical Literature Monograph Series 1 (Philadelphia: SBL Press, 1946), 4.

29. The translation of the superscription of Codex Marchalianus (Q) is by Douglas
R. Hare, *OTP* 1:385.

Daniel made the seven years, which he called seven seasons, become seven months; the mystery of the seven seasons was accomplished in his case, for he was restored in seven months; during the six years and six months [remaining] he prostrated himself to the LORD and confessed his impiety, and after the forgiveness of his wickedness he restored to him the kingdom. He neither ate bread or meat nor drank wine as he made his confession, for Daniel had ordered him to appease the LORD with [a diet of] soaked pulse and greens. (Liv. Pro. 4.4–15)[30]

This depiction of the king's affliction seems reminiscent of the penitential Nebuchadnezzar suggested by the early Church Fathers. During the seven seasons, Nebuchadnezzar undertakes numerous spiritual exercises: prostration (ὑπόπτωσις), confession (ἐξομολόγησις) and abstinence from bread, wine and meat. Though the explicit inclusion of *exomologesis* should immediately remind us of the penitential practices proposed by Tertullian (see above), all these actions follow the pattern for penance in the early church.[31] Indeed, even the fact Daniel reduced the length of Nebuchadnezzar's affliction may reflect tendencies in the fourth-century church to mitigate harsh punishments.[32] These clear parallels have led to the establishment of a fourth-century date for the complete extant form of Liv. Pro. For example, the emphasis on both Nebuchadnezzar's physical metamorphosis and his sorrowful repentance only fully combined in fourth-century Christian literature and are not present in early Jewish interpretation.[33] While this does not preclude the fact that the *Vita* may rely on earlier Jewish tradition and have its roots in Second Temple Judaism,[34] David Satran concludes that 'the legend before us represents a thoroughly

30. Translated by Douglas R Hare: Hare, *OTP* 1:390, though I have divided the text into sections following: Satran, *Biblical Prophets in Byzantine Palestine*, 124. For a critical text, see Schermann, *Prophetarum vitae fabulosae*, 77–79. I have chosen to follow the text from manuscript Q of the *Recensio Anonyma* because it is seen by many as the oldest Greek text still extant and it is also the most accessible text to demonstrate how the *Vita* deals with Nebuchadnezzar's affliction.

31. Satran, *Biblical Prophets in Byzantine Palestine*, 89–91; and David Satran, 'Daniel: Seer, Philosopher, Holy Man', in *Ideal Figures in Ancient Judaism: Profiles and Paradigms*, ed. John J. Collins and George W. E. Nickelsburg, SCS 12 (Chico, CA: Scholars Press, 1980), 33–48 (39).

32. Satran, 'Early Jewish and Christian Interpretation', 355–356. For example, see Basil of Caesarea, *Epist.* 217.74, and John Chrysostom, *Ad Theodorum lapsum* 1.6.

33. Satran, *Biblical Prophets in Byzantine Palestine*, 81 and 86. For further discussion of some early Jewish interpretations of Nebuchadnezzar's metamorphosis, see the later section in this book: §2.5.

34. This is the period in which scholars had previously dated its composition; see Hare, 'Lives of the Prophets', 381 and Torrey, *Lives of the Prophets*, 11–12.

altered, indubitably Christian stage of development. The biblical chapter has been transformed into a fine expression of early Byzantine piety.'[35]

Nevertheless, while the *Vita* is clearly similar to the previous penitential interpretation, the text also takes the narrative down a different route and is distinctive in suggesting Nebuchadnezzar became a hybrid creature.[36] The *Vita* initially states the king 'became a wild animal [θηρίον] and beast [κτηνος]' (Liv. Pro. 4.4), which is later clarified by the more bizarre metamorphosis where '[h]is fore parts with the head were like an ox, and the feet with the hind parts like a lion' (Liv. Pro. 4.5). He thus became a lion/ox hybrid creature, with the lion representing the wild animal (θηρίον) and the ox representing the domestic beast (κτηνος). This hybrid interpretation of Nebuchadnezzar's affliction lacks any apparent parallel, yet the *Vita* offers an explanation for why the king appears this way.[37] His appearance like an ox was because 'he was fond of pleasure and stiff-necked, and because those who belong to Beliar become like an ox under yoke. Tyrants have these (vices) in their youth' (Liv. Pro. 4.6–7). The leonine appearance is explained as a reflection of the fact that in the end tyrants 'become monsters, seizing, destroying, killing, and smiting' (Liv. Pro. 4.7). In his youth, Nebuchadnezzar had formerly been yoked to pleasure thus his fore parts became those of an ox; later he became a cruel, vicious tyrant so his hind parts became leonine. This correspondence of both the love of pleasure with a bestial state, and the actions of a tyrant with a ferocious beast are traditional ones.[38] The *Vita* has thus depicted Nebuchadnezzar as physically metamorphosing into a hybrid animal in order to make his affliction reflect his moral degeneration. By transforming into a lion and an ox, the text of the *Vita* indicates the decline of Nebuchadnezzar from hedonistic slave to harsh tyrant.

The *Vita Danielis* is a uniquely significant point in the history of interpretation of Nebuchadnezzar's transformation due to its articulation of a physical hybrid metamorphosis. This text continued to be transmitted, translated and acknowledged by numerous later writers. Amongst them, it seems that Isidore of Seville omitted mention of the king's metamorphosis,[39] whereas a manuscript of the *Chronicle of*

---

35. Satran, *Biblical Prophets in Byzantine Palestine*, 96.

36. While Paulinus agreed Nebuchadnezzar changed into a beast, he only states he was likened to a lion and an ox. Instead the king became an indeterminate beast; see Paulinus of Nola, *Epist.* 23.20. Cyril describes Nebuchadnezzar as appearing like a lion, but he had no physical bovine features; see Cyril of Jerusalem, *Catecheses* 2.18.

37. It is possible this hybridity may also result from a conflation of the texts of Dan. 4 and Dan. 7:4; for example, see §3.3.2 below.

38. David Satran has shown how this logic is reflected in Greco-Roman literature; see Satran, *Biblical Prophets in Byzantine Palestine*, 82–85.

39. For example, whilst we might expect it, there is no reference to this in Isidore of Seville, *De ortu et orbitu partum*.

Jerahmeel preserves this hybrid transformation of Nebuchadnezzar.[40] There is not space here to go into further depth about the extent of the *Vita's* literary legacy, but its far-reaching influence will become evident later in this chapter.[41]

2.3 Antiochene Denial of Metamorphosis (Fourth–Fifth Century CE)

Not all early Christian interpreters agreed that Nebuchadnezzar underwent a physical metamorphosis in Dan. 4. An alternative interpretation of the king's affliction arose which denied that Nebuchadnezzar had transformed into an animal and suggested that he instead suffered with madness or insanity. Such an interpretation of Dan. 4 can be found in several early Christian writers; for example, the catena on Daniel contains comments by Ammonius of Alexandria who writes that Nebuchadnezzar 'was cast out of his realm as a result of having gone mad' (Ammonius of Alexandria, *In Danielem*, 4.30).[42]

However, this early line of interpretation reached its most complete form in the Antioch tradition.[43] Much has been written about a supposed school of thought and interpretation centred on early Christian figures around the city of Antioch.[44] The idea of such a school has traditionally been proposed, in part, due to the observation that these theological writers share certain methods of biblical

---

40. *Chronicles of Jerahmeel* 46. For an English translation, see Moses Gaster, *The Chronicles of Jerahmeel or, The Hebrew Bible Historiale* (London: Royal Asiatic Society, 1899), 205–207. For further discussion of this, see Satran, *Biblical Prophets in Byzantine Palestine*, 15–16 n. 33–34.

41. For more detailed discussion of the *Vita Danielis*, its different versions, and manuscript witnesses, see Satran, *Biblical Prophets in Byzantine Palestine*, 9–16; Lorenzo DiTomasso, *The Book of Daniel and the Apocryphal Daniel Literature*, STVP 20 (Leiden: Brill, 2005), 339–45.

42. This text is taken from the catena on Daniel; see Angelo Mai, ed., *Scriptorum Veterum Nova Collectio e Vaticanis Codicibus Edita*, 10 vols (Rome: Typis Vaticanis, 1825–38), 1.2.194. The English translation is taken from Satran, 'Early Jewish and Christian Interpretation', 263. The exact date for Ammonius is difficult to pinpoint. Mai situates him in the fifth century CE (Mai, *Scriptorum Veterum*, 1.1.xxxiiii), whereas a third-century date is also suggested; see Michael Faulhaber, *Die Propheten-Catenen nach römischen Handschriften*, BibS(F) 4.2.3 (Freiburg: Herder, 1899), 187–188.

43. For wider studies on biblical interpretation in the Antiochene tradition, see e.g. David S. Wallace-Hadrill, *Christian Antioch: A Study of Early Christian Thought in the East* (Cambridge: Cambridge University Press, 1982), 27–51; Robert C. Hill, *Reading the Old Testament in Antioch*, The Bible in Ancient Christianity 5 (Leiden: Brill, 2005).

44. For a summary of different views on the 'Antioch tradition' see Richard J. Perhai, *Antiochene Theōria in the Writings of Theodore of Mopsuestia and Theodoret of Cyrus* (Minneapolis: Fortress, 2005), 34–43. I have adopted the 'Centrist Approach' which Perhai also follows.

interpretation.[45] First, they seem to have placed somewhat more emphasis on the literal or historical sense of scripture; secondly, there is often thought to be some opposition to the allegorical interpretation favoured by the 'Alexandrian School';[46] and finally, the presence of biblical typologies is noticeable, particularly applied to Old Testament characters and Jesus. However, another common feature of Antiochene biblical interpretation is their assessment of Nebuchadnezzar's affliction in Dan. 4.

Of these Antiochene writers, the first to comment on Daniel was probably the fourth-century writer John Chrysostom (*ca.* 340–407 CE). In the homiletic text *Interpretatio in Danielem prophetam*, Chrysostom tackled the issue of Nebuchadnezzar's transformation and stated that 'he did not change form' (Chrysostom, *Interpretatio* [PG 56:219]).[47] He thus seems to specifically reject the idea that Nebuchadnezzar's affliction involved a metamorphosis. He also argued that Nebuchadnezzar retained his human soul because only then would the king be aware of what had happened to him and realize his awful state (Chrysostom, *Interpretatio* [PG 56:219]).[48]

Another writer in the same tradition was Polychronius, bishop of Apamea (d. 430 CE) who is considered one of the great Antiochene exegetes.[49] He addressed Dan. 4 chiefly in his fragmentary commentary on the book of Daniel and explained Nebuchadnezzar's condition as a form of mental affliction which his physical appearance merely reflected.[50] Polychronius suggested that it was due to this madness that Nebuchadnezzar was chained up: 'they constrained him with bonds and imprisoned him in chains, just as the band of bronze and iron (Dan. 4:12) indicates' (Polychronius, *In Danielem* 4.22).[51] The point at which Nebuchadnezzar lifts his eyes to heaven (Dan. 4:34) Polychronius interpreted as Nebuchadnezzar 'being set free from insanity' (Polychronius, *In Danielem* 4.30).

---

45. This summary is adapted from Adam M. Schor, 'Theodoret on the "School of Antioch": A Network Approach', *Journal of Early Christian Studies* 15 (2007): 517–562 (520–521).

46. Such a simple bifurcation is not so easy to maintain though as, at times, writers in both 'schools' shared similar interpretations. See Wallace-Hadrill, *Christian Antioch*, 29.

47. The English translation is my own.

48. There is considerable doubt over the authenticity of this homily's ascription to Chrysostom; see Otto Bardenhewer, *Geschichte der altkirchlichen Literatur*, 5 vols (Freiburg: Herder, 1913–1932), 3.337; and José A. de Aldama, *Repertorium Pseudochrysostomicum*, Documents, Études et Répertoires publiés par l'Institut de Recherche et d'Histoire des Textes 10 (Paris: Éditions du Centre National de la Recherche Scientifique, 1965), 203–204 (n. 545).

49. For an introduction to Polychronius, see Peter Bruns, 'Polychronius von Apamea: Der Exeget und Theologie', *Studia Patristica* 37 (2001): 404–412.

50. The text of Polychronius' commentary is provided in Mai, *Scriptorum Veterum*, 1.2.105–60.

51. English translations of this text are taken from Satran, 'Early Jewish and Christian Interpretation', 263.

Nevertheless, the most significant witness to the Antiochene interpretation of Dan. 4 may be found in the commentary by Theodoret of Cyrrhus who was born in Antioch around 393 CE and has been called 'the last great theologian' from the city.[52] In 423 CE he was appointed bishop of Cyrrhus and his commentary on Daniel was written about a decade later (*ca.* 433).[53] The way in which Theodoret approached his commentary was to initially outline his general assessment or 'hypothesis' (ὑπόθεσις) about the text of a chapter before turning to a detailed exegesis of the same section. In his hypothesis of Dan. 4, Theodoret stated that, as a result of the conquest of Jerusalem, God was angry with Nebuchadnezzar. After unsuccessful attempts to make Nebuchadnezzar amend his ways, God afflicted the king:

> [God] inflicted the troubles he had threatened; instead of punishing him straight out, he struck with insanity and dementia that arrogant mind that had dreamed of preternatural things. Then when he became wildly enraged, he caused him to be driven out. (Theodoret, *Comm. Dan.* 3.98)

The purpose of his affliction is to make the king recognize the eternal kingdom of God. In Theodoret's commentary, Dan. 4 thus forms the last in a sequence of narratives (Dan. 2–4) where Nebuchadnezzar is challenged to acknowledge this.[54] For Theodoret, the means by which this is finally achieved is by making the king insane.

This same understanding of Nebuchadnezzar's affliction is carried through in Theodoret's subsequent verse-by-verse exegesis. First, his assessment of the band of iron and bronze in Dan. 4:15 reflects previous Antiochene interpretations: 'having fallen victim to madness, insanity, and mental disease, being deranged in a frenzy and raging against everyone, he had to be kept in chains' (Theodoret, *Comm. Dan.* 4.12). For Theodoret, such was Nebuchadnezzar's insanity that it was necessary for him to be restrained. Furthermore, Theodoret explains the phrase 'I lifted up my eyes to heaven, and as soon as I did so, my reason returned to me' (Dan. 4:34) as basically meaning 'I was rid of my derangement and came to my senses, and immediately I became of sound mind again' (Theodoret, *Comm. Dan.* 4.31). Finally, in Theodoret's assessment, the physical ailments of the king also result from his insanity.

> *He ate grass like an ox.* It is typical of deranged people not only to say and do what is irrational and disorderly, but also to eat everything they come upon; even today you could see people possessed by demons acting and suffering this way.

52. Johannes Quasten, *Patrology*, 4 vols (Utrecht: Spectrum, 1950–1986), 3.536.

53. For discussion of the date of this commentary, see Robert C. Hill, ed. and trans., *Theodoret of Cyrus: Commentary on Daniel*, Writings from the Greco-Roman World 7 (Atlanta: SBL Press, 2006), xiii–xiv. The Greek text, along with the English translations used, are also found in this volume.

54. Satran, 'Early Jewish and Christian Interpretation', 254.

Not only was he in the habit of eating grass like an ox, however: *his body was dipped in the dew of heaven*: suffering from exposure, and struggling in his naked body with frost and heat, he inevitably took on a different colour. *Until his hair grew as long as lions' and his nails as long as birds'*: not grooming himself in the usual way or cutting his nails, over time he inevitably had hair and nails like this. (Theodoret, *Comm. Dan.* 4.30)

In all these comments, it is clear that for Theodoret, Nebuchadnezzar's affliction was purely mental or psychological. He became insane, and any physical changes that took place were merely a result of this.

While Polychronius' work has been left in a fragmentary state and debate still exists regarding the attribution of Chrysostom's homily, Theodoret's commentary stands as the most complete survivor of the Antiochene interpretative tradition on Dan. 4. Nevertheless, while his predecessors' work may pose difficulties for modern scholarly use, Theodoret clearly relied on these earlier interpretations and he was dependent on them in numerous places.[55] His assessment of Nebuchadnezzar's affliction is no exception and seems very reminiscent of their earlier comments. For example, both Theodoret and Polychronius interpret the band of iron and bronze as a chain to restrain the mad king; they both comment on Dan. 4:34 as a key verse for seeing a return of the king's sound mind; and both view the physical condition of the king as being the result of his insanity.[56] This close correspondence between these interpreters strongly suggests the Antiochene tradition fostered a particular interpretation of Dan. 4 to understand Nebuchadnezzar as stricken with insanity. It is plausible that this was a direct reaction to previous interpretations which elevated the bestial nature of his transformation.[57] Therefore, this Antiochene denial of an animal transformation may be an attempt to rebut both the penitential and hybrid interpretations discussed earlier.

This Antiochene interpretation of Nebuchadnezzar's affliction can potentially find further support from the writings of Jerome (*ca.* 331–420) who seems to have followed this Antiochene tradition of reading Dan. 4. Between 372 and 382 CE Jerome was regularly in Antioch, and this experience appears to have particularly influenced his biblical interpretation.[58] He adopted the Antiochene interest in the literal or plain sense of scripture over and above the allegorical or spiritual

55. For example, in his symbolic reading of the vision of the tree and in explaining the meaning of 'seven seasons' he seems to be relying upon Polychronius' established interpretation of these narrative elements. See Satran, 'Early Jewish and Christian Interpretation', 259–261.

56. Satran, 'Early Jewish and Christian Interpretation', 263–264. It is possible Eusebius' comments on Dan. 4 could also have influenced him; see Jean-Noël Guinot, *L'Exégèse de Théodoret de Cyr*, ThH 100 (Paris: Beauchesne, 1995), 713–722 and 746–748.

57. This is argued in Satran, 'Early Jewish and Christian Interpretation', 265.

58. See John N. D. Kelly, *Jerome: His Life, Writings, and Controversies* (London: Duckworth, 1975), 36–79.

sense.[59] Thus, when Jerome finished his commentary on Daniel in 407 CE, it is not surprising that he focused on the 'plain' sense of Dan. 4. He began his consideration of the chapter by stating: 'The narrative is clear indeed and requires but little interpretation' (Jerome, *Comm. Dan.* 4.1).[60] Nevertheless, the similarities between Jerome's interpretation and the Antiochene exegesis are more extensive. Jerome also views the king's affliction as insanity: 'Nebuchadnezzar was turned into a madman' (Jerome, *Comm. Dan.* 4.1); his explanation of the iron and bronze band is that 'all maniacs are bound with chains' (Jerome, *Comm. Dan.* 4.20); and he argues that in Dan. 4:34, Nebuchadnezzar 'had lost not his outward appearance but only his mind' (Jerome, *Comm. Dan.* 4.31). Not only does Jerome approach Dan. 4 in an Antiochene manner, he also highlights the same verses of the chapter to demonstrate the insanity of the king.[61] Thus good evidence seems to exist for proposing a conventional early exegesis of Dan. 4, that denied a physical metamorphosis, and read Nebuchadnezzar's affliction as a form of madness. This seems to be most developed in the Antiochene tradition and typically relies on a specific interpretation of both the band of metal in Nebuchadnezzar's vision as well as the king's recovery of his reason (Dan. 4:31 MT).

2.4 Multiple Metamorphoses (Fourth–Ninth Century CE)

The fourth century provides evidence of yet another interpretation of Nebuchadnezzar's affliction which is best found in the Syriac writings of the Persian Christian writer Aphrahat (*ca.* 270–345 CE).[62] Precious few facts are

59. Dennis Brown, *Vir Trilinguis: A Study in the Biblical Exegesis of Saint Jerome* (Kampen: Kok Pharos, 1992), 199.

60. English translations of this commentary are taken from Gleason L. Archer, ed. and trans., *Jerome's Commentary on Daniel* (Eugene, OR: Wipf and Stock, 2009). Jerome's focus on the literal sense is also to avoid Origen's apocalyptic interpretation; see Régis Courtray, *Prophète des temps derniers: Jérôme commente Daniel*, ThH 119 (Paris: Beauchesne, 2009), 329–330. For Jerome's general reluctance to resort to fantastical explanations for biblical imagery, see the discussion of his consideration of Isa. 13:21 in Peter J. Atkins, 'Mythology or Zoology: A Study on the Impact of Translation History in Isaiah 13:21', *Biblical Interpretation* 24 (2016): 48–59 (54–55).

61. For a similar argument, see Satran, 'Early Jewish and Christian Interpretation', 263–64.

62. Aphrahat's dates are taken from Robert Murray, *Symbols of Church and Kingdom: A Study in Early Syriac Tradition* (London: Cambridge University Press, 1975), 29. This section is indebted to the helpful discussions of Aphrahat's interpretation of Dan. 4 in Henze, *Madness of King Nebuchadnezzar*, 147–155; Matthias Henze, 'Nebuchadnezzar's Madness (Daniel 4) in Syriac Literature', in *The Book of Daniel: Composition and Reception*, ed. John J. Collins and Peter W. Flint, VTSup 83 (Leiden: Brill, 2001), 550–571 (550–556); Craig E. Morrison, 'The Reception of the Book of Daniel in Aphrahat's Fifth Demonstration, "On Wars"', *Hugoye: Journal of Syriac Studies* 7 (2017): 55–82.

known concerning his life but, between 337 and 345 CE, he composed twenty-three 'demonstrations' (Syriac: *taḥāṯâ*) or treatises. These *Demonstrations* are saturated with biblical citations and allusions. The book of Daniel is referenced several times, primarily in the fifth demonstration entitled 'On Wars', which addressed the precarious political situation at the time of 337 CE.[63] Christians in Persia were living under the threat of persecution by their Sasanian ruler Shapur II. The Christian Roman emperor Constantine could offer them some support, and Aphrahat was probably writing under the presumption that this assistance would be forthcoming.[64] The demonstration begins with an acknowledgement of the troubling situation for Christians under Shapur II ('evil is stirred up as regards the host that is gathered together by means of the evil and arrogant one who glories' [Aphrahat, *Demonstrations* 5.1]),[65] but also that God controls history ('The times were disposed beforehand by God' [Aphrahat, *Demonstrations* 5.1]), and whoever glorifies themselves will be brought low ('For every one that glories shall be humbled' [Aphrahat, *Demonstrations* 5.3.]). To prove this, Aphrahat refers to a number of biblical figures including Pharaoh, Sennacherib and Nebuchadnezzar.

The key section about Nebuchadnezzar's affliction occurs when Aphrahat begins to discuss the four beasts of Dan. 7 (Aphrahat, *Demonstrations* 5.15–20). He seems most interested in the first beast described in the book of Daniel as follows: '[t]he first was like a lion and had eagles' wings. Then, as I watched, its wings were plucked off, and it was lifted up from the ground and made to stand on two feet like a human being; and a human *heart* was given to it' (Dan. 7:4).[66] Aphrahat's comments on this beast are worth providing here in full:

> Now as to the first beast, he said concerning it, that it was like a lion, and it had the wings of an eagle. For the first beast was the kingdom of Babylon, which was like a lion. For thus Jeremiah wrote saying: – *Israel is a wandering sheep. The lions caused them to wander. First the king of Assyria devoured him. And this last was stronger than he, Nebuchadnezzar king of Babylon.* So Jeremiah called him a lion. And he said: – *He has the wings of an eagle.* For thus it is written that, when Nebuchadnezzar went out to the wilderness with the beasts he grew hair like (the plumage) of an eagle. And he said: – *I saw that its wings were plucked away and it stood upright upon its feet as a man, and a man's heart was given to it.* For

63. In *Demonstrations* 5.6, Aphrahat believed he was writing 648 years after Alexander the Great's reign ended (311 BCE). This puts the date of the fifth Demonstration *ca.* 337 CE.

64. Unbeknown to Aphrahat, Constantine had unfortunately already died; Timothy D. Barnes, 'Constantine and the Christians of Persia', *Journal of Roman Studies* 75 (1985): 126–136 (130).

65. The English translations here are taken from: *NPNF* 2/13:345-412.

66. I have amended the NRSV text so rather than 'human mind' it reads 'human heart'. This reflects the literal sense of the Aramaic term 'וֹלְבַב' and corresponds with the usage in the later quote from Aphrahat. This amendment is italicized.

first, in the vision of the image, he was compared to gold which is more precious than anything which is used in the world. So in the vision of the beasts he is compared to a lion which excels in its might all the beasts. And again he was compared to an eagle which surpasses every bird. Whatsoever was written about him was fulfilled in him. For the Lord said concerning him: – *I have placed a yoke of iron upon the neck of all the nations, and they shall serve the king of Babylon seventy years. And also the beasts of the desert and the birds of heaven have I given to him to serve him.* For since the king was like the head of gold, men served him as a king. And when he went out to the wilderness, the beasts served him as a lion. And when his hair was like (the plumage) of an eagle, the birds of heaven served him as an eagle. But when his heart was lifted up, and he knew not that the power was given to him from heaven, the yoke of iron was broken from the neck of men, and he went forth with the beasts, and instead of the heart of a king there was given him the heart of a lion. And when he was lifted up over the beasts, the heart of a lion was taken away from him, and there was given him the heart of a bird. And when wings grew upon him like those of an eagle, he exalted himself over the birds. And then his wings also were plucked away and there was given to him a humble heart. And when he knew that the Most High has authority in the kingdom of man, to give it to whomsoever He will, then as a man he praised Him. (Aphrahat, *Demonstrations* 5.16)

Aphrahat is primarily attempting to make sense of this strange first creature, but his efforts rely heavily on the narrative of Nebuchadnezzar's affliction in Dan. 4. He initially demonstrates the lion of Dan. 7:4 must allude to Nebuchadnezzar by providing a quotation from Jer. 50:17. So satisfied, he notices the specific parallel between the lion's aquiline wings and the likeness of both Nebuchadnezzar's hair and nails to an eagle in Dan. 4:30. Aphrahat also alludes to the head of gold in Dan. 2, and possibly a version of Jer. 28:14, which all together explain how Nebuchadnezzar was able to rule over humans, animals and birds. Thus, having prepared a portrait of the beast as representing the king, Aphrahat was ready to unveil his depiction of how Nebuchadnezzar's affliction played out. Once he went out to be with the wild animals, Nebuchadnezzar underwent a series of successive transformations – his kingly heart was exchanged for a lion's; his lion's heart was replaced with a bird's and he sprouted wings; his wings were plucked and he returned to a humble heart. For Aphrahat this was an important interpretative move, as he could then demonstrate that if leaders lay aside arrogance and humble themselves before God then they would keep their thrones. This is clearly his wish for Shapur II, but it also forms an important interpretative step in the history of interpretation of Nebuchadnezzar's affliction.[67] By interweaving the texts of Dan. 4 and Dan. 7:4, Aphrahat's Nebuchadnezzar undergoes not just one physical metamorphosis but several. This is a distinctive reading of Nebuchadnezzar's

---

67. For this message about Shapur, see Morrison, 'Reception of the Book of Daniel', 79.

affliction because his animal transformation occurs over multiple stages rather than as one simple event.

However radical it seems, this interpretation may actually precede Aphrahat. While the extent of the influence of Jewish traditions upon Aphrahat is debated, it is not unreasonable to detect parallels between his account of Dan. 4 and contemporary Jewish texts.[68] The manner in which Aphrahat links Isa. 14 with Nebuchadnezzar (Aphrahat, *Demonstrations* 5.4) is very similar to Mekilta of Rabbi Ishmael, Širata 6.[69] They both connect these biblical texts by using the Isaian passage to describe Nebuchadnezzar's pride, then follow it with Dan. 4 to relate his downfall for such hubris.[70] Both show how God reacts to those who oppose him, an assertion which is supported in both Aphrahat and the Mekilta by similar lists of other biblical figures including Pharaoh and Sennacherib. Also paralleled in earlier Jewish texts is Aphrahat's linkage of Nebuchadnezzar's affliction in Dan. 4 with the beast in Dan. 7. This same connection is clearly assumed in the debate between Rabbi Eleazar and Nahman in Leviticus Rabbah 13.5.[71] Here, the rabbis presuppose a relationship between both chapters of Daniel and use it as a means for understanding the affliction of Nebuchadnezzar.[72] While these Jewish texts do not contain the striking series of metamorphoses which Nebuchadnezzar goes through in Aphrahat's *Demonstrations*, they do contain sufficient parallels to suggest this interpretation of Dan. 4 perhaps originated in earlier rabbinic tradition.[73]

Aphrahat's contemporaries do not seem to have followed his interpretation of Dan. 4; however, the idea that Nebuchadnezzar experienced multiple metamorphoses made a reappearance in the ninth-century *Commentary on Daniel* by Ishodad of Merv. In his treatment of Dan. 4, Ishodad cites *The Fast of the House*

---

68. The Mekilta of Rabbi Ishamel may be a fourth-century CE text, although for different theories see Jay M. Harris, 'Midrash Halachah', in *The Late Roman-Rabbinic Period*, ed. Steven T. Katz, *CHJ* 4 (Cambridge: Cambridge University Press, 2006), 336–368 (337 n.1). Jacob Neusner has denied Aphrahat had any contact with rabbinic Judaism; see Jacob Neusner, *Aphrahat and Judaism: The Christian-Jewish Argument in Fourth-Century Iran*, Studia Post-Biblica 19 (Leiden: Brill, 1971), 187. For recent comments on this relationship, see Morrison, 'Reception of the Book of Daniel', 58–60.

69. A critical text can be found in: Jacob Z. Lauterbach, ed. and trans., *Mekhilta de-Rabbi Ishmael: A Critical Edition on the Basis of the Manuscripts and Early Editions with an English Translation, Introduction, and Notes*, 3 vols (Philadelphia: Jewish Publication Society, 1933–1935).

70. Matthias Henze convincingly argues for a link between Aphrahat and the Mekilta; see Henze, *Madness of King Nebuchadnezzar*, 124. He relies heavily on the previous work by Satran, 'Early Jewish and Christian Interpretation', 103.

71. A critical Hebrew text can be found in: Mordechai Margulies, ed. and trans., *Midrash Vayyikra Rabba*, 5 vols (New York: Jewish Theological Seminary of America, 1953–1960).

72. A more thorough discussion is in Henze, *Madness of King Nebuchadnezzar*, 153.

73. This is the conclusion of Henze, *Madness of King Nebuchadnezzar*, 147–155.

of Daniel — a homily purportedly by John Chrysostom. The attribution to Chrysostom is almost certainly inaccurate and the text instead seems to have been copied from a version of the Syro-Hexaplar.[74] Nevertheless, within it there is a lengthy passage on Nebuchadnezzar's affliction which provides a fascinating parallel to the interpretation offered by Aphrahat:

> He cast off the crown and horns grew (him). He left the bread untouched and ate herbs. He cast off the horns and molars grew (him). He left the herbs untouched and ate meat. He cast off the molars and grew talons. He left the meat untouched and ate fowl. He became an ox for two years and four months; then he became a lion for two years and four months; then he became an eagle for two years and four months, and he completed seven years — and seven times passed over him. He lifted up his eyes toward heaven and his reason returned to him. So he cast away the wings and the talons and became entirely human. (Ishodad of Merv, *Commentary on Daniel*, 4:32)[75]

The metamorphosis depicted here is, if anything, more elaborate than that which Aphrahat provides. Nebuchadnezzar now travels between the forms of four different creatures (human, ox, lion and eagle). These different stages are further distinguished by the specific physical features he adopts for each one (crown, horns, molars and talons), and by the diet he must follow while in each form (bread, herbs, meat and fowl). While the exact provenance of this text is unknown, at the very least it does demonstrate the existence of another Christian Syriac source in the ninth century which depicted Nebuchadnezzar's affliction as a series of metamorphoses.

If it were not for this second-hand reference through Ishodad of Merv there would be no evidence of other Christian commentators adopting this interpretative strategy for Dan. 4. However, good evidence exists that this was adopted by at least some Jewish commentators. The rabbi and biblical exegete Saadia Gaon (*ca.* 882– 942) provided a short summary of three different interpretations of the events of Dan. 4 in his commentary on Daniel.[76] One of these reflects the same tradition of multiple metamorphoses:

> At present we need to relate the incident that happened to Nebuchadnezzar. Because many think that from a human being he was altered into an animal.

---

74. Ceslas Van den Eynde, *Commentaire d'Išo'dad de Merv sur l'Ancien Testament: V. Jérémie, Ézéchiel, Daniel*, 2 vols, CSCO 328–329, Scriptores Syri 146–147 (Leuven: Peeters, 1972), xvi, xx; and Satran, 'Early Jewish and Christian Interpretation', 2:266.

75. Critical text is in: Van den Eynde, *Commentaire d'Išo'dad de Merv*, 1:125f. The English translation is taken from Henze, *Madness of King Nebuchadnezzar*, 140.

76. The English translations used, and also a critical edition, of Saadia Gaon's commentary are found in Joseph Alobaidi, ed. and trans., *The Book of Daniel: The Commentary of R. Saadia Gaon: Edition and Translation*, Bible in History 6 (Oxford: Peter Lang, 2006).

Others added that he was altered into a female in order to be subjected, moreover, to the humiliation of the weakness. Others went further to say that he changed from one person to another in every year, every month or every day. (Saadia Gaon, *Commentary on Daniel* [Alobaidi, 165])

Saadia Gaon's comments provide additional evidence that this multiple metamorphoses interpretation was at least still being read in the ninth century and, furthermore, brings into clearer focus the fact that this was not purely a Syriac Christian interpretation, but was familiar to Jewish commentators as well.

2.5 Conscious/Unconscious Metamorphosis (ca. Fifth–Thirteenth Century CE)

Other interpretative traditions, which Saadia Gaon made reference to, seem to be evidenced solely in Jewish texts. The perceived connection between Dan. 4 and Dan. 7 has already been noted and, while helpful for illuminating who the first beast is in Dan. 7 (as per Aphrahat), it poses a problem for interpreting Nebuchadnezzar's affliction in Dan. 4. This connection thus led to two different, yet related, interpretations and both are illustrated in Lev. Rab. 13.5 (*ca.* fifth–sixth century CE):[77]

> Rabbi Eleazar said: It was completely transformed into a lion, but its mind was not affected, as it is written, 'and it was given the mind of a man' (Dan. 7:4). Rabbi Samuel bar Nahman said: Its mind as well was transformed, as it is written, 'Let his mind be altered from that of a man [and let him be given the mind of a beast]' (Dan. 4:13). (Lev. Rab. 13.5)[78]

In their discussion it is clear that the conflation of these two chapters is not altogether successful and the text of Dan. 7:4 appears to conflict with the passage in 4:13. This creates a dilemma: either Nebuchadnezzar had a human mind during his affliction and was conscious (following Dan. 7:4) or he was given an animal mind and was unconscious of his predicament (following Dan. 4:13). Interestingly, there is no debate about whether Nebuchadnezzar physically changed or not. This unspoken assumption of the king's metamorphosis is also presumably down to the conflation of the two texts, as Dan. 7:4 clearly refers to a beast which appears like a lion. Later Jewish tradition developed both of these two interpretative options

---

77. The date of this text is variously dated: Joseph Heinemann, 'Profile of a Midrash: The Art of Composition in Leviticus Rabba', *Journal of the American Academy of Religion* 39 (1971): 141–150; Jacob Neusner, *Judaism and Scripture: The Evidence of Leviticus Rabbah* (Chicago: University of Chicago Press, 1986), 5.

78. English translation is taken from Satran, 'Early Jewish and Christian Interpretation', 109.

(conscious and unconscious metamorphoses). Due to their shared presupposition about the relationship of Dan. 4 and Dan. 7, and their agreement that Nebuchadnezzar metamorphosed, they will be examined together in the following two subsections.

2.5.1 Conscious Metamorphosis (ca. Fifth–ca. Eighth Century CE)

First, conflating Dan. 7:4 with the affliction of Nebuchadnezzar in Dan. 4 made it possible for interpreters to argue that Nebuchadnezzar retained his human mind, and only physically became an animal. This is the view espoused by Rabbi Eleazar in Lev. Rab. and, while there is no further elaboration upon his statement here, later Jewish tradition did.

A developed example of this interpretation is found in Midrash Tanhuma.[79] When the text turns to address Nebuchadnezzar, it first refers to Isa. 14 to explain the hubris of the king. This is accomplished in much the same manner as the Mekilta and Aphrahat did. Once the reason for the events has been made apparent, the text of Midr. Tanh. recounts the affliction of Nebuchadnezzar:

> He exiled him into the wilderness, while he was still on his throne, and nourished him with grass like a beast, as it is said, 'he was fed grass like cattle' (Dan. 5:21; 4:29). And the beasts and the animals saw him in the form of a beast and they would come and have intercourse with him, as it is said, 'And the destruction of the beasts will terrify them' (Hab. 2:17). 'Will terrify them' — this may be likened to what is said, 'Nor shall you marry them' (Deut. 7:3). And despite all this, 'it was given the mind of a man' (Dan. 7:4) – for he knew that he was the ruler of all the world, yet now reduced to copulation with animals and beasts. (Midr. Tanh., Va'era 9)[80]

This seems to be an explication of the narrative in Dan. 4 which describes Nebuchadnezzar's exile in the wilderness. Moreover, the interpretation of the king's affliction is also fairly clear: he seems to have physically metamorphosed because the other animals behold him in 'the form of a beast'. Yet the text of Midr. Tanh. also clearly describes how Nebuchadnezzar kept a human mind. This is achieved through conflating this narrative with Dan. 7:4, in much the same way that Rabbi Eleazar does in Lev. Rab.

The effect of doing so is more pronounced in this case though, because the midrashic text depicts Nebuchadnezzar as being sexually assaulted by animals.

---

79. Midrash Tanhuma probably originates from the period after the Islamic conquest of Palestine; see Marc Bregman, *The Tanhuma-Yelammedenu Literature: Studies in the Evolution of the Versions* (Piscataway, NJ: Gorgias, 2003), 4–5.

80. English translation is taken from Satran, 'Early Jewish and Christian Interpretation', 104.

While a seemingly peculiar addition to the narrative, it is not the only text to depict him this way.[81] It appears to be part of a tradition that aims to depict Nebuchadnezzar as engaging in the same degradation he enforced upon others. Thus Nebuchadnezzar is assaulted by animals because he had also forced the same upon the Judean king, Zedekiah.[82] This can be explained as a kind of 'measure for measure' principle.[83] It is possible that this curious turn in interpretation began by treating Nebuchadnezzar as a cipher for the Roman emperor whom the rabbis saw as engaging in such activities.[84] Equipped with this humiliating depiction of Nebuchadnezzar, the conflation of Dan. 4 with Dan. 7 becomes more important. Only by retaining his human mind can the king be made conscious of the bestial sexual assault. This worsens the punishment that he undergoes as, while still aware he was the great king of the world, he is also conscious that he has been forced into copulation with animals. This quite graphic humiliation and punishment of Nebuchadnezzar is thus reliant on the king's mind remaining intact. His form could change but he retained a human mind so his transformation would be apparent to him.

In this tradition, the affliction of Nebuchadnezzar consisted purely of a physical metamorphosis to force him to remain conscious of his affliction. This seems at least superficially to be a similar rationale to the Christian penitential interpretation seen earlier; however, the justification is different. Rather than attempting to use Nebuchadnezzar as an example penitent, this metamorphic interpretation of his affliction relied on the supposed relationship between Dan. 4 and Dan. 7 in order to intensify the king's humiliation and degrade him as fully as possible. This could only be achieved if the king underwent a physical transformation and remained conscious throughout.

2.5.2 *Unconscious Metamorphosis (ca. Fifth–Thirteenth Century CE)*

The second possible interpretation that resulted from conflating Dan. 4 and Dan. 7, was to suggest Nebuchadnezzar both physically metamorphosed *and* mentally changed into an animal. This results in the king being metamorphosed while remaining unconscious of the transformation. It is this view which Rabbi Samuel bar Nahman proposes in Lev. Rab.

Unfortunately, after the text of Lev. Rab., the only text that is somewhat reminiscent of a similar interpretative tradition is the thirteenth-century Midrash

---

81. For example, see also Tanhuma Buber, Va'era 8; and Exodus Rabbah 8.2.

82. For example Tanhuma Buber, Va'era 18.

83. Satran, 'Early Jewish and Christian Interpretation', 106–108. It is possible too that this may bear some relationship with the phrase 'Behemoth used to come upon him' in the *Vita*. This is suggested by Marc Bregman, 'Textual Witnesses of the Tanhuma-Yelamdenu Midrashim' [Hebrew], in *Proceedings of the Ninth World Congress of Jewish Studies, Division C: Jewish Thought and Literature*, ed. David Assaf (Jerusalem: Magnes, 1986), 49–56.

84. Henze, *Madness of King Nebuchadnezzar*, 132–133.

Daniel. The Midrash, written by Samuel ben Nissim Masnut, does not present the rabbi's own view or original comments but preserves a blend of previous rabbinic interpretations. Furthermore, he often does not provide references for these prior sources.[85] It is therefore possible the author relied on a pre-existing tradition for his comments on Dan. 4:13:

> His sense was altered and his reason departed him and he was given the heart of a beast which has no mind at all. And all this (was done) in order that he be able to endure the punishment inflicted upon him: for if his mind and reason had remained intact, he would have gone mad and died. He was given the appearance of a beast and animal in order that he not die but endure all his sufferings during the seven seasons. (Midr. Dan. 4.13)[86]

This seems to accord with Rabbi Nahman's opinion that Nebuchadnezzar's mind changed in addition to his form. David Satran has considered the possibility there is some link between Midr. Dan. and Lev. Rab., and found some points of comparison.[87] The commentary here is nevertheless slightly more developed as Rabbi Masnut does not explicitly rely on Dan. 7 for his interpretation but on his consideration of Nebuchadnezzar's affliction. Whereas previous commentators suggested the king kept his mind and remained conscious of his affliction in order to make Nebuchadnezzar's punishment worse, the Midr. Dan. suggests the opposite. The sheer horrendousness of the affliction meant Nebuchadnezzar could not have kept his mind otherwise he would not have endured the ordeal at all. This interpretation, and thus the apparent metamorphosis of Nebuchadnezzar it describes, seems to be motivated by the mere fact that Nebuchadnezzar survived and was able to praise God afterward.

2.6 Early Medieval Denial of Metamorphosis (Tenth–Thirteenth Century)

In his tenth-century commentary on Daniel, the great Jewish exegete Saadia Gaon described three different interpretations of Nebuchadnezzar's affliction (these were covered in §2.4, §2.5.1 and §2.5.2 above). Each of these he deemed to be incorrect and it was only after he had described each in turn that Saadia revealed his own assessment: 'The correct (interpretation) whoever [sic], is that

---

85. Israel M. Ta-Shma, 'Masnut, Samuel Ben Nissim', *EncJud* 11:1097–1098.

86. The text can be found in Isaac S. Lange and Samuel Schwartz, eds and trans, *Midrash Daniel and Midrash Ezra Rabbi Samuel Ben Rabbi Nissim Masnut* [Hebrew] (Jerusalem: Mekize Nirdamim Society, 1968), 45. English translation is from Henze, *Madness of King Nebuchadnezzar*, 154 n. 9.

87. Satran, 'Early Jewish and Christian Interpretation', 149–150 n. 36.

Nebuchadnezzar's physical aspect did not change. What changed was his mind' (Saadia Gaon, *Commentary on Daniel* [Alobaidi, 165–6]). The other 'incorrect' interpretations he had previously referenced all proposed that Nebuchadnezzar had undergone a physical metamorphosis, whereas Saadia suggested the 'correct' understanding is to suppose only his mind changed. Thus nothing physical was altered and there was no metamorphosis.

Saadia then immediately referred to 1 Sam. 16:14 to support his argument. King Saul is here tormented by an evil spirit and, as this does not result in him being physically altered, by Saadia's logic the same must therefore be true for Nebuchadnezzar (Saadia Gaon, *Commentary on Daniel* [Alobaidi, 166]). Thus, as the instances are equivalent for Saadia, the comparison serves to highlight the lack of physical change that Nebuchadnezzar would have undergone. He then returns to the events in Daniel:

> As to Nebuchadnezzar, his difficulty was immense, which is the total disappearance of the human mind from him. That is why he said: *My reason came back to me.* He reached the point that he abandoned the human company. (Saadia Gaon, *Commentary on Daniel* [Alobaidi, 166])

Saadia seems to view this incident as a purely mental affliction and uses Dan. 4:34 as evidence. He expands on what this means a little earlier in his commentary when wrestling with how to understand the phrase in Dan. 4:13 MT 'the heart of an animal'. He translated it: '"animal imagination" following the necessity of the context. In fact men of science attribute discernment to human beings, no [*sic*] to animals. However, they attribute imagination to them' (Saadia Gaon, *Commentary on Daniel* [Alobaidi, 165]). In this passage Saadia reveals the theoretical basis upon which he supports his interpretation of the king's affliction. The reference to 'men of science' who attribute 'discernment to human beings' appears to be a reference to the medieval Jewish doctrine of the three-fold nature of the human soul. This doctrine claimed the human soul consisted of three parts: the rational soul which governed discursive knowledge, or discernment; the animal soul which was responsible for instinct (or imagination), locomotion and sensory perception; and the vegetative soul which was responsible for generation, growth and nourishment.[88] Thus Saadia appears to reinterpret the phrase 'the heart of an animal' (Dan. 4:13) in light of this doctrine and explains that Nebuchadnezzar lost the human capabilities of the soul (discernment etc.) being left with only the animal and vegetative parts (and thus an animal heart). By applying this doctrine of the soul to Dan. 4, Saadia's interpretation clearly demonstrates how the king's animalising affliction affected only his rational capacities and was evidently not a physical metamorphosis.

Curiously, Saadia Gaon's interpretation differs considerably from previous Jewish interpretations on this passage as it seems more rationalistic, and

---

88. See Alfred L. Levy, 'Soul', *EncJud* 19:33–35.

additionally he uses support from 1 Sam. rather than linking Dan. 4 with Dan. 7.[89] It is therefore plausible that Saadia's new exegetical proposal was influenced by a different interpretative tradition entirely, for example that which is associated with the Antiochene tradition. Interestingly, there are some striking similarities between this Antiochene interpretation and that of Saadia Gaon.[90] Both interpret Nebuchadnezzar's affliction as a mental condition and appeal to Dan. 4:34 MT ('my reason returned to me') as evidence the king had lost his mind.[91] Furthermore, Saadia's commentary is much more focused on the plain sense of the biblical text than preceding Jewish interpretation on this narrative. This is again a shared characteristic with Antiochene interpretation. Finally, it is clear that within his commentary on Daniel, Saadia was indeed aware of and engaged in reading Christian interpretations of the book. Often in his commentary on Daniel, Saadia seems to respond specifically to a Christian exegesis of the text.[92] He could only do this by gaining an intimate knowledge of these Christian writings, something which he seemed to have acquired.[93] While there is no obvious indication that Saadia Gaon's interpretation of Nebuchadnezzar's affliction relied upon this earlier Antiochene trend, nevertheless there *is* evidence which may be suggestive of such an influence.

This apparent reaction of Saadia Gaon to earlier metamorphic interpretations of Dan. 4 nonetheless seems to characterise commentary on Nebuchadnezzar's affliction for the next few centuries; Medieval Jewish commentators who looked specifically at Daniel interpreted the narrative in largely similar ways. For example, the Karaite commentator Jephet Ibn Ali, writing around 1000 CE, stated:

89. He does link Dan. 4 and 7 together, but only when interpreting the vision in Dan. 7; see Saadia Gaon, *Commentary on Daniel* (ed. Alobaidi, *Book of Daniel: Commentary of R. Saadia Gaon*), 226–227.

90. David Satran has also noted the resemblance between Saadia's interpretation and that of the Antiochene tradition; see Satran, 'Early Jewish and Christian Interpretation', 150 n. 39.

91. The one noticeable difference is that Saadia does not mention the metal band in Dan. 4:12 as representing the restraining of a mad king. However, the later Jewish commentator Jephet Ibn Ali does; see Jephet Ibn Ali, *A Commentary on the Book of Daniel*, 4.20. English translations are taken from David S. Margoliouth, ed. and trans., *A Commentary on the Book of Daniel by Jephet ibn Ali the Karaite* (Oxford: Clarendon, 1889), 22.

92. Robert Chazan has shown how Saadia did this with Dan. 9:24–27; see Robert Chazan, 'Daniel 9:24–27: Exegesis and Polemics', in *Contra Iudaeos: Ancient and Medieval Polemics between Christians and Jews*, ed. Ora Limor and Guy G. Stroumsa (Tübingen: Mohr Siebeck, 1996), 143–159. For a more general assessment, see Eliezer Schlossberg, 'Concepts and Methods in the Commentary on Daniel by R. Saadia Gaon' [Hebrew] (PhD diss., Bar Ilan University, 1988).

93. See Daniel J. Lasker, 'Saadya Gaon on Christianity and Islam', in *The Jews of Medieval Islam: Community, Society, and Identity*, ed. Daniel Frank (Leiden: Brill, 1995), 165–77.

> Let his heart be changed refers to the cessation of his reason, and his becoming deprived of the power of discrimination which he had. Three things, it is to be observed, are literal: (1) grass like an ox, etc.; (2) let it be wet with the dew of heaven; (3) let his heart be changed; the rest are all symbolical. (Jephet Ibn Ali, *A Commentary on the Book of Daniel*, 4.20)

For Ibn Ali, the cessation of the king's reason was the full extent of his affliction and he explained any physical changes as symbolic (rather than literal) statements of Nebuchadnezzar's transformation into an animal. While Ibn Ali tends to polemicise against Saadia Gaon throughout his commentary, he often agrees with him about the most crucial points, and the interpretation of Dan. 4 seems to be one such example.

Abraham Ibn Ezra also explicitly refuted the idea of Nebuchadnezzar's physical metamorphosis into an animal. In his commentary on Dan. 4:28 (*ca.* 1155), he wrote: 'Do not let it occur to you that Nebuchadnezzar actually turned into an animal, neither male nor female, for the verse says only that he lived among the animals and ate grass like them' (Abraham Ibn Ezra, *Commentary on Daniel* 4:28).[94] Ibn Ezra specifically denied previous interpretations that suggested Nebuchadnezzar metamorphosed, instead he argued that the king lost his mind and other people simply assumed the king was an animal as he had begun moving around on his hands and feet.[95] Scholars suggest that Ibn Ezra tended to explain away seemingly extraordinary or suspicious biblical events in order to make a more rational account, and his assessment of Dan. 4 may be an example of this.[96] To support his idea that Dan. 4 describes a type of madness, Ibn Ezra provided a contemporary anecdote: 'Indeed, I have been told by one of my trustworthy friends that on a certain island called Sardinia, a certain Gentile lost his sanity, escaped from his family, and lived among the rams for many years, walking on all fours' (Abraham Ibn Ezra, *Commentary on Daniel* 4:28). By including an anecdotal quotation, Ibn Ezra could justify his own interpretation of the passage and demonstrate how credible the story of Nebuchadnezzar's affliction was. However, like Saadia, Ibn Ezra may also be reliant upon the medieval Jewish doctrine of the three-fold soul to explain Nebuchadnezzar's affliction.[97] Thus, for Ibn Ezra, rather

---

94. English translations are taken from David I. Shyovitz, *A Rememberance of His Wonders: Nature and the Supernatural in Medieval Ashkenaz* (Philadelphia: University of Pennsylvania Press, 2017), 138.

95. See Judah J. Slotki, *Daniel, Ezra, Nehemiah: Hebrew Text and English Translation with Introductions and Commentary*, Soncino Books of the Bible (London: Soncino, 1951), 37. Ibn Ezra's reference to Nebuchadnezzar becoming female seems to be directed at the earlier interpretation whereby the king had intercourse with other animals; see above: §2.5.1.

96. For example: Shyovitz, *A Rememberance of His Wonders*, 138.

97. Timothy R. Ashley, 'The Book of Daniel Chapters I–VI: Text, Versions and the Problems of Exegesis' (PhD diss., University of St Andrews, 1975), 371–372.

than explaining the king's animalising affliction as a physical metamorphosis, Nebuchadnezzar was viewed as suffering from a psychological affliction which made him lose his rational judgement and become mad.

This trend for early medieval Jewish commentators to deny a metamorphosis in Dan. 4 is also found in Christian writings of the same period. A prime example is the comment made in one of the most influential medieval Christian texts, the twelfth-century *Historia scholastica* by Peter Comestor. When tackling Nebuchadnezzar's affliction in Dan. 4, Comestor wrote:

> From this it appears, and Epiphanius attests, that he did not suffer a physical metamorphosis, but he lost his reason, and he lost the use of his tongue to speak, and grass was given as food for his human nature. And it seemed to him that he was an ox in front, and a lion at the rear. (Peter Comestor, *Historia scholastica* [PL 198:1452a–b])[98]

As with other commentators of the period, Comestor here conveys the opinion that Nebuchadnezzar did not experience a physical metamorphosis but experienced delusions so he only believed that he had.[99] This is surprising given that he explicitly relies on the tradition from the Epiphanius recension of the *Vita Danielis*.[100] He evidently has access to the text and treats its information with some credibility, yet does not follow its assertion that the king physically metamorphosed into an animal (see above). However, Comestor read very widely and it is probable he also had access to other commentaries on Dan. 4. For example, one of his main sources was the commentary made by Jerome which Comestor accessed through the *Glossa ordinaria*.[101] He is also known to have been exposed to earlier Jewish commentaries and frequently refers to '*Hebraei tradunt*' or 'Hebrew reports'.[102] Both Jerome and previous Jewish commentators denied a physical metamorphosis in Dan. 4 and this may have influenced Comestor here too. If this is the case, Comestor appears to have produced a blend whereby he was influenced by

---

98. The English translation is my own.

99. For a similar assessment of Comestor's interpretation, see Penelope B. R. Doob, *Nebuchadnezzar's Children: Conventions of Madness in Middle English Literature* (London: Yale University Press, 1974), 70.

100. Comestor's interpretation of Dan. 4 is addressed by Roling, *Physica Sacra*, 242. Unfortunately, Roling does not notice that Comestor is relying on the *Vita* and not just the biblical narrative.

101. See Mark A. Zier, 'The Medieval Latin Interpretation of Daniel: Antecedents to Andrew of St Victor', *Recherches de théologie ancienne et médiévale* 58 (1991): 43–78 (esp. 64); David A. Wells, 'The Medieval Nebuchadnezzar: The Exegetical Tradition of Daniel IV and Its Significance for the Ywain Romances and for German Vernacular Literature', *Frühmittelalterliche Studien* 16 (1982): 380–432 (398 and 410).

102. James H. Morey, 'Peter Comestor, Biblical Paraphrase, and the Medieval Popular Bible', *Speculum* 68 (1993): 6–35 (11–14).

previous commentators who denied Nebuchadnezzar's metamorphosis, whilst also simultaneously incorporating aspects of the metamorphic narrative in the *Vita*.[103] Nevertheless, for Comestor, the result was that Nebuchadnezzar did not change physically, but only imagined himself to have metamorphosed into an ox–lion hybrid. Thus, despite acknowledging the text of the *Vita*, Comestor still denied a metamorphosis in the narrative of Dan. 4.

Other twelfth-century Christian commentators continued this denial of a physical metamorphosis. For example, Andrew of St Victor stated Nebuchadnezzar retained his human form during his affliction (Andrew of St Victor, *Expositio super Danielem*, 4.13–33).[104] During the thirteenth century, Albert the Great (*ca.* 1193–1280) wrote another explicit rejection of Nebuchadnezzar's metamorphosis: 'we do not read that he lost his external form, but that his heart shall be changed from that of a human' (Albert the Great, *Commentarii in librum Danielis* 4.33).[105] He then stated how the depiction of Nebuchadnezzar results instead from the loss of his reason. This early medieval period is thus fairly uncontroversial for interpretation of Dan. 4 as it seems to be almost entirely represented by interpreters who saw Nebuchadnezzar's condition as a mental affliction, and which also simultaneously downplayed the metamorphic reading of this Danielic text.

There are a number of possible explanations for this more restrained trend in medieval interpretation of Dan. 4. A prominent probable influence upon medieval Christian commentators at this time was the wider attitude in the church to such metamorphoses. Two sources were particularly influential. One of these was Augustine of Hippo's view that stories of demonic transformations from human into animal were either false or were too extraordinary to be believed.[106] Secondly,

---

103. It is possible Peter Comestor had access to a corrupted form of the *Vita* that suggested Nebuchadnezzar's transformation was not physical. However this is unlikely as no other commentators on this passage read the *Vita* as advocating a non-physical transformation. It is more likely Comestor has reinterpreted the *Vita* to cohere with other commentaries he had read. Hints at a similar interpretation are potentially provided by illustrations in the eleventh century *Roda Bible*; see Anat Tcherikover, 'The Fall of Nebuchadnezzar in Romanesque Sculpture (Airvault, Moissac, Bourg-Argental, Foussais)', *Zeitschrift für Kunstgeschichte* 49 (1986): 288–300.

104. For an example of another similar medieval Christian interpretation, see Thomas Aquinas, *In Danielem Prophetam Expositio* 4 in Stanislai E. Fretté and Pauli Maré, eds, *Doctoris Angelici Divi Thomae Aquinatis Sacria Ordinis F. F. Praedicatorum Opera Omnia*, 34 vols. (Paris: Vivès, 1871–1880), 31:224–225.

105. This text can be found in: Augustus Borgnet, ed., *B. Alberti Magni Opera Omnia*, 38 vols. (Paris: Vivès, 1890–1899), 18:522. The English translation is my own.

106. Augustine, *De civitate Dei* 18.18 (PL 41:574–576). He did accept transformations through divine power which could potentially have included the events in Dan. 4, but Augustine does not provide a direct comment on this chapter.

the *Canon episcopi* (*ca.* 900) explicitly denounced belief in human–animal metamorphoses as blasphemous and illusory.[107] Both these texts were commonly repeated and accepted amongst early medieval theologians and church lawyers, and together these texts dampened belief in metamorphoses among Western Christians.[108] It is probable that they thereby influenced Christian interpreters of Dan. 4 to deny Nebuchadnezzar's transformation too. Without official support for the possibility of lycanthropic transformations and other metamorphoses, medieval interpretations of Dan. 4 were relatively moderate.[109]

2.7 Substantial Lycanthropic Metamorphosis (Twelfth–Seventeenth Century)

While the dominant view in the medieval Christian church was to dismiss tales of metamorphoses, not all were content to accept these prevailing views. The continued popularity of belief in werewolves meant some individuals still considered human–animal metamorphoses to be entirely plausible. During the twelfth and thirteenth centuries there was a renewed interest in lycanthropy which some have called a 'werewolf renaissance'.[110] Amongst several others, the two writers who characterize this resurgence most are Gerald of Wales and Gervase of Tilbury.[111] Both recount tales of humans who turn into wolves and treat them as reliable accounts of actual events.[112] However, they also frame these narratives within discussions about the nature and possibility of metamorphoses more generally and they are careful to justify their belief in the credibility of such stories.

It is amongst these writings that evidence can be found of a renewed metamorphic interpretation of Dan. 4 linked to lycanthropy.[113] Though Gerald of

---

107. See Henry Charles Lea, *Materials toward a History of Witchcraft*, ed. Arthur C. Howland, 3 vols (Philadelphia: University of Pennsylvania Press, 1939), 1:178–180.

108. Dennis M. Kratz, 'Fictus Lupus: The Werewolf in Christian Thought', *Classical Folia* 30 (1976): 57–78; Jeffrey A. Massey, '*Corpus Lupi*: The Medieval Werewolf and Popular Theology' (PhD diss., Emory University, 2003), 59–93.

109. See Roling, *Physica Sacra*, 319.

110. See Caroline Walker Bynum, *Metamorphosis and Identity* (New York: Zone Books, 2001), 94; David I. Shyovtiz, 'Christians and Jews in the Twelfth-Century Werewolf Renaissance', *Journal of the History of Ideas* 75 (2014): 521–543.

111. For information on the wider interest in werewolves at this time, see Caroline Walker Bynum, 'Metamorphosis, or Gerald and the Werewolf', *Speculum* 73 (1998): 987–1013 (1000 n. 60).

112. Gerald of Wales, *Topographia hibernica* 2.19; Gervase of Tilbury, *Otia imperialia*, 3.120.

113. Prior to this, Rupert of Deutz (*ca.* 1080–1129) had also disputed the prevailing medieval idea that Nebuchadnezzar did not physically transform; see Rupert of Deutz, *De victoria verbi Dei* 6.29 (PL 169:1358a-c).

Wales makes no mention of Nebuchadnezzar, Gervase of Tilbury begins his section on werewolves by considering the events of Dan. 4:

> The question is often raised among the learned as to whether Nebuchadnezzar was really changed into an ox by divine power for the period of penitence imposed on him: for it is surely easier to make a creature by transformation than to create one out of nothing. Many writers think that he adopted the lifestyle of a beast, feeding like an ox that eats hay, but without adopting its nature. One thing I know to be of a daily occurrence among the people of our country: the course of human destiny is such that certain men change into wolves according to the cycles of the moon. (Gervase of Tilbury, *Otia imperialia*, 3.120)[114]

This text from the *Otia imperialia* (*ca.* 1215)[115] does not necessarily appear to advocate a metamorphic understanding of Nebuchadnezzar's affliction, Gervase merely seems to document and describe how people have previously viewed the narrative. However, he never dismisses the possibility Nebuchadnezzar did metamorphose and suggests the king's physical transformation would be relatively easy to achieve. In the context of Gervase's discussion of other werewolf stories, which he evidently believes,[116] the Danielic text appears yet as another example of a human–animal transformation. Gervase's mention of Dan. 4 in this context therefore evidences an early link between Nebuchadnezzar and lycanthropy[117] while also indicating that such a transformation of the king into an animal was deemed possible.

The suggestion of a bovine metamorphosis in Dan. 4 was returned to by later writers when, during the fifteenth and sixteenth centuries, there was another resurgence of interest in lycanthropy. With the issue of the papal bull *Summis desiderantibus affectibus* in 1484, Pope Innocent VIII effectively recognized the existence and efficacy of witches and approved their punishment by the church. This officially reopened the possibility of demonic lycanthropic metamorphoses and thus the possibility of seeing Nebuchadnezzar as undergoing a similar transformation.

Arguably the most significant articulation of a lycanthropic-inspired interpretation of Dan. 4 came when Jean Bodin wrote his major work *De la*

---

114. The English translation is taken from S. E. Banks and J. W. Binns, eds and trans, *Gervase of Tilbury: Otia Imperialia: Recreation for an Emperor* (Oxford: Clarendon, 2002), 812–813. Gerald of Wales refers instead to the story of Lot's wife in Gen. 19 and the transformation of the bread in the Eucharist; see Gerald of Wales, *Topographia hibernica* 2.19.

115. For this dating, see Banks and Binns, *Gervase of Tilbury*, xxxviii-xl.

116. For example, see Gervase of Tilbury, *Otia imperialia*, 1.15.

117. While originally 'lycanthropy' referred just to human–wolf transformations, it eventually became a broader term which was used about the transformation of a human into any animal.

Démonomanie des Sorciers in 1580. He touched upon the issue of lycanthropy principally in the sixth chapter of the second book entitled 'De la Lycanthropie & si les esprits peuvent changer les hommes en bestes'. Initially, he provided a range of contemporary anecdotal evidence, including legal cases, about specific individuals who had been identified as werewolves.[118] He admitted that such stories seemed far-fetched; nevertheless the possibility of lycanthropy was proven, for Bodin, by appealing to sacred scripture of which the most critical text is Dan. 4:

> [Lycanthropy] seems incredible and almost impossible to human sense. And nonetheless it is quite certain, that this is confirmed by the sacred history of King Nebuchadnezzar, about whom the Prophet Daniel speaks, he was converted and transformed into an ox.[119]

He returned to the Danielic narrative again at the close of the chapter as he sums up his case for the reality of lycanthropy.

> And if we confess the truth of the sacred story in Daniel, which cannot be called into doubt, and the story of Lot's wife changed into immobile stone, it is certain that the changing of a human into ox or into stone is possible, and also into many other animals.[120]

Bodin's primary objective appears to be to advocate the reality of werewolves and the possibility of such human–animal transformations. The affliction of Nebuchadnezzar was utilized as irrefutable evidence that lycanthropic stories could be believed. Therefore, to establish the existence of werewolves, Bodin's interpretation of events in Dan. 4 cast Nebuchadnezzar as an archetypal werewolf, or perhaps more accurately a 'werecow'. He repeated his argument about lycanthropy again in his *Réfutation des Opinions de Jean Wier*, a response to Johann Weyer's denial of the reality of werewolves,[121] which was appended to Bodin's *Démonomanie*.[122] Here Bodin strengthened his case by arguing how a similar kind of transformation in humans could be completed by Satan. Amidst this discussion Bodin again returned to Nebuchadnezzar:

> Also Weyer cannot deny that Nebuchadnezzar Emperor of Assyria was changed into an ox grazing the grass seven whole years; his skin, hair, nails, and whole

---

118. Jean Bodin, *De la Démonomanie des Sorciers* (Paris: Jacques Du Puys, 1580), 94–98. All quotations from the *De la Démonomanie des Sorciers* are from this first edition.

119. Bodin, *Démonomanie*, 101. The English translations of this text are my own.

120. Bodin, *Démonomanie*, 104.

121. Johann Weyer, *De Praestigiis Daemonum et Incantationibus ac Venificiis* (Basel: Oporinus, 1563).

122. He makes a similar statement in: Jean Bodin, *Universae Naturae Theatrum* (Frankfurt: Wechel, 1597), 537.

form being changed, and then restored in his figure: as the history of Daniel the Prophet teaches us. If he dictates that this change of King Nebuchadnezzar is true, as holy Scripture says and not a fabulous illusion, he must also confess that the same change can be made of the human figure into wolves.[123]

This passage provides a glimpse at Bodin's reasoning behind his interpretation of Dan. 4. To support the assertion that Nebuchadnezzar metamorphosed into an animal, Bodin appeals to aspects of the text itself: the king's consumption of grass; the change of his nails, hair, skin. Bodin does not seem interested in defending his interpretation but assumes that the idea Nebuchadnezzar metamorphosed is plain to see. This suggests that a metamorphic interpretation was, to Bodin, obvious from a simple reading of the text.

However, the primary influence upon Bodin's interpretation of Dan. 4 was probably his view of what actually took place in such lycanthropic transformations. Throughout his work, Bodin was clear that the only result of such metamorphoses was a change in physical appearance. The mind and 'reason', which Bodin considered the essential human features, were unaffected.[124] Thus it is not possible to explain away these transformations as mental afflictions because a person's 'reason' had to be unchanged to ensure the individual remained essentially human throughout the experience. In Bodin's view, werewolves (and thus Nebuchadnezzar) would remain human but only appear physically bestial. This is motivated, at least in part, by Bodin's desire to remain broadly in agreement with prior tradition and specifically with the previously mentioned *Canon episcopi*.[125] By casting Nebuchadnezzar as an example of a lycanthropic transformation, Bodin must also propose that the king's bovine change was solely physical.

Bodin's lycanthropic understanding of Nebuchadnezzar's transformation had a significant influence upon most subsequent interpretations of Dan. 4. His view was initially received fairly positively. For example the only evidence needed to convince the German philosopher Rudolph Goclenius that Nebuchadnezzar metamorphosed into an ox was his high opinion of Bodin's intellectual ability.[126] Similarly, the seventeenth-century Catholic demonologist Francesco Torreblanca Villalpando, despite being sceptical of the views of the Protestant Bodin, came to the same

---

123. Bodin, *Démonomanie*, 244–245.

124. Bodin, *Démonomanie*, 102.

125. For Bodin's approach to the *Canon episcopi*, see Johannes Dillinger, '"Species", "Phantasia", "Raison": Werewolves and Shape-Shifters in Demonological Literature', in *Werewolf Histories*, ed. Willem de Blécourt, Palgrave Historical Studies in Witchcraft and Magic (Basingstoke: Palgrave Macmillan, 2015), 142–158 (151).

126. Rudolph Goclenius, *Scholae seu Disputations Physicae, More Academic Fere Propositae et Haitae Plaeraeque Omnes in Schola Illustri Cattorum* (Marburg: Paul Egenolphus, 1591), 86 [Disputation 12.42].

opinion that Nebuchadnezzar physically transformed into an animal.[127] In 1667, Jacobus Thomasius addressed the issue of human–animal transformations in an extended work: *De transformatione hominum in bruta dissertationem philosophicam*. While he commented on werewolves at length in his dissertation, referencing Bodin several times in the process,[128] he doubted the appropriateness of linking lycanthropy with the king's affliction in Dan. 4.[129] Nevertheless, even Thomasius concluded that Nebuchadnezzar's transformation was a substantial, physical change into an animal form.[130] Such was the impact of the lycanthropic debate, and especially Bodin's contribution to it, that during the sixteenth and seventeenth centuries the idea that Nebuchadnezzar physically metamorphosed had become once again quite prevalent.

However, after the publication of Bodin's *Démonomanie* and the popularization of the depiction of Nebuchadnezzar as a werewolf, the lycanthropic interpretation of Dan. 4 attracted more hostile reactions from other demonologists of the time. For example, Reginald Scot in his *The Discoverie of Witchcraft* addressed Bodin's interpretation of Nebuchadnezzar by specifically claiming 'he was neither in bodie nor shape transformed at all, according to their grosse imagination; as appeareth both by the plaine word of the text, and also by the opinions of the best interpretors thereof'.[131] Similar statements about Bodin's interpretation were later made by Henri Boguet and Pierre de Lancre.[132] There was thus a significant reaction against the proposal of Bodin. Nonetheless this substantial lycanthropic interpretation of Dan. 4 gained widespread notoriety, occasioned probably by the level of controversy it garnered among other demonologists of the sixteenth and seventeenth centuries.

2.8 Denial of Lycanthropic Metamorphosis as Illusory (Fifteenth–Seventeenth Century)

Not all those writing about lycanthropy at this time concluded that Nebuchadnezzar's affliction was a genuinely physical metamorphosis; yet neither

---

127. Francesco Torreblanca Villalpando, *Daemonologia Sive de Magia Naturali, Daemoniaca, Licita et Illicita, Deque Aperta et Occulta* (Mainz: Schoenwetterus, 1623), 241–242.

128. Jacobus Thomasius (praes.) and Fredericus Tobius Moebius (resp.), *De Transformatione Hominum in Bruta Dissertationem Philosophicam* (Leipzig: Hahnius, 1667), fols. E3vf–E4rf [§§120–123].

129. Thomasius, *De Transformatione Hominum*, fols. Bvf, B3v [§§17–19 and §§30–31].

130. Thomasius, *De Transformatione Hominum*, fol. C2rf [§§48–49].

131. Reginald Scot, *The Discoverie of Witchcraft* (London: William Brome, 1584), 101. For a discussion of Scot's interpretation of Nebuchadnezzar's affliction, see Philip C. Almond, *England's First Demonologist: Reginald Scot and 'The Discoverie of Witchcraft'* (London: I. B. Tauris, 2011), 103–104.

132. Henri Boguet, *Discours Exécrable des Sorciers*, 2nd ed. (Lyon: Pierre Rigaud, 1608), 346–53; Pierre de Lancre, *Tableau de L'Inconstance des Mauvaius Anges et Démons* (Paris: Nicholas Buon, 1612), 273–274 [book 4, discourse 3].

did they explain it simply as a form of madness. Instead this apparent metamorphosis was explained as a form of illusion whereby the eyes of both the afflicted and those who viewed the afflicted were deceived into seeing the appearance of an animal when no actual change had taken place.

This interpretation of Nebuchadnezzar's affliction can trace its roots to some of the writings of early demonologists.[133] Heinrich Kramer and Jacob Sprenger in their *Malleus maleficarum* (*ca.* 1486) systematically explained lycanthropic transformations.[134] However in their view, while these transformations were created through actual demonic acts, they were not physical metamorphoses. Instead, for Kramer and Sprenger, these transformations were illusions that were conjured by demons through the obstruction of people's perception of the world. A demon could cause imaginary pictures of animals to appear in an individual's mind, making an individual's eyes detect these images in the external world. This could thus make another person appear to be an animal, although it would be a demonic illusion and no such animal metamorphosis would have actually taken place.[135] The result of this demonic intervention was that an individual could appear to be an animal both to themselves and to any spectators. Later writers would agree with Kramer and Sprenger that lycanthropic transformations were caused by demonic illusions.[136]

These demonologists' doubts over the actuality of werewolf transformations led commentators to express similar doubts over Nebuchadnezzar's metamorphosis in Dan. 4. Primary examples of this were again Kramer and Sprenger who specifically cited Nebuchadnezzar as an example of this demonic illusory process:

> Those who seemed to others to have been changed into other appearances also seemed to themselves to have been converted into wild beasts, just as happened to Nebuchadnezzar that, when seven times were changed over him, he ate hay like an ox. (Kramer and Sprenger, *Malleus maleficarum*, 120B)

---

133. For a more detailed discussion of this interpretation, see Roling, *Physica Sacra*, 258–264. This interpretation of Dan. 4 also seems to be a return to the view of lycanthropic metamorphoses expressed in the *Canon episcopi* that all witchcraft was seen as illusory; see above: §2.6.

134. Citations and pagination of the *Malleus maleficarum* are taken from the first-edition facsimile in: André Schnyder, ed., *Malleus Maleficarum von Heinrich Institoris (alias Kramer) unter Mithilfe Jakob Sprengers aufgrund der dämonologischen Tradition zusammengestellt: Widergabe des Erstdrucks von 1487 (Hain 9238)* (Göppingen: Kümmerle Verlag, 1993). English translations are taken from: Christopher S. MacKay, ed. and trans., *The Hammer of Witches: A Complete Translation of the Malleus Maleficarum* (Cambridge: Cambridge University Press, 2009).

135. Heinrich Kramer and Jacob Sprenger, *Malleus maleficarum*, 61C–61D.

136. For example, see Ulrich Molitor, *De Lamiis et Pithonicis Mulieribus* (Strasbourg: Johann Prüss, 1489), fols. C5r–C6v.

In this interpretation, Nebuchadnezzar appeared to be an ox both to himself and anyone who saw him; however, this was enacted only through a demonic distortion of perception. A little later in 1521, Silvestro Mazzolini argued similarly that Nebuchadnezzar became an animal only in his imagination.[137] The Franciscan theologian Miguel de Medina came to a similar conclusion in 1564 when he discussed metamorphoses of people in *Christianae Paraenesis sive de Recta in Deum Fide Libri Septem*. He saw the king's affliction as the result of sorcery; however, the sorcerers did not truly enact Nebuchadnezzar's transformation into an animal and only made it appear so. Instead Nebuchadnezzar suffered a *fascinatio oculorum,* or a bewitching of his eyesight, so he saw himself as an animal.[138] Anyone else who looked at the king during this time also saw him like an animal in appearance. An actual metamorphosis of Nebuchadnezzar was unnecessary, and it was much simpler to suggest he appeared like an animal while actually remaining human. This interpretation continued into the sixteenth century in works by commentators like Peter Binsfeld[139] and is referenced by Walter Raleigh who claims about Nebuchadnezzar: 'not that he was changed in figure external, according to Mediana, insomuch as he appeared a beast to other men's eyes'.[140]

2.9 Rationalistic Denials of Metamorphosis (Sixteenth–Nineteenth Century)

The early modern period saw other trends in comments on Dan. 4 which appear to be reactions to the highly metamorphic reading also generated around this time. While many suggested anew that Nebuchadnezzar physically metamorphosed into a beast, a variety of different commentators used more rationalistic approaches to refute these statements.

137. Silvestro Mazzolini, *De Strigimagarum Daemonumque Mirandis Libri Tres* (Rome: In Aedibus Populil Romani, 1575), 182–183. The first edition, which unfortunately does not have clear pagination, was published in 1521 in Rome by Antonio Blado.

138. Miguel de Medina, *Christianae Paraenesis sive de Recta in Deum Fide Libri Septem* (Venice: Jordani Zileti, 1564), 61.

139. Peter Binsfeld, *Tractatus De Confessionibus Maleficarum et Sagarum* (Trier: Heinrich Bock, 1596), 207–210 [conclusion 3].

140. Raleigh also rejects the idea that Nebuchadnezzar became a hybrid creature, which is suggested in Liv. Pro. 4.4–15, by stating that nor was he 'made a Monster as *Dorotheus* and *Epiphanius* dreamed'; see Walter Raleigh, *The History of the World in Five Books* (London: William Stansby, 1614), 3.1.11.21. A survey of this hybrid interpretation of Dan. 4, and the ascription of Liv. Pro. to Dorotheus and Epiphanius, was conducted earlier, see §2.2 above. For Raleigh's text, I follow the citation style in Nicholas Popper, *Walter Ralegh's 'History of the World' and the Historical Culture of the Late Renaissance* (London: University of Chicago Press, 2012), xv.

2.9.1 Rationalistic Denial as Limitation of Reason (Sixteenth–Seventeenth Century)

The first of these rationalistic denials of Nebuchadnezzar's metamorphosis was based on an interpretation of his affliction as a suspension of his rational faculties. Though similar to earlier medieval denials of the king's transformation, these later commentators were characterized by a few key shared points: they interpreted Nebuchadnezzar's affliction as a change of mental state; emphasized the importance of preserving his human substance; and noted how the king's mental change could also account for the difference in his physical presentation.

Around the time immediately preceding the publication of Bodin's work in 1580, there were some biblical commentators who were beginning to use Nebuchadnezzar's affliction as the foundation for defending the possibility of physical metamorphosis too.[141] In a series of lectures on the book of Daniel between 1559 and 1560, John Calvin addressed this controversial interpretation:

> Some think that Nebuchadnezzar was changed into an animal, but that is too harsh and absurd. So we are not to imagine some metamorphosis. But he was so rejected from human society that, save for his human shape, he differed nothing from the brute beasts; more, such a deformity took place in that banishment that he became a horrible sight – ás we shall see later, all the hair of his body increased so much that they grew like the feathers of an eagle, and his nails were like birds' claws. This is what he had in likeness to the animals; for the rest he kept his human shape. But either Nebuchadnezzar was seized by insanity, or while he was mad he left human society, or he was ejected, as often happens to tyrants. It was a memorable example, that he lived with the beasts for a time. And yet it is probable that he was quite stupefied; God left him his human shape but took away his reason, as will better appear from the context.[142]

When faced with the animalising affliction of Nebuchadnezzar in Dan. 4, Calvin declared that the metamorphosis interpretation was 'absurd', instead concluding that the king merely lost his reason and was seized with madness. He also argued that this deprivation of rationality and subsequent exile led to a deformation of Nebuchadnezzar's human shape. By living in the wilderness away from society, Nebuchadnezzar's body underwent significant change, explaining the king's long nails and hair in Dan. 4. While Calvin adopted a psychological understanding of

---

141. A prominent example is Johannes Oecolampadius, *Commentarium In Danielem Prophetam Libri Duo* (Basel: Ioannem Bebel, 1530), 1.61. While he does not see Nebuchadnezzar as undergoing a lycanthropic transformation, Oecolampadius is fairly insistent about the possibility of such transformations.

142. John Calvin, *Praelectiones in Librum Prophetiarum Danielis* (CO 40:681). English translations of this text are taken from T. H. L. Parker, trans., *Daniel I: Chapters 1–6*, Calvin's Old Testament Commentaries 20 (Carlisle: Paternoster, 1993).

the king's affliction, he was also careful to state Nebuchadnezzar did not completely lose his human reason:

> From this we gather that he was for a time out of his mind. Yet in my judgement he was not so senseless that he could not feel his evils, but he was chafing at the bit and was like a madman. Others would have him a complete maniac. I will not argue for this; for me it is sufficient that he was out of his mind, so that he had something of the beast in him. But to me it is probable that there were some remnants of intelligence, so that he should feel some torment from his ruin.[143]

This need to preserve the king's rationality is important for Calvin as this is the defining characteristic of humanity.[144] Even those people who seem to lack basic reason or be entirely irrational have, for Calvin, remnants of intelligence which differentiate them from other animals.[145] Thus, if Nebuchadnezzar did not transform into an animal, he must have retained some vestige of rationality to enable him to remain human. Calvin therefore was pulled in two directions: On the one hand, he viewed a physical metamorphosis as absurd, so a mental transformation makes better sense of Dan. 4; yet the faculty of reason could not be lost through this miraculous event, otherwise Nebuchadnezzar's humanity would be utterly and definitively altered. His solution was to suggest that while Nebuchadnezzar's reason was affected, some part of it must have remained. Most other commentators of Calvin's time were generally of the same opinion that Nebuchadnezzar cannot have physically transformed and instead lost his mind.[146] The emphasis on preserving Nebuchadnezzar's humanity through a kind of mental affliction, and the resulting physical disfigurement this brought, would become key interpretative moves for future commentators.

The publication of Bodin's *Démonomanie* and the greater prominence of such lycanthropic readings of Dan. 4 led to a proliferation of such rationalistic comments on Nebuchadnezzar's affliction. Juan Maldonado (1533–1583) wrote that the king's reason was merely *limited* for a time which led to his strange appearance.[147] By arguing Nebuchadnezzar's reason was only limited, Maldonado could advocate a mental change in Nebuchadnezzar without having to resort to a complete alteration in the king's essence. This interpretative position was rigorously defended by Maldonado's Jesuit compatriot Benedict Pereira. In his 1587 commentary on the events of Dan. 4, Pereira distinguished four possible types of

---

143. John Calvin, *Praelectiones in Librum Prophetiarum Danielis* (CO 40:684).

144. John Calvin, *Institutes of the Christian Religion* 1.15.3 (CO 2:136–138), 2.2.13 (CO 2:197); John Calvin, *Commentarius in Evangelium Ioannis* (CO 47:5 and 9).

145. John Calvin, *Institutes of the Christian Religion* 2.2.12 (CO 2:196), 2.2.17 (CO 2:200).

146. For example: Johann Wigand, *Danielis Prophetae Explicatio Brevis: Tradita in Academia Ienensi* (Jena: Hüttlich, 1571), 147 and 153.

147. Juan Maldonado, *Commentaria in Prophetas Quattor: Ieremiam, Baruch, Ezechielem et Danielem* (Tournon: Horace Cardon, 1611), 564–566 [In Danielem, chapter 4].

transformation.[148] The first was a complete change in nature and substance, spoken of in literature like Apuleius' *The Golden Ass*, though Pereira thought this type was probably not actually possible. The second type were commonplace transformations in the natural world which obey strict rules, for example the metamorphosis of tadpole into frog. The third were magical rituals or demonic transformations. The final type was *transformatio divina*, transformations enacted through God's power, examples of which include the change of Lot's wife into salt (Gen 19:26) and transubstantiation at the Eucharist.[149] It is this final type of transformation which Pereira concluded happens in Dan. 4. Like Calvin, however, Pereira contended that this transformation could not have taken away the king's rationality completely. To do so would require the destruction of Nebuchadnezzar's rational soul, which when recreated would not be the same; Nebuchadnezzar's very identity would be lost in the process. To avoid this issue, instead of a complete loss of rationality, Pereira proposed that God simply blocked Nebuchadnezzar's rational faculties for the ordained amount of time. This made him behave like an animal which in turn led to a severe change in his physical appearance.[150] Therefore, while still retaining a rational soul, Nebuchadnezzar was deprived of the use of his reason and as a result took on a superficial resemblance to an animal.

Pereira's conclusions about Nebuchadnezzar's change were adopted and cited by a vast range of different commentators in the following century. The later Jesuit commentators Caspar Sanctius and Cornelius Lapide are unmistakably indebted to Pereira's earlier contribution to understanding the narrative.[151] Seventeenth-century English biblical commentators display the same interpretative moves, tracing back to Calvin,[152] as do continental European biblical commentators.[153]

148. Benedict Pereira, *Commentariorum in Danielem Prophetam Libri Sexdecim* (Antwerp: Aedibus Petri Belleri, 1594), 264–266 [*In Danielem*, book 5]. For discussion of these, see Roling, *Physica Sacra*, 276–279.

149. Pereira, *Commentariorum in Danielem Prophetam*, 266.

150. Pereira, *Commentariorum in Danielem Prophetam*, 267–268 [In Danielem, book 5].

151. Caspar Sanctius, *In Danielem Prophetam Commentarii cum Paraphrasi* (Lyon: Horatii Cardon, 1619), 199a–203C; Cornelius Lapide, *Commentaria in Quattor Prophetas Maiores* (Antwerp: Iacobum Meursium, 1675), 1300a–1301f. Lapide first published his commentary in 1622.

152. For example: Andrew Willet, *Hexapla in Danielem* (Cambridge: Cambridge University Press, 1610), 131–132; and John Mayer, *A Commentary upon all the Prophets Both Great and Small* (London: Abraham Miller and Ellen Cotes, 1652), 529–533.

153. Abraham Calov, *Biblia Veteris et Novi Testament Illustrata*, 4 vols (Frankfurt: Wustius, 1672–1676), 2:605b; Martin Geier, *Praelectiones Academicae in Danielem Prophetam Habitae Antehac Lipsiae* (Leipzig: Lanckisch, 1667), 370–374. Salomon Gesner also largely follows a similar interpretation, however, he is open to the possibility of a demonic role in Nebuchadnezzar's transformation; see Salomon Gesner, *Daniel Propheta Disputationibus XII. Et Praefatione Chronologica Breviter Explicatus* (Wittenberg: Martin Henckel, 1606), unpaginated [Disputatio 4, §25, 113–123]. For a wider examination of such an interpretation during this period, see Roling, *Physica Sacra*, 274–297.

Thus, amidst the early modern period, most biblical commentators on Dan. 4 argued against a metamorphic interpretation of the narrative and concluded that the king remained human throughout. The affliction of Nebuchadnezzar, including the behavioural and physical changes described in the text, were frequently explained as the effects of the restricting, or limiting, of the king's rational faculties.

2.9.2 Rationalistic Denial as Fiction (Eighteenth Century)

These previous rationalistic denials of the metamorphosis of Nebuchadnezzar all maintain a sense that the biblical narrative is reasonable and could be explained. The king was not metamorphosed nor was he transformed by a demonic power; instead, through an act of God, his reason had simply been restricted for a time. However, not all those in the early modern period reacting to metamorphic readings of Dan. 4 agreed that this narrative could be explained.

During the eighteenth century, a number of people began to dismiss the Bible's authority based on certain 'unreasonable' passages and incorrect statements contained therein.[154] One such 'unreasonable' narrative was found to be that in Dan. 4. For example, while discussing various metamorphoses in his *La Philosophie de L'Histoire*, including werewolves and Ovid's *Metamorphoses*, Voltaire refers to the affliction of Nebuchadnezzar as another example of such events.[155] He did not imagine that this actually took place as a historical event but recognized that '[w]hat gives weight to the belief in all these prodigies and transmutations, is that no formal proof can be given of their impossibility. There is no argument to be opposed.'[156] Thus these stories of transmutations are unable to be disproved through the use of reason and remain popular only because they strike a person's imagination or amusement.

Émilie du Châtelet, Voltaire's long-time collaborator, commented much more expansively on Dan. 4 in her *Examens de la Bible* (*ca.* 1742). She assumed Dan. 4 referred to a supposed physical transformation of Nebuchadnezzar, though she thought it was ridiculous to conceive of it ever happening historically.[157] She stated that in order for a man to be turned into an ox, 'it would be necessary to annihilate the man and create the ox, and this ox would have no more relation with this man

---

154. For example, see John Locke, *The Reasonableness of Christianity as Delivered in the Scriptures* (London: Awnsham and John Churchill, 1695). For further discussion on this trend, see Bertram Eugene Schwarzbach, 'Reason and the Bible in the So-Called Age of Reason,' *Huntington Library Quarterly* 74 (2011): 437–470.

155. Voltaire, *Philosophie de L'Histoire* (Amsterdam: Changuion, 1765), 130–131.

156. Voltaire, *Philosophie de L'Histoire*, 131. The English translation is taken from Voltaire, *The Philosophy of History* (Glasgow: Robert Urie, 1766), 164.

157. See Émilie du Châtelet, *Examens de la Bible*, ed. Betram Eugene Schwarzbach, 3 vols (Paris: Honoré Champion, 2011), 1:462. For discussion of her interpretation of Dan. 4, see Schwarzbach, 'Reason and the Bible,' 456.

than with any other. It is therefore physically and metaphysically impossible'.[158] Therefore, in agreement with Pereira, she refutes the idea of a total transformation of the king on the basis that a total destruction of his humanity would destroy his identity. With his identity gone, the event would no longer function as a legitimate transformation. However, rather than propose an alternative theory about the text, as Pereira had done by suggesting God only limited Nebuchadnezzar's reason, du Châtelet dismissed the text's events as impossible and thus fictive. Therefore, for du Châtelet and Voltaire, Dan. 4 does refer to a physical metamorphosis, yet the narrated events must be thought of as purely fictional.

2.9.3 Rationalistic Denial as a Medical Illness (Sixteenth–Twenty-First Century)

In addition to the previous rationalistic denials of Nebuchadnezzar's metamorphosis, another interpretative trend which stemmed from early medical conceptions of mental illness gradually seemed to predominate. While the idea that Nebuchadnezzar's affliction was mental and not physical had been proposed by previous commentators,[159] this interpretative trend sought to go further by specifically diagnosing the king's condition and aligning it with current medical thought. By doing so, this trend was able to develop further than previous rationalistic denials.

Between the fourth and seventh centuries, several early Byzantine physicians had identified and written extensively on a disorder they called lycanthropy.[160] This was not a belief in lycanthropic metamorphosis (as examined above), rather it was understood as a mental illness which made the patient act like a wolf or dog. Though some saw it as a type of mania, mainly it was viewed as a type of melancholy. As Hippocrates had proposed melancholy resulted from an excess of black bile, it was therefore often thought to be curable by bloodletting.[161] The Persian physician Avicenna adapted these insights and included lycanthropy in his *Canon of medicine* (1025 CE), though instead of linking it to a wolf he likened it to a type of water strider (*cucubuth*).[162] He described how the illness made the sufferer restless and agitated. For these writers, lycanthropy was not a physical metamorphosis, but

---

158. Émilie du Châtelet, *Examens de la Bible*, 1:462. The English translation is my own.

159. For example, interpreters like John Calvin and Benedict Pereira; see earlier: §2.9.1.

160. Oribasius, *Synopsis ad eustathium* 8.9 (CMG 6.3.250); Aetius of Amida, *Libri medicinales*, 6.11 (CMG 8.2.151–153); Paul of Aegina, *Pragmateia* 3.16 (CMG 9.1.159–160). For a broader discussion, see E. Poulakou-Rebelakou et al., 'Lycanthropy in Byzantine times (AD 330–1453)', *History of Psychiatry* 20 (2009): 468–479.

161. Hippocrates, *De aere aquis et locis*, 10 (CMG 1.1.66).

162. Avicenna, *Canon of medicine* 3.1.4.20. He also included *mania lupina* in his work which he connected with lupine behaviour; see Avicenna, *Canon of medicine* 3.1.4.15. See Nadine Metzger, 'Battling Demons with Medical Authority: Werewolves, Physicians and Rationalization', *History of Psychiatry* 24 (2013): 341–355.

rather described a medical affliction that made the individual behave like an animal.

As such texts received few Latin translations, these medical observations remained largely unknown to Western scholars. It was not until the dawn of the early modern era amidst a renewed interest in ancient Greek sources that extensive translation work was undertaken. During the sixteenth century, physicians began to apply these rediscovered medical observations to Dan. 4. An early example is the Spanish physician Francisco Vallés who, in 1587, attempted to explain Nebuchadnezzar's affliction as *canina melancholia*, a type of insanity. This made him imagine that he had turned into the form of another animal, either a wild ass or an ox.[163] Vallés explained that this delusion exacerbated the king's neglect leading to the other physical changes described in the biblical narrative. While Vallés does not cite the work of the earlier Byzantine physicians, his debt to them is revealed when he refers to the *canina melancholia* condition in both Greek and Arabic.[164] While discussing lycanthropy, Girolamo Mercuriale also classified Nebuchadnezzar's affliction as this form of melancholy in 1598.[165] Medical writers into the seventeenth century also continued to use Nebuchadnezzar's affliction in Dan. 4 as an example of an illness called lycanthropy.[166]

Fairly soon after Nebuchadnezzar was described as a sufferer of melancholy, these observations by medical writers began to be included in biblical commentaries. The Italian Bible translator Giovanni Diodati was one of the first biblical commentators to describe the king's illness in this way in his 1607 *Annotationes in Biblia*:

> Being (through God's judgement) taken with a disease called Lycanthropy, which is a kind of frenzy and madness, whereby one loseth all humane sense, and use of reason, and becomes brutish, fierce, and ravenous, like a beast, living in the fields wandering, and to hinder him from doing hurt, he must be kept bound and chained. Wherein questionlesse there is much diabolicall operation, and possession: as Mat 5:3–4. Luke 8:29.[167]

---

163. Francisco Vallés, *De Iis Quae Scripta sunt Physice in Libris Sacris* (Turin: Nicola Beuilaquae, 1587), 605. This kind of interpretation can also be found in earlier demonological works; for example, see Scot, *Discoverie of Witchcraft*, 102.

164. Vallés, *De Iis Quae Scripta*, 605. Another example of a sixteenth-century interpreter reliant on these earlier medical traditions is Isaac Abarbanel, *Ma'ayeni Hayeshu'ah* 5.5.

165. Girolamo Mercuriale, *Variarum Lectionum in Medicinae Scriptoribus et Alijs Libri VI* (Venice: Apud Iuntas, 1598), book 6, chapter 20, 136.

166. For example: Anton Deusing, *Fasciculus Dissertationum Selectarum* (Groningen: Johannis Colleni, 1660), 137–139.

167. Giovanni Diodati, *Pious Annotations upon the Holy Bible*, trans. Robert Gentili, 3rd edition; (London: James Flesher, 1651), fol. Aaaa2, [Dan. 4:25].

The influence of medical writings is clear in these annotations. Diodati attributed Nebuchadnezzar's affliction to the disease lycanthropy that he described as an individual becoming 'brutish' and 'like a beast'. However, Diodati's comments also betray other influences, for example, he states the king only acted like a beast once he lost his ability to reason. This is reminiscent of the previous rationalistic interpretation of the king's affliction as a limitation of reason (see §2.9.1 above). This combination of medical explanation with suspension of the king's reason can be found in other seventeenth-century commentators too.[168] Equally, Diodati's assertion that there was a demonic role in the illness may illustrate how his conception of the events in Dan. 4 was still affected by the debate over werewolves and the devil's role in such transformations. Nevertheless, there began to be a more widespread understanding of Nebuchadnezzar's affliction as a genuine medical illness in the seventeenth century. Often, this medical interpretation was used to directly refute the suggestion Nebuchadnezzar physically metamorphosed. For example, William Pemble stated '[s]ome have said that Nebuchadnezzar was metamorphosed into a very beast: but it is the truer opinion to say, that his malady was in mind not in body. God struck him with a kind of melancholy madness.'[169] The insights of early medicine thus became a means to disprove the notion of an actual metamorphosis.

Towards the latter half of the seventeenth century a new genre of biblical interpretation emerged called '*medica sacra*'. These texts attempted to systematically explain all illnesses and diseases in sacred scripture using contemporary medical knowledge, and were thus often written by physicians.[170] Their scope included any incredible biblical events for which a medical explanation could be found and it is unsurprising that Nebuchadnezzar's affliction features prominently in this genre. A prime example is *De Morbis Biblicis Miscellanea Medica* by the Danish physician Thomas Bartholin in 1672. Unlike the earlier biblical interpreters, he explains the events of Dan. 4 in solely medical terms and does not resort to incorporating other ideas; for example, he denies outright any involvement by the devil.[171] Bartholin instead decided the king was afflicted with a form of melancholy whereby he imagined himself an animal.[172] The only doubt he had about the king's condition was the exact role God had in enacting it:

168. For example: John Trapp, *Annotations upon the Old and New Testament,* 5 vols (London: Robert White, 1662), 3:537–539; Samuel Clarke, *The Life and Death of Nebuchadnezzar the Great* (London: William Miller, 1665), 23.

169. William Pemble, *The Period of the Persian Monarchie* (London: Richard Capel, 1631), 62.

170. On the creation and name of this genre, see Sandra Pott, *Medizin, Medizinethik und schöne Literatur: Studien zu Säkularisierungsvorgängen vom frühen 17. bis zum frühen 19. Jahrhundert,* Säkularisierung in den Wissenschaften seit der Frühen Neuzeit 1 (Berlin: De Gruyter, 2002), 83–84; Roling, *Physica Sacra,* 305–311.

171. Thomas Bartholin, *De Morbis Biblicis Miscellanea Medica* (Frankfurt: Danielis Paulli, 1672), 69–70.

172. Bartholin, *De Morbis Biblicis Miscellanea Medica,* 70.

This infliction of punishment on Nebuchadnezzar is assigned in Daniel 4,28 and 34 to God alone, who either of himself disturbed the wits of the proud king or permitted secondary causes, perhaps an innate melancholy, to produce their effects. Certainly the king was not of sound mind before: otherwise he would not so arrogantly have extolled his works above those of God. Hence by endless reflexion on his own greatness the humours became heated and adust and gave occasion to the melancholic madness which was to follow.[173]

Bartholin was confident the affliction was divinely enacted due to the content of the narrative itself, although he could not be certain how direct this activity was. He was more confident in asserting the mechanics of how the affliction happened. Bartholin reasoned that Nebuchadnezzar must not have been of 'sound mind' to be able to praise his own works and not God's in Dan. 4:30. This self-obsession resulted in an imbalance of the humours making him melancholic. Bartholin then described the effects of melancholy and, using insights from previous physicians like Aetius and Paul of Aegina, classified Nebuchadnezzar's as a form of *insania lupine*.[174] Finally, he went to great length to explain how melancholy could also explain the king's physical changes:

> The harmful juices of black bile are driven towards the surface of the skin, where malignant ulcers arise which are very difficult to cure. The same working of nature gave rise not only to the long hair which we read of in Nebuchadnezzar, but to the nails which grew like birds' claws.[175]

Bartholin was evidently satisfied with a medical explanation for the narrative's events as this specific melancholic condition was able to cause the physical changes described within the narrative. In Bartholin's assessment, modern medicine provided all the necessary information to explain the narrative, making the proposal of a metamorphosis here redundant.

Many other seventeenth-century examples of this genre described Nebuchadnezzar's affliction as a form of melancholy known as lycanthropy.[176] This idea was widely adopted by subsequent writers of commentaries on the Bible too. Augustin Calmet in his *Dissertation sur la Métamorphose de Nabuchodonosor* categorised the different interpretations of Dan. 4 and, citing

---

173. Bartholin, *De Morbis Biblicis Miscellanea Medica*, 70–71. English translations taken from James Willis, ed. and trans., *On Diseases in the Bible: A Medical Miscellany, 1672*, eds Johan Schioldann-Nielsen and Kurt Sorensen, Acta Historica Scientiarum Naturalium et Medicinalium 41 (Copenhagen: Danish National Library of Science and Medicine, 1994), 68.

174. Bartholin, *De Morbis Biblicis Miscellanea Medica*, 71.

175. Bartholin, *De Morbis Biblicis Miscellanea Medica*, 72.

176. For example: Vicente Molés, *De Morbis in Sacris Litteris Pathologia* (Madrid: Juan Sanchez, 1642), 117.

Vallés, Mercuriale and Bartholin, concluded the king had fallen into a mania caused by a melancholy called lycanthropy.[177] Other eighteenth-century commentators likewise adopted lycanthropy as the name of the disease Nebuchadnezzar was afflicted with.[178]

However not all were satisfied with lycanthropy as the name of Nebuchadnezzar's illness. In 1682, Valentin Vogler agreed with the previous medical consensus, however he expressed doubt about whether it was accurate to say Nebuchadnezzar had lycanthropy or a more general form of melancholy.[179] The eighteenth century saw many more writers of *medica sacra* become reticent in proposing lycanthropy as a legitimate form of medical illness. A good illustration of this tendency is the 1749 *Medica Sacra* by Richard Mead:

> All these circumstances agree so perfectly well with hypochondriacal madness, that to me it appears evident, that Nebuchadnezzar was seized with this distemper, and under its influence ran wild into the fields: and that, fancying himself transformed into an ox, he fed on grass in the manner of cattle. For every sort of madness is, as I shall specify more particularly hereafter, a disease of disturbed imagination; which this unhappy man laboured under full seven years. And thro' neglect of taking proper care of himself, his hair and nails grew to an excessive length; whereby the latter growing thicker and crooked, resembled the claws of birds. Now, the ancients called persons affected with this species of madness λυκανθρώποι or κυνανθρώποι; because they went abroad in the night, imitating wolves or dogs.[180]

Mead's diagnosis was '*insano & melancholico*', which suggests Nebuchadnezzar had a disturbed imagination and imagined himself to have transformed into an ox. The physical changes described in the text are again explained as a result of this mental illness. However, now these physical changes were understood as an

---

177. Augustin Calmet, *Commentaire Litteral sur Tous les Livres de L'Ancien et du Nouveau Testament: Ezechiel, et Daniel* (Paris: Pierre Emery, 1715), 543–546. Calmet's assessment of previous interpretations is not always accurate, for example he states Bodin thought the king was changed in form, body and soul. In actual fact, Bodin denied there was any change in the king's soul; see Bodin, *Démonomanie*, 102.

178. For example: Thomas Stackhouse, *A New History of the Holy Bible: From the Beginning of the World to the Establishment of Christianity*, 6 vols (Edinburgh: Alexander Donaldson, John Wood and James Meuros, 1767), 4:312–314; Johann Jacob Scheuchzer, *Physica Sacra Iconibus Aeneis Illustrata*, 4 vols (Augsburg: Johannes Andreas Pfeffel, 1731–1735), 4:1258a–1259b.

179. Valentin Heinrich Vogler, *De Rebus Naturalibus ac Medicis, Quarum in Scripturis Sacris fit Mentio Commentarius* (Helmstedt: George Wolfgang Hamm, 1682), 200–206. For more discussion, see Roling, *Physica Sacra*, 308–309.

180. The English translation is taken from Richard Mead, *Medica Sacra; or, A Commentary on the Most Remarkable Diseases Mentioned in the Holy Scriptures*, trans. Thomas Stack (London: J. Brindley, 1755), chap. 7, 58–59.

indirect result of Nebuchadnezzar's neglect in the wilderness, rather than a direct result of melancholy, as per Bartholin. Beyond suggesting melancholy, Mead does not claim lycanthropy as the specific diagnosis and only mentions that the ancients spoke of such people as lycanthropes. This reluctance to speak of lycanthropy as a distinct medical condition in and of itself is found in other eighteenth-century writers of this genre,[181] and perhaps culminated in the work of writers like Johann David Michaelis who no longer referred to lycanthropy at all, but rather just to madness and frenzy.[182] Even some nineteenth-century commentators who adopt a medical understanding of the narrative continued to refrain from using the word lycanthropy to describe the king's affliction.[183]

Not all those who gave medical interpretations of Dan. 4 were willing to surrender the term lycanthropy though. Around the middle of the nineteenth century Nebuchadnezzar's affliction became known by a different name: *insania zoanthropica*. This was a wider term developed by physicians of the time to denote a form of insanity whereby the individual thought themselves to be any type of animal.[184] Lycanthropy was only one type of this delusion. One of the early commentators to diagnose Nebuchadnezzar with *insania zoanthropica* was the physician Johannes B. Friedrich. Due to the contents of the text, he suggested the specific type of the disease Nebuchadnezzar suffered from should instead be called boanthropy.[185] Later commentators followed this model, for example the American professor John Dynely Prince wrote in 1899: 'The disease as described by the writer of Daniel is the form of Melancholia known as *Insania Zoanthropia*.'[186]

The effect of this surge in medical interpretations meant that by the nineteenth century the explanation of the narrative's events as an actual physical metamorphosis

---

181. Another example is Jonathan Harle, *An Historical Essay on the State of Physick in the Old and New Testament and the Apocryphal Interval* (London: Richard Ford, 1729), 115–117. Although some were still suggesting lycanthropy as the diagnosis, for example: Christian Tobias Ephraim Reinhard, *Bibelkrankheiten welche im alten Testamente vorkommen,* 2 vols. (Frankfurt-Leipzig: Günther, 1767), 2:310–317.

182. Johann David Michaelis, *Deutsche Übersetzung des Alten Testaments mit Anmerkungen für Ungelehrte. Der Zehnte Theil welcher Ezechiel und Daniel enthalt* (Göttingen: Vandenhoeck, 1781), Anmerkungen zum Propheten Daniel, 39–41.

183. Moses Stuart, *A Commentary on the Book of Daniel* (Boston: Crocker and Brewster, 1850), 126.

184. N. Parker, 'On Lycanthropy or Wolf-madness, a Variety of Insania Zoanthropica', *The Asylum Journal* 1.4 (1854): 52–53.

185. Johannes B. Friedrich, *Analekten zu Natur-und Heilkunde,* 2nd edition, 3 vols (Ansbach: Carl Brügel, 1846), 3:50–51; Edward B. Pusey, *Daniel the Prophet: Nine Lectures, Delivered in the Divinity School of the University of Oxford* (Oxford: John Henry and James Parker, 1864), 427.

186. John Dynely Prince, *A Critical Commentary on the Book of Daniel* (New York: Lemcke & Buechner, 1899) 34. For further examples, see Johann P. Trusen, *Die Sitten, Gebräuche und Krankheiten der alten Hebräer,* 2nd edition (Breslau: W. G. Korn. 1853), 214; Carl F. Keil, *Biblischer Kommentar über den Propheten Daniel* (Leipzig: Dörffling und Franke, 1869), 133.

had become increasingly unfavourable. In his 1853 notes on Daniel, Albert Barnes recognized how some commentators interpreted Nebuchadnezzar's affliction as a metamorphosis, but argued that 'it may seem, perhaps, to be undignified even to *refer* to such opinions now', and later suggested that 'it is indeed painful to reflect that such absurdities and puerilities have been in any way connected with the interpretation of the word of God'.[187]

Such medical interpretations have proved to be long-lasting and commentators throughout the twentieth and twenty-first centuries who regarded historical events as underlying the narrative of Dan. 4 continued to explain the king's affliction in Dan. 4 as a form of either the illness lycanthropy[188] or zoanthropy.[189] While many other scholars from this period have begun to doubt these particular medical diagnoses and appear less interested in understanding the precise affliction of the king, due to a shift in interpretative focus towards contextualizing Nebuchadnezzar's affliction within the ancient Near East or on understanding the historical basis (or lack thereof) for any such event, they continue to refer to the depiction of the king's affliction as either simply a mental illness, madness or insanity.[190] This choice

187. Albert Barnes, *Notes, Critical, Illustrative, and Practical on the Book of Daniel* (New York: Leavitt & Allen, 1853), 220.

188. For example: James A. Montgomery, *A Critical and Exegetical Commentary on the Book of Daniel*, ICC (Edinburgh: T&T Clark, 1927), 220; Joyce Baldwin, *Daniel: An Introduction and Commentary*, TOTC (Leicester: InterVarsity, 1978), 109–110; André Lacocque, *The Book of Daniel*, trans. David Pellauer (London: SPCK, 1979), 80; Ernest C. Lucas, *Daniel*, Apollos Old Testament Commentary (Leicester: InterVarsity, 2002), 111–112; Paul R. House, *Daniel: An Introduction and Commentary*, TOTC (London: InterVarsity, 2018), 99. Lycanthropy seems to continue to be the term customarily used by medical professionals when referring to the psychological condition in general; for example, see Petra Garlipp et al., 'Lycanthropy – psychopathological and psychodynamical aspects', *Acta Psychiatrica Scandinavica* 109 (2004): 19–22.

189. Norman W. Porteous, *Daniel: A Commentary*, OTL (London: SCM Press, 1965), 70; Louis F. Hartman and Alexander A. Di Lella, *The Book of Daniel*, AB 23 (Garden City, NY: Doubleday, 1978), 177.

190. For example, John J. Collins recognizes that 'scholars have argued that Nebuchadnezzar's transformation can be understood as an example of the disease of zoanthropy or lycanthropy' but due to 'the tradition history of the story and its original association with Nabonidus, such arguments are beside the point'. However, he still refers to the affliction as 'madnesss', 'psychological' and 'insanity'; see John J. Collins, *Daniel: A Commentary on the Book of Daniel*, Hermeneia (Minneapolis: Fortress, 1993), 209 and 227–228. For an example of a scholar who refers to the affliction as a 'mental illness', see Thomas S. Cason, 'Confessions of an Impotent Potentate: Reading Daniel 4 through the Lens of Ritual Punishment Theory', *JSOT* 39 (2014): 79–100 (97). The arguments about the narrative's context and historicity are not addressed in the present chapter as they do not attempt to explicitly address the issue of a possible physical metamorphosis of Nebuchadnezzar in the narrative. Nevertheless, I engage with them in detail elsewhere. For a discussion of the historicity of Nebuchadnezzar's affliction, see §3.1. For ancient contextualizing approaches to Dan. 4, see §4.1.

of language which commentators continue to employ seems to be inherited from earlier medical interpretations of Dan. 4.[191]

However, despite the prevalence of these medical explanations, such is the historical controversy over whether Dan. 4 presents Nebuchadnezzar as physically metamorphosing or not that this interpretative thread was not completely eradicated. Multiple twentieth-century commentators had to explicitly refute this potential explanation in order to convincingly establish the (by now more popular) medical interpretation.[192] Nevertheless, some commentators in both the twentieth and twenty-first centuries continue to advocate a physical metamorphosis in place of this medical interpretation.[193] As a consequence of this unresolved dispute about the precise nature of his supposed affliction, the legacy of this controversial debate over Nebuchadnezzar's possible metamorphosis in Dan. 4 has continued to impact interpretation of the text well into the twentieth and twenty-first centuries.

2.10 Summary

It is clear from this survey that the possibility of a metamorphosis in Dan. 4 has been a particularly controversial issue for interpreters and crucially there seems to be a split between two broad interpretative trends. On the one hand there are commentators who see in the events surrounding Nebuchadnezzar an actual/ intended physical metamorphosis of a human king into an animal form. This interpretation is taken in several different distinct directions by commentators. For example, the writer(s) of the *Vita Danielis* understood the king as metamorphosing into a hybrid lion-ox animal. Others, for example Aphrahat, suggested Nebuchadnezzar metamorphosed several times into different creatures. This range of metamorphic interpretations seem to be motivated by different factors. For example, early church fathers like Cyril of Jerusalem were keen for Nebuchadnezzar's form to change so his mind remained unaffected and he was able to repent; whereas later writers like Jean Bodin saw Nebuchadnezzar as an example of a lycanthropic metamorphosis in order to prove the existence of werewolves. Despite these differences, these various interpretations all view Nebuchadnezzar as undergoing a metamorphosis into animal form.

On the other hand, some interpreters of Dan. 4 vehemently dismissed claims of a metamorphosis, rejecting any notion of an animal transformation. In place of a metamorphosis various alternatives were proposed. Many commentators, like

---

191. Jared Beverly argues that '*the vast majority of scholars continue to uncritically employ the medicalizing language*'. See Jared Beverly, 'Nebuchadnezzar and the Animal Mind (Daniel 4)', *JSOT* 45 (2020): 145–157 (147).

192. For example, see Montgomery, *Critical and Exegetical Commentary on Daniel*, 220; Porteous, *Daniel*, 70.

193. Examples include: Otto Plöger *Das Buch Daniel*, Kommentar zu Alten Testamentum 18 (Gütersloh: G. Mohn, 1965), 77; William B. Nelson, *Daniel*, Understanding the Bible Commentary Series (Grand Rapids: Baker Books, 2013), 120.

Theodoret of Cyrrhus and Saadia Gaon, viewed the king's affliction as a type of insanity or madness which then resulted in changes to the king's appearance and behaviour. Others, including Miguel de Medina, viewed Nebuchadnezzar's supposed metamorphosis as an illusion such that the king actually retained his human form throughout the ordeal. These interpretations were also influenced by a variety of different factors. For instance, Abraham Ibn Ezra seemed to be persuaded by contemporary anecdotes about insanity which he heard, while apparent advances in medical knowledge led physicians like Francisco Vallés to understand Nebuchadnezzar's affliction as melancholy or mania, rather than metamorphosis.

This survey has demonstrated how the animalising affliction of Nebuchadnezzar has been a highly contentious issue throughout the history of the interpretation of Dan. 4. The debate over whether to understand the king's condition as a physical metamorphosis has largely been considered by interpreters to be synonymous with the question of whether Nebuchadnezzar transformed into an animal or not. This has led to a persistent division between those who see the Babylonian king as physically transforming into an animal and those who entirely reject any animal transformation in the narrative. It could even be suggested that, due to the longevity of this debate, Nebuchadnezzar's animal transformation has been the dominant interpretative concern for commentators on Dan. 4. However, as will be seen in later discussion, neither of these lines of interpretation best reflect the narrative events in Dan. 4.

Chapter 3

THE QUESTION OF METAMORPHOSIS IN THE TEXTS OF DANIEL 4

The history of the interpretation of Nebuchadnezzar's affliction has been shown to be pervaded by a basic division of opinion between whether the king is presented as having experienced a physical metamorphosis into an animal or whether an animal transformation should be entirely rejected as a valid interpretation of Daniel 4. Given this, the focus of this chapter will examine the textual evidence of Dan. 4 to address this interpretative conflict. This assessment of the various texts of Dan. 4 will be conducted with a careful eye for any evidence that may suggest an intended physical metamorphosis of the king into the form of an animal.

In order to do this, however, there are some complications. First, the extant versions of Dan. 4 seem to be drawing on earlier source material. Indeed, these sources may themselves be the origin of any supposed animal metamorphosis in the text. Thus, before proceeding to examine the texts of Dan. 4 themselves for such a transformation, it will be useful to see whether any commonly suggested potential sources for the Danielic narrative seem to describe a metamorphosis and identify whether such a transformation is inherent to the tradition behind Dan. 4. Secondly, the textual history of Dan. 4 is somewhat complex and there seem to be various different editions of the narrative (in particular, one Aramaic and two Greek editions). This chapter will thus also examine the variety of available principal texts and manuscript witnesses of Dan. 4 to uncover the level of complexity behind the tale. It will then outline the probable ways in which these divergent traditions relate to each other. Finally, once the variety of textual information has been laid out, each of the main textual traditions will be examined for evidence that could support an interpretation of Nebuchadnezzar's affliction as a physical metamorphosis. Ultimately it will be argued that, despite the use of animal imagery, the textual evidence of Dan. 4 (including the material upon which it may draw) does not seem to envisage an actual physical metamorphosis of the king into an animal. The traditions that underlie Dan. 4 seem to have an almost complete lack of animal imagery. Moreover, the animalising imagery used in both Greek editions of Dan. 4 will be shown to be reliant on the Aramaic edition. This Aramaic edition, which can be considered the primary edition of Dan. 4 when considering the animalisation of the king, seems to emphasise behavioural and spatial changes of the king and these are characterised predominantly by a loss of reason rather than any physical metamorphosis.

3.1 Searching for a Metamorphosis in the
Potential Sources of Daniel 4

Initially, and before investigating the text of Dan. 4 itself, it is necessary to examine the potential sources for the Danielic narrative to determine whether evidence for an intended metamorphosis of the king can be detected here. An analysis of this 'prehistory' of Dan. 4 will help determine whether the material which may have influenced the early forms of this narrative brought with it the idea that the king suffered a physical metamorphosis into an animal.

It is now commonly thought that the book of Daniel was not originally composed as a single literary whole but was compiled from a range of earlier material.[1] Hence there have been a number of prominent source-critical studies of Dan. 4 which have argued that the chapter is an arrangement of several older pre-existent traditions, though only two scholars have attempted this in any depth. The first of these was Ernst Haag who distinguished two principal sources for Dan. 4: a Dream Interpretation source (corresponding to Dan. 4:1–23 MT); and a Wall Pronouncement and Exile source (corresponding to 4:25–30 MT) which he considered to describe the king's animalisation.[2] A second major attempt to decipher the sources of Dan. 4 has since been made by Lawrence Wills who focused explicitly on the Old Greek (OG) edition of Dan. 4. Wills agreed with Haag in identifying the Dream Interpretation source (corresponding to Dan. 4:1–25 OG); however, he then effectively separated Haag's second source into two, and argued for the existence of a Wall Pronouncement source (corresponding to Dan. 4:26–30 OG), and a Bull Sojourn source (corresponding to Dan. 4:30a–33 OG).[3] While Wills' theory is based upon the primacy of Dan. 4 OG, which will be shown to be an inadequate

1. Even H. H. Rowley, who goes to great lengths to argue for the unity of the book of Daniel, proposes that the early chapters of the book contain material 'taken from various sources, oral and written'; see H. H. Rowley, 'The Unity of the Book of Daniel', *HUCA* 23 (1950–1951): 233–273 (271). For an example of how scholars have tried to isolate the sources for Daniel, see Esther Eshel, 'Possible Sources of the Book of Daniel', in *The Book of Daniel: Composition and Reception*, ed. John J. Collins and Peter W. Flint, VTSup 83 (Leiden: Brill, 2001), 387–94.

2. This was part of his wider project to distinguish the sources for the whole section of Dan. 4–6. Ernst Haag, *Die Errettung Daniels aus der Löwengrube: Untersuchungen zum der Ursprung der biblischen Danieltradition*, SBS 110 (Stuttgart: Katholisches Bibelwerk, 1983), 23–88.

3. Lawrence M. Wills, *The Jew in the Court of the Foreign King*, HDR 26 (Minneapolis: Fortress, 1990), 87–121. He also notes the doxology (Dan. 4:34–34a OG), which he attributes to the redactor of the finished chapter, and the letter from Nebuchadnezzar (Dan. 4:34b—34c OG) which he concludes was part of the 'Bull Sojourn' source see Wills, *Jew in the Court of the Foreign King*, 110–11.

understanding of the relationship between the different editions of Dan. 4, this does not affect the legitimacy of his conclusions.[4] His identification of these main sources generally holds up even when considering Dan. 4 MT and OG as double literary editions, and thus both editions will be referred to in the ensuing discussion.[5] Moreover, the division devised by Wills is overall more detailed and more convincing than Haag's because he relates his sources to extant extra-biblical texts. The existence of a Wall Pronouncement source was suggested to Wills by the similarities between Dan. 4:26–30 OG and the Abydenus fragment, while similarities between Dan. 4:30a–33 OG and the tradition surrounding Nabonidus, typified by *The Prayer of Nabonidus,* suggested the existence of his so-called Bull Sojourn source.[6] To understand the potential influences or sources for Nebuchadnezzar's affliction in Dan. 4, Wills' proposal therefore functions as a good starting point. However, of the three sources that he discerned, Wills only considered the Wall Pronouncement or the Bull Sojourn as potential sources for the king's animalisation.[7] Thus, when considering whether Dan. 4 has inherited from this potential source material any concept of a physical metamorphosis on the part of the king, this analysis will be restricted to these two potential sources and their associated extant texts. This analysis will first look at the various traditions about Nabonidus' sojourn in Teima (corresponding to Wills' Bull Sojourn source), then secondly at the Abydenus fragment (corresponding to Wills' Wall Pronouncement source).

While there is seemingly nothing in the lifetime of Nebuchadnezzar II (r. 643–562 BCE) which provides a basis for the king's affliction in Dan. 4, it has long been

4. Wills asserts that Dan. 4 OG is 'the better witness to the original text' see Wills, *Jew in the Court of the Foreign King*, 88. For discussion of how to understand the relationship between the MT and OG, see §3.2.2.

5. For an attempt to study different sources whilst maintaining the theory that the MT and the OG should be considered double literary editions of Dan. 4, see Amanda M. Davis, 'A Reconsideration of the MT and OG Editions of Daniel 4' (MA diss., Emory University, 2012), 16–31.

6. For discussion of these two texts, see §3.1.4 and §3.1.5. Both Wills and Haag discern the Dream Interpretation source without comparing it to another relevant text, however various parallels have been found with Dan. 4:1–25 to justify the existence of another source; see Geo Widengren, *The King and the Tree of Life in Ancient Near Eastern Religion (King and Saviour IV)*, UUA 1951:4 (Uppsala: Lundequist, 1951), 45–58; Louis F. Hartman, 'The Great Tree and Nabuchodonosor's Madness', in *The Bible in Current Catholic Thought*, ed. John L. McKenzie (New York: Herder & Herder, 1962), 75–82; Peter W. Coxon, 'The Great Tree of Daniel 4', in *A Word in Season: Essays in Honour of William McKane*, ed. James D. Martin and Philip R. Davies, JSOTSup 42 (Sheffield: JSOT Press, 1986), 91–111.

7. Wills, *Jew in the Court of the Foreign King*, 95–98.

suspected that events during Nabonidus' reign (556–539 BCE) may.[8] After the death of Nebuchadnezzar's successor Amel-Marduk (560 BCE), the reign of his murderer Neriglissar (560–556 BCE), and Neriglissar's son Labashi-Marduk (556 BCE), Nabonidus seized the throne to become the sixth king of the Neo-Babylonian Empire.[9] A link between Nabonidus and Dan. 4 was first indicated in 1854 when an inscription was discovered in Ur which referred to Bēl-šarra-uṣur as the son of Nabonidus.[10] This heir was recognized as the biblical Belshazzar of Dan. 5 who must have been Nabonidus' and not Nebuchadnezzar's as the book claimed in Dan. 5:2.[11] The implication of this is that the preceding chapter (Dan. 4) might thus have some connection with Belshazzar's actual father, Nabonidus. Soon after, various cuneiform documents were published which seemed to describe Nabonidus' absence from the throne of Babylon for ten years while he stayed at the desert oasis in Teima.[12] The resemblance of these events to the narrative in Dan. 4 (where the Babylonian king is similarly absent from the throne for a number of years) immediately led many scholars to propose that the Danielic

8. Attempts to find, amongst extra-biblical sources, a reference to an incident in Nebuchadnezzar's life which matches the events in Dan. 4 have proven vain. Such efforts have involved considering Josephus' account that Nebuchadnezzar died of an illness (Josephus, *C. Ap.* 1.20), or appealing to a vague and fragmentary text that perhaps refers to unusual behaviour on behalf of Nebuchadnezzar (BM 34113) in Albert K. Grayson, *Babylonian Historical-Literary Texts,* Toronto Semitic Texts and Studies 3 (Toronto: University of Toronto Press, 1975), 87–92. For this second argument, see Gerhard F. Hasel, 'The Book of Daniel: Evidences Relating to Persons and Chronology', *AUSS* 19 (1981): 37–49 (41–42); and Paul Ferguson, 'Nebuchadnezzar, Gilgamesh, and the "Babylonian Job"', *JETS* 37 (1994): 321–331 (321–323). However, the texts these arguments are based upon are too ambiguous and fragmentary to ultimately be convincing. It can therefore be agreed that 'there is no evidence that he was ever absent from Babylon for any extended period of time, aside from that required for his numerous military conquests' see Amanda M. Davis Bledsoe, 'The Identity of the "Mad King" of Daniel 4 in Light of Ancient Near Eastern Sources', *Christianesimo nella storia* 33 (2012): 743–758 (745).

9. Nabonidus was purportedly part of the plot which conspired to kill and replace Labashi-Marduk. This is claimed by the priest Berossus writing around 280 BCE. See Stanley M. Burstein, *The Babyloniaca of Berossus*, Sources from the Ancient Near East 1.5 (Malibu, CA: Udena, 1978), 28.

10. The discoveries are detailed in: Cyril J. Gadd, *History and Monuments of Ur* (London: Chatto & Windus, 1929), 34–36.

11. For a survey of discussion of this, see Werner Dommershausen, *Nabonid im Buche Daniel* (Mainz: Grünewald, 1964), 35–37.

12. For an outline of the evidence and an attempt to reconstruct historical information about Nabonidus' sojourn in Teima, see Paul-Alain Beaulieu, *The Reign of Nabonidus King of Babylon 556–539 B.C.,* YNER 10 (New Haven: Yale University Press, 1989), 149–185.

narrative was originally based around Nabonidus' sojourn in the desert.[13] Further evidence emerged at Qumran (e.g., the *Prayer of Nabonidus*) which seemingly confirmed that Dan. 4 drew upon such Nabonidus traditions and many scholars now agree that the underlying narrative behind Dan. 4 may have originally concerned Nabonidus rather than Nebuchadnezzar.[14] Therefore, it is necessary to briefly examine the various documentary material about Nabonidus' sojourn in Teima, which may potentially lie behind Dan. 4, to see on the one hand whether there is any evidence that these texts functioned as originating sources for the affliction of Nebuchadnezzar and, on the other, whether this affliction was conceived of as an animal metamorphosis.[15]

13. For example, see Paul Riessler, *Das Buch Daniel: Textkritische Untersuchung,* Kurzgefasster wissenschaftlicher Kommentar zu den Heiligen Schriften des Alten Testaments 3.3.2 (Stuttgart: Roth, 1899), 43; Fritz Hommel, 'Die Abfassungszeit des Buches Daniel und der Wahnsinn Nabonids', *Theologisches Literaturblatt* 23 (1902): 145–150; Hugo Winckler, *Altorientalische Forschungen,* 3 vols (Leipzig: Eduard Pfeiffer, 1893–1905), 2:200–201; Raymond P. Dougherty, *Nabonidus and Belshazzar: A Study of the Closing Events of the Neo-Babylonian Empire,* YOSR 15 (New Haven: Yale University Press, 1929); Wolfram von Soden, 'Eine babylonische Volksüberlieferung von Nabonid in den Danielerzählungen', *ZAW* 53 (1935): 81–89. Teima is often stated as being in the desert because the occupants of the huge city of Babylon likely would have thought this small settlement of Teima was distantly separated from human society; see Bledsoe, 'Identity of the "Mad King" of Daniel 4', 750. More recently, Alasdair Livingstone has argued that Teima was not actually as remote and unconnected as has been previously thought. See Alasdair Livingstone, 'Taimā' and Nabonidus: It's a Small World', in *Writing and Ancient Near East Society: Papers in Honour of Alan R. Millard,* ed. Piotr Bienkowski, Christopher Mee and Elizabeth Slater, LHBOTS 426 (London: T&T Clark, 2005), 29–39.

14. For example, see Bledsoe, 'Identity of the "Mad King" of Daniel 4', 743–58; Jonathan Stökl, 'Nebuchadnezzar: History, Memory and Myth-Making in the Persian Period', in *Remembering Biblical Figures in the Late Persian and Early Hellenistic Periods: Social Memory and Imagination,* ed. Diana V. Edelman and Ehud Ben Zvi (Oxford: Oxford University Press, 2013), 257–69 (261–2). For a more doubtful assessment of their relationship, see Takayoshi M. Oshima, 'Nebuchadnezzar's Madness (Daniel 4:30): Reminiscence of a Historical Event or Legend?' in *"Now It Happened in Those Days": Studies in Biblical, Assyrian, and Other Ancient Near Eastern Historiography Presented to Mordechai Cogan on his 75th Birthday,* ed. Amitai Baruchi-Unna et al. (Winona Lake, IN: Eisenbrauns, 2017), 645–676 (650–660).

15. For the most part, I intend to avoid inferring that any of these texts actually functioned as direct sources for the Danielic narrative, nevertheless scholars tend to agree that some oral or written traditions about this historical event probably lie behind Dan. 4.

3.1.1 The Nabonidus Chronicle

The first text to be discovered which described Nabonidus' time in Teima was *The Nabonidus (-Cyrus) Chronicle* which came to light in 1879.[16] The only surviving tablet of the *Chronicle* dates from either the Hellenistic or Parthian period, but a putative sixth-century original is widely assumed.[17] This cuneiform text documents the events surrounding the end of the Neo-Babylonian Empire under Nabonidus, the rise of Persia under Cyrus, and the first years of Persian rule over Nabonidus' old territory. Amongst the chief information related by the tablet, one recurrent event during Nabonidus' regnal years is his persistent absence from Babylon in favour of spending time in Teima:

> The seventh year: The king (was) in Tema (while) the prince, his officers, (and) his army (were) in Akkad. [The king] did not come to Babylon. (*The Nabonidus Chronicle* ii.5–6)[18]

This statement of the king's absence from Babylon is almost exactly repeated when the *Chronicle* describes events during the ninth, tenth and eleventh years of Nabonidus' reign. Thus this text describes how Nabonidus dwelt in Teima for at least four years of his reign and, due to the presence of lacunae in the tablet, it is possible that this statement was repeated for other years too. The *Chronicle* is not commonly thought of as having a direct influence upon Dan. 4 but is merely part of the context which has suggested that Dan. 4 may refer to an event in Nabonidus' life. Nevertheless, while recounting a similarly lengthy absence from the throne, it is worth emphasizing that there is nothing in this account which even remotely suggests that the king is presented as undergoing a metamorphosis.[19]

16. The *Chronicle* was first published in 1882 in Theophilus G. Pinches, 'On a Cuneiform Inscription Relating to the Capture of Babylon by Cyrus and the Events which Preceded and Led Up to It', *Transactions of the Society of Biblical Archaeology* 7 (1882): 139–76. A more recent edition, and the one quoted here, is in Albert K. Grayson, *Assyrian and Babylonian Chronicles*, TCS 5 (Winona Lake, IN: Eisenbrauns, 1975), no. 7.

17. For the dating of the *Chronicle*, see Sidney Smith, *Babylonian Historical Texts Relating to the Capture and Downfall of Babylon* (London: Methuen, 1924), 98. Caroline Waerzeggers has recently questioned how much of the extant form of the *Chronicle* can be thought of as a reliable guide to sixth-century history or to an original sixth-century edition of the text; see Caroline Waerzeggers, 'Facts, Propaganda, or History? Shaping Political Memory in the Nabonidus Chronicle', *Political Memory in and after the Persian Empire*, ed. Jason M. Silverman and Caroline Waerzeggers, ANEM 13 (Atlanta: SBL Press, 2015), 95–124.

18. This translation is taken from Grayson, *Assyrian and Babylonian Chronicles*, 106.

19. The text even refrains from passing judgement on Nabonidus' actions which elicit no negative response in the text; see Paul-Alain Beaulieu, 'Nabonidus the Mad King: A Reconsideration of His Steles from Harran and Babylon', in *Representations of Political Power: Case Histories from Times of Change and Dissolving Order in the Ancient Near East*, ed. Marlies Heinz and Marian H. Feldman (Winona Lake, IN: Eisenbrauns, 2007), 137–166 (137–138).

3.1.2 The Verse Account of Nabonidus

In 1880, shortly after the discovery of *The Nabonidus Chronicle,* another cuneiform tablet was uncovered which contained a text, now known as *The Verse Account of Nabonidus,* which also narrated Nabonidus' self-imposed exile from Babylon.[20] The extant text is fragmentary and thought to have been composed in the late sixth century BCE.[21] The *Verse Account* is often labelled as polemical in style as it seems to vilify Nabonidus, while simultaneously showing sympathy with the Persian conquerors and justifying why Cyrus was able to conquer Babylon.[22] According to this text, Nabonidus 'entrusted the military camp to his first born' (*Verse Account* II.17–20),[23] then marched into the Arabian desert, conquered the oasis called Teima, and set up his dwelling there:

> He took distant paths (and) roads. As soon as (he) arri[ved], he slew the ruler of Teima [wi]th wea[pons], and slaught[ered] the inhabitants of the city a[nd] the country (and) their herds. As for himself, he took up residence (in) [Tei]ma, the forces of Akkad [staying with him? He em]bellished the city and built [his palace] (there) like the palace of Babylon. (*The Verse Account of Nabonidus* II.24–29)[24]

Unlike the *Chronicle,* the *Verse Account* provides a narration of Nabonidus' conquest of Teima, however there is little evidence in this text to suggest that Nabonidus' sojourn there was linked to an affliction of any form. Yet some translations of this fragmentary text reconstruct in the *Verse Account* a reference to the king's madness. The fourth column has only a few preserved words of legible text, one of which has been translated as 'the king is mad'.[25] While the *Verse Account* has no direct textual link with Dan. 4, this verse may potentially reveal the historical reason for the king's wilderness sojourn and may suggest the king was mentally afflicted, or at least

---

20. The *Verse Account* was published in 1924 in Smith, *Babylonian Historical Texts,* 27–97, plates V–X. For the latest edition, see Hanspeter Schaudig, *Die Inschriften Nabonids von Babylon und Kyros' des Großen samt den in ihrem Umfeld entstandenen Tendenzschriften. Textausgabe und Grammtik,* AOAT 256 (Münster: Ugarit-Verlag, 2001), 563–78.

21. For the dating of this text, see Smith, *Babylonian Historical Texts,* 27; Schaudig, *Die Inschriften Nabonids,* 47–8.

22. For the propagandistic character of the text, see Smith, *Babylonian Historical Texts,* 231; Kabalan Moukarzel, 'The Religious Reform of Nabonidus: A Sceptical View', in *Melammu: The Ancient World in an Age of Globalization,* ed. Markham J. Geller, Max Planck Research Library for the History and Development of Knowledge Proceedings 7 (Berlin: Edition Open Access, 2014), 129–189 (169); Beaulieu, 'Nabonidus the Mad King', 137.

23. Translation taken from Beaulieu, *Reign of Nabonidus,* 150.

24. Translation taken from Beaulieu, *Reign of Nabonidus,* 171.

25. Translation taken from 'Nabonidus and the Clergy of Babylon', trans. Adolf L. Oppenheim, *ANET,* 314, col. iv.

perceived as such. While this could be a useful point of comparison with Dan. 4, it does seem unlikely that the *Verse Account* depicts Nabonidus' absence as resulting from madness. Similar pro-Persian texts do not suggest Nabonidus was mad, and the reference in the *Verse Account* is within a large section of indecipherable text which provides no context for understanding the phrase.[26] Furthermore, none of the Akkadian words which could suggest madness are present in the text and the madness which appears in the English translation is probably better understood as anger rather than insanity.[27] Paul-Alain Beaulieu proposes 'the intimation of madness, if any, stems from the allegedly unusual nature of the decision made by the king, not from a diagnosis of his mental state.'[28] Therefore, the account of Nabonidus' sojourn in Teima within the *Verse Account* provides no evidence that this event was linked to a genuine affliction of the king, much less any sort of perceived metamorphosis into an animal.

3.1.3 *The Harran Inscriptions*

Further confirmation of Nabonidus' sojourn in Teima was provided by the publication of two inscriptions on three stelae found at Harran in 1958.[29] The first inscription (H1, B) is by Nabonidus' mother Adad-guppi, while the second (H2, A and B) is by the king himself. This second inscription, which must date from before 539 BCE, provides Nabonidus' own account of his experience in Teima:[30]

> And as for me, I removed myself out of my city Babylon, and (I proceeded) on the way (to) Teima, Dadanu, Padakku, Ḫibra, Yadiḫu, and as far as Yatribu. During ten years I went back and forth between them (and) did not enter my city Babylon. (H2 I.22–27)[31]

This is followed later in the inscription by a description of the king's return to Babylon:

> (After) ten years the appointed time arrived, fulfilled were the days which Nannar, the king of the gods, had said. On the seventeenth day of Tašrītu, 'a day (upon which) Sîn is propitious,' is its (ominous) meaning. (H2 II.10–14)[32]

---

26. The Cyrus Cylinder condemns Nabonidus but does not hint at his madness; see Schaudig, *Die Inschriften Nabonids*, 550–556.

27. Edwin M. Yamauchi, 'Nabonidus', *ISBE* 3:470.

28. Beaulieu, 'Nabonidus the Mad King', 137.

29. The inscriptions were published in Cyril J. Gadd, 'The Harran Inscriptions of Nabonidus', *AnSt* 8 (1958): 35–92. The numbering of the stelae will be followed here.

30. For the date of this inscription, see Beaulieu, *Reign of Nabonidus*, 32.

31. Translation taken from Beaulieu, *Reign of Nabonidus*, 150–151. Other translations of H2 are available in Gadd, 'Harran Inscriptions of Nabonidus', 56–65; 'Nabonidus and His God', trans. Adolf L. Oppenheim, *ANET*, 562–563.

32. Translation taken from Beaulieu, *Reign of Nabonidus*, 151.

Unlike the previously observed fragmentary evidence, this inscription provides Nabonidus' own take on his sojourn in the desert near Teima. Interestingly, as well as describing the king's absence from Babylon, this inscription bears many significant and specific similarities with Dan. 4: the summary of the text as a work or sign of a deity (H2 I.1; cf. Dan. 3:31–32 MT); a first-person public address (H2 I.7; cf. Dan. 4:1 MT); self-deprecating references (H2 I.7–11; cf. Dan. 4:14, 31, 33 MT); a revelatory dream (H2 I.11; cf. Dan. 4:15 MT); a set term of absence (H2 II.11–12; cf. Dan. 4:22, 31 MT); subsequent praise of the deity (H2 II.14–20; cf. Dan. 4:31 MT); a return to Babylon wherein the king is greeted by his subjects (H2 III.4–9; cf. Dan. 4:33 MT); and a concluding praise of the deity (H2 III.28–29; cf. Dan. 4:34 MT).[33] While some of these points of comparison between Dan. 4 and H2 may merely be coincidental, the degree of their similarity has prompted scholars to argue that the Danielic narrative seems to display knowledge of Nabonidus' portrayal of events in the Harran inscriptions.[34] More recently, Carol Newsom has proposed a method by which the Danielic author may have received such knowledge.[35] Recognizing both the public nature of the inscriptions at Harran and the evidence for oral recitation of such texts, she suggests that the author of Dan. 4 probably received knowledge of the Harran inscription orally through its public reading.[36] It is therefore possible that the H2 inscription has exerted some influence upon the narrative of Dan. 4.

Nevertheless, while there are clear similarities between the inscriptions at Harran and Dan. 4 (including the descriptions of their respective kings as

33. For an outline of such similarities, see Carol A. Newsom, 'Why Nabonidus? Excavating Traditions from Qumran, the Hebrew Bible, and Neo-Babylonian Sources', in *The Dead Sea Scrolls: Transmission of Traditions and Production of Texts*, ed. Sarianna Metso, Hindy Najman and Eileen Schuller, STDJ 92 (Leiden: Brill, 2010), 57–79 (77–79); Carol A. Newsom, 'Now You See Him, Now You Don't: Nabonidus in Jewish Memory', in *Remembering Biblical Figures in the Late Persian and Early Hellenistic Periods: Social Memory and Imagination,* ed. Diana V. Edelman and Ehud Ben Zvi (Oxford: Oxford University Press, 2013), 270–282 (278–279).

34. Rudolf Meyer, *Zur Geschichte und Theologie des Judentums in hellenistisch-römischer Zeit* (Berlin: Evangelische Verlagsanstalt, 1989), 111; Klaus Koch, 'Gottes Herrschaft über das Reich des Menschen: Daniel 4 im Licht neuer Funde', in *The Book of Daniel in the Light of New Findings,* ed. Adam S. van der Woude, BETL 106 (Leuven: Leuven University Press and Peeters, 1993), 77–120 (89–98).

35. Newsom, 'Now You See Him', 278–279.

36. In the ancient world, texts were read or performed aloud; see Karel van der Toorn, *Scribal Culture and the Making of the Hebrew Bible* (Cambridge, MA: Harvard University, 2007), 11–14; Mogens T. Larsen, 'The Mesopotamian Lukewarm Mind: Reflections on Science, Divination and Literacy', in *Language, Literature, and History: Philological and Historical Studies Presented to Erica Reiner,* ed. Francesca Rochberg-Halton, AOS 67 (New Haven: American Oriental Society, 1987), 202–225 (219). The placement of the Harran inscriptions also seems deliberately public; see Gadd, 'Harran Inscriptions of Nabonidus', 90.

undergoing a set term of absence from Babylon), there is very little commonality between them when it comes to describing the experience of the king during this sojourn. There is, for example, certainly no parallel in the Harran inscriptions for the animalising imagery used to describe Nebuchadnezzar. The only perceptible connection is that the king's absence might be divinely ordained. This is suggested by some alternate translations of H2 which portray the moon god Sin as being responsible for Nabonidus' sojourn in Teima.[37] For example, Adolf Oppenheim renders H2 I.22–25 as 'He (Sin) decimated the inhabitants of the country, but he made me leave my city Babylon on the road to Tema, Dadanu, Padakku, Hibra, Jadihu even as far as Jatribu.'[38] This divine cause of Nabonidus' exile is doubtful and many other versions of the text translate this passage differently without the god's involvement in the events,[39] nevertheless most translators do agree that the inscriptions at Harran describe Sin as continuing to protect Nabonidus in the supposedly hostile Arabian territory.[40] Thus, while there is no evidence in these inscriptions for an animal metamorphosis or even something that might approximate to the specific affliction of Nebuchadnezzar in the Danielic narrative, Nabonidus' absence does still involve a deity's intervention while absent from Babylon.

3.1.4 The Prayer of Nabonidus

These suspicions of a link between Nabonidus and Dan. 4 were seemingly confirmed by the discovery of a first-century BCE document at Qumran labelled 4Q242 which has since become known as *The Prayer of Nabonidus* (4QPrNab).[41] Initially four fragments (1, 2a, 3 and 4) were published in 1956 by Józef Milik,[42] and later Rudolf Meyer published a further fifth fragment (2b) in 1962.[43] There is

---

37. This similarity is also suggested by Newsom ('Why Nabonidus?', 78) but I include it as a supplementary similarity due to the uncertainty regarding its presence in the inscription.

38. 'Nabonidus and His God', trans. Adolf L. Oppenheim, *ANET,* 562, col i.

39. For example, see Beaulieu's translation of the same passage above. For other possible reasons for Nabonidus' decision to leave Babylon, see Oshima, 'Nebuchadnezzar's Madness', 654.

40. See the translation of H2 I.27–II.10 in Beaulieu, *Reign of Nabonidus,* 172–173.

41. For the text, see John J. Collins, '4QPrayer of Nabonidus ar', in *Qumran Cave 4.XVII: Parabiblical Texts, Part 3,* ed. George J. Brooke et al., DJD 22 (Oxford: Clarendon, 1996). For the approximate date of this manuscript, see Frank M. Cross, 'Fragments of the Prayer of Nabonidus', *IEJ* 34 (1984): 260–264 (260).

42. Józef T. Milik, ,'"Prière de Nabonide" et autres écrits d'un cycle de Daniel', *RB* 63 (1956): 407–415.

43. Rudolf Meyer, *Das Gebet des Nabonid: Eine in den Qumran-Handschriften wiederentdeckte Weisheitserzählung,* Sitzungsberichte der Säcsischen Akademie der Wissenschaften zu Leipzig, Philologisch-historische Klasse 107.3 (Berlin: Akademie, 1962), 16.

general agreement over how these fragments should line up, but exactly how they relate to each other is still disputed: for example the appropriate size of each lacuna between the fragments is unclear.[44] This manuscript relates a story about Nabonidus, a king of Babylon, who is afflicted with a disease for seven years in Teima. He prays unsuccessfully to idols, but after being healed he is told by a Jewish diviner to praise God. The structure of the material has been explained as containing a title in lines 1–2a, a first-person summary of the story in lines 2a–5, and the actual recounting of Nabonidus' experiences in line 5 to the end.[45] The text is introduced to the reader as a prayer, however the text contains nothing that resembles one.[46] The extant text is perhaps best classified as an 'idol parody narrative' as it seems to highlight Nabonidus' conversion from worshipping idols to praising the Jewish God:[47]

> [1]The words of the p[ra]yer which Nabonidus, king of [Baby]lon, [the great]king, prayed [when he was smitten] [2]with a bad disease by the decree of G[o]d in Teima. [I, Nabonidus, with a bad disease] [3]was smitten for seven years and sin[ce] G[od] set [his face on me, he healed me] [4]and as for my sin, he remitted it. A diviner (he was a Jew fr[om among the exiles) came to me and said:] [5]'Pro[cla]im and write to give honour and exal[tatio]n to the name of G[od Most High', and I wrote as follows:] [6]I was smitten by a b[ad] disease in Teima [by the decree of the Most High God.] [7]For seven years [I] was praying [to] the gods of silver and gold, [bronze, iron,] [8]Wood, stone, clay, since [I thoug]ht that th[ey were] gods [9][...] their [...] (4Q242 frags. 1–3 lines 1–9)[48]

> [1][...] apart from them. I was made strong again [2][...]from it he caused to pass. The peace of [my] repo[se returned to me [...] [3][...] my friends. I was not able [...] [4][...] how you are like [...] [5][...] (4Q242 frag. 4 lines 1–5)[49]

44. A prominent example is the scholarly disagreement over the size of the lacuna between fragments 1, 2a and 2b.

45. Wills, *Jew in the Court of the Foreign King*, 91.

46. Some scholars speculate that a prayer may have been originally inserted within the larger surviving narrative sections; see Collins, '4QPrayer of Nabonidus ar', 87; and Andrew B. Perrin, *The Dynamics of Dream-Vision Revelation in the Aramaic Dead Sea Scrolls*, JAJSup 19 (Göttingen: Vandenhoeck & Ruprecht, 2015), 74.

47. Wills, *Jew in the Court of the Foreign King*, 91. This genre of literature is described in detail in Lawrence M. Wills, *The Jewish Novel in the Ancient World*, Myth and Poetics Series (Ithaca, NY: Cornell University Press, 1995), 62. For an example of someone who classifies the *Prayer* as a wisdom tale, see Florentino García Martínez, *Qumran and Apocalyptic: Studies on the Aramaic Texts from Qumran*, STDJ 9 (Leiden: Brill, 1992), 135.

48. Translation from Collins, '4QPrayer of Nabonidus ar', 89.

49. Translation from Collins, '4QPrayer of Nabonidus ar', 92.

The *Prayer* was almost immediately associated with the narrative in Dan. 4 due to several shared features.[50] Both are about a Babylonian king who is stricken by God; the affliction lasts for a seven-year period; and he recovers due to a Jewish seer's advice to return to God.[51] They also contain parallel paeans to God, as well as both third- and first-person sections of their respective stories.[52] Furthermore, as well as the narrative content, these texts both seek to demonstrate God's power over and against the futility of trusting false gods.[53]

While the *Prayer* shares a number of features with Dan. 4 there are also significant differences between the two narratives. These include: the name of the king (Nebuchadnezzar in Dan. 4, but Nabonidus in the *Prayer*); the name of the secondary Jewish character (Daniel in Dan. 4, but unnamed in the *Prayer*);[54] the affliction of the king (Nebuchadnezzar's affliction involves some degree of animalisation, while Nabonidus simply suffers from a disease); the setting (Nebuchadnezzar is afflicted in Babylon, but Nabonidus is afflicted in Teima); and the advice given to the king (Daniel tells him to repent and be merciful, whereas Nabonidus is told to glorify God).[55]

The close similarity in the stories appears to indicate that these two texts bear some relation to each other, but, due to the marked dissimilarities, the nature of this relationship has been contested since the first publication of *The Prayer of Nabonidus* in 1956.[56] There have been several different theories which try to explain this supposed relationship.[57] It has been tempting for scholars to claim the

50. Milik, '"Prière de Nabonide" et autres écrits', 407–415.

51. For a list of parallels and differences between the narratives, see Andrew Steinmann, 'The Chicken and the Egg: A New Proposal for the Relationship Between the *Prayer of Nabonidus* and the *Book of Daniel*,' *RevQ* 20 (2002): 557–70 (560 especially Table 1 and 2).

52. These are parallels with the MT of Daniel, but Lawrence Wills has compared the *Prayer* with the OG text. He claims that the first-person account in the *Prayer* is formally more similar to the OG. See Wills, *Jew in the Court of the Foreign King*, 92.

53. García Martínez, *Qumran and Apocalyptic*, 129.

54. This is only a difference in the extant text. It is possible that in the complete text this unnamed Jewish seer within the *Prayer* was explicitly connected with Daniel, though this is admittedly mere speculation.

55. The advice offered to both kings is not completely different as both kings do end up repenting and glorifying God.

56. A minority of scholars maintain that the two texts are entirely independent, documenting separate events that happened to both Nebuchadnezzar and Nabonidus. See Hasel, 'Book of Daniel', 37–49; Roland K. Harrison, *Introduction to the Old Testament* (Grand Rapids: Eerdmans, 1969), 1117–1120. However, the degree of similarity between the texts makes it extremely unlikely that they are completely independent. For other dismissals of this theory, see Henze, *Madness of King Nebuchadnezzar*, 69; García Martínez, *Qumran and Apocalyptic*, 129–130.

57. A useful and brief summary of the main theories is provided in Perrin, *Dynamics of Dream-Vision Revelation*, 74.

Prayer as a rare example of an extant direct source for a biblical text.[58] However the existence of glaring narrative differences between the *Prayer* and Dan. 4 is enough to effectively disregard this theory.[59] Most often, scholars have been more cautious and have instead described the *Prayer* as representing an older, more primitive or more conservative tradition.[60] This option recognizes that the *Prayer* perhaps contains more accurate historical information (e.g., the character of Nabonidus and the setting in Teima) alongside aspects that are similar to the Danielic narrative (e.g., the seven-year period and the king's affliction). Such observations often lead to the conclusion that the *Prayer* occupies 'an intermediate place' between the Babylonian evidence of Nabonidus' absence from Babylon and the Danielic narrative, while preserving evidence of the formative tradition that antedated and gave rise to Dan. 4.[61] However, as the tradition about Nabonidus' sojourn seems to be pluriform and retold in different texts, the assumption that the relationship between Dan. 4 and the *Prayer* can fit into a linear chain of literary development from the same basic written text is both forced and unnecessary.[62] More recently, by embracing both the evident plurality in the Nabonidus tradition and the lack of explicit correspondence between the texts, scholars have situated Dan. 4 and the

58. One scholar who views it as a direct source for Dan. 4 is Esther Eshel, who claims: 'the biblical author adapted the prayer according to his worldview by making specific changes'. See Eshel, 'Possible Sources', 387–94.

59. See David N. Freedman, 'The Prayer of Nabonidus', *BASOR* 145 (1957): 31–32 (31); Milik, '"Prière de Nabonide" et autres écrits', 410; Newsom with Breed, *Daniel: A Commentary*, 128.

60. Collins, '4QPrayer of Nabonidus ar', 86; John J. Collins, 'New Light on the Book of Daniel From the Dead Sea Scrolls', in *Perspectives in the Study of the Old Testament and Early Judaism: A Symposium in Honour of Adam S. van der Woude on the Occasion of His 70th Birthday*, ed. Florentino García Martínez and Ed Noort (Leiden: Brill, 1998), 180–196 (195–196); Frank M. Cross, *The Ancient Library of Qumran*, 3rd ed. (Sheffield: Sheffield Academic Press, 1995), 123–124; García Martínez, *Qumran and Apocalyptic*, 130; Michael A. Knibb, 'The Book of Daniel in Its Context', in *The Book of Daniel: Composition and Reception*, ed. John J. Collins and Peter W. Flint, VTSup 83 (Leiden: Brill, 2001), 16–36 (24); Loren T. Stuckenbruck, 'The Formation and Re-formation of Daniel in the Dead Sea Scrolls', in *The Bible and the Dead Sea Scrolls: Volume One: Scripture and Scrolls*, ed. James H. Charlesworth (Waco, TX: Baylor University Press, 2006), 101–130 (106); Freedman, 'Prayer of Nabonidus', 31; Milik, '"Prière de Nabonide" et autres écrits', 411; Pierre Grelot, 'Nabuchodonosor changé en bête', *VT* 44 (1994): 10–17 (11).

61. Quotation from: Collins, '4QPrayer of Nabonidus ar', 86. See also Peter W. Flint, 'The Daniel Tradition at Qumran', in *Eschatology, Messianism, and the Dead Sea Scrolls*, ed. Craig A. Evans and Peter W. Flint (Grand Rapids: Eerdmans, 1997), 41–60 (58); Stuckenbruck, 'Formation and Re-formation of Daniel', 103. These scholars do not suggest that the extant version of the *Prayer* is older than Dan. 4, nor that the author of Dan. 4 even knew of the *Prayer*.

62. This is convincingly argued by Henze, *Madness of King Nebuchadnezzar*, 69.

Prayer as distinct recollections of the same tradition. For Matthias Henze, this best explains the general thematic similarities between the texts whilst allowing for specific literary differences.[63] This has been further advanced by Carol Newsom who argued that early forms of both these texts resulted from a basic remembered narrative of Nabonidus' exile inherited from the Harran inscriptions. By hearing public readings of these inscriptions, the authors of the *Prayer* and Dan. 4 would have remembered a template of the content of the stele, which then subsequently and independently underwent the process of conceptual blending with other known traditions.[64] Thus, while these two Jewish narratives can trace some lineage back to the same traditions about Nabonidus, Newsom argues that they were constructed independently of one another through the blending of concepts. Although there are significant issues with maintaining the complete independence of the *Prayer* from Dan. 4, the general structural and functional commonality between the two texts is nevertheless best explained if they shared a common oral origin.[65]

The fact that these two texts plausibly share the same origins may thus mean that the text of the *Prayer* can shed light upon whether an early source of Dan. 4 contained any suggestion of the king's transformation into an animal. Indeed there are some scholars who have suggested a reconstruction of the lacunae whereby the

---

63. Henze, *Madness of King Nebuchadnezzar*, 70–73. See also Klaus Koch, *Daniel: Kapitel 1,1–4,34*, BKAT 22.1 (Neukirchen-Vluyn: Neukirchener Verlag, 2005), 408–415.

64. Newsom, 'Why Nabonidus?', 57–79; Newsom, 'Now You See Him', 270–82. For a similar argument, see Reinhard G. Kratz, 'Nabonid in Qumran', in *Babylon: Wissenskultur in Orient und Okzident*, ed. Eva Cancik-Kirschbaum, Margarete van Ess and Joachim Marzahn, Topoi 1 (Berlin: De Gruyter, 2011), 253–70. Joseph Angel suggests this blending of a nucleus of early traditions also resulted in the text known as the *Book of Giants*. See Joseph L. Angel, 'The Humbling of the Arrogant and the "Wild Man" and "Tree Stump" Traditions in the *Book of Giants* and Daniel 4', in *Ancient Tales of Giants from Qumran and Turfan: Contexts, Traditions, and Influences*, ed. Matthew Goff, Loren T. Stuckenbruck and Enrico Morano, WUNT 360 (Tübingen: Mohr Siebeck, 2016), 61–80.

65. There are compelling reasons that should make us sceptical of the notion that the *Prayer* and Dan. 4 are entirely independent recollections of public recitations of the Harran inscriptions. The level of similarity between these two texts suggests that they have used and interpreted such received information in a similar way. This includes fundamental aspects of the narratives; for example, they each concern a pagan king converting to worship the Jewish God; they use the event to demonstrate the deity's supremacy; and they agree that the king was absent from Babylon for seven years. Thus, if these texts did arise through the recitation of the Harran inscriptions, as Newsom suggests, then they may have arisen from the same received narrative template which then was adjusted or blended in different places or times so as to form the two different narratives.

Prayer would have originally included a bestial affliction similar to that in Dan. 4.[66] Frank Moore Cross adjusted the positioning of the fragments of the *Prayer* and proposed inserting a reference to Nabonidus becoming like a beast after fragment 2a. He suggested that in 4Q242 1–3.3 the reconstruction should be influenced by Dan. 5:21 resulting in: 'for seven years, and from [that] (time) I was like [unto a beast and I prayed to the Most High]'.[67] Cross explained that the king's likeness to a beast consists only of the fact that he is forced to live separately from society. However, by comparing Dan. 4 OG with this reconstruction of the *Prayer*, Lawrence Wills has taken this possibility further and argued for the existence of an earlier source for the Danielic narrative called the Bull Sojourn which he concluded depicted the king as transforming into a domesticated bull.[68] This argument would thus provide evidence that an animal transformation of the king was part of the earlier material that influenced the Danielic narrative.

However, Cross' reconstruction of the *Prayer* to include a reference to a bestial transformation has been called 'paleographically impossible',[69] and was not included in the official publication of the *Prayer* as it was deemed 'highly questionable'.[70] Moreover, there is nothing in the extant fragments of the *Prayer* that logically indicates the text ever made any reference to the king becoming animal-like or indeed to animals at all. The only reason to suspect that the *Prayer* might contain animalising imagery is the existence of the parallel story in Dan. 4 and alone this is not sufficient reason to propose a similar reconstruction of the *Prayer*. Cross' reconstruction is thus overly reliant on Dan. 4 and does not pay enough heed to the text of the *Prayer* itself which seems to have no place for the king's change to resemble an animal.[71] Thus both Cross' reconstruction of the *Prayer* and Wills' suggestion of an earlier bull transformation source behind Dan. 4 must be rejected.

Instead of depicting an animal transformation of any kind, the *Prayer* suggests that Nabonidus' sojourn in Teima is linked to his affliction with a bad disease (4Q242 1–3.2 and 6). While the specifics of this illness are not described, it is likely

---

66. An early attempt at this was the suggestion that a reference to the king's animalisation could be included in the lacuna between fragments 1 and 2a, see Haim M. Y. Gevaryahu, 'The Prayer of Nabonidus of the Scrolls of the Judean Desert' [Hebrew], in *Studies on the Scrolls of the Judean Desert*, ed. Jacob Liver (Jerusalem: Israel Society for Biblical Research, 1957), 12–23; Adam S. van der Woude, 'Bemerkungen zum Gebet des Nabonid', in *Qumrân: Sa Piété, Sa Théologie et Son Milieu*, ed. Mathias Delcor (Leuven: Leuven University Press, 1978), 120–129. This possibility has now been mostly discounted by scholars.

67. Cross, 'Fragments of the Prayer of Nabonidus', 263.

68. Wills, *Jew in the Court of the Foreign King*, 95, 110–111.

69. García Martínez, *Qumran and Apocalyptic*, 123.

70. Collins, '4QPrayer of Nabonidus ar', 90.

71. Collins, '4QPrayer of Nabonidus ar', 89–90 for the more commonly-agreed reconstruction of 4Q242 1–3.3.

a reference to some form of skin disease.[72] It has been noted by scholars that this affliction is reminiscent of those described in cuneiform curse formulas.[73] For example:

> [419][May Sin], the brightness of heaven and earth clothe you with [420][a lep]rosy; [may he forbid your entering into the presence of the gods] [421][or king (saying): 'Roam the desert] like the wild-ass (and) the gazelle.' (*Vassal-Treaties of Esarhaddon* v.419–421)[74]

The similarity of skin affliction in these *Vassal-Treaties* with the *Prayer* is immediately apparent, but so is the cursed man's isolation in the wilderness. The fact that Nabonidus' favoured deity, the moon God Sin, is the one who brings this about is especially pertinent. If this comparison with such curse formulae is legitimate, it may suggest that the king's skin disease in the *Prayer* would have been also connected with living in the wilderness like an animal. This is perhaps the closest we can get to animalising imagery about the king within a text relating to Nabonidus. However, while the *Vassal-Treaties of Esarhaddon* refer to wild-asses and gazelles, no similar references to animals can be found in the text of the *Prayer* itself. Furthermore, even if this imagery were present in the *Prayer*, it would not be indicative of a metamorphosis of the king into an animal, rather in such curse formulae the likeness to an animal is based purely on their shared location of habitation. Thus, in the extant text, the *Prayer* appears to simply describe the king as suffering from a skin ailment which meant he was forced to stay away from the city of Babylon. There is no tangible evidence that the *Prayer* depicted an animalising affliction of the king, and this text should not be seen as a witness to a potential source for the animal transformation in the Dan. 4 tradition.

3.1.5 The Abydenus Fragment

Unlike the previous material, the final text which will be investigated as a potential source for Dan. 4 is not related to Nabonidus. Instead it concerns Nebuchadnezzar himself and thus potentially holds a quite different relationship with Dan. 4

---

72. The Aramaic term used here שׁחִין is also the same Hebrew form used to describe the plague of boils in Exod. 9:8–11 and Deut. 28:27. Marcus Jastrow defined the Aramaic form as one of a variety of skin ailments; see Jastrow, s.v. 'שְׁחִין.'

73. Kazuko Watanabe, 'Die literarische Überlieferung eines babylonisch-assyrischen Fluchthemas mit Anrufung des Mongottes Sin', *ASJ* 6 (1984): 99–119; Grelot, 'Nabuchodonosor changé en bête', 14–15; Antoine Cavigneaux, 'Shulgi, Nabonide, et les Grecs', in *An Experienced Scribe Who Neglects Nothing: Ancient Near Eastern Studies in Honor of Jacob Klein*, ed. Yitschak Sefati et al. (Bethesda, MD: CDL, 2005), 63–72.

74. Translation taken from: Donald J. Wiseman, 'The Vassal-Treaties of Esarhaddon', *Iraq* 20 (1958): 1–99 (60).

than the other previously examined texts. In the early fourth century CE, the Christian historian Eusebius of Caesarea wrote *Praeparatio Evangelica* in which he claimed to have discovered a story in a work entitled *Concerning the Assyrians* by the second-century CE historian Abydenus, who in turn relied to some extent on the Greek writer and diplomat Megasthenes (358–290 BCE). This text details a statement which Nebuchadnezzar is alleged to have made from within Babylon:

> It is, moreover, related by the Chaldeans, that as he went up into his palace he was possessed by some god; and he cried out, and said: 'Oh! Babylonians, I, Nebucodrosorus [Nebuchadnezzar] foretell unto you a calamity which must shortly come to pass, which neither Belus my ancestor, nor his queen Beltis, have the power to persuade the Fates to turn away. A Persian mule shall come, and by the assistance of your gods shall impose upon you the yoke of slavery; the author of which shall be a Mede, the foolish pride of Assyria. Before he should thus betray my subjects, Oh! That some sea, or whirlpool, might receive him, and his memory be blotted out forever; or that he might be cast out to wander through some desert, where there are neither cities nor the trace of men; a solitary exile among rocks and caverns, where beasts and birds alone abide. But for me, before he shall have conceived these mischiefs in his mind, a happier end will be provided.' (Eusebius, *Praep. ev.* 9.41.6)[75]

The relation of this text to Dan. 4 seems to have been proposed by Eberhard Schrader in 1881, who suggested the Abydenus fragment preserved an earlier form of a Babylonian legend that was modified in Dan. 4.[76] There have since been a variety of theories about their relationship, some following Schrader,[77] others who have dismissed the relationship entirely.[78] However such theories arose due to the remarkable similarity the story bears to Dan. 4. These include: Nebuchadnezzar as the protagonist; the setting around his palace; the divine decree which is received about his kingdom's fate; the emphasis on Nebuchadnezzar's might; and the solitary exile of the king.[79] This resemblance is perhaps even closer when the fragment is compared with the Old Greek edition of Dan. 4 as they share references

---

75. This translation is taken from Ronald H. Sack, *Images of Nebuchadnezzar: The Emergence of a Legend*, 2nd rev. and exp. ed. (London: Associated University Presses, 2004), 22.

76. Eberhard Schrader, 'Die Sage vom Wahnsinn Nebuchadnezzars', *Jahrbücher für protestantische Theologie* 4 (1881): 618–629 (623–624).

77. For example Samuel R. Driver, *The Book of Daniel*, The Cambridge Bible for Schools and Colleges (Cambridge: Cambridge University Press, 1900), 59–60.

78. Charles C. Torrey, 'Notes on the Aramaic Part of Daniel', *Transactions of the Connecticut Academy of Arts and Sciences* 15 (1909): 239–82 (266).

79. See Koch, 'Gottes Herrschaft', 87–88.

to the king's successor.[80] This level of commonality lends considerable weight to the idea that this text is related to Dan. 4. Nevertheless, while this Abydenus fragment shares several elements with Dan. 4 there are some clear differences too, examples of which include: Nebuchadnezzar is the recipient of the divine decree in Dan. 4 but he delivers it in the Abydenus fragment; Nebuchadnezzar is the subject of the decree in Dan. 4 whereas in the fragment it concerns 'a Mede' (which most probably should be identified with Cyrus the Persian).[81] Due to these differences, and the fact that the extant text of the Abydenus fragment is later in date than the text of Dan. 4 and so may have received later amendment *towards* the Danielic narrative, a direct literary relationship between these two cannot necessarily be maintained. Furthermore, the complexity surrounding the transmission and purported authorship of the Abydenus fragment means that at best it can be said they share a common tradition.[82] It is this purported common tradition which Wills argues gave rise to a Wall Pronouncement source for Dan. 4.

This proposed underlying common tradition reflected in both the Abydenus fragment and Dan. 4 has been suggested by Haag as a potential source for Nebuchadnezzar's animalisation.[83] Indeed, the references to wild beasts within the Abydenus fragment may, on a cursory reading of the text, support such a claim. However, evidence that this earlier source described the king's animalisation is actually fairly weak. Importantly, the comparative material in the Abydenus fragment does not depict the king in animalising terms. The Mede is said to 'wander through the desert' as 'a solitary exile among rocks and caverns, where beasts and birds alone abide' (Eusebius, *Praep. ev.* 9.41.6). While this resembles Dan. 4:29 MT, it is far short of the entire affliction related in the rest of Dan. 4 MT and only incorporates the reference to animals in order to illustrate the location of his exile. Additionally, while the Persian conqueror is called a 'mule', there is no reason to think that the 'Mede' in the Abydenus fragment is actually supposed to resemble an animal at all. This is most likely simply a metaphor designed to comment disparagingly upon the incoming Persian conqueror (perhaps a reference to his parentage), rather than to assign an equine nature to the king.[84] Thus there is no actual evidence for a bestial affliction in this comparative text and it seems to simply hope for Cyrus to go into exile. The animalising imagery that does occur in

---

80. See Wills, *Jew in the Court of the Foreign King*, 95–98; Collins, *Daniel: A Commentary*, 219. The king's successor is mentioned in Dan. 4:28 OG. For the text of the Old Greek, see Appendix B.

81. Dommershausen, *Nabonid im Buche Daniel*, 65–66.

82. Koch, 'Gottes Herrschaft', 77–119.

83. Haag, *Die Errettung Daniels aus der Löwengrube*, 87–89.

84. A similar usage may be how Jesus calls Herod a fox in Luke 13:32. For a detailed study on animal insults in the ancient world, see Manfred Faust, 'Metaphorische Schimpfwörter', *Indogermanische Forschungen* 74 (1969): 54–125. For the use of mule metaphors as a reference to Cyrus' parentage, see Anise K. Strong, 'Mules in Herodotus: The Destiny of Half-Breeds', *The Classical World* 103 (2010): 455–464 (457–459).

Dan. 4 (i.e., eating grass like an ox; see 4:29–30 MT; 4:29 OG) has no parallel in the Abydenus fragment and thus it is unlikely that the shared common tradition lying behind both texts contained such a depiction. Instead, the specific similarities between Dan. 4 OG and the Abydenus fragment suggest that the proposed underlying tradition about Nebuchadnezzar's wall pronouncement was more concerned with the political implications of the exile rather than the king's animalisation.[85] Therefore, while it may be useful to think of the Abydenus fragment as witnessing to an earlier tradition behind the Danielic narrative, there is again no evidence in this tradition for an animal transformation of the king.

3.1.6 Summary

By assessing the fragmentary evidence which appears to hold some relationship with the narrative of Dan. 4, it has been shown that none of these other texts depict the king as physically metamorphosing into an animal. Despite the conclusions of Wills and Haag, who each suppose an earlier source or tradition as being the origin of the animalising affliction of the king, there is no evidence that any underlying material behind Dan. 4 referred to the king's affliction in such striking animalising terms. The textual evidence relating to Nabonidus suggests that the king's time in Teima was a divine punishment and involved a specific physical affliction (e.g., H2 I.22–25; 4Q242 1–3, 2). The evidence from the Abydenus fragment, and the purported source lying behind both it and Dan. 4, potentially contains some animal imagery but this only seems to describe *where* the king lived rather than the affliction itself. However, the presence of such animal imagery in the underlying tradition, while not a direct source for the king's animalisation, might not be merely coincidental.[86] While there is no evidence of any animal transformative imagery in the purported tradition that underlies this section of Dan. 4 and the Abydenus fragment, it is entirely possible that the imagery about the king wandering with the beasts (Eusebius, *Praep. ev.* 9.41.6, and possibly also in the Wall Pronouncement source of Dan. 4:26–30) may have influenced or contributed to the development of the more elaborate animalisation that was eventually depicted in Dan. 4. We could speculate that the animalising affliction present in the tradition of Dan. 4 may have developed out of a combination of this animal imagery in the Wall Pronouncement source mixed with a remembrance of the king's divine punishment present in the

---

85. Due to the similarities between Dan. 4 OG and the Abydenus fragment, it seems best to follow Wills in proposing that the animalising imagery in Dan. 4:29–30 is a later addition rather than deriving from a possible underlying shared source; see Wills, *Jew in the Court of the Foreign King*, 100–101.

86. Wills suggests that this animal imagery in the Abydenus fragment and the supposed Wall Pronouncement source for Dan. 4 is only coincidental and had no influence on the animalising affliction in Dan. 4; see Wills, *Jew in the Court of the Foreign King*, 111–12. However, this seems to be an unnecessary overstatement and it is difficult to discount any relationship between this imagery and Nebuchadnezzar's affliction.

Nabonidus tradition.[87] This potential influence has to remain speculative but should still not be categorically ruled out. Nevertheless, even taking into account this possibility, it is clear that there is no evidence in the potential sources of Dan. 4 for any sort of *explicit* physical metamorphosis of the king. Therefore, if such an animal transformation is present in the Danielic narrative, as the interpretation of Dan. 4 at least suggests, it must be innovative to the textual editions of Dan. 4 itself or result from a subsequent development of the text.[88]

3.2 Describing the Textual Traditions of the Book of Daniel

Before we can examine the text of Dan. 4 for evidence of an animal metamorphosis, first it is necessary to understand the range of textual evidence available. Whilst the main features of Dan. 4, including Nebuchadnezzar's great tree dream and divine affliction, seem to be critical parts of the narrative, its textual history is far from uniform.[89] There are numerous distinct textual traditions which each retell Nebuchadnezzar's affliction slightly differently. While there is a wide array of ancient textual material of Daniel, only the three main variant editions will be examined here in detail: the Hebrew-Aramaic text (MT), the Old Greek text (OG), and the Greek Theodotion (Θ) translation.[90] These each provide a complete version of Dan. 4,

87. This assumes that Newsom is correct in arguing that Dan. 4 and the *Prayer* both resulted from a remembered template of recitations of the Harran inscriptions; see Newsom, 'Why Nabonidus?', 57–79; Newsom, 'Now You See Him', 270–282.

88. In this, I agree with Wills that the more blatant animalising imagery is the result of later redaction; see Wills, *Jew in the Court of the Foreign King*, 95.

89. For recent studies highlighting the pluriformity of the Danielic textual tradition, see Anathea Portier-Young, 'Three Books of Daniel: Plurality and Fluidity among the Ancient Versions', *Interpretation* 71 (2017): 143–153; Hans Debel, 'Retracing Authoritative Traditions behind the Scriptural Texts: The Book of Daniel as a Case in Point', in *The Process of Authority: The Dynamics in Transmission and Reception of Canonical Texts*, ed. Jan Dušek and Jan Roskovec, DCLS 27 (Berlin: De Gruyter, 2016), 117–138.

90. These roughly correspond to the variant editions outlined by Eugene Ulrich, 'The Text of Daniel in the Qumran Scrolls', in *The Book of Daniel: Composition and Reception*, ed. John J. Collins and Peter W. Flint, VTSup 83 (Leiden: Brill, 2001), 573–85 (582). In addition to the texts analysed here, there are at least two other fragmentary early Greek texts of Daniel: Aquila and Symmachus. For an analysis of these texts, see Jason T. Parry, '18.3.2 Daniel: Primary Translations: Other Greek Versions Prior to the Hexapla', *THB* 1c:554–558. There are also a range of other early versions in Syriac, Latin and Arabic. For an overview of these versions, see Collins, *Daniel: A Commentary*, 11–12. See also Richard A. Taylor, '18.3.3 Daniel: Primary Translations: Peshitta', *THB* 1c:558–560; Michael Graves, '18.3.6 Daniel: Primary Translations: Vulgate', *THB* 1c:568–570; Miriam Lindgren Hjälm, '18.3.7 Daniel: Primary Translations: Arabic Translations', *THB* 1c:571–4. These other texts are less important for this study as they largely seem to rely on the Hebrew-Aramaic or Theodotion texts; see Collins, *Daniel: A Commentary*, 11–12.

however they also vary significantly in their retelling of Nebuchadnezzar's affliction and have each been influential in affecting interpretation of the narrative. This range of textual material inevitably complicates any attempt to examine the narrative of Dan. 4 and thus each edition must be understood in order to satisfactorily address the supposed presence of an animal metamorphosis in the text.

3.2.1 *The Hebrew-Aramaic Edition (MT)*

First, the book of Daniel is found in bilingual Hebrew-Aramaic manuscripts. This textual tradition begins in Hebrew (1:1–2:4a), changes to Aramaic (2:4b–7:28), then switches back to Hebrew again towards the end (8:1–12:13). It comprises twelve chapters that are evenly split between court narratives (Dan. 1–6) and apocalyptic visions (Dan. 7–12). This textual tradition contains the narrative about Nebuchadnezzar's affliction entirely within an Aramaic narrative section in Dan. 3:31–4:34, as well as a later description of it by Daniel within Dan. 5:17–22.

Unfortunately, early manuscript evidence for this Aramaic text is fairly elusive. The only complete Hebrew-Aramaic texts of Daniel are found in medieval Masoretic manuscripts which contain diacritical marks and notes on the consonantal text. The primary extant manuscript with a complete text is Codex Leningradensis B19[A], which dates back to 1008–1009 CE, and it is from this manuscript that most modern critical editions and translations are derived.[91] Other similar manuscript evidence can be found in, e.g., Codex Sassoon 1053 (tenth century CE), while a number of manuscripts of Daniel were also found in the Cairo Genizah.[92]

The earliest complete Hebrew-Aramaic version of Daniel is therefore medieval, yet the discovery of the Qumran scrolls near the Dead Sea brought to light much older fragments of this edition of Dan. 4. Amongst this Qumran corpus, eight different manuscripts of Daniel have been discovered making it one of the most evidenced of any scriptural text found at Qumran.[93] These manuscripts were found in three of the eleven caves: two in Cave 1, five in Cave 4 and one papyrus in Cave

---

91. This includes the *Biblia Hebraica Stuttgartensia* (BHS) which is the critical Hebrew-Aramaic text referred to throughout this study. Karl Elliger and Wilhelm Rudolph, eds, *Biblia Hebraica Stuttgartensia*, 5th ed. (Stuttgart: Deutsche Bibelstiftung, 1977).

92. For ancient Hebrew-Aramaic manuscript evidence of Daniel, see Michael Segal, '18.2.2 Daniel: Ancient Hebrew-Aramaic Texts: Masoretic Texts and Ancient Texts Close to MT', *THB* 1c:532–537.

93. While it is not the largest of books, only eight other non-sectarian texts have been found more frequently. These are the books of Psalms, Deuteronomy, Isaiah, Genesis, Exodus, Leviticus and the extra-biblical books of Jubilees and 1 Enoch. Additionally, it is unlikely that during this period the book of Daniel was a fixed entity; thus there is also a range of other Qumran material which may be classed as to some extent 'Danielic'. For discussion of this other material, see Stuckenbruck, 'Formation and Re-formation of Daniel', 113–120.

6.[94] The oldest of these (4QDan[c]) can be roughly dated to the late second century BCE,[95] thus the Qumran fragments have revealed portions of a text of Daniel which is more than a millennium older than any other extant Hebrew-Aramaic version and significantly closer to the text's supposed formation.[96] Not all of these fragments seem to reflect a text precisely aligned with the Masoretic text,[97] however most scholars tend to consider these fragments as confirming the antiquity of this Hebrew-Aramaic textual tradition.[98] The bilingual nature of the Hebrew-Aramaic version is attested,[99] and there appear to be no additional insertions that may indicate a different textual edition.[100] While some minor variants from the later Masoretic manuscripts are present, most seem to be morphological or orthographic variances.[101] Furthermore, the order of the Danielic chapters seems to be reflected in these

94. The texts in full are: 1QDan[a] (1Q71), 1QDan[b] (1Q72), 4QDan[a] (4Q112), 4QDan[b] (4Q113), 4QDan[c] (4Q114), 4QDan[d] (4Q115), 4QDan[e] (4Q116), and 6QpapDan. (6Q7).

95. Eugene C. Ulrich, '114. 4QDan[c]', in *Qumran Cave 4.XI Psalms to Chronicles*, ed. Eugene Ulrich et al., DJD 16 (Oxford: Clarendon, 2000), 269–78 (270).

96. It is possible that these Danielic Qumran scrolls are closer in date to the initial composition than any other documentary evidence of a book in the Hebrew Bible. See Cross, *Ancient Library of Qumran*, 43–44.

97. 1QDan[b] may be 'unaligned' or 'semi-Masoretic'. See Kipp Davis and Torleif Elgvin, '1QDan[b] (1Q72) with MS 1926/4b (Dan. 3.26–27)', in *Gleanings from the Caves: Dead Sea Scrolls and Artefacts from the Schøyen Collection*, ed. Torleif Elgvin, Kipp Davis, and Michael Langlois, LSTS 71 (London: T&T Clark, 2016), 257–270. See also Armin Lange, '18.2.1 Daniel: Ancient Hebrew-Aramaic Texts: Ancient Manuscript Evidence', *THB* 1c:528–532.

98. Michael Segal, '18.2.3 Daniel: Ancient Hebrew-Aramaic Texts: Other Texts', *THB* 1c:537–542; Eugene Ulrich, 'Pluriformity in the Biblical Text, Text Groups, and Questions of Canon', in *The Madrid Qumran Congress: Proceedings of the International Congress on the Dead Sea Scrolls - Madrid, 18–21 March, 1991*, ed. Julio Trebolle Barrera and Luis Vegas Montaner, STDJ 11 (Leiden: Brill, 1992), 1:23–41 (39–41); Eugene Ulrich, 'Orthography and Text in 4QDan[a] and 4QDan[b] and in the Received Masoretic Text', in *Of Scribes and Scrolls: Studies on the Hebrew Bible, Intertestamental Judaism, and Christian Origins Presented to John Strugnell on the Occasion of his Sixtieth Birthday*, ed. Harold W. Attridge, John J. Collins and Thomas H. Tobin, College Theological Society Resources in Religion 5 (Lanham, MD: University Press of America, 1990), 29–42.

99. The switch from Hebrew to Aramaic at Dan. 2:4b is evidenced in 1QDan[a], as well as the shift back to Hebrew in Dan. 8 (4QDan[b] and 4QDan[d]).

100. For example, the addition found in Greek texts after Dan. 3 appears to be absent (1QDan[b] and 4QDan[d]).

101. Stephen Pfann identified a total of 144 variants from the MT within the Aramaic scrolls of Daniel and Ezra; Stephen Pfann, 'The Aramaic Text and Language of Daniel and Ezra in the Light of Some Manuscripts from Qumran', *Textus* 16 (1991): 127–137 (129). See also Ulrich, 'Text of Daniel in the Qumran Scrolls', 580.

Qumran manuscripts,[102] and only Dan. 12 is not attested.[103] Therefore, the Danielic text in these Qumran fragments is generally reflective of the Masoretic text and substantiates its antiquity. Nevertheless, despite the plethora of evidence for Daniel at Qumran, the fragmentary nature of the material means that Nebuchadnezzar's affliction is only attested in three of the manuscripts: 4QDan[a] contains sections from Dan. 4:29–30 and 5:16–19; 4QDan[b] contains Dan. 5:19–22; and 4QDan[d] has sections from Dan. 4:5–9 and 4:12–16.

Together, this range of manuscript evidence attests to the same general textual tradition. While it is clear that this tradition antedates the Masoretes due to its presence within the Qumran material, a complete version of this text is only preserved in the Masoretic tradition. In order to refer to a whole Aramaic copy of Dan. 4, the Masoretic text must therefore be heavily relied upon. For ease of reference throughout the following discussion this Hebrew-Aramaic textual tradition will thus be discussed using the abbreviation MT (Masoretic Text).

3.2.2 The Old Greek Edition (OG)

The second variant edition of Daniel, commonly referred to as the Old Greek (OG), is preserved in an early Greek translation that can be dated to the late second or early first century BCE.[104] For the most part it preserves similar content to the MT, though there are several significant differences. Most notably, the OG contains the so-called Additions to Daniel which are: The Prayer of Azariah and the Song of the Three Young Men inserted after Dan. 3:23; then two further narratives known as Susanna, and Bel and the Dragon both appended after Dan. 12. The second major difference compared with the MT edition is that the OG contains widely divergent narratives in Dan. 4–6. These differences are far more extensive than the usual discrepancies between translations, such as those found between the MT and OG in Dan. 1–3 and 7–12. The disparity between the MT and OG in Dan. 4–6 is also not consistent as Dan. 4 OG is longer than the MT, whereas Dan. 5 OG is shorter than the respective section in the MT. A key divergence is that the OG lacks the return to Nebuchadnezzar's

---

102. Holm, *Of Courtiers and Kings*, 221, n.151.

103. However, Dan. 12:10 is quoted in 4QFlor (4Q174) which suggests that the chapter was known at Qumran and perhaps simply did not survive.

104. This is due to a perceived dependency of the Greek text of 1 Maccabees (dated around 100 BCE) upon this textual edition; see August Bludau, *Die alexandrinische Übersetzung des Buches Daniels und ihr Verhältniss zum massoretischen Texten*, BibS(F) 2.2.3 (Freiburg: Herder, 1897), 7–8. This dating evidence has more recently been called into question by Sharon Pace Jeansonne, *The Old Greek Translation of Daniel 7–12*, CBQMS 19 (Washington, DC: Catholic Biblical Association, 1988), 16–18. Nevertheless, it does seem to have been widely known by the time of the composition of the New Testament (e.g., Matt. 24:30; Rev. 1:14; 4:1).

affliction in 5:17–22.[105] The events surrounding Nebuchadnezzar's transformation are thus, in the OG edition, narrated exclusively within the divergent version of Dan. 4.

There are very few manuscript witnesses to the OG edition of Daniel. While long known from some patristic citations, the publication of a text from the library of the Chigi family in Rome in 1772 initially confirmed this edition's existence.[106] This cursive manuscript, known as Codex Chisianus 88,[107] can be dated between 800 and 1000 CE[108] and was initially the only extant Greek copy of the OG. The second manuscript witness to the OG is the ninth-century Syro-Hexaplar Codex Ambrosianus which was first published by Cajetanus Bugati in 1788, then later Antonio Ceriani added photographic facsimiles in 1874.[109] This contains a Syriac translation of the Greek text created by Bishop Paul of Tella around 616–617 CE.[110] While a Syriac translation, the manuscript's extreme fidelity to the underlying Greek has been noted and thus is of great use as a witness to the OG narrative tradition. [111] However both of these copies of the OG are problematic due to being Hexaplaric recensions. The Hexapla was a large critical edition of the Hebrew Bible constructed by Origen (*ca.* 240 CE) and arranged into six individual columns, each containing a different version of the text.[112] When there was a conflict of word order (e.g., when the same scene or sentence occurred in multiple texts but in different places) the Hexapla followed the order of the MT edition. This meant that the original order of the OG edition was, in places, completely altered to match the MT. Furthermore, some sections of the OG were deliberately 'corrected' to match the MT text.[113] Therefore, due to such transpositions and alterations,

---

105. For a list of other additions and omissions, see R. Timothy McLay, 'The Old Greek Translation of Daniel Chapters IV–VI and the Formation of the Book of Daniel', *VT* 55 (2005): 304–323 (305).

106. Simon D. Magistris, *Daniel secundum Septuaginta ex tetraplis Origenis nunc primum editus e singulari Chisiano codice* (Rome: Typis Propagandae Fidei, 1772).

107. Sometimes known as Codex Chisianus 87 due to incorrect listing. See Montgomery, *Critical and Exegetical Commentary on Daniel*, 26.

108. Bludau, *Die alexandrinische Übersetzung*, 25.

109. Antonio M. Ceriani, *Codex syro-hexaplaris Ambrosianus photolithographice editus*, Monumenta sacra et profana 7 (Milan: Pogliani, 1874).

110. Henry B. Swete, *An Introduction to the Old Testament in Greek* (Cambridge: Cambridge University Press, 1902), 112.

111. Swete claims it provides 'an exact reflexion of the Hexaplaric LXX'; see Swete, *Introduction to the Old Testament*, 114.

112. The six texts are: the Hebrew-Aramaic text; a Greek transliteration of the Hebrew-Aramaic text; Aquila; Symmachus; the Old Greek text; and Theodotion.

113. Swete, *Introduction to the Old Testament*, 68.

these Hexaplaric recensions cannot be considered reliable guides for the original OG edition of Daniel.[114]

Nevertheless, more recently an extant pre-Hexaplaric text was discovered in 1931 in Egypt. Known as Papyrus 967, it is part of a collection of twelve manuscripts known as the Chester Beatty Biblical Papyri and contains sections of Esther and Ezekiel, as well as a fragmentary text of Daniel. The papyrus was published gradually, but the first publication in 1937 contained the text of Dan. 4.[115] It contains substantial variances from the other OG texts of Daniel, for example, while Codex Chisianus 88 includes Susanna then Bel and the Dragon after Dan. 12, Papyrus 967 switches this sequence including Susanna last.[116] Furthermore the order of the book is significantly different (Dan. 7–8 are placed before Dan. 5; see Appendix A). This chapter sequence is commonly explained as an attempt by the Greek translator(s)/editor(s) to improve the chronology of the book of Daniel.[117] Despite this, Papyrus 967's chapter sequence should be considered the primary guide for the original form of Dan. OG. Not only is it the sole pre-Hexaplaric witness to the OG edition, but it is much older than either of the other OG texts of Daniel, dated around 100–200 CE and predating both by at least six centuries.[118] It is therefore reasonable to think this was the original order of the OG text before Origen's Hexaplaric recension in 240 CE. Furthermore, another witness to this chapter sequence is found in *Liber Promissionum* by the fifth-century bishop of Carthage named Quodvultdeus. As *Liber Promissionum* also follows the order attested in Papyrus 967, this suggests that it was not a unique variant tradition. Due to this evidence, and its pre-Hexaplaric form and earlier date, it seems reasonable to agree that Papyrus 967 preserves an ancient order of the chapters in the Greek

114. See Ernst Würthwein, *The Text of the Old Testament: An Introduction to the Biblia Hebraica*, trans. Errol F. Rhodes, 2nd ed. (Grand Rapids: Eerdmans, 1995), 58.

115. Frederic G. Kenyon, *The Chester Beatty Biblical Papyri: Descriptions and Texts of Twelve Manuscripts on Papyrus of the Greek Bible* (London: Walker, 1937), fasc. 7, 17–38.

116. Codex Ambrosianus also has a different sequence of Additions as it includes a so-called 'Book of Women' by collecting together Ruth, Susanna, Esther and Judith. Thus Ruth interrupts the Danielic material; see Appendix A.

117. Collins, *Daniel: A Commentary*, 4–5; and Henze, *Madness of King Nebuchadnezzar*, 22. This is argued because chs 7–8 are set during Belshazzar's reign, who has already disappeared after the end of Dan. 5.

118. See Winfried Hamm, *Der Septuaginta-Text des Buches Daniel, Kap. 1–2, nach dem Kölner Teil des Papyrus 967*, Papyrologische Texte und Abhandlungen 21 (Bonn: R. Habelt, 1969), 18; and Angelo Geissen, *Der Septuaginta-Text des Buches Daniel, Kap. 5–12, zusammen mit Susanna, Bel et Draco, nach dem Kölner Teil des Papyrus 967*, Papyrologische Texte und Abhandlungen 5 (Bonn: R. Habelt, 1968), 18.

book of Daniel.[119] This manuscript has therefore assumed primary importance for understanding the OG text.[120]

Together these three manuscripts seem to attest the same general form of Daniel and a critical composite text has been created from these principal sources to reflect this distinct edition of the book.[121] Traditionally, this edition of Daniel was known as the Septuagint (LXX) version, however scholars now commonly refer to it as the Old Greek textual tradition (OG). This change in terminology avoids potentially misleading connotations associated with the LXX and is also somewhat occasioned by the fact that a second Greek text ended up supplanting the OG within Greek Bibles.[122] It is this text which will be dealt with in the next section.

If we are to assess this OG edition of Dan. 4 and its presentation of Nebuchadnezzar's affliction, then we need to understand why it differs so markedly from the MT edition. These differences have raised significant questions about how these editions

119. Johan Lust proposed that the order in Papyrus 967 should have priority over that of the MT and he considered it the 'original' chapter sequence; see Johan Lust, 'The Septuagint Version of Daniel 4–5', in *The Book of Daniel in the Light of New Findings*, ed. Adam S. van der Woude, BETL 56 (Leuven: Leuven University Press and Peeters, 1993), 39–53. This was followed in: Pablo S. David, 'The Composition and Structure of the Book of Daniel: A Synchronic and Diachronic Reading' (PhD diss., Katholieke Universiteit, 1991), 87–96. While I agree that in Greek manuscripts the antiquity of the order in Papyrus 967 is easily demonstrable, Lust fails to demonstrate why this necessitates an early Semitic text which reflected this same sequence. He also fails to address how or why this alternate order was maintained by the OG; this is especially puzzling as he emphasises the historic popularity of the MT order. A similar theory was later proposed by Olivier Munnich, 'Texte Massorétique et Septant dans la Livre de Daniel', in *The Earliest Text of the Hebrew Bible: The Relationship between the Masoretic Text and the Hebrew Base of the Septuagint Reconsidered*, ed. Adrian Schenker, SCS 52 (Atlanta: SBL Press, 2003), 93–120. He suggests that Papyrus 967 reflected an earlier Semitic *Vorlage* which was an alternative literary edition of the Semitic text of Daniel. This theory suffers from similar issues to Lust's proposal and was systematically critiqued in: McLay, 'Old Greek Translation of Daniel Chapters IV–VI', 310–318.

120. Papyrus 967 may even provide scholarship with a rare example of the *Grundtext* from which Origen formulated his Septuagint text in the Hexapla; see Eugene Ulrich, 'Origen's Old Testament Text: The Transmission History of the Septuagint to the Third Century C.E.', in *Origen of Alexandria: His World and His Legacy*, ed. Charles Kannengiesser and William L. Peterson, Christianity and Judaism in Antiquity 1 (Notre Dame: University of Notre Dame, 1988), 3–33 (12).

121. The most current example, and the one referred to here for both the OG and Θ, is Joseph Ziegler and Olivier Munnich, eds, *Susanna, Daniel, Bel et Draco*, 2nd ed., Septuaginta: Vetus Testamentum Graecum 16.2 (Göttingen: Vandenhoeck & Ruprecht, 1999).

122. For an explanation of why OG is preferable to LXX here, see Robert A. Kraft, 'Septuagint', in *IDBSup*, 811.

relate, and a variety of solutions have been proposed to understand their relationship. Traditionally the merits of the OG have been unappreciated and it was assumed in antiquity that, when it represented a different text to the MT, the OG was in error. Jerome, for example, stated that the OG should be rejected because it differs so much from 'the truth',[123] which he thought was revealed in the Hebrew-Aramaic text. Even in the nineteenth century, the OG was generally thought of as inferior or incorrect and purely the result of a bad translator.[124] However, while some modern critical scholars have proposed that the general discrepancies between the texts are simply the result of a different theological *Tendenz* of the translator of the OG,[125] others view the unique OG material as to some extent resulting from a different Semitic *Vorlage* which lay behind the Greek translation. This was likely originally in Aramaic, although Hebrew has also been suggested as a possibility.[126]

Despite doubt surrounding the translation of the OG as a whole, the existence of the previously-mentioned divergences between Dan. 4–6 OG and MT has commonly been used to confirm the existence of a differing *Vorlage* for these chapters alone. This was initially suggested by August Bludau, who proposed that Dan. 4–6 OG represents a textual tradition equally as ancient as the MT,[127] and led

123. Jerome, *Prologus in Danihele Propheta*. The Latin text is in: Robert Weber, ed., *Biblia Sacra iuxta vulgatam versionem,* 2nd ed., 6 vols (Stuttgart: Würtembergische Bibelanstalt, 1975), 1:1341. The translation is my own.

124. For example, the OG is explained as 'a chaos of accretions, alterations, and displacements' in Anthony A. Bevan, *A Short Commentary on the Book of Daniel* (Cambridge: Cambridge University Press, 1892), 46. For a survey of nineteenth-century interpretation, see Bludau, *Die alexandrinische Übersetzung*, 29–33.

125. Bludau, *Die alexandrinische Übersetzung*; F.F. Bruce, 'The Oldest Greek Version of Daniel', in *Instruction and Interpretation: Studies in Hebrew Language, Palestinian Archaeology and Biblical Exegesis*, ed. Hendrik. A. Brongers et al., OtSt 20 (Leiden: Brill, 1977), 22–40; Arthur McCrystall, 'Studies in the Old Greek Translation of Daniel' (PhD diss., University of Oxford, 1980), 76.

126. For an underlying Aramaic *Vorlage,* see Jeansonne, *Old Greek Translation;* and Dean O. Wenthe, 'The Old Greek Translation of Daniel 1–6' (PhD diss., University of Notre Dame, 1991). For a Hebrew original, see Pierre Grelot, 'La Septante de Daniel IV et son substrat sémitique', *RB* 81 (1974): 5–23; and Haag, *Die Errettung Daniels aus der Löwengrube*. More recently, Dalia Amara has cast doubt over whether the original language can possibly be known for certain; see Dalia Amara, 'The Old Greek Version of Daniel: The Translation, the *Vorlage* and the Redaction' [Hebrew] (PhD diss., Ben Gurion University of the Negev, 2006), ii.

127. Bludau, *Die alexandrinische Übersetzung*, 31–33, 143–154. Recently, Arie van der Kooij has questioned whether these divergences require diverse ancient versions of 4–6, suggesting instead the possible role of translation and retelling. See Arie van der Kooij, 'Compositions and Editions in Early Judaism: The Case of Daniel', in *The Text of the Hebrew Bible and Its Editions: Studies in Celebration of the Fifth Centennial of the Complutensian Polyglot*, ed. Andrés P. Otero and Pablo T. Morales, Supplements to the Textual History of the Bible 1 (Leiden: Brill, 2017), 428–448.

to James Montgomery's proposal that Dan. 4–6 originally circulated independently as a shorter story collection which subsequently underwent later development resulting in the two diverse extant versions of these chapters.[128] Since then various similarities have been noted across Dan. 4–6 OG which appear to unify this collection of tales: for example Rainer Albertz revealed linguistic keyword links such as between 4:19 OG (ὑψώθη σου ἡ καρδία) and 5:2 OG (ἀνυψώθη ἡ καρδία αὐτου);[129] and Lawrence Wills noted some eight shared redactional characteristics in 4–6 OG.[130] These observations seem to corroborate the conclusion that Dan. 4–6 OG was an independent collection, and indicate they subsequently circulated and underwent redaction together.[131] Thus the differences between Dan. 4–6 MT and OG recommend the existence of two different ancient Semitic versions of these chapters.[132]

However, while an important step, this supposition about the multiplicity of ancient versions of Dan. 4–6 did not settle debate about how the OG and MT relate. Instead, it has since generated a new dispute over which of these is superior, and which derives from the other. There have been three main scholarly opinions.[133] One view, which grew out of Bludau's initial suggestion, was to advocate the priority of the OG text. Early versions of this argument asserted that the OG reflects an earlier Hebrew *Vorlage* which was actually more 'original' than the MT.[134] This idea did not meet with much early support, but the case for OG's priority has been revived more recently. Rainer Albertz studied Dan. 4–6 and concluded that these chapters in the OG 'represent an independent shape of the Daniel stories which in my view is even older than the Aramaic, perhaps not in all

128. Montgomery, *Critical and Exegetical Commentary on Daniel*, 35–37.

129. Rainer Albertz, *Der Gott des Daniel: Untersuchungen zu Daniel 4–6 in der Septuagintafassung sowie zur Komposition und Theologie des aramäischen Danielbuches*, SBS 131 (Stuttgart: Katholisches Bibelwerk, 1988), 91–92, 159–160.

130. Wills, *Jew in the Court of the Foreign King*, 87–152.

131. There may also be evidence suggestive of these chapters being translated by a different hand from the rest of Dan. OG; see Albertz, *Der Gott des Daniel*, 164; R. Timothy McLay, *The OG and Th Versions of Daniel*, SCS 43 (Atlanta: Scholars Press, 1996), 109, 145, 212. This has however been questioned in Amara, 'Old Greek Version of Daniel'.

132. Despite this, Tawny Holm has attempted to argue that Dan. 4–6 OG never circulated together; see Holm, *Of Courtiers and Kings*, 270–271. This seems unlikely based on the similarities and shared traits outlined above.

133. For an outline of these, see Amanda M. Davis Bledsoe, 'The Relationship of the Different Editions of Daniel: A History of Scholarship', *CurBR* 13 (2015): 175–190 (181–184).

134. Riessler, *Das Buch Daniel*, 33, 44, 52; Gustav Jahn, *Das Buch Daniel nach dem Septuaginta hergestellt* (Leipzig: Pfeiffer, 1904), iii–vi. This was also followed, though more conservatively, by Robert H. Charles, *A Critical and Exegetical Commentary on the Book of Daniel* (Oxford: Clarendon Press, 1929), l–lviii.

their details, but in their basic narrative plot'.[135] Other scholars have highlighted the character and age of Papyrus 967 to support the OG's superiority.[136] Moreover, Lawrence Wills compared the MT and OG editions of Daniel and found indications of later redaction in the MT. He concluded that the MT was 'a great improvement over the OG' and that the MT redactor was attempting to 'make sense of illogical images in the OG'.[137] Thus for Wills, the MT reflects a smoother adjusted text, and therefore the Greek text is a better witness to the original form of the *Vorlage* of this chapter.

Conversely, there have been a number of scholars who have continued to advocate the priority of the MT. Pierre Grelot proposed an underlying Hebrew text of the OG although he insisted this should be considered secondary to the MT.[138] David Satran looked at some difficulties within the MT text and argued that the OG was an attempt to adjust these apparent tensions within the Aramaic text. He concluded that the OG has a 'secondary, derivative nature', and can be described as 'the first extended interpretation of the biblical narrative'.[139] Thus the OG should be seen as comparable to a later corrective midrash on the text, whereas the MT would be considered more original. The most recent proponent of the MT's primacy is Dalia Amara who conducted a complete analysis of the OG. She argued that the influence of the OG's translator means that its *Vorlage* is very difficult to reconstruct and, even when it can be, this underlying text appears to be secondary to the MT.[140] Nevertheless, she does recognize a few cases, usually where it has a shorter text, where the OG should be given priority over the MT.

These two sets of views, while working with largely the same evidence, arrive at starkly contrasting conclusions. Yet they share the assumption that one of these textual editions (either MT or OG) must be inferior and rely upon the other.

135. Rainer Albertz, 'The Social Setting of the Aramaic and Hebrew Book of Daniel', in *The Book of Daniel: Composition and Reception,* ed. John J. Collins and Peter W. Flint, VTSup 83 (Leiden: Brill, 2001), 171–204, 180. See also: Albertz, *Der Gott des Daniel,* 13–42, 77–84, 113–128.

136. David, 'Composition and Structure'; Lust, 'Septuagint Version of Daniel 4–5', 39–53; Olivier Munnich, 'Les versions grecques de Daniel et leur substrats sémitiques', in *VIII Congress of the International Organization for Septuagint and Cognate Studies,* ed. Leonard Greenspoon and Olivier Munnich, SCS 41 (Atlanta: Scholars Press, 1995), 291–308; Munnich, 'Texte Massorétique et Septant', 93–120; Olivier Munnich, 'The Masoretic Rewriting of Daniel 4–6: The Septuagint Version as Witness', in *From Author to Copyist: Essays on the Composition, Redaction, and Transmission of the Hebrew Bible in Honor of Zipi Talshir,* ed. Cana Werman (Winona Lake, IN: Eisenbauns, 2015), 149–172; Géza Xeravits, 'Poetic Passages in the Aramaic Part of the Book of Daniel', *BN* 124 (2005): 29–40.

137. Wills, *Jew in the Court of the Foreign King,* 109.

138. Grelot, 'La Septante de Daniel IV', 22.

139. Satran, 'Early Jewish and Christian Interpretation', 83–84.

140. Amara, 'Old Greek Version of Daniel'; Dalia Amara, '18.3.2. Daniel: Primary Translations: Septuagint', *THB* 1c:547–551.

A growing consensus amongst modern scholars has questioned this basic assumption and argued that, due to the significant differences between the OG and MT, both editions should be simply seen as alternate versions. Thus, neither should be thought of as *more* original. The most prominent proponent of this theory is Eugene Ulrich who, by recognizing the fluid nature of texts during the Second Temple period, described what he called 'double literary editions'. These he defines as:

> a literary unit ... appearing in two (or more) parallel forms in our principal textual witnesses, which one author, major redactor, or major editor completed and which a subsequent reader or editor intentionally changed to a sufficient extent that the resultant form should be called a revised edition of that text.[141]

When Ulrich applied this idea to the MT and OG editions of Dan. 4–6, he proposed that both should be understood as '*expanding in different directions* beyond an earlier common edition which no longer survives'.[142] They are thus both witnesses to the same original form of the narrative but, through independent processes of expansion or alteration, they eventually resulted in these two variant editions (OG and MT). Neither edition therefore relies on nor directly results from the other. This theory was later followed by a number of other scholars who focused on Dan. 4–6.[143] Given the evidence for secondary expansion in both editions, this third view, that Dan. 4–6 MT and OG should be considered variant editions going back to the same narrative core, will be largely adopted here.

Although Dan. 4 OG and MT will mostly be treated as independent editions of the Dan. 4 tradition, this view requires a couple of nuances. First, it must be acknowledged that, while being parallel editions of the same narrative, both Dan. 4

---

141. Eugene Ulrich, 'Double Literary Editions of Biblical Narratives and Reflections on Determining the Form to be Translated', in *Perspectives on the Hebrew Bible: Essays in Honor of Walter J. Harrelson,* ed. James L. Crenshaw (Macon, GA: Mercer University, 1988), 101–116 (102).

142. Eugene Ulrich, 'The Canonical Process, Textual Criticism, and Latter Stages in the Composition of the Bible', in *The Dead Sea Scrolls and the Origins of the Bible,* Studies in the Dead Sea Scrolls and Related Literature (Grand Rapids: Eerdmans, 1999), 51–78 (72).

143. Wenthe, 'Old Greek Translation'; Henze, *Madness of King Nebuchadnezzar,* 38–49; Collins, *Daniel: A Commentary,* 221; Birte Braasch, *Die LXX-Übersetzung des Danielbuches: Eine Orientierungshilfe für das religiöse und politisch-gesellschaftliche Leben in der ptolemäischen Diaspora: Eine rezeptionsgeschichtliche Untersuchung von Daniel 1-7* (PhD diss., Fachbereich Evangelische Theologie der Universität Hamburg, 2004), 290–291; Koch, *Daniel,* 378–379; Emanuel Tov, 'Three Strange Books of the LXX: 1 Kings, Esther, and Daniel Compared with Similar Rewritten Compositions from Qumran and Elsewhere', in *Die Septuaginta: Texte, Kontexte, Lebenswelten,* ed. Martin Karrer et al., WUNT 219 (Tübingen: Mohr Siebeck, 2008), 369–393 (385); Holm, *Of Courtiers and Kings,* 230–231.

MT and OG contain their own secondary expansions of the narrative. Many of the observations by proponents of the primacy of the MT or OG (e.g., those by Satran or Wills) demonstrate evidence of later redaction or expansion in each edition of Dan. 4. Michael Segal has recently incorporated such evidence into an understanding of these two texts as double literary editions and has identified several original and secondary readings in both the MT and OG.[144] He concludes that the MT and OG cannot therefore simply be considered as distinct original texts of Dan. 4, rather they have each undergone expansion and both seem to be essentially secondary in nature. Secondly, while Segal's argument is for the most part accepted here, it is unwise to assume that *all* the secondary elements in each narrative arose independently from one another. It remains possible, given their coexistence, that there may have been some direct or indirect influence of one edition upon the other. As such, when examining these two distinct editions of Dan. 4 it will be worth considering whether some aspects of the texts may be more complexly interrelated.[145]

3.2.3 *The Theodotion Edition (Θ)*

The reason for the paucity of sources that attest to the OG of Daniel is due to its eventual replacement in Greek Bibles by another version known as the Theodotion text (Θ). This text bears a much greater similarity to the MT when compared to the OG, though the Θ does include the Additions (albeit Susanna is placed before Dan. 1). It is most likely due to this closer resemblance to the MT that the Θ almost entirely usurped the OG version of Daniel within the Christian tradition.[146] Most of the major witnesses to the Greek Bible contain the Θ text including the uncial manuscripts: Codex Vaticanus (*ca.* 300–325 CE), Codex Alexandrinus (*ca.* 400–440 CE), and Codex Marchalianus (*ca.* 500–600 CE). Codex Vaticanus is probably the best extant witness to this edition of Daniel though all Θ manuscripts display some Hexaplaric influence.[147] The various evidence for the Θ can be placed into four main groups: the codices Vaticanus, Alexandrinus, Marchalianus, along with other dependent manuscripts; a Hexaplaric group; a Lucianic group; and a Catena group.[148]

This Θ edition has traditionally been associated with the second-century Theodotion, whom Irenaeus named as making a translation of the Old

---

144. Michael Segal, *Dreams, Riddles, and Visions: Textual, Contextual, and Intertextual Approaches to the Book of Daniel*, BZAW 455 (Berlin: De Gruyter, 2016), 94–131.

145. This will become clear when examining evidence for a metamorphosis; see especially §3.3.2.

146. According to Sidney Jellicoe, this took place in the second half of the third century CE; see Sidney Jellicoe, *The Septuagint and Modern Study* (Oxford: Clarendon, 1968), 86–87.

147. See James A. Montgomery, 'The Hexaplaric Strata in the Greek Texts of Daniel', *JBL* 44 (1925): 289–302. For information on each of these manuscripts, see Appendix A.

148. Ziegler and Munnich, *Susanna, Daniel, Bel et Draco*, 44–57.

Testament[149] and whom Epiphanius dated during the reign of Emperor Commodus (*ca.* 180–192 CE).[150] However this textual edition surely predates Theodotion himself as various New Testament authors appear to reference this version of the text (e.g., compare Heb. 11:33 and Dan. 6:22 Θ).[151] Possible explanations for this have included either an 'Ur-Theodotion' (an early, Hellenistic version of Daniel)[152] or a 'Proto-Theodotion' *kaige* recension (a revised form of the OG to more closely reflect the MT) which were then later adapted by the translator Theodotion.[153] However, extensive studies have recently concluded that Dan. Θ does not belong to the same translational tradition as the Theodotion translation of the rest of the Hebrew Bible.[154] It therefore seems most reasonable to view the Θ edition as a separate translation of Daniel that was not reworked by the historical figure Theodotion at all.[155] Nevertheless, this edition will still be referred to by the abbreviation Θ to avoid creating confusion.[156] This Θ text was probably produced in Palestine around the onset of the first century CE, given apparent allusions/ quotations in the New Testament, though an exact date and location is difficult to discern.[157]

In addition to debates over its connection to the historical Theodotion, it is also important to understand how the Θ edition of Daniel relates to both the MT and OG editions. It seems to generally reflect the MT and, when it does depart from this edition, it appears to align with the OG (for example, the Additions to Daniel

---

149. Irenaeus, *Haer.* 3.24 (PG 7:946).

150. Epiphanius, *De mensuris et ponderibus* 17.

151. Montgomery, *Critical and Exegetical Commentary on Daniel,* 49 and 159; Charles, *Book of Daniel,* liv; Pierre Grelot, 'Les versions grecques de Daniel', *Bib* 47 (1966): 381–402 (390). For a list of all allusions to the Θ edition within the New Testament, see Alexander A. Di Lella, 'The Textual History of Septuagint-Daniel and Theodotion-Daniel', in *The Book of Daniel: Composition and Reception,* ed. John J. Collins and Peter W. Flint, VTSup 83 (Leiden: Brill, 2001), 586–607 (593).

152. Montgomery, *Critical and Exegetical Commentary on Daniel,* 50; John Gwynn, 'Theodotion', *DCB* 4:970–979.

153. Dominique Barthélemy, *Les Devaniers d'Aquila: Première publication intégrale du texte des fragments du Dodécaprophéton,* VTSup 10 (Leiden: Brill, 1963), 148; also Grelot, 'Les versions grecques', 392; Jeansonne, *Old Greek Translation,* 16–22.

154. Armin Schmitt, *Stammt der sogenannte 'Th' Text bei Daniel wirklich von Theodotion?,* MSU 9 (Göttingen: Vandenhoeck & Ruprecht, 1966); and Armin Schmitt, 'Die griechischen Danieltexte und das Theodotionsproblem', *BZ* 36 (1992): 1–29. This view was critiqued by Collins (*Daniel: A Commentary,* 10–11) but was nevertheless seemingly confirmed by McLay (*OG and Th Versions of Daniel,* 239–240).

155. Hartman and Di Lella, *Book of Daniel,* 80–82; Di Lella, 'Textual History of Septuagint-Daniel and Theodotion-Daniel', 595–596.

156. This practice is adopted and defended by Hartman and Di Lella, *Book of Daniel,* 82.

157. Di Lella, 'Textual History of Septuagint-Daniel and Theodotion-Daniel', 596. See also Hartman and Di Lella, *Book of Daniel,* 79–83; Amara, '18.3.2. Septuagint', 544.

inserted after Dan. 3:23, and Dan. 8:11, 13).[158] Nevertheless, there are also specific instances where the Θ departs from both previously-examined editions of Daniel.[159] To understand this text, scholars have proposed several theories. Firstly, some have suggested that the Θ is a recension of the OG which was adapted to better reflect the MT. This was initially proposed by James Montgomery to account for the general similarities with the OG but also the convergences with the MT.[160] This was supported by later studies, but perhaps most prominently by Sharon Pace Jeansonne who advanced the idea that the Θ is largely a reworking of the OG based on the degree of similarity between them.[161] Alternatively, the other principal position on the relationship of the Θ to the other editions is to view it as an entirely independent translation of the MT. For example, Alexander Di Lella considered the Θ as a fresh translation based on the MT, albeit with an eye on the OG text.[162] This theory was advanced most notably by R. Timothy McLay who studied their respective translation techniques and argued that similarities between the editions could not simply be attributed to the Θ drawing upon the OG.[163] He noted twenty-nine

---

158. The case of the Additions to Daniel is complicated. The OG and Θ texts display significant differences in 3:24–25 and 46 which may indicate they have both revised the expanded version of Dan. 3; see Gerhard J. Swart, 'Divergences between the OG and Th Versions of Daniel 3: Evidence of Early Hellenistic Interpretation of the Narrative of the Three Young Men in the Furnace?' *Acta Patristica et Byzantina* 16 (2005): 106–120. While the differences between 'the Prayer' and 'the Song' in the OG and Θ are minimal, these two versions of Bel and the Dragon agree with each other only 80 per cent of the time; see Collins, *Daniel: A Commentary*, 409. Moreover, Susanna exhibits even more striking differences with several phrases added and others seemingly deleted; see Carey A. Moore, *Daniel, Esther, and Jeremiah: The Additions*, AB 44 (Garden City, NY: Doubleday, 1977), 78–79.

159. Timothy J. Meadowcroft, *Aramaic Daniel and Greek Daniel: A Literary Comparison*, JSOTSup 198 (Sheffield: Sheffield Academic Press, 1995), 281–285.

160. Montgomery, *Critical and Exegetical Commentary on Daniel*, 39–42.

161. Jeansonne, *Old Greek Translation*. See also Sharon Pace Jeansonne, 'The Stratigraphy of the Text of Daniel and the Question of Theological *Tendenz* in the Old Greek', *BIOSCS* 17 (1984): 15–35; Karen H. Jobes, 'A Comparative Syntactic Analysis of the Greek Versions of Daniel: A Test Case for New Methodology', *BIOSCS* 28 (1995): 18–41; Olivier Munnich, 'Les nomina sacra dans les versions grecques de Daniel et leurs suppléments deuterocanoniques', in κατα τους ό: *Selons les Septante: Trente études sur la Bible Grecque des Septante,* ed. Gilles Dorival and Olivier Munnich (Paris: Cerf, 1995), 93–120 (145–167).

162. Hartman and Di Lella, *Book of Daniel*, 80–82; Di Lella, 'Textual History of Septuagint-Daniel and Theodotion-Daniel', 596. See also Grelot, 'Les versions grecques', 381, 394–395.

163. McLay, *OG and Th Versions of Daniel*; R. Timothy McLay, 'The Relationship between the Greek Translations of Daniel 1–3', *BIOSCS* 37 (2004): 29–54; R. Timothy McLay, 'It's a Question of Influence: The Theodotion and the Old Greek Texts of Daniel', in *Origen's Hexapla and Fragments: Papers Presented at the Rich Seminar on the Hexapla*, ed. Alison Salvesen, TSAJ 58 (Tübingen: Mohr Siebeck, 1998), 231–254. See also Chukwudi J. Obiajunwa, 'Semitic Interference in Theodotion-Daniel' (PhD diss., The Catholic University of America, 1999), iv.

instances where the OG is influenced by the Θ, as opposed to five times the Θ has been influenced by the OG. In twenty-four cases the direction of dependence was unclear.[164] The minimal evidence of the Θ drawing on the OG demonstrated, for McLay, that the Θ only consulted the OG when confronted with a difficult passage.[165] This more complicated understanding of the relationship between editions has been further enhanced by the work of Dalia Amara who concluded that, when the *Vorlage* of the OG and Θ was presumably identical, the Θ translation seems to offer a different translation to the OG, though freely uses it at times. Nevertheless, the Θ has influenced the OG during the transmission process too.[166] This is the account which best addresses the complexity of the information and possible points of contact. Thus, on the whole, the Θ can be considered a fresh translation of a Semitic text close to the MT which nevertheless occasionally draws upon the OG. It will therefore be considered here separately from the other versions of Daniel.

However, while the general relationship of the Θ with the OG and the MT has been addressed, the situation for the narrative of Nebuchadnezzar's affliction in Dan. 4 is slightly different. It has already been shown how, for Dan. 4–6, the OG appears to reflect a completely different *Vorlage* to the MT. However, Dan. 4–6 Θ appears to be a translation of a *Vorlage* remarkably similar to the MT though perhaps with some minor differences.[167] Daniel 4 Θ does nevertheless display evidence that its translator(s) interpreted the underlying Semitic text in the act of translation, which has adjusted the extant text.[168] Its relationship to Dan. 4 OG appears to be much more distant. There is very little shared vocabulary or verbal agreements between them which suggests not only that these specific points of contact are secondary, but also that on the whole the Θ caused emendations to Dan. 4 OG.[169] However, as the

---

164. McLay, *OG and Th Versions of Daniel*, 246–248.

165. McLay, *OG and Th Versions of Daniel*, 15.

166. Amara, '18.3.2. Septuagint', 547. See also Amara, 'Old Greek Version of Daniel', 25. Daniel Olariu has since demonstrated evidence suggestive of a closer link between the Θ and OG; see Daniel Olariu, 'Criteria for Determining the Common Basis of the Greek Versions of Daniel', *Textus* 28 (2019): 105–124.

167. For evidence of a slightly different *Vorlage*, see Meadowcroft, *Aramaic Daniel and Greek Daniel*, 281, 285–286. See also Di Lella, 'Textual History of Septuagint-Daniel and Theodotion-Daniel', 596; R. Timothy McLay, 'The Greek Translations of Daniel 4–6', in *The Temple in Text and Tradition: A Festschrift in Honour of Robert Hayward*, ed. R. Timothy McLay, LSTS 83 (London: Bloomsbury T&T Clark, 2015), 211–238 (187, 213–214).

168. Meadowcroft, *Aramaic Daniel and Greek Daniel*, 285–286. See also Heinz-Dieter Neef, 'Menschliche Hybris und göttliche Macht. Dan. 4 LXX und Dan. 4 Th im Vergleich', *JNSL* 31 (2005): 59–89 (86).

169. McLay, 'Greek Translations of Daniel 4–6', 198. Origen's Hexaplaric project also affected the Θ text, though this probably only involved slight revisions and additions through the influence of the later Aquila text of Daniel; see Montgomery, *Critical and Exegetical Commentary on Daniel*, 51–53; and Ziegler and Munnich, *Susanna, Daniel, Bel et Draco*, 50–53.

Θ does occasionally draw upon the OG elsewhere, it is nevertheless advisable to be attentive to any situations where the Θ may be influenced by the OG. Daniel 4 Θ therefore seems to largely reflect a text similar to the MT, though with some alteration, and has in turn had some probable effect upon the OG edition.

3.2.4 Summary

Essentially, there are three key textual editions of Dan. 4 that are important to focus on: the MT, the OG, and the Θ. Each differs significantly, and it is possible to refer to them as different traditions of the text of Dan. 4. The MT and the OG should be considered as double literary editions and are best viewed as essentially variant forms of the same narrative which nevertheless seem to have undergone secondary expansion themselves. The Θ appears to occupy a distinct position in relation to these two other traditions. Its version of the narrative of Dan. 4 should be viewed as a fresh Greek translation of a Semitic text that was in the same tradition as the MT, but which has nevertheless been subsequently adjusted through the translation process (in some cases towards the OG).

3.3 Searching for a Metamorphosis in the Textual Traditions of Daniel 4

These varying textual traditions of Dan. 4 are all different witnesses to the narrative concerning Nebuchadnezzar's animalising affliction in the wilderness. Each of these three editions of Dan. 4 will now be examined in turn to assess how they present Nebuchadnezzar's affliction and the extent to which this is presented as a physical metamorphosis. Although the texts contain various instances of animalising imagery, ultimately it will be shown that none of them appear to envisage a physical metamorphosis on the part of the king.

3.3.1 Metamorphosis in the Aramaic Text (MT)

The text of Dan. 4 MT provides ample description of Nebuchadnezzar's divine affliction. Over the course of the chapter the exact affliction that both the tree and Nebuchadnezzar experience is described several times: first when Nebuchadnezzar describes his dream (Dan. 4:11–14); again when Daniel recites the king's dream (4:20); when Daniel interprets the dream (4:22); as the voice from heaven pronounces the affliction (4:29); and again when the affliction actually takes place (4:30).[170] Nebuchadnezzar's affliction is even retold once more in Dan. 5:20–21. While this

---

170. The verse numbering in this section follows that of the MT, which differs from that commonly found in most English translations (e.g., NRSV). For a comparison of equivalent verse numberings, see Appendix B.

repetition of the different elements of the divine affliction is remarkable, it is also interesting to notice that these separate lists are all subtly different (see Table 1).[171]

Each of these passages that describe the affliction (of either Nebuchadnezzar or the tree in his dream) include or exclude different specific parts of this experience. While Dan. 4:11–14 appears to contain the fullest account of the affliction, there is no single definitive list of all the effects that take place. In order to assess all the different descriptions of Nebuchadnezzar's affliction in the MT edition, each of these different passages will need to be considered.

Initially, it should be noted that much of the description of Nebuchadnezzar's affliction in Dan. 4 MT is not in any way suggestive of an animal metamorphosis. For example, the statement that he will be 'wet with the dew of the heavens [ובטל שמיא יצטבע]' (Dan. 4:12, also: 4:20, 22, 30; 5:21), while plainly indicating a physical effect of his lack of shelter, is not itself indicative of any animalising change of form. Some aspects of the king's affliction do explicitly relate it to animals; for example, he is told that he will be 'driven out from humanity [טרדין מן־אנשא]' (Dan. 4:22, also: 4:29, 30; 5:21) and 'with the animals of the field will be your dwelling [ועם־חיות ברא להוה מדרך]' (Dan. 4:22, see also 4:29; 5:21). This does suggest that the king will somehow live like an animal, however the change is spatial (living away from humans) rather than anything physical.[172]

More specific evidence might be found in the command that 'with the animals [ועם־חיותא], let its portion [חלקה] be in the grass of the earth' (Dan. 4:12 MT, cf. 4:20).[173] This reference plainly associates Nebuchadnezzar (or the tree that represents him) with the animals in some way, though the specifics of this interaction rely upon how we understand the word חלקה (portion). Two principal interpretations of this word present themselves. Firstly, some scholars see חלקה as simply meaning 'a tract of land' or 'territory', an interpretation bolstered by the only other use of חלק in the Aramaic portions of the Hebrew Bible (Ezra 4:16).[174] Thus, this passage would be further evidence of the spatial change effected by Nebuchadnezzar's affliction. The king is again spatially separated from other people as the portion of land given to him is that inhabited by the wild animals. However, on account of the passage's context, other scholars see חלקה as instead referring to a portion of food.[175] This interpretation suggests that Nebuchadnezzar

---

171. When a passage omits a particular symptom, this is indicated by '---'.

172. For further discussion of such phraseology, see Grelot, 'Nabuchodonosor changé en bête', 15.

173. Various textual work has been conducted on 4:12 and many scholars suppose 'in the grass of the earth' is a gloss that should be omitted (see Montgomery, *Critical and Exegetical Commentary on Daniel*, 235). Charles Torrey suggested inserting some further words here to resolve the ambiguity in the passage; see Torrey, 'Notes on the Aramaic Part of Daniel', 269–270.

174. Montgomery, *Critical and Exegetical Commentary on Daniel*, 235; Collins, *Daniel: A Commentary*, 227. See also: BDB, s.v. 'חֲלָק'.

175. For example, John E. Goldingay, *Daniel*, WBC 30 (Dallas: Word, 1988), 80–81.

Table 1 Symptoms of the Divine Affliction in each iteration in Dan. 4–5 MT

Dan. 4:11–14	Dan. 4:20	Dan. 4:22–23	Dan. 4:29	Dan. 4:30	Dan. 5:20–21
Tree is cut down [גדו אילנא]	Tree is cut down and destroyed [גדו אילנא וחבלוהי]	--	--	--	--
Branches cut off [וקצצו ענפוהי]	--	--	--	--	--
Leaves stripped off [אתרו עפיה]	--	--	--	--	--
Fruit scattered [ובדרו אנבה]	--	--	--	--	--
Wild animals and birds flee [תנד חיותא מן תחתוהי וצפריא מן ענפוהי]	--	--	--	--	--
Stump of its roots left in field with metal band [ברם עקר שרשוהי בארעא שבקו ובאסור די פרזל ונחש בדתאא די ברא]	Stump of its roots left in field with metal band [ברם עקר שרשוהי בארעא שבקו ובאסור די פרזל ונחש בדתאא די ברא]	Stump of the tree's roots left [עקר שרשוהי שבקו]	--	--	--
Its heart changed from human to animal [לבבה מן אנושא ישנון ולבב חיוה יתיהב לה]	--	--	--	--	Heart became like an animals' [ולבבה עם חיותא שוי]
Seven times pass over [ושבעה עדנין יחלפון עלוהי]	Seven times pass over [ושבעה עדנין יחלפון עלוהי]	Seven times pass over [ושבעה עדנין יחלפון עלוהי]	Seven times pass over [ושבעה עדנין יחלפון עלוהי]	--	--
--	--	Driven away from humanity [ומן אנשא לך טרדין]	Driven away from humanity [טרדין לך מן אנשא]	Driven away from humanity [ומן אנשא לך טרדין]	Driven away from sons of humanity [ומן בני אנשא טריד]
--	--	Dwells with animals [ועם חיות ברא להוה מדרך]	Dwells with animals [ועם חיות ברא מדרך]	--	Dwells with wild asses [ועם ערדיא מדורה]
Its portion is grass of the earth [ובחלקה עם חיות ברא בעשב ארעא]	--	Fed grass like oxen [ועשבא כתורין לך יטעמון]	Fed grass like oxen [ועשבא כתורין לך יטעמון]	Ate grass like oxen [עשבא כתורין יאכל]	Fed grass like oxen [ועשבא כתורין יטעמונה]
--	--	--	--	Hair like eagles and nails like birds' [עד די שערה כנשרין רבה וטפרוהי כצפרין]	--

ate his portion of grass in the field, an idea that recurs with increased specificity later in Dan. 4: 'he was eating grass like oxen' (4:30; cf. 4:22, 29; 5:21). Nevertheless, this again has only limited use as evidence for a supposed animal metamorphosis of Nebuchadnezzar. While it may suggest a change in the king's diet, there is no reason to think the text indicates an alteration in the king's physiology in order to digest this. Amidst the context it seems to rather indicate a behavioural alteration in the king whereby he simply adopts the behaviour of oxen. This element of the passage therefore only appears to provide evidence for a behavioural change, not a change in the king's physical form.

Thus far, the varying descriptions of Nebuchadnezzar's affliction in the MT seem to only portray a change in either the king's behaviour or the location of his habitation. Perhaps more substantial evidence for an animal metamorphosis might be indicated when, during Nebuchadnezzar's dream, it is stated that 'its heart [לבב] be changed from that of a human, and let the heart [לבב] of an animal be given to it' (Dan. 4:13). A similar sentiment is repeated in Dan. 5:21 MT: 'his heart became like that of an animal'. This element of the king's affliction plainly links the condition of the king's heart with that of an animal, however there is little to commend interpreting this as being indicative of a physical metamorphosis. While the semantic range of the Aramaic term לבב (heart) potentially includes a physical sense as a reference to an internal organ, such usage is incredibly rare in Aramaic texts.[176] Instead לבב was primarily used to denote 'the centre of inner experience', which was associated with feelings, thoughts, and desires, and this is how it seems to be used in Daniel too (e.g., Dan. 2:30, 7:28).[177] Furthermore, the context of Dan. 4:13 MT corroborates this non-physical understanding of Nebuchadnezzar's heart. If Nebuchadnezzar's 'inner experience' becomes like an animal's it would be expected that he would begin to think, feel, and behave like one; this is exactly what has been described in 4:12.[178] These references to Nebuchadnezzar's heart becoming animal-like thus provide further evidence for a behavioural change of the king.

The most prominent potential evidence that Nebuchadnezzar may have experienced a physical metamorphosis is mentioned only once. Towards the end of Dan. 4:30 MT, the king's appearance is described as changing significantly:

> until when his hair grew long like that of eagles and his nails were like those of birds.

עד די שׂערה כנשׁרין רבה וטפרוהי כצפרין (Dan. 4:30 MT)[179]

176. The only clear examples are found in Aramaic fragments of the book of Tobit found at Qumran, e.g., 4Q197 4.1.12 (Tob. 6:7) and 4Q196 14.1.11 (Tob. 6:17). See Holger Gzella, 'לב', *TDOT* 16:384.

177. For example, 1QapGen ar 2.1. Many more examples are provided in Gzella, *TDOT* 16:384–388.

178. House, *Daniel*, 96.

179. English translations of Dan. 4 MT are my own unless otherwise stated.

This undoubtedly describes an alteration of the king's outward aspect and could theoretically relate to a transformation of the king's physical form into that of some kind of bird. However there are problems with such an interpretation. This description of the king is conveyed entirely through the utilisation of similes: Nebuchadnezzar's hair is only *like* that of eagles and his nails *like* those of birds. Rather than suggesting that the king actually grew the hair (feathers) of an eagle or grew bird's claws, his features are simply described as growing long during his time in the wilderness and so ultimately appearing similar to these avian attributes. The passage does not denote a metamorphosis of Nebuchadnezzar into a different physical creature, instead it seems to employ specific animal imagery in an attempt to convey how the king appeared. There is, in fact, an interesting parallel for such imagery in the *Story of Ahiqar* which was a well-known text in the ancient Near East and may date back to the seventh century BCE.[180] This text has been preserved in a range of early modern and medieval manuscripts in languages including Ethiopic, Armenian, Arabic, and Syriac, however the earliest Aramaic fragments found at Elephantine date to the fifth century BCE.[181] It relates how the protagonist Ahiqar, described as a wise counsellor to the Assyrian kings Sennacherib and Esarhaddon, is falsely accused of treason and condemned to death.[182] He hides beneath a house until, when he is needed by the king once more, he returns to the court. When he emerges from his hiding place, Ahiqar describes his appearance:

> The hair of my head had grown down on my shoulders [*s'r' dršy rm' 'l ktpty*], and my beard reached my breast; and my body was foul with the dust, and my nails were grown long like eagles' [*wṭpry 'rykyn 'yk dnšr'*]. (*Story of Ahiqar* 5.11–12 [Syriac recension])[183]

180. For the date and ancient influence of the story of Ahiqar, see James M. Lindenberger, 'Ahiqar', in *OTP* 2:279–293.

181. For the dating of these fragments, see Ada Yardeni, 'Maritime Trade and Royal Accountancy in an Erased Customs Account from 475 B.C.E. on the Aḥiqar Scroll from Elephantine', *BASOR* 293 (1994): 67–78.

182. See also Tob. 1:21–22; 14:10.

183. Translation from Frederick C. Conybeare, James R. Harris and Agnes S. Lewis, *The Story of Ahikar from the Aramaic, Syriac, Arabic, Armenian, Ethiopic, Old Turkish, Greek and Slavonic Versions,* 2nd ed. (Cambridge: Cambridge University Press, 1913), 116; Syriac text c. 5.11–12. Due to its fragmentary nature, this section has sadly not survived amongst the earliest Aramaic sources, however the Syriac version quoted here is thought to be the closest recension to the Aramaic. For a translation of the Aramaic text, see Bezalel Porten and Ada Yardeni, *Textbook of Aramaic Documents from Ancient Egypt, vol. 3: Literature, Accounts, Lists* (Jerusalem: Hebrew University Press, 1993).

Just like Nebuchadnezzar, Ahiqar's hair and nails grow long and, using similes, his appearance is likened to that of an eagle.[184] However, there is no suggestion that Ahiqar's unusual description is intended to convey any literal change into an animal and instead the narrative seems to be concerned with signposting the length of time that Ahiqar was hidden underground. Firstly, after being secreted away, 'a few days'[185] go by before more food is brought to him. Then enough time passes for news to reach Egypt and, finally, there is a further delay as Pharaoh writes a letter which takes a few weeks to reach the Assyrian king.[186] The unusual description of Ahiqar may be another way in which the narrative describes the passage of time, conveying the sense that he had been hidden long enough for his hair and nails to grow long. If this is the case in *Ahiqar*, and due to the clear parallels with Nebuchadnezzar's appearance in Dan. 4 MT, it is probable that the Danielic text also employs such imagery to illustrate the extreme length of time that Nebuchadnezzar had been in social isolation.[187] This usage is even suggested by the preposition 'until' (עַד) which introduces Nebuchadnezzar's description. Thus, rather than denoting a literal animal metamorphosis, the imagery in Dan. 4:30 MT should be understood simply as an illustration of a prolonged period of extreme neglect.

Finally, it is worth noting that, after his period of exile is complete and Nebuchadnezzar returns to Babylon, there is no mention of his transformation back into a human form (as would presumably be required if he was indeed now a bird of some sort!). Instead, once the appointed period of time is complete Nebuchadnezzar states that 'my reason returned to me, and for the honour of my kingdom my glory and my splendour returned to me' (Dan. 4:33 MT). This suggests that during his affliction Nebuchadnezzar only lost some of his regal splendour and rational faculties. If the king had undergone a metamorphosis into

---

184. For a look at the parallels between the texts, see George A. Barton, 'The Story of Ahikar and the Book of Daniel', *AJSL* 16 (1900): 242–247. James R. Harris suggested that the *Story of Ahiqar* may be a source for Dan. 4; see Conybeare, Harris and Lewis, *Story of Ahikar*, lxi–lxii. However, there is minimal evidence for any kind of dependence, so it is safer to think of *Ahiqar* as part of the literary context which Dan. 4 grew out of; see Collins, *Daniel: A Commentary*, 41. This imagery has also been explained by other parallels with the Heroic Encounter in Achaemenid-era iconography; see Brian Charles DiPalma, 'The Animalistic Nebuchadnezzar and the Heroic Encounter: Daniel 4:30 Iconographically Revisited', *JBL* 139 (2020): 499–520.

185. Conybeare, Harris and Lewis, *Story of Ahikar*, 114.

186. Conybeare, Harris and Lewis, *Story of Ahikar*, 114. This same argument about the passage of time is made in Hector Avalos, 'Nebuchadnezzar's Affliction: New Mesopotamian Parallels for Daniel 4', *JBL* 133 (2014): 497–507 (501–502). He also refutes the suggestion that Ahiqar is depicted as descending to the netherworld made in Christopher B. Hays, 'Chirps from the Dust: The Affliction of Nebuchadnezzar in Daniel 4:30 in Its Ancient Near Eastern Context', *JBL* 126 (2007): 305–325 (323).

187. This is argued by, for example, Sack, *Images of Nebuchadnezzar*, 106–107.

animal form, the resolution of such a transformation would doubtless be mentioned here too. The lack of such a statement seemingly confirms that any physical aspects of the king's affliction were superficial rather than substantial, and instead appears to show that the change was characterised by a loss of reason.

This assessment of Nebuchadnezzar's affliction in Dan. 4 MT has shown that, despite the range of descriptions in the narrative, there is no particular evidence to suggest that the king is presented as transforming into the physical form of an animal. Instead, the text provides sufficient evidence that the king changed in both behaviour and location of habitation. Pierre Grelot is thus right to conclude that 'il ne s'agit pas d'une metamorphose corporelle comme on en touve dans la mythologie grecque, mais d'une modification du comportement'.[188] The king's affliction is therefore presented in Dan. 4 MT as a time when Nebuchadnezzar lived in the wilderness and *behaved* (or was treated) like an animal. Rather than an external transformation, Nebuchadnezzar's affliction is presented as an internal change which affected his thoughts and behaviour.

3.3.2 Metamorphosis in the Old Greek Text (OG)

The parallel OG edition of Dan. 4 includes some material which closely reflects the description of Nebuchadnezzar's affliction in the MT. For example, Nebuchadnezzar is again described as eating grass like an animal (Dan. 4:12, 13, 14a, 29, 30a OG) and as being driven away from people into the wilderness (Dan. 4:21, 22, 29 OG).[189] Both these themes are evident in v. 29:

> And the angels will drive you for seven years, and you will never be seen nor will you ever speak with any human. They will feed you grass like an ox, and your pasture will be the tender grass of the earth. (Dan. 4:29 OG)[190]

However, rather than simply indicating a change in the king's behaviour or location, this same material is used to depict Nebuchadnezzar as being forcibly punished by angels. This theme of divine castigation is evident throughout Dan. 4 OG, where the king's affliction is elaborately described in terms unique to the OG. Firstly, the great tree, representing Nebuchadnezzar in his dream, is 'dragged and it was put down' before 'it was delivered into prison, and it was bound in copper manacles and shackles by them' (Dan. 4:14a). When Daniel interprets the dream, he states that 'the Most High and his angels will pursue you. They will lead you away to prison' (4:21–22). Daniel then warns Nebuchadnezzar that 'they are preparing against you and they will whip you and they will bring judgements against you'

---

188. Grelot, 'Nabuchodonosor changé en bête', 12.

189. The verse numbering in this section follows that of the OG, which differs from that commonly found in most English translations (e.g., NRSV). For a comparison of equivalent verse numberings, see Appendix B.

190. All English translations of Dan. 4 OG are my own unless otherwise stated.

(Dan. 4:23). Later, the heavenly voice announces to the king that 'the angels will drive you for seven years' and 'they will bind you' (Dan. 4:29). Finally, Nebuchadnezzar himself admits that he 'was bound seven years' (Dan. 4:30a). This penalty appears to be completely enacted by divine figures, whether it is the angel and divine voice who proclaim the sentence (Dan. 4:10–14, 28–30) or the angels who directly carry it out (Dan. 4:29–30a). Thus, in the OG, the king's affliction involves severe divine punishment such as flogging, forced transportation, enchainment and imprisonment. Indeed, this appears to be the principal way in which the OG depicts Nebuchadnezzar's affliction.[191]

The reason for the inclusion of this punishment motif is perhaps suggested by the OG's emphasis on the king's sins (ἁμαρτια) which are referred to repeatedly (Dan. 4:19, 24, 30a, 30c OG), compared to only one reference in the MT (חטי, Dan. 4:24).[192] The king is also linked to a very specific sin: the desolation of 'the house of the living God' (Dan. 4:19 OG). This seems to refer to the destruction of Jerusalem's temple by Nebuchadnezzar's forces under the command of Nebuzaradan (2 Kgs 25:8–11; Jer 52:12–15). The link between Dan. 4 and the temple's destruction is further suggested by another piece of unique OG material at the beginning of the narrative. A chronological note in the OG situates the opening of Dan. 4 'in the eighteenth year of his reign' (4:1). Thus, 'after twelve months' (Dan. 4:26), Nebuchadnezzar is afflicted during the nineteenth year of his rule. This matches perfectly with the date of Nebuchadnezzar's destruction of the temple (2 Kgs 25:8; Jer. 52:12). The precise timing of his affliction in the OG suggests a connection between it and the temple's desolation during the same year. Indeed both of these passages (Dan. 4:19 and 4:26), which are found exclusively in the OG, seem to indicate that Nebuchadnezzar's affliction is brought about as a direct result of his destruction of the Jerusalem temple. The OG edition of Dan. 4 therefore seems to frame Nebuchadnezzar's affliction as an appropriate divine punishment for his sins, particularly his responsibility for the desolation of Jerusalem's temple.

With this emphasis on punishment in Dan. 4 OG, the narrative is less focused upon depicting Nebuchadnezzar's affliction as an animalisation. Thus, the OG edition of Dan. 4 is generally less interested in animals than the MT. The respective

191. Satran, 'Early Jewish and Christian Interpretation', 77–78; Holm, *Of Courtiers and Kings*, 257. In addition to divine punishment, the OG also seems to stress that Nebuchadnezzar's affliction was a political exile. In contrast to the brief statement in 4:28 MT, the unique material in 4:28 OG provides an extended account of exactly how the political situation changed. A variety of explanations for this have been proposed, but importantly it reveals that the OG text has an increased emphasis on the political implications of the king's exile and has an interest in the person who succeeded Nebuchadnezzar when he left the throne.

192. This difference is, at least in part, due to the elaboration of the royal repentance in the OG; see Segal, *Dreams, Riddles, and Visions*, 123; Satran, 'Early Jewish and Christian Interpretation', 80–81.

term for 'animal' is used eight times in both the MT (חיוא in Dan. 4:12, 14, 15, 16, 21, 23, 25, 32 MT) and Θ (θηριον in Dan. 4:9, 11, 12, 13, 18, 20, 22, 29 Θ), whereas the OG only refers to 'animals' on four occasions (θηριον in Dan. 4:9, 12, 14a, 30b OG).[193] This reduced interest in animals is especially evident when it comes to the OG's description of Nebuchadnezzar's affliction. However, despite this there are some passages which may potentially be taken to indicate that he undergoes a bodily transformation into an animal form. One such passage can be found when Nebuchadnezzar is described as being affected by the dew of the heaven (Dan. 4:13 OG). Rather than simply being made wet by it (as in Dan. 4:12 MT), the OG describes how the king's 'body [το σωμα] may be changed [ἀλλοιωθη] from the dew of the heaven' (Dan. 4:13 OG). This statement seems suggestive of a bodily change of the king and has been suggested as perhaps the closest any edition of Dan. 4 comes to describing a physical metamorphosis.[194] Significantly though, it does not contain any specific information on how his body was altered, nor is his body likened to an animal in any way (unlike 4:13 MT). Therefore, even if Dan. 4:13 OG is understood as depicting a bodily metamorphosis (which is by no means clear), there is no evidence to suggest his body changed into an animal's. This lack of specificity or comprehensibility in the passage has led many scholars to postulate some historic corruption or the elision of certain words here.[195] However, even if the passage is simply read in its extant form, Dan. 4:13 OG is not particularly compelling as evidence for an animal metamorphosis. Taken on its own, this passage only really attests to a physical effect of the king's affliction upon his body.

The key passage in the OG regarding Nebuchadnezzar's affliction occurs later in the narrative when the king recounts it in more detail:

> My hairs became like wings of an eagle, my nails like those of a lion. My flesh and my heart were changed. I was walking about naked with the animals of the earth.

> και αἱ τριχες μου ἐγενετο ὡς πτερυγες ἀετου, οἱ ὀνυχες μου ὡσει λεοντος· ἠλλοιωθη ἡ σαρξ μου και ἡ καρδια μου, γυμνος περιεπατουν μετα των θηριων της γης. (4:30b OG)

This section of narration contains various descriptions of the king that are unique to the OG edition. Firstly, it contains the only reference to Nebuchadnezzar's heart changing in Dan. 4 OG and this differs markedly in a number of ways from

---

193. Dean Wenthe suggests an explanation for this evidence by postulating that the OG is rendering a Semitic original that was less focused on animals; see Wenthe, 'Old Greek Translation', 134.

194. Satran, 'Early Jewish and Christian Interpretation', 91, n. 39.

195. Montgomery, *Critical and Exegetical Commentary on Daniel*, 235; Ziegler and Munnich, *Susanna, Daniel, Bel et Draco*, 294, n. 13; Grelot, 'La Septante de Daniel IV', 19.

the parallel section in 4:13 MT. These differences include: the later position in the narrative (Dan. 4:30b OG rather than 4:13 MT); the lack of an explicit statement that his heart was changed into animal's; and in the OG this heart change is clearly coupled with a change in the king's flesh (σαρξ). A second remarkable feature of this passage is that it closely connects the king's change of heart with the change to his hair and nails (whereas in the MT these occur in Dan. 4:13 MT and 4:30 MT respectively). However, this imagery differs markedly from the MT as the similes are no longer purely avian; instead Nebuchadnezzar's nails are like those of a lion (rather than a bird cf. Dan. 4:30 MT). Moreover, while in the MT his hair is simply compared with an eagle's (כנשרין), the OG provides additional detail and likens his hair to a specific aquiline feature: the wings (πτερυγες). The final noteworthy aspect of this passage is that it uniquely describes Nebuchadnezzar as being 'naked' (γυμνος), an observation entirely lacking in the MT. All these unique aspects of Nebuchadnezzar's affliction in 4:30b OG seem to be specifically tailored to illustrate a physical change in the appearance of the king.[196] This is suggested by the additional references to both the change of Nebuchadnezzar's flesh and the description of the king's nakedness. Furthermore, in this different context, the similes about his hair and nails no longer unambiguously function as indicators of the passage of time. Unlike the MT, the OG edition omits the word 'until' and, without this preposition, the length of his hair and nails are not connected with the length of his exile. Instead, the likening of Nebuchadnezzar's features to those of animals seems purely intended to describe how the king physically appeared. At this point, we can presume that the OG edition seems to be modifying and repositioning aspects of the description of Nebuchadnezzar's affliction in order to more carefully depict the physical changes undergone by the king.

To fully explicate why the OG differs so markedly from the MT here and how exactly it presents the affliction, it is worth comparing the description of Nebuchadnezzar with that of the first beast in Dan. 7:4:[197]

> The first was like a lion and had eagles' wings. Then, as I watched, its wings were plucked off, and it was lifted up from the ground and made to stand on two feet like a human being; and a human mind [lit. heart] was given to it. (Dan. 7:4 NRSV)

> קדמיתא כאריה וגפין די־נשר לה חזה הוית עד די־מריטו גפיה ונטילת מן־ארעא ועל־רגלין כאנש הקימת ולבב אנש יהיב לה: (Dan. 7:4 MT)

---

196. See Meadowcroft, *Aramaic Daniel and Greek Daniel*, 237.

197. It has also been suggested that 4:30b OG simply results from textual corruption; see Dominique Barthélemy, *Critique textuelle de l'Ancien Testament: Tome 3. Ézéchiel, Daniel et les 12 Prophètes*, OBO 50/3 (Göttingen: Vandenhoeck & Ruprecht, 1992), 446. While there may be evidence for this, the evidence of a relationship with Dan. 7:4 is more compelling.

το πρωτον ώσει λεαινα έχουσα ώσει πτερα άετου έθεωρουν έως ου έτι τα πτερα αύτης και ήρθη άπο της γης έπι ποδων άνθρωπων έσταθη και άνθρωπινη καρδια έδοθη αύτη. (Dan. 7:4 OG)[198]

The description of this beast in Dan. 7:4 bears considerable resemblance to that of Nebuchadnezzar and it is commonly agreed that this passage is an adapted form of Dan. 4:13 and 31 (MT).[199] Not only do they share similar terminology and imagery, John Collins has suggested that the positive assessment of the beast in Dan. 7:4 may also be evidence of the influence of Dan. 4.[200] This reliance of Dan. 7:4 upon Dan. 4 has been questioned by Michael Segal who argues that the direction of influence runs the opposite way from Dan. 7 to Dan. 4 MT.[201] He suggests that the MT's reference to Nebuchadnezzar receiving an animal heart (Dan. 4:13 MT) is secondary, principally because it is not repeated when the king's affliction is described again in 4:20, and therefore this verse is an adaptation based on Dan. 7:4. However this argument is unconvincing because, as has been demonstrated in Table 1 above, each time the king's affliction is described in the MT a different list of symptoms is recounted. For example, the change of the king's heart is not the only aspect of the affliction described in Dan. 4:11–13 but omitted in 4:20's repetition (e.g., 4:20 also omits the shaking of leaves, the scattering of fruit, and the flight of the animals from beneath the tree). This imperfect repetition of symptoms just seems to be part of the way in which the MT narrative is constructed.[202] Furthermore, Alexander Di Lella has demonstrated that Dan. 4:13 is an integral part of the poetic structure in Dan. 4:7–14 MT.[203] The weight of

198. For the most part this passage follows Ziegler's critical text, though when the manuscript evidence differs I have included the variants found in Papyrus 967 as this is both older in date and bears better comparison with Dan. 4 OG.

199. This has recently been defended by Carlos Olivares, 'El Léon con Alas de Águila en Daniel 7:4: Un Resumen de la Locura y Restauración de Nabucodonosor (Dn 4)', *DavarLogos* 4 (2002): 149–158. Examples of other modern commentators who hold this view include Reinhard G. Kratz, 'The Visions of Daniel' in *The Book of Daniel: Composition and Reception*, ed. by John J. Collins and Peter W. Flint, VTSup 83 (Leiden: Brill, 2001), 91–113 (95–96); Eric W. Heaton, *The Book of Daniel: Introduction and Commentary*, TBC (London: SCM Press, 1956), 176; Porteous, *Daniel*, 105; Anne E. Gardner, 'Decoding Daniel: The Case of Dan. 7,5', *Bib* 88 (2007): 222–33 (229). For a list of commentators who hold a similar view, see Jürg Eggler, *Influences and Traditions Underlying the Vision of Daniel 7:2-14*, OBO 177 (Göttingen: Vandenhoeck & Ruprecht, 2000), 39.

200. Collins, *Daniel: A Commentary*, 297.

201. Segal, *Dreams, Riddles, and Visions*, 106–107.

202. See Coxon, 'Great Tree of Daniel 4', 99–100.

203. Alexander A. Di Lella, 'Daniel 4:7–14: Poetic Analysis and Biblical Background', in *Mélanges bibliques et orientaux en l'honneur de M. Henri Cazelles*, ed. André Caquot and Mathias Delcor, AOAT 212 (Neukirchen-Vluyn: Neukirchener Verlag, 1981), 247–258 (248–255).

evidence therefore suggests that Dan. 4:13 is not secondary in the MT and supports the argument that Dan. 7:4 has in turn been influenced by it.[204]

Nevertheless, there is good evidence for the influence of Dan. 7:4 upon Dan. 4 OG and this can potentially explain the distinctive adjustment to Nebuchadnezzar's affliction in Dan. 4:30b OG. The first key indicator of the influence of Dan. 7:4 is the change in animalising imagery in 4:30b OG. Here, unlike the MT, the OG distinctively refers to Nebuchadnezzar's hair as like wings (πτερυγες) of an eagle and likens his nails to a lion's (λεοντος). Both these unique descriptions reflect the depiction of the beast in Dan. 7:4 which has eagle's wings (πτερα) and otherwise appears as a lion (λεαινα) and thus would have leonine claws. Unlike the MT, the imagery in the OG almost exactly correlates with that in Dan. 7:4.[205] The additional mention of the king's flesh (σαρξ) changing might also be a reference to the depiction of the composite creature in 7:4.[206] Moreover, the influence of Dan. 7:4 is also suggested by the repositioning of the change of the king's heart (4:13 MT) in the OG to be within close proximity to the animalising imagery (4:30b OG). This closer connection between these two descriptions exactly parallels Dan. 7:4, even in the order in which they are referred to (both passages describe the appearance of hair and then relate the change of heart). There is also a possible point of contact between the unique OG passage describing the king as 'walking about naked with the animals' (Dan. 4:30b) and the description in Dan. 7:4 of the beast being 'lifted up from the ground and made to stand on two feet like a human'. The description in Dan. 4:30b OG appears to anticipate the 'lifting up' in 7:4 as, in order to for this to occur, the individual must first have been walking like an animal (which might in turn suggest that the king in 4:30b OG is considered to be on all fours). These close connections suggest an inherent relationship between Dan. 7:4 and 4:30b OG. Such a relationship is given even greater credence by that the fact that the oldest manuscript witness to Dan. 4 OG (Papyrus 967) positions Dan. 7 straight after Dan. 4 in the sequence of the book (see Appendix A). This alternate sequencing, which is presumably original to the OG edition (see §3.2.2), may have encouraged such connections to be made between these Danielic chapters.

Based on these connections, it is proposed here that the depiction of Nebuchadnezzar's affliction in Dan. 4 OG has been influenced by and amended

---

204. It remains possible that the entirety of Dan. 4 MT could have been influenced by Dan. 7:4, rather than just Dan. 4:13 MT specifically. However, this explanation would require the author/editor of Dan. 4 MT to have intentionally divorced the heart-change (4:13 MT) from the animalising imagery about hair and nails (4:30) which are united in Dan. 7:4. This seems significantly less plausible than the alternative explanation that the author/editor of Dan. 7:4 united this varying animalising imagery into a single depiction of the beast.

205. Satran, 'Early Jewish and Christian Interpretation', 76–77. Interestingly, it is worth noting that the gender of the lion differs in Dan. 7:4 OG and Dan. 4:30b OG.

206. Alternatively, it has been suggested that σαρξ (flesh) is somehow a rendition of the word בשׂר (body) in 4:30 MT; see Ashley, 'The Book of Daniel Chapters I–VI', 239.

towards Dan. 7:4. Furthermore, it is possible that Dan. 4:30b OG was specifically adapted in order to highlight the connection between these texts and to help interpret the confusing imagery in Dan. 7:4. For example, the editor(s) of Dan. 4 OG may have attempted to explicitly identify Nebuchadnezzar with the first beast in Dan. 7:4 by adapting the description of the king's affliction. To some extent Dan. 4:30b OG could then function as a prequel to the subsequent passage in Dan. 7:4, shedding light upon the identity of this first beast and how this character ended up in such a condition. It would appear, therefore, that the only animalising imagery in Dan. 4 OG (4:30b) seems to depend upon the portrayal of the beast in Dan. 7:4, which in turn draws upon Dan. 4 MT. The animalising imagery in Dan. 4 OG can therefore be considered to be secondary when compared with the MT.[207] In light of these conclusions, and despite being double literary editions, Dan. 4 MT should be considered the primary evidence when considering the possible animalisation of Nebuchadnezzar in the Dan. 4 tradition. Thus, while the OG predominantly portrays Nebuchadnezzar's affliction as a divine punishment, it does incorporate animalising imagery in 4:30b OG however this is ultimately dependent upon the MT, albeit indirectly.

Nevertheless, while the description of Nebuchadnezzar's affliction in this passage is closely related to the portrayal of the beast in Dan. 7:4, the imagery in 4:30b OG is not necessarily indicative of a literal metamorphosis of the king into an animal. It has commonly been agreed that Dan. 4:30b OG stops some way short of a true or explicit animal metamorphosis.[208] Despite the more physical portrayal of his affliction in 4:30b OG, Dan. 4 OG only describes more general changes of the king which have no explicit connection with an animalising change at all. The only actual reference to Nebuchadnezzar resembling an animal in any way is the description of his nails and hair, and this animalising imagery is still only conveyed through similes. The text does not suggest that the king *actually* assumed an eagle's wings or a lion's claws. Unlike Dan. 4 MT, the OG text appears to have redeployed this imagery in order to explicitly draw attention to the connections between Dan. 4 and the beast in Dan. 7:4. However, while connections with the entirely physically bestial creature in Dan. 7:4 have clearly been emphasised, this itself should not dictate how the intended change of Nebuchadnezzar in 4:30b should be understood. Such textual connections between these passages do not require the king to be

---

207. It has been argued by some scholars that Dan. 4:30b OG was originally absent and Dan. 4 OG thus originally lacked any trace of animalising imagery; e.g., see Wills, *Jew in the Court of the Foreign King*, 95; Segal, *Dreams, Riddles, and Visions*, 106, n. 23. Rather than argue for this, I am simply claiming that, in its current form, the animalising imagery in Dan. 4 OG (found solely in 4:30b) has been influenced by Dan. 4 MT. The MT should thus be considered the primary extant evidence for the animalising imagery used to describe Nebuchadnezzar's affliction.

208. In this, I agree with David Satran's assessment; see Satran, 'Early Jewish and Christian Interpretation', 76; and Henze, *Madness of King Nebuchadnezzar*, 30.

literally metamorphosed into a similar composite creature and are more likely indicators to the reader to link these two texts together.

However, while perhaps not depicting a metamorphosis in the truest sense, the OG edition appears to be responsible for most of the prominent metamorphic interpretations of Dan. 4 (including those surveyed in chapter 2 above). The trend of interpreting Nebuchadnezzar's affliction as a form of penitential metamorphosis, whereby he performed an act of penance in the wilderness (see the first section of chapter 2), is reliant on the OG edition's references to Nebuchadnezzar's prayers and petitions (Dan. 4:30a) as well as his subsequent confessions (Dan. 4:34 OG).[209] Similarly, the hybrid metamorphosis, depicted most notably in the *Vita Danielis* (see §2.2), also shows evidence of reliance on the OG and not MT edition of Dan. 4. The *Vita* describes how Nebuchadnezzar's 'foreparts with the head were like an ox, and the feet with the hind parts like a lion' (Liv. Pro. 4.5)[210] which matches the unique depiction in the OG edition of the king's leonine nails (Dan. 4:30a OG) which are on the feet of such a creature. Presumably his foreparts were interpreted in the *Vita* as being like an ox in order for him elsewhere to consume 'grass like an ox' (Dan. 4:30a OG). This range of imagery in Dan. 4 OG has thus been combined in the *Vita* resulting in a visual depiction of Nebuchadnezzar as a composite creature.[211] Therefore, despite lacking unequivocal evidence for an actual or intended metamorphosis in the text itself, the change of emphasis in the OG towards depicting the king as experiencing physical effects from his affliction has directly facilitated interpretations of Dan. 4 which to explain the events as Nebuchadnezzar metamorphosing into an animal.

Through this assessment of the OG edition of Dan. 4 it has been shown that the primary focus in this version of the narrative is on depicting Nebuchadnezzar's affliction as a divine punishment. The animalising nature of the king's affliction is therefore significantly underplayed, at least when compared with the MT. On the few occasions when a change in the king is suggested, Dan. 4 OG appears to be influenced by Dan. 7:4, yet still does not unambiguously suggest that Nebuchadnezzar underwent a physical metamorphosis into an animal. At most we

---

209. The influence of the OG edition is especially clear in Tertullian's writings. For the influence of the OG on Tertullian, see Montgomery, *Critical and Exegetical Commentary on Daniel*, 29–32, 43–46; Satran, 'Early Jewish and Christian Interpretation', 213–215; Henze, *Madness of King Nebuchadnezzar*, 190.

210. Translation from Hare, 'Lives of the Prophets', 390 v. 4.5.

211. Despite noting the leonine correlation, Satran states that there is no evidence for this lion-ox hybrid creature in the biblical versions: Satran, 'Early Jewish and Christian Interpretation', 346; Satran, *Biblical Prophets in Byzantine Palestine*, 83. However he fails to note that by creating this hybrid creature with an ox's head, the *Vita* is visually depicting the ability of Nebuchadnezzar to consume grass. The reliance of the *Vita* upon the OG can also be seen in how, unlike the MT, they both explicitly mention that the king will be unable to speak; compare Hare, 'Lives of the Prophets', 390 v. 4.10, and Dan. 4:29 OG.

can conclude that, by emphasising the physical effect of his wilderness isolation, the OG's representation of the king's affliction is a step towards a metamorphosis which is thus ultimately responsible for early metamorphic interpretations. It is fair to conclude then that Dan. 4 OG is perhaps a witness to an early alteration of the narrative to accord with Dan. 7:4, which has in turn led to later interpretations of Nebuchadnezzar's affliction as a metamorphosis.

3.3.3 Metamorphosis in the Theodotion Text (Θ)

The final edition of Dan. 4 which will be assessed here for evidence of an animal metamorphosis is the Theodotion (Θ) edition. As might be expected, due to their close relationship, the presentation of Nebuchadnezzar's affliction in the Θ edition of Dan. 4 differs very little from the MT's depiction of events (see Appendix B). The many parallels between these editions will not be discussed here in detail, though it should be acknowledged that because of this textual connection the Θ edition likewise portrays Nebuchadnezzar as behaving and living like an animal. However, there are a couple of unique adjustments in this edition which are of interest when considering whether there is evidence of an intended metamorphosis.

Firstly, the Θ offers a slightly different description of the changes to Nebuchadnezzar's physical features. The king is described as being in the wilderness 'until when his hair lengthened like that of lions [λεοντων] and his nails were like those of birds [ὀρνεων]' (Dan. 4:30 Θ). This differs significantly from both the MT and the OG in that his hair is compared with a lion's, rather than an eagle's. The resemblance to a lion has suggested to some scholars a potential link between the Θ and OG editions as each use leonine imagery to describe the king.[212] To assess this possibility and understand this final and unique restatement of the animalising imagery about Nebuchadnezzar we will compare it with the previous imagery noticed thus far:

Dan. 4:30 MT   Until when his hair grew long like that of eagles [כנשרין] and his nails were like those of birds [כצפרין].

Dan. 4:30b OG   And my hairs became like wings of an eagle [ὡς πτερυγες ἀετου], my nails like those of a lion [λεοντος].

Dan. 4:30 Θ   Until when his hair lengthened like that of lions [λεοντων] and his nails were like those of birds [ὀρνεων].

Dan. 7:4   The first was like a lion [λεαινα] and had eagles' wings [ὡσει πτερα ἀετου].[213]

---

212. See Montgomery, *Critical and Exegetical Commentary on Daniel*, 245; Satran, 'Early Jewish and Christian Interpretation', 76–77; Segal, *Dreams, Riddles, and Visions*, 124.

213. Though the Greek texts of Dan. 7:4 use the same terminology to refer to the beast's 'eagles' wings' in Dan. 7:4, each text puts them in a slightly different sequence: Dan. 7:4 Θ — πτερα αὐτη ὡσει ἀετου; Dan. 7:4 OG [Papyrus 967] — ωσει πτερα αετου; Dan. 7:4 OG [Chigi 88] — πτερα ὡσει ἀετου. I have followed the sequence in Papyrus 967 as it again illustrates the closer parallel between this manuscript and Dan. 4 OG.

Such a connection, between the Θ and OG depictions of Nebuchadnezzar, does not seem straightforward. While admittedly they both refer to lions (OG: λεοντος; Θ: λεοντων), the OG uses this comparison to describe Nebuchadnezzar's nails (ὄνυχες; Dan. 4:30b OG) and the Θ uses it to describe his hair (τριχες; Dan. 4:30 Θ). Furthermore, while the OG appears to deploy lion imagery to specifically match Nebuchadnezzar with the beast in Dan. 7:4, the Θ's use of similar imagery does not match this later Danielic passage. For example, the beast in Dan. 7:4 appears like a lion and would have lion's claws, whereas in 4:30 Θ Nebuchadnezzar's nails are likened to the claws of a bird rather than a lion. Equally, if the Θ were trying to match Dan. 7:4, we would expect it to maintain the likeness to an eagle (ἀετου) in its description, however this comparison is replaced by the lion imagery whilst the comparison to a bird (ὀρνεων), which has no parallel in Dan. 7:4, is preserved. This may suggest that the inclusion of leonine imagery is used for an entirely different purpose in the Θ, rather than to match Dan. 7:4 (as the OG does).[214] Instead it is plausible to suggest that this Θ change resulted from the translator's desire to make the passage more illustrative.[215] While rendering the Aramaic text, the Θ translator(s) may have struggled with the potentially difficult image of the king's hair being like an eagle's (given that eagles have feathers rather than hair). As the Θ translator(s) seem to draw upon the OG elsewhere when confronted with a difficulty in the Aramaic text, it is probable that the Θ also relied upon the OG in this circumstance too and incorporated the Greek leonine imagery into its own translation in order to better illustrate the length of Nebuchadnezzar's hair.[216] Likening the king's long hair to a lion's mane probably seemed more appropriate a comparison and one which more clearly illustrated Nebuchadnezzar's condition. Therefore, by using the OG to make sense of a difficult phrase in the MT, Dan. 4:30 Θ could be considered the result of a blend of both the MT's and OG's animal imagery. While seemingly unaware of any connection with Dan. 7:4 at all, the Θ nevertheless seems to be indirectly influenced by this later passage through its reliance upon Dan. 4:30b OG.[217]

214. The absence of a connection between Dan. 7:4 and Dan. 4:30 Θ is also suggested by the order of Dan. Θ manuscripts. Unlike Papyrus 967, which places Dan. 7 after Dan. 4, all Greek manuscripts of the Θ follow the order of the MT (i.e., Dan. 4, 5, 6, 7; see Appendix A). This ordering of the book of Daniel in the Θ obscures any potential links between Dan. 7 and Dan. 4.

215. Satran, 'Early Jewish and Christian Interpretation', 76–77. This kind of solution also seems to be inferred by the brief comment in Lacocque, *Book of Daniel*, 85.

216. For the theory that Θ occasionally relied upon the OG, see earlier: §3.2.3. For a list of situations where the Θ appears to rely on the OG, see McLay, *OG and Th Versions of Daniel*, 247.

217. Unfortunately, in his comparison of these editions of Dan. 4, McLay ('Greek Translations of Daniel 4–6') does not attend to this connection between Dan. 4:30 Θ and Dan. 4:30b OG.

The second major departure from the MT, and one with more bearing on a possible metamorphosis, is in Dan. 4:33 Θ. Upon the completion of his exile, Nebuchadnezzar states that 'my reason was returned to me, and I came into the honour of my kingdom, and my form [ἡ μορφη μου] returned to me' (Dan. 4:33 Θ). The statement that the king's 'form' returned is distinctive to the Θ edition and can likely be explained as the result of translating the underlying Aramaic word זיו (Dan. 4:33 MT). In Second Temple texts, this Aramaic term seems to specifically denote either a person's majesty or the shine of their visage.[218] Timothy Meadowcroft has proposed that the Aramaic text of Daniel appears to play with these various meanings of זיו, by using it to refer equally to physical countenance and royal splendor.[219] As the Greek term μορφη seems to cover a similar semantic range as the Aramaic term, signifying a person's countenance or appearance,[220] Meadowcroft concluded that the Θ translation probably used μορφη in an attempt to translate this range of meanings.[221] This seems to be part of a larger translational tendency as Dan. Θ tends to render זיו as μορφη elsewhere in Daniel (Dan. 5:6, 9, 10; 7:28 Θ).[222] Thus it is possible that the reference to the king's form changing (Dan. 4:33 Θ) arose due to an attempt by the Greek translator to satisfactorily capture the sense of an underlying Aramaic word.

However, while μορφη covers a similar semantic range to the Aramaic, the primary function of this Greek word is usually to denote the outward shape or form of a person.[223] For example, Isa 44:13 LXX describes an idol being in 'the form [μορφη] of a man' (NETS) which clearly uses this word to refer to the shape of a human being.[224] Consequently, while 4:33 Θ appears to be a suitable translation of the Aramaic reference to the king's royal splendour, by rendering זיו as μορφη this Greek text also introduces the implication that Nebuchadnezzar is returning to his human form or shape. This specific terminological choice in Dan. 4:33 Θ therefore suggests that the king's human form or shape (μορφη) had been changed which may further indicate that during his affliction he had experienced some

218. E.g., 4Q531 8:4; 11Q10 34:6; Dan. 2:31 MT. The plural form occurs elsewhere in Daniel (Dan. 5:6, 9, 10; 7:28 Θ), though this form appears to denote 'a person's sanguine complexion, which pales in view of a threatening divine message'; see Klaus Beyer, 'זיו,' *TDOT* 16:235. Gzella, *TDOT* 16:384.

219. Meadowcroft, *Aramaic Daniel and Greek Daniel*, 79.

220. LEH, s.v. 'μορφή'.

221. This is instead of a perhaps more direct translation of the Aramaic which may have been ὅρασις, as rendered in Dan. 5:6 OG.

222. The only instance where Dan. Θ uses an alternate Greek word to translate זיו is Dan. 2:31 where it is rendered ὅρασις.

223. LEH, s.v. 'μορφή'.

224. Similar examples can be found in e.g., Job 4.16 LXX; 4 Macc. 15:4.

kind of physical metamorphosis. While this specific implication may not have been intended by the translator and presumably was not suggested by the underlying Aramaic, through the act of translation the Θ edition has created a text which is perhaps a step further down the road towards depicting a plausible metamorphosis. With this rendition of Dan. 4:33, the Θ edition can thus be read as implying that Nebuchadnezzar underwent an animal metamorphosis.

The possibility of an implied metamorphosis in Dan. 4 Θ also seems evident in some early metamorphic interpretations of Nebuchadnezzar's affliction. Those who view Nebuchadnezzar as undergoing a physical metamorphosis into an animal as an act of penance (see §2.1) tend to rely upon the Θ. While most commentators who follow this interpretative trend draw upon the OG too, they also describe Nebuchadnezzar as having a lion's mane which explicitly reflects Dan. 4:30 Θ.[225] In fact, in his *Catecheses,* Cyril of Jerusalem seems to provide a description of Nebuchadnezzar which results from a blend of both Greek textual editions by describing the king has having a lion's mane (presumably derived from Dan. 4:30 Θ) and lion's claws (presumably from Dan. 4:30b OG).[226] It is probable that this penitential metamorphic interpretation is therefore influenced by passages from both the OG and the Θ editions of Dan. 4. The return of the king's form in Dan. 4:33 Θ also seems to have influenced this interpretation which can be seen, for example, in Tertullian's comments that the king was exiled from human form (*ab humana forma*).[227] However, the potentially ambiguous nature of Dan. 4:33 Θ is such that even those who deny a metamorphosis can still read the text as supporting their view (see §2.3). For instance, John Chrysostom quotes this passage about the return of the king's form (μορφη), and yet elsewhere specifically denies that the king was changed in form (μορφη) during his affliction.[228] Furthermore, Theodoret of Cyrrhus also specifically references the return of the king's form (Dan. 4:33 Θ) but he explains this as simply referring to the unkempt appearance of Nebuchadnezzar.[229] Therefore, we can see that the implied nature of the king's change of form in Dan. 4 Θ has meant that this text has supported both metamorphic interpretations and denials of such transformations within the narrative.

This brief assessment of the Θ edition of Dan. 4 has shown that it differs only in detail from the MT in its description of Nebuchadnezzar's affliction and thus

---

225. Tertullian, *De paenitentia* 12.7–8; Paulinus of Nola, *Epist.* 23.19–20; Cyril of Jerusalem, *Catecheses* 2.18. It has been suggested that Tertullian's similarity to 4:30 Θ may be a result of textual corruption; see Satran, 'Early Jewish and Christian Interpretation', 239 n. 14.

226. Cyril of Jerusalem, *Catecheses* 2.18.

227. Tertullian, *De patientia* 13.4 in E. Decker et al., *Tertullianus Opera I. Opera Catholica. Adversus Marcionem,* Corpus Christianorum: Series Latina 1 (Turnhout: Brepols, 1954), 314.

228. John Chrysostom, *Interpretatio in Danielem prophetam* (PG 56:219, 221). Jerome also comments that Nebuchadnezzar did not lose his form; see Jerome, *Comm. Dan.* (PL 25:517).

229. Theodoret, *Comm. Dan.* 4.33 (PG 81:1373B). Theodoret was probably reading the Lucianic recension of the Θ text; see Hill, *Theodoret of Cyrus,* xvi.

preserves the animalising imagery of the Aramaic text. Nevertheless, the couple of minor variations between the MT and Θ editions are significant. The subtle change to the description of Nebuchadnezzar in Dan. 4:30 Θ provides evidence that the Θ has also been influenced by the OG edition. Furthermore, and more significantly, the distinctive terminological choice in Dan. 4:33 Θ has perhaps produced an edition of Dan. 4 which implies that Nebuchadnezzar underwent an animal metamorphosis. It seems unlikely that this portrayal of the king's affliction was intended, but this implication is borne out by the influence of the Θ edition upon subsequent metamorphic interpretations of the narrative by later commentators. This edition of Dan. 4 therefore arguably comes closest to depicting Nebuchadnezzar's affliction as a physical transformation into an animal by implying a metamorphosis that is certainly more apparent than in the MT.

3.3.4 Summary

Through this assessment of the different editions of Dan. 4, each has been shown to portray Nebuchadnezzar's affliction significantly differently. Firstly, the MT describes few physical changes to the king and, by depicting his affliction as a change in both behaviour and in the location of his habitation, seems to chiefly characterise his animalising change as a loss of reason. The OG describes more physical effects of the king's change but still does not contain unequivocal evidence that Nebuchadnezzar underwent a physical metamorphosis into an animal. In any case, the OG is primarily focused on depicting his affliction as a divine punishment for the desolation of Jerusalem's temple rather than anything relating to an animalisation. Finally, the Θ translates the animalising imagery from the underlying Aramaic but also includes some significant variations which imply Nebuchadnezzar underwent a physical change of form. Additionally, and in light of these conclusions, it is possible to suggest the existence of a particular redactional layer in both the MT and the OG editions. The OG seems to have been redacted towards Dan. 7:4, generating its more physical description of Nebuchadnezzar's affliction (Dan. 4:30b OG), while Dan. 4 MT seems to have influenced Dan. 5 MT due to the repetition of the king's animalisation contained therein (Dan. 5:18–22). These unique connections with other Danielic chapters seem to be occasioned by the differing chapter sequence in each edition of the book (Dan. 4 OG immediately precedes Dan. 7 OG, whereas Dan. 4 MT precedes Dan. 5 MT; see Appendix A). Thus, both the MT and OG portrayals of Nebuchadnezzar's animalising affliction seem to have undergone separate redactional layers which were induced by their respective proximity to different Danielic chapters.

    Based on these observations, it is possible to attempt explanations for why some later metamorphic interpretations of Dan. 4 came about. To a greater or lesser extent, both the OG and the Θ editions enable a transformative understanding of Nebuchadnezzar's affliction and suggest physical changes of the king. These have demonstrably been used, or even perhaps combined, by commentators who have suggested that a physical animal metamorphosis is described in the narrative. Furthermore, these more transformative elements of the OG and Θ themselves resulted from either a perceived connection with Dan. 7:4 (i.e., Dan. 4:30b) or the result of specific translational choices (i.e., Dan. 4:33 Θ). Therefore, as the transformative descriptions in both the OG and Θ are the result of later amendments, it seems that the primary version of Nebuchadnezzar's animalisation is found in the MT where it did not originally appear to be intended as one of metamorphosis. This does not mean that Dan. 4 MT as a whole should be thought of as the primary edition (as it has already been demonstrated that both the MT and OG are best understood as double literary editions; see §3.2.2), instead the MT should simply be considered the earliest or most basic tradition about Nebuchadnezzar's animalisation. Thus the earliest witness to the tradition about Nebuchadnezzar's animalisation, found in the MT, does not appear to be intended as one of metamorphosis.

3.4 Conclusion

While Nebuchadnezzar's affliction in Dan. 4 often seems to be interpreted as a physical metamorphosis into an animal, this assessment of the potential sources and texts of Dan. 4 has shown that the actual evidence for such a transformation is slight. A number of texts have been suggested as possible influences on Dan. 4 and these have allowed scholars to theorise about what sources the Danielic narrative might be reliant upon. However, within these potential sources, there is little evidence of animalising imagery and certainly nothing that suggests the affliction of the king was portrayed as an animal metamorphosis. From this assessment, it seems that any animal transformation of Nebuchadnezzar in the narrative must result, not from an underlying source, but from the editing or subsequent development of the Danielic text itself.

The actual textual evidence for the narrative in Dan. 4 about Nebuchadnezzar's affliction has been preserved in three main variant editions: an Aramaic text (MT) and two Greek versions (OG and Θ). The MT and the OG versions of Dan. 4 should be treated primarily as different literary editions of the same narrative core which have undergone their own secondary expansion. Not all of these expansions took place independently of one another, as we have also seen how the depiction of Nebuchadnezzar's affliction in the OG is influenced by Dan. 7:4 and thus indirectly by the MT. Thus, in terms of how it depicts the animalising effects of the king's affliction, the MT should be considered the primary text. The Θ is essentially a fresh Greek translation of the Aramaic text and therefore also relies upon the MT edition. Nevertheless, there is evidence that occasionally the Θ has interpreted and adjusted the underlying Semitic text, and sometimes these emendations seem to be influenced by the OG edition.

However, while there are various examples of animalising imagery in each text, none of these variant editions of Dan. 4 contain any substantial or compelling evidence that Nebuchadnezzar was intentionally depicted as metamorphosing into an animal. The primary depiction of Nebuchadnezzar's affliction in the MT contains a variety of animal imagery but this is used to illustrate a change in the king's behaviour and place of abode brought about through a loss of reason. These changes are superficial, not substantial, and do not describe a physical metamorphosis. By contrast, both Greek editions seem to emphasise the king's transformation through subsequent adjustments to the narrative. While the OG is primarily interested in depicting Nebuchadnezzar's affliction as a divine punishment for the destruction of the Jerusalem Temple, when it does incorporate animalising imagery it is reliant upon Dan. 7:4, which in turns relies upon Dan. 4 MT. This textual connection has increased the physical description of the king's animalising affliction in the OG, but the evidence is still not sufficient to claim that it portrays an unequivocal metamorphosis of Nebuchadnezzar. Nevertheless, this edition clearly allows for such an interpretation as many metamorphic interpretative trends about Dan. 4 are reliant upon the OG. The Θ may perhaps be seen as being closest to a depiction of an animal metamorphosis. While it seems unlikely that a physical metamorphosis was intended by the translator of the Θ, the narrative underwent minor changes from the MT and, in the case of the translation of 4:33 Θ, resulted in a text that could imply a physical change of the king's form.

This chapter has therefore begun to address the controversial issue of whether the king's affliction in Dan. 4 should be interpreted as a metamorphosis into an animal or whether an animal transformation should be denied. By demonstrating that animalising imagery is almost entirely absent in the potential sources for Dan. 4, and that the presence of such imagery in both the OG and the Θ is ultimately secondary, it can thus be concluded that the earliest evidence for the king's affliction being framed in explicitly animalising terms is contained in the MT edition. While the Greek editions both seem to be the originating point for the development of interpretations that support a metamorphosis, in the primary evidence of Nebuchadnezzar's animalising affliction in the MT text there is no compelling evidence that this should be understood as a metamorphosis. Nevertheless, while the suggestion of a *metamorphosis* seems unsupported by the earliest form of the king's animalisation in Dan. 4, this does not mean that this Danielic tale of Nebuchadnezzar's affliction did not intend to depict the king as becoming an animal. Rather than a physical transformation, the primary description of the king's animalisation in the MT seems to focus on the king's loss of reason and, as will be argued in the following chapters, in the ancient context of this narrative this might indicate a rather different and somewhat more significant form of human–animal transformation.

Chapter 4

THE HUMAN–ANIMAL BOUNDARY IN THE ANCIENT NEAR EAST

While investigations into the textual evidence of Daniel 4 have shown that there is no reasonable basis to see an intended physical metamorphosis in the text, and certainly nothing in the primary edition of Nebuchadnezzar's animalising affliction in Dan. 4 MT, this conclusion does not preclude the possibility of any animal transformation in the narrative at all. Focus will now turn to assess the narrative of Dan. 4 in terms of its ancient Near Eastern context to see how these traditions may assist in understanding the affliction in the narrative. This will delineate how the boundary between human and animal was understood in the ancient Near East and thus also demonstrate what an animal transformation in this context would entail. Such an assessment will be conducted with the aim of subsequently describing (in chapter 5) how the narrative of Dan. 4, while not containing a metamorphosis per se, in fact contains a rather more significant crossing of the human–animal boundary.

4.1 Previous Scholarly Readings of Daniel 4 in its Ancient Near Eastern Context

Much recent scholarly work on Dan. 4 has employed comparative ancient Near Eastern evidence to reach important insights into how to understand Nebuchadnezzar's affliction and the animal imagery used to describe it. Most often, scholars have placed Dan. 4 into the context of a Mesopotamian belief in primordial wild humanity.[1] These first early humans are supposed to have originally lived a savage or wild type of existence, dwelling in the wilderness away from urban centres. Eventually they developed through a civilizing process

---

1. For example, Peter W. Coxon, 'Another Look at Nebuchadnezzar's Madness', in *The Book of Daniel in the Light of New Findings*, ed. Adam S. van der Woude, BETL 106 (Leuven: Leuven University Press and Peeters, 1993), 211–22 (218–20); Ferguson, 'Nebuchadnezzar, Gilgamesh, and the "Babylonian Job"', 325–6; Henze, *Madness of King Nebuchadnezzar*, 93–9; Jeffrey H. Tigay, 'Paradise', *EncJud* 15:625.

into full humanity who then created settlements and cities.² Scholars have therefore suggested that an explanation for Nebuchadnezzar's condition could be found in these Babylonian traditions about the primordial wild man, particularly in the civilising process which they underwent.³ When placed into this context, Nebuchadnezzar's affliction essentially becomes a reversal of the process that eventually civilized these primordial humans. In Henze's words, Dan. 4 'is a piece of Babylonian mythology, borrowed by the ancient Israelite author, turned upside-down, and applied to King Nebuchadnezzar, Israel's enemy of the first rank'.⁴

Another theory has been proposed by Silviu Bunta which identifies a different Mesopotamian basis for Nebuchadnezzar's experience.⁵ He claims the imagery of the tree in Dan. 4 is an appropriation of the *mēsu*-tree – the Mesopotamian concept of an enormous tree used as an icon for the divine. Thus, when the tree is cut down it symbolizes Nebuchadnezzar losing his function as a legitimate divine icon to be worshipped. Instead he is depicted as one of the animals that had previously subsisted on the tree. For Bunta, this depiction should be interpreted as Nebuchadnezzar becoming an angel who serves and worships the divine image.⁶ Yet, his argument for Nebuchadnezzar's 'angelization' does not have much discernible support in the text of Dan. 4, and nor has it received much scholarly support since. The principal reason that he rejects the primordial reading of Nebuchadnezzar's affliction is that he claims the idea of a primordial animalistic state is not evidenced at all in the Hebrew Bible. However, the primordial argument cannot be so easily dismissed because we do get a suggestion of it in the narrative in Gen. 2–3, something which even Bunta himself admits.⁷

Christopher Hays has argued for a different understanding of Nebuchadnezzar's affliction.⁸ He states that the primordial human argument is an 'unsatisfying

---

2. For works on wild men in Mesopotamian and world literature, see Roger Bartra, *Wild Men in the Looking Glass: The Mythic Origins of European Otherness* (Ann Arbor, MI: University of Michigan Press, 1994); David A. Wells, *The Wild Man from the Epic of Gilgamesh to Hartmann von Aue's Iwein: Reflections on the Development of a Theme in World Literature*, New Lecture Series 78 (Belfast: Queen's University Press, 1975); Gregory Mobley, 'The Wild Man in the Bible and the Ancient Near East', *JBL* 116 (1997): 217–233 for a specific analysis of the Bible in relation to wild men.

3. Particularly the work of Henze, *Madness of King Nebuchadnezzar*, 93–99.

4. Henze, *Madness of King Nebuchadnezzar*, 99.

5. Silviu N. Bunta, 'The *Mēsu*-Tree and the Animal Inside: Theomorphism and Theriomorphism in Daniel 4', in *The Theophaneia School: Jewish Roots of Eastern Christian Mysticism*, ed. Basil Lourié and Andrei Orlov, Scrinium 3 (St Petersburg: Byzantinorossica, 2007), 364–384.

6. Bunta, 'The *Mēsu*-Tree', 381–383.

7. Bunta, 'The *Mēsu*-Tree', 381.

8. Hays, 'Chirps from the Dust', 305–325.

solution' because there is no evidence in Mesopotamian texts that the primordial state of humankind could result from a deity's curse.[9] He also rightly observes that, while there is evidence of uncivilized peoples, only one 'transformation' (of Enkidu in *The Gilgamesh Epic*) is offered as a parallel to Dan. 4 and this is the opposite of Nebuchadnezzar's transformation in Dan. 4. Instead Hays turns to different parallels in the ancient Near Eastern prayer genre and notices that the animal imagery of the king in Dan. 4 is reminiscent of descriptions of underworld/netherworld gods and demons. He then attempts to show how this animal-like depiction of underworld beings is transferred onto the individuals who these supernatural beings afflict. Thus people who are suffering are depicted as taking on these animal-like forms, so Hays can conclude that 'it is Nebuchadnezzar's *suffering* at the hand of God, rather than his madness, that this imagery should evoke'.[10] Thus the animal imagery symbolizes an individual's affliction by divine powers.

This apparent disagreement between understanding Nebuchadnezzar's animal affliction as either reflective of a reversal to a primordial bestial state (Henze) or of a netherworld punishment (Hays) has been addressed in a recent article by Hector Avalos.[11] He problematizes the second view by rightly observing that there is no indication of the netherworld, death, or even pits, present in Dan. 4.[12] Moreover, he resolves Hays' major issue with the primordial wild human understanding of Dan. 4 by providing evidence that it could result from a deity's curse. However, to do so, he draws upon prayer genre texts which Hays suggested were useful to interpret Dan. 4. Avalos utilizes the *dingir.šà.dib.ba* incantations, a set of magico-medical Akkadian and Sumerian texts from Late Assyrian and Babylonian libraries, to demonstrate that returning to a wild primordial existence could result from a divine curse.[13] These incantations describe someone being cursed, made to be an animal and then eat plants like animals because of their sins.[14]

Takayoshi Oshima has conducted a similar and more extensive study of ancient Near Eastern prayer parallels to Dan. 4 and concluded that, rather than indicating a divine affliction, such animal imagery indicates both the adversities brought about by sin, and the limited knowledge humans have of divine things.[15] He notes (contra Hays) that those suffering from divine affliction are only depicted with

9. Hays, 'Chirps from the Dust', 306–307.

10. Hays, 'Chirps from the Dust', 308.

11. Avalos, 'Nebuchadnezzar's Affliction'.

12. Avalos, 'Nebuchadnezzar's Affliction', 501–502.

13. Avalos, 'Nebuchadnezzar's Affliction', 503–505. The incantations were initially provided by Wilfred G. Lambert, 'dingir.šà.dib.ba Incantations', *JNES* 33 (1974): 267–322.

14. Lambert, 'dingir.šà.dib.ba Incantations', 285, lines 2–8.

15. Oshima, 'Nebuchadnezzar's Madness', 666–667.

animal features, whereas Nebuchadnezzar also behaves like an animal.[16] He instead understands the animal imagery as a device for visualizing the individual's despair during suffering, something which he does not appear to think incompatible with Henze's argument for a return to a primordial state.[17]

These previous ancient Near Eastern comparisons with Dan. 4 have been fruitful and scholars have suggested numerous legitimate and useful parallels to Nebuchadnezzar's affliction. However, these studies have been insufficiently attentive to the implications of these parallels for the delicate boundary between the human and animal.[18] No one has yet focused on the position of the animal in such comparative texts to discover how the human-animal boundary is negotiated and affected by the events surrounding Nebuchadnezzar. To attempt to answer the question of whether Nebuchadnezzar can legitimately be regarded as becoming an animal or not, such previously-suggested ancient Near Eastern parallels to Nebuchadnezzar's affliction will be combined with other scholarly work which has endeavoured to reconstruct the ontological boundary between gods and humans in the ancient Near East.

This work on the divine–human divide can be traced back at least to the work of Johannes Pedersen.[19] He attempted to analyse the parallel ways in which both ancient Near Eastern texts and the Old Testament represented the relative position of the gods and humankind within creation. By looking at Mesopotamian literature, Pedersen stated that humans primarily relate and approximate to the gods in their possession of wisdom. This similarity or resemblance would be complete if humans were given possession of immortality too, though this would make them no longer human but divine.[20] He also stated that humankind occupies an intermediate position which is lower than the gods but still set apart from all other creatures. This position creates a tension whereby humans seek for more and the gods vehemently defend their superiority.[21]

---

16. Oshima, 'Nebuchadnezzar's Madness', 663.

17. Oshima is actually quite positive about Henze's arguments; see Oshima, 'Nebuchadnezzar's Madness', 660–662.

18. In her commentary on Dan. 4, Carol Newsom attempts to relate this text to ancient Near Eastern boundaries between humans, gods and animals, but her comments lack a detailed assessment of how such boundaries were constructed; see Newsom with Breed, *Daniel: A Commentary*, 141.

19. Johannes Pedersen, 'Wisdom and Immortality', in *Wisdom in Israel and in the Ancient Near East: Presented to Professor Harold Henry Rowley*, ed. Martin Noth and David W. Thomas, VTSup 3 (Leiden: Brill, 1955), 238–246 and Johannes Pedersen, 'The Fall of Man', in *Interpretationes ad Vetus Testamentum pertinentes SIgmundo Mowinckel septuagenario missae*, ed. Nils A. Dahl and Arvid S. Kapelrud (Oslo: Forlaget Land og Kirke, 1955), 162–172.

20. Pedersen, 'Wisdom and Immortality', 244.

21. Pedersen, 'Wisdom and Immortality', 240.

Building on these insights by Pedersen, a similar assessment of boundaries in Mesopotamian literature was composed by Shlomo Izre'el.[22] In his view, the possession of both wisdom/intelligence and immortality was a divine privilege. These were two keys features of the divine. One of these features (wisdom) had been granted to humanity, therefore the only difference between gods and humans was the possession of eternal life.[23] More recently, this proposal has been picked up by Tryggve Mettinger who argued that 'there was in Mesopotamian literature a traditional line of demarcation between gods and humans: wisdom and immortality are divine prerogatives.'[24] Humans possess the divine attribute of wisdom, but only gods are able to possess both. Mettinger suggests that the idea of two key divine attributes, which humankind cannot fully participate in, is a standard concept within the ancient Near Eastern world. Therefore, these two qualities of wisdom and immortality are the markers which indicate the ontological boundary between humans and deities.[25]

While the description of this perceived ontological boundary between gods and humans is helpful, it opens the possibility for further such boundaries between other beings, for instance between humans and animals. There seems to be a lack of interest in the human–animal boundary in the work of Pedersen and Mettinger, but Izre'el does incorporate animals into his assessment of such boundaries.[26] He suggests that just as immortality separates gods from humans, wisdom (the other divine characteristic) distinguishes humans from animals. Life is common to animals, humans, and gods – but intelligence is shared only by humans and the

22. Shlomo Izre'el, *Adapa and the South Wind: Language Has the Power of Life and Death*, MC 10 (Winona Lake, IN: Eisenbrauns, 2001), 120–130. Despite Tryggve Mettinger's claims to the contrary (Mettinger, *Eden Narrative*, 99), Izre'el does reference Pedersen regarding wisdom and immortality; see Izre'el, *Adapa and the South Wind*, 120. The same kind of concepts were referred to by Bernard F. Batto, *Slaying the Dragon: Mythmaking in the Biblical Tradition* (Louisville, KY: Westminster John Knox, 1992), 57–59.

23. Izre'el, *Adapa and the South Wind*, 121.

24. Tryggve Mettinger, *The Eden Narrative: A Literary and Religio-Historical Study of Genesis 2–3* (Winona Lake, IN: Eisenbrauns, 2007), 99.

25. Mettinger, *Eden Narrative*, 126. While this assessment is useful, it should be noted that these distinctions between gods and humans can become complicated and blurred; see Gebhard J. Selz, 'Who is a God? A Note on the Evolution of the Divine Classifiers in a Multilingual Environment', in *Libiamo ne' lieti calici: Ancient Near Eastern Studies Presented to Lucio Milano on the Occasion of his 65th Birthday by Pupils, Colleagues and Friends*, ed. Paola Corò et al., AOAT 436 (Münster: Ugarit-Verlag, 2016), 605–614. For recent work on the relationship between human and the divine in the ancient Near East, see Tyson L. Putthoff, *Gods and Humans in the Ancient Near East* (Cambridge: Cambridge University Press, 2020).

26. Pedersen does suggest humans are separated from other creatures but does not elaborate on precisely how; see Pedersen, 'Wisdom and Immortality', 240.

gods.[27] Thus for Izreʾel, the ontological boundary between humans and animals in the Mesopotamian world was indicated by the possession of the attribute of wisdom. They share life, but not wisdom. This wisdom or intelligence (Izreʾel uses these terms almost interchangeably) is most clearly symbolised through language which is the basic means by which the possession of wisdom is identified.[28] Izreʾel's sketch of an ancient Near Eastern ontological boundary between human and animal is useful, nevertheless it is fairly cursory and is principally, though not exclusively, restricted in scope to the text of *Adapa*. This chapter will therefore attempt a more thorough survey of ancient Near Eastern texts to expand upon Izreʾel's comments and provide a solid basis from which statements about this particular system of boundaries in the ancient Near East can then be made. This variety of texts reveal useful clues that indicate towards a particular hierarchical and tripartite division of creatures into deities, humans, and animals. Much of the Near Eastern material covered here is not new to Danielic scholarship and neither is this the first time in which many of these texts have been considered in relation to boundaries. However, there has not thus far been a satisfactory attempt to assess them all together in relation to a tripartite division between divine–human–animal. By undertaking this endeavour, it will be shown how the attributes of wisdom and immortality play crucial roles in distinguishing between gods, humans and animals.

4.2 The Boundary between Gods and Humans in the Ancient Near East: Immortality

First, I will survey the ancient Near Eastern material which seems to show the perceived ontological boundary between gods and humans based on the possession of immortality. As previously stated, this boundary has been readily described by previous scholars and this survey will therefore rely upon this earlier scholarship. Over the course of this section a range of key ancient Near Eastern texts will be assessed, examining each individually for evidence of the divine characteristic of immortality. It will become clear that, in these texts, while the gods possess both wisdom and immortality, humankind, while often seeking or striving for immortality, only possesses wisdom.

4.2.1 The Sumerian Flood Myth

The first text of interest is *The Sumerian Flood Myth* (*SFM*) which is also known by a variety of other names including the *Eridu Genesis*[29] and the *Epic of*

---

27. Izreʾel illustrates this is a basic table. For the table and his related discussion of it, see Izreʾel, *Adapa and the South Wind*, 122–123.

28. Izreʾel, *Adapa and the South Wind*, 130–135.

29. Thorkild Jacobsen, 'The Eridu Genesis', *JBL* 100 (1981): 513–529.

Ziusudra.[30] The only currently known preserved form of the myth is contained on part of the damaged tablet from Nippur CBS 10673 + CBS 10867.[31] This tablet dates from *ca.* 1600 BCE though *SFM* itself was almost certainly composed much earlier.[32] Thorkild Jacobsen has suggested that there are two other witnesses to parts of this text:[33] a Sumerian and Akkadian bilingual fragment from the library of Ashurbanipal in Nineveh dated to 600 BCE (K 11261 + 11624),[34] and a Sumerian fragment from Ur which dates from a similar period to the Nippur tablet (*UET* 6.61).[35] However, the relationship of these other fragments to the Nippur tablet proved contentious and is still being debated.[36]

After an initial lacuna, the fragmentary Nippur tablet of *SFM* begins with the establishment of several cities by the god Enki (*SFM* i.37–50, ii.84–100).[37] Then follows another gap, after which some of the gods seem unhappy over a decision

30. Matthew A. Collins, 'An Ongoing Tradition: Aronofsky's *Noah* as 21st-Century Rewritten Scripture', in *Noah as Antihero: Darren Aronofsky's Cinematic Deluge,* ed. Rhonda Burnette-Bletsch and Jon Morgan, Routledge Studies in Religion and Film 9 (London: Routledge, 2017), 8–33 (10).

31. Recently another tablet has been recognized as a probable witness to this text in the Schøyen Collection (MS 3026). This is being edited by Konrad Volk and Jana Matuszak. While at the time of writing it has not yet been made available, it is due to be published in the forthcoming volume: Konrad Volk and Jana Matuszak, *Sumerische literarische Texte in der Martin Schøyen Collection* (Bethesda, MD: CDL, forthcoming).

32. For the dating of the tablet, see Ed Noort, 'The Stories of the Great Flood: Notes on Gen 6:5–9:17 in its Context of the Ancient Near East', in *Interpretations of the Flood,* ed. Florentino G. Martínez and Gerard P. Luttikhuizen, TBN 1 (Leiden: Brill, 1998), 1–38 (5). Examples of attempts to date the composition of *SFM* are: Ruth E. Simoons-Vermeer, 'The Mesopotamian Floodstories: A Comparison and Interpretation', *Numen* 21 (1974): 17–34 (28) who dates it during the second millennium BCE; and John D. Pleins, *When the Great Abyss Opened: Classic and Contemporary Readings of Noah's Flood* (Oxford: Oxford University Press, 2003), 102 who suggests it was composed in the third millennium BCE.

33. Jacobsen, 'Eridu Genesis', 513–514.

34. This was published by Wilfred G. Lambert, ed., *Cuneiform Texts from Babylonian Tablets in the British Museum Part XLVI: Babylonian Literary Texts* (London: Trustees of the British Museum, 1965), pl xxiii n. 5.

35. For information regarding this text's numbering and provenance, see Jeremiah Peterson, 'The Divine Appointment of the First Antediluvian King: Newly Recovered Content from the Ur Version of the Sumerian Flood Story', *JCS* 70 (2018): 37–51 (37 n. 1).

36. For example, see Samuel N. Kramer, 'The Sumerian Deluge Myth: Reviewed and Revised', *AnSt* 33 (1983): 115–21 (116 n. 2), and more recently Peterson, 'The Divine Appointment'.

37. Unless stated otherwise, the line numberings and translation will be taken from Kramer, 'Sumerian Deluge Myth', 115–121.

to destroy humanity (*SFM* iii.140–144). The king Ziusudra is warned of this and is told a flood will sweep over the human cities (*SFM* iii.145–160). The text breaks off yet again only to pick up at the exact moment of the deluge, which Ziusudra survives thanks to his boat (*SFM* v.201–211). There is another lacuna, then the extant text ends once Ziusudra is presented before the gods An and Enlil who reward him for his survival (*SFM* vi.251–261).[38]

It is at this point, when Ziusudra is granted a final reward, that evidence of the exclusively divine attribute of immortality can be traced. Once Ziusudra is presented before An and Enlil, it is written that: 'Life like a god they give him. Breath eternal like a god, they bring down to him' (*SFM* vi.257–258). There are two important things to notice about this gift. First, Ziusudra is depicted as receiving something which is usually only possessed by the gods. His gift of life is twice referred to as being 'like a god', indicating that what he receives is typically a uniquely divine characteristic. Secondly, this divine type of life is indicated to be eternal. It is described as 'breath eternal', sometimes translated as simply 'eternal life'.[39] This is possibly also indicated by the new habitation Ziusudra is given. He is made to dwell in 'the land of Dilmun' (*SFM* vi.261) which has been understood as a land without death that the gods visit.[40] Ziusudra's gifts therefore demonstrate a clear link between life without end (or immortality) and the gods. Thus, while the gods are portrayed as possessing eternal life, humans on the other hand are not. The entire *SFM* has been based on the idea that humankind is mortal; a destructive flood would be entirely futile without it. Clearly Ziusudra functions as an exception to this normal state of affairs. As a reward for surviving an event which was intended to kill all of humankind, Ziusudra is given that which was denied to his fellow humans – eternal life. Still, this unusual extension of immortality to Ziusudra does not contradict the essentially divine status of this attribute. It merely demonstrates that the perceived indicator of the divine–human boundary is not completely rigid, and the boundary can, on occasion, be crossed.

4.2.2 The Atrahasis Epic

Another seemingly related version of this deluge myth can be found within the *Atrahasis Epic*. This is an Akkadian text found in a variety of fragments from

---

38. The narrative in *SFM* is considerably similar to, and probably influenced, the flood narratives in *The Atrahasis Epic* III, *The Gilgamesh Epic* II, and Genesis 6–9.

39. Miguel Civil, 'Sumerian Flood Story', in *Atra-ḫasīs: The Babylonian Story of the Flood*, ed. Wilfred G. Lambert and Alan R. Millard (Winona Lake, IN: Eisenbrauns, 1999), 138–145 (145, line 257).

40. For links between Dilmun and immortality, see Samuel N. Kramer, 'Dilmun: Quest for Paradise', *Antiquity* 37 (1963): 111–115; and Clifford C. Lamberg-Karlovsky, 'Dilmun: Gateway to Immortality', *JNES* 41 (1982): 45–50. The interpretation of Dilmun as an eternal paradise has recently been critiqued by Keith Dickson, 'Enki and Ninhursag: The Trickster in Paradise', *JNES* 66 (2007): 1–32.

the Old Babylonian to the Late Babylonian period, the earliest of which dates to the reign of King Ammisaduqa *ca.* 1646–1626 BCE.[41] The contents of *Atrahasis* are broader than *SFM,* incorporating a fuller creation narrative which describes the creation of humans in order to work for the gods (*Atrahasis* I.1–339).[42] After humankind seems to overpopulate the world, the deity Enlil convinces the other gods to make attempts to decrease the human population through pestilence (*Atrahasis* I.352–416) and then through drought (*Atrahasis* II). Both times the human Atrahasis is assisted by the god Enki who helps humankind survive. Eventually, however, *Atrahasis* moves onto a deluge myth of its own (*Atrahasis* III). After the gods decide to destroy humankind (*Atrahasis* II.vii-viii), Atrahasis is again warned and told to construct a boat (*Atrahasis* III.i.11–37). This enables Atrahasis to survive the flood after which he offers a sacrifice to the gods (*Atrahasis* III.v.30–35).

Scholarship has long been aware of the *Atrahasis Epic*'s interest in bounding and demarcating the positions of both gods and humans.[43] Immortality and mortality still play key roles in constructing this divine-human boundary, yet it has been proposed that *Atrahasis* describes the origin of mortality significantly differently. Unlike *SFM,* which depicts human mortality as being instituted from the beginning, *Atrahasis* may be part of a different Mesopotamian tradition whereby humans were originally created immortal.[44] The argument for this originates in Wilfred Lambert's specific reconstruction of *Atrahasis* III.vi.47–48 as: '[You, O mother]-goddess, who creates destinies, [assign death] to the people.'[45]

41. Yi S. Chen, *The Primeval Flood Catastrophe: Origins and Early Development in Mesopotamian Traditions* (Oxford: Oxford University Press, 2013), 3. This has also been assumed to be the approximate date of composition for *Atrahasis,* though von Soden has suggested it may originate significantly earlier: Wolfram von Soden, 'Konflikte und ihre Bewältigung in babylonischen Schöpfungs- und Fluterzählungen. Mit einer Teil-Übersetzung des Atramḫasīs-Mythos', *MDOG* 111 (1979): 1–33 (5). For a recent survey of all the manuscript evidence for the *Atrahasis Epic,* see Helge S. Kvanvig, *Primeval History: Babylonian, Biblical, and Enochic: An Intertextual Reading,* JSJSup 149 (Leiden: Brill, 2011), 13–19.

42. The translated text, tablet and line numberings will follow Wilfred G. Lambert and Alan R. Millard, eds, *Atra-ḫasīs: The Babylonian Story of the Flood* (Winona Lake, IN: Eisenbrauns, 1999).

43. For example: Wolfram von Soden, 'Der Mensch bescheidet sich nicht: Überlegungen zu Schöpfungserzählungen in Babylonien und Israel', in *Symbolae Biblicae et Mesopotamicae Francisco Mario Theodoro de Liagre Böhl dedicatae,* ed. Martinus A. Beek et al. (Leiden: Brill, 1973), 349–58; and Robert A. Oden, 'Divine Aspirations in Atrahasis and in Genesis 1–11', *ZAW* 93 (1981): 197–216.

44. Wilfred G. Lambert, 'The Theology of Death', in *Death in Mesopotamia: Papers Read at the XXVIᵉ Rencontre Assryiologique Internationale,* ed. Bendt Alster, Mesopotamia, Copenhagen Studies in Assyriology 8 (Copenhagen: Akademisk Forlag, 1980), 53–66 (58).

45. The sections in square brackets are those postulated in Lambert, 'Theology of Death', 58. Interestingly, Lambert did not include this reconstruction within his later co-edited edition of *Atrahasis;* see Lambert and Millard, *Atra-ḫasīs,* 102–103.

Lambert reasoned that since death does not seem to be instituted for humans upon their creation in *Atrahasis*, it must have been dealt with as part of the regulations at the end of the epic.[46] However, Joshua J. Van Ee has problematized this logic by noting that the fragmentary nature of the first tablet of *Atrahasis* means specifically what was and what was not addressed at humankind's creation is uncertain. He also notes that there is no necessity for *Atrahasis* to address the institution of death at all.[47] Possible support for Lambert's reconstruction has been claimed to exist in the Sumerian text *The Death of Bilgamesh* M.72-7 || 162–167, however this probably suggests simply that no human besides Ziusudra would receive immortality.[48]

However, even those scholars who argue that *Atrahasis* depicts humans as originally immortal would claim that by the end of the epic immortality is the key distinction between gods and humans. After being thwarted in his attempts to eradicate humankind, the god Enlil imposes new 'regulations for the human race [*ú-ṣú-ra-at ni-ši*]' (*Atrahasis* III.vii 5 R) and these regulations are understood as limitations upon the vitality and natural lifespan of humankind.[49] These regulations seem to include shortening the duration of human life, establishing categories of women who cannot bear children, and introducing the *Pāšittu*-demon who takes away children from their mothers (*Atrahasis* III.vii.1–8). Bernard F. Batto argues that in these actions we see a clarification of the essentially mortal status of humankind and the clear boundary between human and deity.[50] Thus, even if it is assumed that humans possessed immortality originally, it still forms the definitive dividing line between gods and humans. This key boundary was perhaps instituted secondarily rather than established from the outset. Therefore, regardless of how one views the original state of humankind in *Atrahasis*, it is widely agreed that by the end of the epic immortality is depicted as a distinctly divine characteristic.

The principally divine nature of immortality may also be reaffirmed later in *Atrahasis*. In the extant versions of the text there are no references to immortality

---

46. Lambert, 'Theology of Death', 57–58.

47. Joshua John Van Ee, 'Death and the Garden: An Examination of Original Immortality, Vegetarianism, and Animal Peace in the Hebrew Bible and Mesopotamia' (PhD diss., University of California, 2013), 44.

48. For the proposal that this text suggests original human immortality, see Andrew R. George, *The Babylonian Gilgamesh Epic: Introduction, Critical Edition and Cuneiform Texts*, 2 vols. (Oxford: Oxford University Press, 2003), 1.507–508 (this will henceforth be referred to as *BGE*). For the alternative understanding, see Van Ee, 'Death and the Garden', 45–49. The relevant text of *The Death of Gilgamesh* can be found in: Antoine Cavigneaux and Farouk N. H. Al-Rawi, *Gilgameš et la Mort. Textes de Tell Haddad VI*, CM 19 (Groningen: Styx, 2000), 28, 31.

49. Batto, *Slaying the Dragon*, 31.

50. Batto, *Slaying the Dragon*, 31.

being granted to the hero of the epic.[51] However, it has long been presumed that such an event ought to be found in the text and the relevant references to it simply did not survive in the extant fragments.[52] This probability has been significantly bolstered by evidence from an abridged and fragmented form of *Atrahasis* from ancient Ugarit (R.S. 22.421).[53] This single tablet dates from *ca.* the fourteenth century BCE and would seem to be a form of *Atrahasis* as the character identifies himself with this name (obv. 6).[54] Crucially, the text of the tablet concludes with the statement that 'Life like the gods [you will] indeed [possess]' (rev. 4). This 'life like the gods' can reasonably be explained as Atrahasis' acquisition of eternal life, akin to what was found in *SFM* vi.257–258. This description further confirms the idea that immortality was essentially a divine characteristic. While Atrahasis may have received immortality, he clearly remains the exception as the other humans are defined by their mortality.

4.2.3 The Gilgamesh Epic

The divine attributes of immortality and wisdom are also raised in *The Gilgamesh Epic*. There is manuscript evidence of this Akkadian text across a wide time period, with extant fragments and tablets from the Old Babylonian Period (*ca.* 2000–1600 BCE) and Middle Babylonian Period (*ca.* 1500–1100 BCE) amongst other witnesses.[55] *Gilgamesh* itself also seems to have been preceded by numerous separate Sumerian works concentrated on the figure of Gilgamesh (or Bilgamesh in Sumerian) which may be more than 1900 years older than the latest Babylonian text of *Gilgamesh*.[56] Additionally, there may be some evidence of a historical king

51. Not even the most recently published tablets refer to this, for example: Andrew R. George and Farouk N. H. Al-Rawi, 'Tablets from the Sippar Library VI. Atrahasis', *Iraq* 58 (1996): 147–190.

52. See William L. Moran, 'Atrahasis: The Babylonian Story of the Flood', *Biblica* 52 (1971): 51–61 (53).

53. This was published by Jean Nougayrol et al., *Ugaritica V: nouveaux textes accadiens, hourrites et ugaritiques des archives et bibliothèques privies d'Ugarit. Commentaires des textes historiques (première partie)*, Mission de Ras Shamra XVI (Paris: Librairie Orientaliste Paul Geuthner, 1968), 300–304, text number 167.

54. Nevertheless, the exact relationship between this fragment and *Atrahasis* is unclear. For an example of one scholar who argues this Ras Shamra fragment is not a version of *Atrahasis*, see Jeffrey Tigay, *The Evolution of the Gilgamesh Epic* (Wauconda, IL: Bolchazy-Carducci, 2002), 215. For the dating of this tablet, see Lambert and Millard, *Atra-ḫasīs*, 131. The translated text and line numberings are taken from Lambert and Millard, *Atra-ḫasīs*, 132–133.

55. For a comprehensive overview of the different manuscripts of *The Gilgamesh Epic*, see George, *BGE*, 1.159–417.

56. George, *BGE*, 1.4. For descriptions of the range of Sumerian literature about Gilgamesh, see George, *BGE*, 1.4–17; and Tigay, *Evolution of Gilgamesh*, 23–38.

Gilgamesh who ruled the Sumerian city of Uruk and who may perhaps be the figure upon whom *Gilgamesh* ultimately is based.[57] Despite this vast variety of ancient textual witnesses, we will focus here on what is known as the 'Standard Babylonian version' (SB) of the *Gilgamesh* text.[58] The evidence for this chiefly comes from libraries at Nineveh (*ca.* 700–600 BCE) though tablets survive which seem to date up until *ca.* 130 BCE.[59] This SB version is the most developed version of *Gilgamesh* as it is spread across twelve tablets.[60] It was also probably recognized as the most established or influential version of *Gilgamesh* and thus will be most useful for assessing wider attitudes to divine–human–animal boundaries in the Near East.[61]

The text of *Gilgamesh* focuses principally upon the exploits of Gilgamesh the king of Uruk who, by oppressing the city's inhabitants, causes the gods to create Enkidu (*Gilgamesh* I). Enkidu functions as Gilgamesh's narrative counterpart and they become companions (*Gilgamesh* II). Together they slay Ḫumbaba the guardian of the Cedar Forest, spurn the advances of Ishtar, and kill the Bull of Heaven (*Gilgamesh* III–VI). The gods respond by causing Enkidu to fall sick and die (*Gilgamesh* VII). Gilgamesh then becomes consumed by grief and sets out on a journey to find the secret of eternal life (*Gilgamesh* VIII–IX). After finding the flood-survivor Utnapishtim and learning through him of the impossibility of gaining immortality, he returns back to Uruk with a new recognition of the frailties of humanity (*Gilgamesh* X–XI).

A central concern throughout tablets VII–XI of *Gilgamesh* is the possibility of attaining immortality. This narrative interest seems to be initially spawned by the death of Enkidu after which Gilgamesh declares:

> I shall die, and shall I not then be like Enkidu? Sorrow has entered my heart. I became afraid of death, so go roaming the wild. (*Gilgamesh* IX.4–5)

While he has recognized his own human mortality before (*Gilgamesh* II.234–5), this fresh realization plagues Gilgamesh and he describes his fear of death afresh each time he encounters a new character in the narrative (*Gilgamesh* X.70–71, 138–139, 147–148, 238–239). This awareness of human mortality drives Gilgamesh

---

57. The material, historical or otherwise, which concerns the figure of Gilgamesh is addressed in: George, *BGE*, 1.91–138; Tigay, *Evolution of Gilgamesh*, 13–16.

58. All references will therefore be to the SB unless otherwise noted. The translation will be taken from George, *BGE*. For all quotations from *Gilgamesh*, it should be noted that: text in square brackets indicates words restored where the tablet is broken; italics mark uncertain renderings; and round brackets indicate insertions to create a better English translation.

59. George, *BGE*, 381.

60. The twelfth tablet is widely regarded as being of a later date due to its lack of harmony with the rest of *Gilgamesh*. See George, *BGE*, 47–54.

61. This version is ascribed to the professional scholar Sîn-lēqi-unninni who is commonly claimed by Babylonian intellectuals to be their ancestor; see George, *BGE*, 28–33. For the authoritative status of the SB, see Mettinger, *Eden Narrative*, 111.

to seek out Utnapishtim who, along with his wife, are the sole humans to have acquired immortality and thus may be able to advise Gilgamesh on how to attain it. Yet the essentially mortal nature of humankind is only reemphasized by Utnapishtim when Gilgamesh eventually meets him. Utnapishtim declares:

> Man is one whose progeny is snapped off like a reed in the canebrake: the comely young man, the pretty young woman, *all* [*too soon in*] their very [*prime*] death abducts (them). No one sees death, no one sees the face [of death,] no one [hears] the voice of death: (yet) savage death is the one who hacks man down. (*Gilgamesh* X.301–307)

This articulation describes the usual and general state of humankind which is to be ultimately destined for death. Gilgamesh's effort to transcend his human condition and become immortal is therefore fruitless. There *is* room in *The Gilgamesh Epic* to allow for immortality to be imparted by the gods to humans, Utnapishtim and his wife being the unique examples. At Gilgamesh's invitation, Utnapishtim recounts the story of the flood which he and his wife survived (*Gilgamesh* XI.8–206).[62] His narrative concludes once the god Enlil gifts immortality to both Utnapishtim and his wife as a reward for being able to survive his attempts to destroy them (*Gilgamesh* XI.203–205). Nevertheless, while one couple are granted immortality, they remain the unique exceptions just like flood-survivors in other ancient Near Eastern texts (*SFM* vi.257–258; R.S. 22.421 rev. 4). At the end of his tale, Utnapishtim asks Gilgamesh 'But now, who will bring the gods to assembly for you, so you can find the life that you search for?' (*Gilgamesh* XI.207–208). Mettinger has pointed out the rhetorical nature of this question, which implies there is no one who is able to find the eternal life Gilgamesh seeks.[63] This gift of immortality cannot be repeated, and Gilgamesh is therefore unable to avoid his inevitable death. In *Gilgamesh* humankind is therefore depicted as essentially and inescapably *mortal*.[64]

While Gilgamesh is unable to attain true immortality, Utnapishtim does reveal to him the function of a specific plant which will supposedly allow him to 'recapture his vitality' (*Gilgamesh* XI.296). Gilgamesh names this plant 'The Old Man Has Grown Young' (*Gilgamesh* XI.299). While not able to give true immortality, this plant does seem capable of returning Gilgamesh to his youth (*Gilgamesh* XI.300). Gilgamesh nevertheless eventually loses the herb before he can benefit from its

---

62. This flood narrative is not evidenced in either the Old or Middle Babylonian versions of *Gilgamesh,* and it is likely to be a later interpolation of *Atrahasis;* see Tigay, *Evolution of Gilgamesh,* 216–240. It does however differ significantly, most notably in the name of the main characters (though Utnapishtim is once referred to as 'Atra-hasis', meaning 'the exceeding wise', in XI.197). For an explanation of the differing names, see Jean Bottéro, *L'épopée de Gilgameš: Le grand homme qui ne voulait pas mourir* (Paris: Galimard, 1992), 66 n. 3.

63. Mettinger, *Eden Narrative,* 118.

64. This is also conveyed in the Sumerian text *The Death of Bilgames* M.72–77//162–167; see Cavigneaux and Al-Rawi, *Gilgameš et la Mort,* 28, 31.

effects (*Gilgamesh* XI.303–307), but his continued interest in immortality is emphasised by his search for this plant. It is possible that his preoccupation with achieving some kind of immortality is also behind his attempt to slay Humbaba, thus achieving some relative immortality through his reputation.[65] Additionally, this craving for immortality may also be reflected in Gilgamesh's statement to the ferryman upon his return to Uruk:

> Go up, Ur-šanabi, on to the wall of Uruk and walk around, survey the foundation platform, inspect the brickwork! (See) if its brickwork is not kiln-fared brick, and if the Seven Sages did not lay its foundations! (*Gilgamesh* XI.323–326)

In ancient Mesopotamia, enduring construction projects were seen as a way to indirectly achieve immortality.[66] This was especially believed to be the case if a person's name was inscribed upon the buildings, as then their name would also be carried into perpetuity.[67] It is possible that Gilgamesh's statement about Uruk reflects this idea that he can receive some measure of immortality through the renown brought about by building the city.[68] Certainly he records his name and deeds during the building process (*Gilgamesh* I.10–14). Nevertheless, no matter what effort Gilgamesh may go to, the clear message of the text is that true immortality is out of reach for him.

The mortality of humankind is a central theme in *The Gilgamesh Epic*; however, it relies on the simultaneous assertion that immortality is a characteristic unique to the gods.[69] When Utnapishtim's acquisition of immortality is described, the god Enlil declares:

> In the past Ûta-napišti was (one of) mankind, but now Ûta-napišti and his woman shall be like us gods! Ûta-napišti shall dwell far away, at the mouth of the rivers! (*Gilgamesh* XI.203–205)

---

65. Berit Thorbjørnsrud, 'What can the Gilgamesh Myth Tell Us about Religion and the View of Humanity in Mesopotamia?' *Temenos* 19 (1983): 112–137 (130–131).

66. Thorbjørnsrud, 'What can the Gilgamesh Myth Tell Us', 130, 135; Tigay, *Evolution of Gilgamesh*, 7, 144–146.

67. Fritz R. Kraus, 'Altmesopotamisches Lebensgefühl', *JNES* 19 (1960): 117–32 (128–31); Richard S. Ellis, *Foundation Deposits in Ancient Mesopotamia*, YNER 2 (New Haven: Yale University Press, 1968), 166–167.

68. For this understanding of the text, see Tigay, *Evolution of Gilgamesh*, 144; Thorbjørnsrud, 'What can the Gilgamesh Myth Tell Us', 135; Adolf L. Oppenheim, *Ancient Mesopotamia: Portrait of a Dead Civilisation*, ed. Erica Reiner, rev. ed. (Chicago: University of Chicago Press, 1977), 257. For an alternative understanding of these passages from *Gilgamesh*, see George, *BGE*, 1.526.

69. For discussion of the central theme of *The Gilgamesh Epic*, see Herman L. J. Vanstiphout, 'The Craftmanship of *Sîn-leqi-unninni*', *OLP* 21 (1990): 45–79 (61–68); and Mettinger, *Eden Narrative*, 120–121.

Here immortality is once again clearly linked to the nature of the gods (and seemingly dependent upon *SFM* vi.257–258). Furthermore, it also functions as a clear divider between humankind and the divine. Initially Utnapishtim is described as being simply a member of the human race, yet once he is given immortality he becomes 'like us gods'.

This function of immortality, as a dividing line or boundary between humans and gods, is also expressed in a fragment of the Old Babylonian (OB) version of *Gilgamesh*. The ale-wife Siduri tells Gilgamesh: 'You cannot find the life that you seek: when the gods created mankind, for mankind they established death, life they kept for themselves' (*Gilgamesh* OB VA+BM iii.2–5). Here again, humankind is separated from the gods by their ability to die. While they may share some attributes with the gods, immortality is withheld as a uniquely divine characteristic. *Gilgamesh* is therefore clear that true immortality belongs to the gods; humankind cannot acquire it.

4.2.4 Adapa and the South Wind

The final text which makes most explicit the characteristics of both immortality and wisdom is *Adapa and the South Wind*. This is known from three principal traditions: the Sumerian recensions from the second millennium BCE found at Tell Haddad (or ancient Meturan) and Nippur;[70] the Middle Babylonian Akkadian recension found at Tell el-Amarna from about the fourteenth century BCE (Fragment B); and a series of Neo-Assyrian Akkadian fragments from the library of Ashurbanipal at Nineveh dated *ca.* seventh century BCE (fragments A, A1, C, D and E).[71] The same general narrative about Adapa is recounted in each of the recensions, though the Sumerian recension has an additional incantation at the end of the text and a long introduction which sets the myth in an immediate postdiluvian world.[72] Though supplementary material from the Nineveh fragments will be referenced, discussion will largely focus here on Fragment B from the Amarna recension of *Adapa* as this is not only the largest extant fragment but also

70. The Sumerian versions from Tell Haddad and one fragment from Nippur were published in Antoine Cavigneaux, 'Une versions sumérienne de la légende d'Adapa. Textes de Tell Haddad X', *ZA* 104 (2014): 1–41. Another fragment of the Adapa myth from Nippur has recently been published by Jeremiah Peterson, 'A Middle Babylonian Sumerian Fragment of the Adapa Myth and an Overview of the Middle Babylonian Sumerian Literary Corpus at Nippur', in *The First Ninety Years: A Sumerian Celebration in Honor of Miguel Civil*, ed. Lluís Feliu, Fumi Karahashi and Gonzalo Rubio, Studies in Ancient Near Eastern Records 12 (Berlin: De Gruyter, 2017), 255–276.

71. The fragments of both of the Akkadian recensions are published in Izre'el, *Adapa and the South Wind*.

72. For a comparison between the Sumerian and Akkadian recensions, see Sara J. Milstein, 'The Origins of Adapa', *ZA* 105 (2015): 30–41.

seems to contain the more original version of the narrative.[73] However, Fragment A will also be referred to as it conveys a similar interpretation of Adapa's state in relation to wisdom and immortality.[74]

The first legible lines of the myth begin with Ea's perfection of the fisherman Adapa (*Adapa* A.i.1–22).[75] After cursing and breaking the wings of the South Wind for capsizing his boat (*Adapa* B.1–7), Adapa is summoned to appear before the god Anu to answer for the chaos he has caused (*Adapa* B.7–14). Before appearing, though, the god Ea gives him instruction not to eat or drink any divine victuals as Ea claimed these would cause Adapa's death (*Adapa* B.14–34). However, after reaching the heavens (*Adapa* B.34–60), it transpires that Adapa is actually offered the food and water of *life* by Anu but, due to his prior instruction, Adapa refuses it (*Adapa* B.60–65).[76] Adapa explains his actions then Ea returns him to earth, at which point fragment B breaks off.

Adapa's concern with the twin concepts of wisdom and immortality is signalled at the initial introductory sequence narrated in fragment A. Here we find a description of how Ea made Adapa:

> He perfected him with great intelligence [*uzna rapašta*], to give instruction about the ordinance of the earth. To him he gave wisdom [*nēmeqa*], he did not give him eternal life [*napišta darīta*].f (*Adapa* A.i.3–4)

The human Adapa is granted intelligence and wisdom, but immortality is withheld from him. This not only sets up the events of the ensuing narrative, but also the human relationship to both of these divine attributes.

The wisdom of Adapa continues to be emphasized in Fragment A:

> In those days, in those years, the sage, a native of Eridu, Ea made him (his) follower among people. The sage's [*apkallu*] speech – no one repudiates; Skilled, foremost in understanding [*atra-ḫasīsa*] of the Annunaki is he. (*Adapa* A.i.5–8)

Adapa's wisdom is made clear in several ways: his wisdom is granted by Ea, the god of wisdom; he is described as being 'foremost in understanding' (*atra-ḫasīsa*);[77]

---

73. For the claim about the Amarna recension's originality, see Izre'el, *Adapa and the South Wind*, 60.

74. For a discussion of the relation of these fragments see Izre'el, *Adapa and the South Wind*, 111–19.

75. Line numberings and quotations follow the translated text in: Izre'el, *Adapa and the South Wind*.

76. This twist on the food offered to Adapa is not present in the Sumerian recension nor the Neo-Assyrian fragments.

77. Note that this is the name given to the hero of *Atrahasis*, and also used to describe Utnapishtim in *Gilgamesh* XI.197.

and he is described as a sage or wise-man (*apkallu*).[78] Furthermore, Adapa's wisdom and intelligence is manifested in his use of language. Just before Adapa is given great intelligence (*Adapa* A.i.3) and wisdom (*Adapa* A.i.4), his speech (*qibītu*) is also changed: 'Let his [s]peech be [...] like the speech of [Anu]' (*Adapa* A.i.2). There seems to be a parallel here between Adapa's wisdom, intelligence, and words – all three are gifted to him by Ea at the same moment. Again, when his wisdom is further described, his sage words (*qibītu*) are also described as unquestionable (*Adapa* A.i.7). If Izre'el is correct when he claims 'in the mythology of ancient Mesopotamia, language symbolises intelligence', then Adapa's keen use of language again displays his wisdom.[79]

Divine immortality and humankind's inability to acquire it, while already referenced in *Adapa* A.i.4, are re-encountered in Fragment B of *Adapa*. At the end of the fragment, Adapa refuses Anu's gift of the food and water of *life* due to a prior warning by Ea that he would be offered the food and water of *death*. Anu then responds to Adapa:

> Come, Adapa, why did you not eat or drink? Hence you shall not live [*lā balṭāta*]!
> Alas for inferior humanity! (*Adapa* B.67–68)

Thus because Adapa has refused the food and water of life he will not receive eternal life and will remain in the inferior human condition. This section of the narrative has generated a large variety of different interpretations, especially over the apparent discrepancy between Ea's warning and Anu's gift.[80] The most common

---

78. For more on Adapa as a wise man, see Benjamin R. Foster, 'Wisdom and the Gods in Ancient Mesopotamia', *Orientalia* 43 (1974): 345–354.

79. Izre'el, *Adapa and the South Wind*, 130–136 esp. 135.

80. Some insist that, while Ea advised against eating the food and water of death, Adapa could have consumed the food and water of life, he simply chose not to. For this interpretation, see Dietz O. Edzard, 'Eas doppelzüngiger Rat an Adapa: ein Lösungsvorschlag', *Orientalia* 71 (2002): 415–416. Other explanations rely on linguistic puns; see Stephanie Dalley, *Myths from Mesopotamia: Creation, the Flood, Gilgamesh, and Others* (Oxford: Oxford University Press, 1989), 188; Anne Kilmer, 'Verse Translation of Adapa (Amarna Version)', in *Mesopotamian Poetic Language: Sumerian and Akkadian*, ed. Marianna E. Vogelzang and Herman L. J. Vanstiphout, CM 6, Proceedings of the Groningen Group for the Study of Mesopotamian Literature 2 (Groningen: Styx, 1996), 111–14 (111); Jack M. Sasson, 'Another Wrinkle on Old Adapa', in *Studies in Ancient Near Eastern World View and Society presented to Marten Stol on the occasion of his 65th birthday*, ed. Robartus V. van der Spek et al. (Bethesda, MD: CDL, 2008), 1–10 (4). Finally, others have simply denied the discrepancy and claimed that all heavenly food was deadly for mortals; see Franz Marius Theodor de Liagre Böhl, 'Die Mythe vom weisen Adapa', *WO* 2 (1959): 416–431; Paolo Xella, 'L'inganno di Ea nel mito di Adapa', *OrAnt* 12 (1973): 257–266; Giorgio Buccellati, 'Adapa, Genesis, and the Notion of Faith', *UF* 5 (1973): 61–70. Liverani has shown that this solution seems to be at odds with the narrative itself: Mario Liverani, 'Adapa, guest of the gods', in *Myth and Politics in Ancient Near Eastern*

interpretation, however, is that Ea deliberately deceives Adapa in order to prevent humankind from acquiring eternal life and thus to maintain the correct relationship between humankind and the gods.[81]

Conversely, Giorgio Buccellati has argued that the issue of immortality is not actually at stake in this fragment at all. He claims that this passage 'does not contain any reference to the hero's acquiring of eternal life'.[82] This doubt over the presence of immortality rests on the use of the verb *balāṭu* found in the phrase 'you shall not live' (*lā balṭāta*) which some earlier translations suggest is a reference to eternal life.[83] This verb typically means 'to live', or 'to stay alive', which would not constitute a reference to immortality at all.[84] Nevertheless, Buccellati's denial of the theme of immortality has met fierce resistance from a range of scholars. The principal objection has come from John Daniel Bing who notes that, in other texts from the same period, *balāṭu* refers to eternal life.[85] The OB fragments of *Gilgamesh* use this word to refer to the life which Gilgamesh seeks, but which the gods have kept for themselves (*Gilgamesh* OB VA+BM i.8; iii.2 and 5).[86] This same usage of the word is carried through into the SB of *Gilgamesh* when Utnapishtim refers to the type of life Gilgamesh is unable to acquire (*Gilgamesh* XI.7 and 208).[87] These parallel occurrences of the word *balāṭu* indicate a link with divine or eternal life. A similar view was advocated by Izre'el who suggested that the verb *balāṭu* in B.67–8 can work on several levels, the deepest level of which may indicate immortality.[88] Additionally, Tryggve Mettinger recalled attention to the statement about Adapa that Ea 'did not give him eternal life' (*Adapa* A.i.4). He uses this 'as the keynote to our understanding of the myth', which then provides a reason to look for eternal life in the other

Historiography, ed. Zainab Bahrani and Marc Van De Mieroop (London: Cornell University Press, 2004), 3–26 (16–18) [originally published as 'Adapa ospite degli dei', in *Religioni e civiltà: Scritti in memoria di Angelo Brelich*, ed. Vittorio Lanterinari, Marcello Massenzio, and Dario Sabbatucci (Bari: Dedalo libri, 1982), 293–319]. For a recent summary of different proposals, see Milstein, 'Origins of Adapa', 35 n. 26.

81. This has been suggested for example by Thorkild Jacobsen, 'The Investiture and Anointing of Adapa in Heaven', *AJSL* 46 (1930): 201–203 (203); and more recently: William W. Hallo, 'Adapa Reconsidered: Life and Death in Contextual Perspective', *Scriptura* 87 (2004): 267–277. For a survey of other scholars who support this view, see Buccellati, 'Adapa, Genesis, and the Notion of Faith', 62.

82. Buccellati, 'Adapa, Genesis, and the Notion of Faith', 63.

83. For example, the translation in: 'Adapa', trans. Ephraim A. Speiser, *ANET*, 102, fragment B[4], line 68.

84. For a treatment of this term's meaning, see *CAD* 2, s.v. 'balāṭu'.

85. John D. Bing, 'Adapa and Immortality', *UF* 16 (1984): 53–56; and John D. Bing, 'Adapa and Humanity: Mortal or Evil?' *JANES* 18 (1986): 1–2 (2 n. 5).

86. George, *BGE*, 276–279.

87. George, *BGE*, 702–703 and 716–717.

88. Izre'el, *Adapa and the South Wind*, 31–32.

fragments of the text.[89] Moreover, Adapa does not die following Anu's pronunciation but continues to live, implying that something other than simply 'staying alive' is meant here by *balāṭu*.[90] These arguments convincingly demonstrate that it is eternal life that is specifically denied Adapa by refusing the food and water offered to him.

Finally, the divine characteristics of wisdom and immortality are also indicated by the four items Adapa is offered when he is in heaven: food, water, a garment and anointing oil. These items seem to symbolize the four basic necessities of human life in Mesopotamian tradition, indicated for example in the incantation series *Utukkū Lemnūtu* IV.158–169.[91] Mario Liverani has noticed a further distinction between the elements: those used internally (water and food) and those used externally (oil and clothing).[92] The two internal elements are fundamental to all living creatures including animals, humans and gods, whereas external elements have a cultural function that hints towards civilization and intelligence. It is therefore notable that Ea instructs Adapa that while in heaven he can accept the external elements (garment and anointing oil) but must reject internal elements (the food and water) (*Adapa* B.28–32). Izre'el has suggested this command directly relates to the division between humans and gods.[93] As Adapa is a human, he can accept the heavenly external elements representing civilization and intelligence as he already shares these divine characteristics. However, he cannot accept the heavenly internal elements, which represent life itself, as he does not share divine life which is eternal.

The *Adapa* myth therefore depicts the two key divine characteristics of wisdom and immortality and describes how the position of humankind relates to them. The human Adapa participates in the divine possession of wisdom or intelligence, but eternal life remains out of reach.

4.2.5 Summary

This survey of ancient Near Eastern texts has demonstrated a sustained tradition which recognizes the importance of the characteristics of wisdom and immortality. These two attributes are principally divine characteristics and are possessed by the deities. However, while wisdom seems to be associated with humankind too, immortality is not and thus the human destiny is to remain mortal. This inability to receive eternal life creates a core distinction between divine and human.[94] The

---

89. Mettinger, *Eden Narrative*, 106.

90. I am grateful to Dr Matthew A. Collins for pointing this out to me.

91. For the text of these incantations, see Markham J. Geller, *Healing Magic and Evil Demons: Canonical Udug-hul Incantations* (Berlin: De Gruyter, 2016), 163–165. For further examples, see Liverani, 'Adapa, guest of the gods', 9–14.

92. Liverani, 'Adapa, guest of the gods', 9–10.

93. Izre'el, *Adapa and the South Wind*, 121–3.

94. See Niels-Erik Andreasen, 'Adam and Adapa: Two Anthropological Characters', *AUSS* 19 (1981): 179–194 (185 n. 30).

definitive boundary between human and divine in this Mesopotamian tradition has therefore been identified as principally based upon the concept of immortality.

4.3 The Boundary between Humans and Animals in the Ancient Near East: Wisdom

In light of this divine–human boundary, which was established in the previous section, focus will now move to the other ontological boundary: that which seemingly exists between humans and other animals. This boundary has received little previous attention within ancient Near Eastern scholarship, however I will seek to describe it through a second survey of ancient Near Eastern material. This material will demonstrate the role of wisdom in distinguishing human from animal and thus its importance for signalling the position of the human-animal boundary in the ancient Near Eastern world.

The textual evidence for a human–animal boundary in ancient Mesopotamia is closely related to conceptions of the creation of humankind, or anthropogenesis. There are diverse accounts of this in the ancient Near East and there have been a variety of scholarly assessments of them.[95] Jan van Dijk discerned two Mesopotamian explanations for the formation of humankind: *emersio* and *formatio*.[96] *Emersio* was the idea that humans, almost like plants, emerged from the earth itself, whereas *formatio* explained humankind as being originally formed out of clay by the gods. Giovanni Pettinato accepted this division though argued that *emersio* took place in two stages:[97] firstly humans emerged from the earth, and secondly they underwent a civilizing process to complete the creation of humankind. He found both types of anthropogenesis in Sumerian literature, though in Akkadian texts Pettinato only found evidence for an augmented *formatio* where humankind is formed out of both clay and divine blood/flesh. This augmentation to include a god's blood or flesh was later designated by Marianne Luginbühl as a *sacrificatio* type.[98] Most recently, Jan Lisman has conducted a study in which he made diachronic observations on anthropogenesis in Mesopotamia.[99] He found no evidence for

---

95. For a survey of previous scholarship on anthropogenesis in relation to Mesopotamian thought, see Jan J. W. Lisman, *Cosmogony, Theogony and Anthropogeny in Sumerian Texts*, AOAT 409 (Münster: Ugarit-Verlag, 2013), 9–22.

96. Jan J. A. van Dijk, 'La Motif Cosmique dans la Pensée Sumérienne', *AcOr* 28 (1964): 1–59 (23–24); Jan J. A. van Dijk, 'Sumerische Religion', in *Handbuch der Religionsgeschichte* I, ed. Jes P. Assmussen and Jorgen Læssøe (Göttingen: Vandenhoeck & Ruprecht, 1971), 431–496 (489).

97. Giovanni Pettinato, *Das altorientalische Menschenbild und die sumerischen und akkadischen Schöpfungsmythen* (Heidelberg: Carl Winter, Universitätsverlag, 1971), 31–36.

98. Marianne Luginbühl, *Menschenschöpfungsmythen. Ein Vergleich zwischen Griechenland und dem Alten Orient* (Paris: Peter Lang, 1992), 30–31.

99. Lisman, *Cosmogony, Theogony, and Anthropogeny*, 204–207.

emersio at all, and thus instead divided Mesopotamian ideas of anthropogenesis into peaceful and violent creation methods. He concluded that the general view in Sumerian texts was that humankind was made out of clay and involved no divine violence, whereas later Akkadian texts suggested humans were made out of both clay and the blood/flesh of a dead god.[100]

Though I remain sceptical about his suggestion of completely rejecting *emersio*, Lisman's division is the most helpful way to generally distinguish between different Mesopotamian views of anthropogenesis and will be followed here. Therefore, this examination of Mesopotamian texts about humankind's creation will be split into two halves. Firstly, Sumerian texts about human creation will be analysed, and then secondly Akkadian texts which depict human creation involving divine blood. Both of these two main Mesopotamian ideas about the creation of humankind are helpful for demonstrating how humans were regarded as differing from animals, and thus the nature of the perceived boundary between humans and animals in the ancient Near East.[101] In the first understanding of anthropogenesis, found in Sumerian texts, humankind is originally made in exactly the same way as other animals. They are then only secondarily made distinct from animals through the acquisition of wisdom or intelligence.[102] The second understanding, which is found in Akkadian texts, suggests humankind is made differently to other creatures from the beginning. Humankind possess a unique quality that distinguishes them from animals, and this can also be equated with wisdom or reason. Accordingly, wisdom/reason is either acquired (generally in Sumerian texts) or inherent

---

100. For his articulation of this separation between Sumerian/peaceful and Akkadian/violent, see Lisman, *Cosmogony, Theogony, and Anthropogeny*, 74.

101. Depictions of anthropogenesis in other ancient Near Eastern cultures are less helpful for this study. Canaanite traditions attribute the creation of humans to the god El, but there are no details on what this act of creation was like; see Richard J. Clifford, *Creation Accounts in the Ancient Near East and in the Bible*, CBQMS 26 (Washington, DC: Catholic Biblical Association of America, 1994), 119. Similarly, there are few details within the Egyptian material beyond a few descriptions of humans being formed from a god's tears; see Clifford, *Creation Accounts*, 115.

102. Pettinato has previously suggested that the civilising of humankind is a second stage in the process of anthropogenesis and thus the creation of humankind is only complete when they have undergone this process: Pettinato, *Das altorientalische Menschenbild*, 31–5. See also: Clifford, *Creation Accounts*, 44. This proposal has been criticized by Lambert and Lisman who see no reason for this civilizing process to be regarded as part of humankind's creation: Wilfred G. Lambert, review of *Das altorientalische Menschenbild und die sumerischen und akkadischen Schöpfungsmythen*, by Giovanni Pettinato, *BSOAS* 35 (1972): 134–135 (135a); Lisman, *Cosmogony, Theogony, and Anthropogeny*, 19. While I agree that the civilising process should not be considered as part of anthropogenesis itself, I propose that it does nevertheless result in a significant change within human creatures which distinguishes them from other animals.

(generally in Akkadian texts). Thus, by assessing these different Mesopotamian conceptions of anthropogenesis, we will be able to detect how the human-animal boundary was constructed in the ancient Near East.

4.3.1 Humankind's Acquisition of Wisdom

The first Mesopotamian conception of anthropogenesis to be examined is that which is found chiefly in Sumerian texts. This is the suggestion that the process of humankind's creation did not require the death of a god, but instead humans were formed out of clay or the earth. This method of anthropogenesis will be tackled in three stages. First, I will describe how humans are initially formed and how this occurs in a very similar way to how the creation of animals is portrayed in Sumerian texts. Secondly, this idea will be confirmed by further Sumerian texts that describe early humans as acting exactly like other animals. Finally, we will see how humans and animals are only distinguished, and the boundary between them effectively drawn, through the human acquisition of wisdom. This understanding of human creation and eventual distinction from animals will be demonstrated through appeal to a variety of early Mesopotamian texts.

4.3.1.1 Creation of Humans and Animals
Initially, descriptions of how humans and animals were created in such textual material will be examined.

4.3.1.1.1 Enki and Ninmah
The earliest known Sumerian text that deals with humankind's creation is *Enki and Ninmah* (composed *ca.* 1800 BCE) and is found in three incomplete Old Babylonian-period tablets.[103] One of these tablets, which was found at Nippur and dates from the eighteenth century BCE, tells how the god Enki instigates the creation of humankind in order to take over the hard work from the gods:

> He [Enki] said to his mother Namma: 'My mother, the creature you planned will really come into existence. Impose on him the work of carrying baskets. You

---

103. Jacob Klein, ed., 'Enki and Ninmah', in *The Context of Scripture I: Canonical Compositions from the Biblical World*, ed. William W. Hallo (Leiden: Brill, 1997), 516–522 (516). The text and translation is taken from Jeremy A. Black et al., eds, '1.1.2 Enki and Ninmah', *ETCSL*. For information on this text's manuscript history and dating, see Wilfred G. Lambert, *Babylonian Creation Myths*, MC 16 (Winona Lake, IN: Eisenbrauns, 2013), 330–335; and Manuel Ceccarelli, *Enki und Ninmah: Eine mythische Erzählung in sumerischer Sprache*, Orientalische Religionen in der Antike 16 (Tübingen: Mohr Siebeck, 2016), 86–87. The text known as *Gilgamesh, Enkidu, and the Netherworld* 1–10 may also refer to the creation of humankind; however, it will not be referred to here as it offers no valuable information beyond a simple statement.

should knead clay from the top of the abzu; the birth-goddesses (?) will nip off the clay and you shall bring the form into existence. Let Ninmah act as your assistant; and let Ninimma, Cu-zi-ana, Ninmada, Ninbarag, Ninmug, … and Ninguna stand by as you give birth. (*Enki and Ninmah* l.29–36)

This process of humankind's creation initially consisted of a small amount of clay which was kneaded (*Enki and Ninmah* ll. 31–32), and then nurtured and birthed by the goddess Namma (*Enki and Ninmah* ll.32–36).[104] The actual material used to form the human is 'clay from the Abzu'.[105] This is therefore a clear example of *formatio* creation, as humans are formed out of clay by the gods.[106]

4.3.1.1.2 The Song of the Hoe
Another description of anthropogenesis is given in *The Song of the Hoe*.[107] This was part of the Decad, a set of ten Sumerian scribal training texts from the Old Babylonian period (*ca.* 2500 BCE).[108] The exact method of human creation in this text has been disputed. This was a key example of *emersio* for van Dijk who relied on line 3: 'Enlil, who will make the human seed of the Land come forth from the earth.' However, the description of the actual event of creation by Enlil is described later:

he had it place the first model of mankind in the brick mould. His Land started to break through the soil towards Enlil. He looked with favour at his black-headed people. (*The Song of the Hoe* 19–21)[109]

104. The initial human is referred to as a clay foetus in Frans A. M. Wiggermann, 'Nammu', *RlA* 9:138.

105. Lambert attempts to translate this text to include a reference to a god's blood; however, this interpretation seems to be based on an unwarranted comparison with *Atrahasis*; see Wilfred G. Lambert, 'The Relationship of Sumerian and Babylonian Myth as Seen in Accounts of Creation', in *La Circulation des Biens, des Personnes et des Idées dans le Proche-Orient Ancien. Actes de la XXXVIIIe Rencontre Assyriologique Internationale (Paris, 8–10 juillet 1991)*, ed. Dominique Charpin and Francis Joannès (Paris: Éditions Recherche sur les Civilisations, 1992), 129–135 (131–132); Lambert, *Babylonian Creation Myths*, 334. It is therefore better to follow Lisman's interpretation that this divine material was not used to create humankind in *Enki and Ninmah*; see Lisman, *Cosmogony, Theogony, and Anthropogeny*, 304.

106. This is used as a key example of *formatio* in: van Dijk, 'La Motif Cosmique', 30.

107. The text and translation is taken from: Jeremy A. Black et al., eds, '5.5.4 The Song of the Hoe', *ETCSL*.

108. The contents of the Decad also included the text of *Enki's Journey to Nibru*; see Steve Tinney, 'On the Curricular Setting of Sumerian Literature', *Iraq* 61 (1999): 159–172 (168–170). For the approximate date, see Clifford, *Creation Accounts*, 30.

109. The Sumerians referred to themselves as 'the black-headed people'.

A brick mould is thus used to create and form the shape of the early human. While the exact material the human being is made out of is not specified, Lisman has noted that this description of using a brick mould to form a human is much more indicative of *formatio* creation out of clay.[110] This text thus likely depicts humankind being formed out of clay through the use of a brick mould.

4.3.1.1.3 Enki's Journey to Nibru

The Sumerian text of *Enki's Journey to Nibru* also contains a possible reference to humankind's genesis.[111] The text, whose composition dates from the Old Babylonian period (*ca.* 1900–1600 BCE),[112] opens with a description of primeval times: 'In those remote days, when the fates were determined; in a year when An brought about abundance, and people broke through the earth like herbs and plants' (*Enki's Journey to Nibru* ll.1–3). This seemingly depicts humans as being created out of the earth itself, and was the prime evidence van Dijk drew upon for human creation by *emersio*.[113] Lisman has proposed that this is a bad translation of the text and suggests that 'it was not "people" but "abundance"' that broke through the earth like plants'.[114] This would mean *Enki's Journey to Nibru* does not contain an account of anthropogenesis at all. However, while there is admittedly doubt over the correct translation of the text, Lisman's counter-translation has so far been rejected by scholars and his suggestion does not seem able to stand up to scrutiny.[115] It is therefore best to accept the original translation of *Enki's Journey to Nibru* which thus provides a depiction of anthropogenesis as humankind being born out of the earth.

4.3.1.1.4 The Sumerian Flood Myth

From the Sumerian texts surveyed so far it is clear that humans could potentially be formed out of clay or from the earth itself. For a final Sumerian text that describes anthropogenesis, many scholars turn again to *The Sumerian Flood Myth*.[116] It does not contain a detailed description of humankind's creation, but it

---

110. Lisman, *Cosmogony, Theogony, and Anthropogeny*, 59.

111. The text and translation is taken from: Jeremy A. Black et al., eds, '1.1.4 Enki's Journey to Nibru', *ETCSL*.

112. For dating this text, see Lisman, *Cosmogony, Theogony, and Anthropogeny*, 179 n. 812.

113. van Dijk, 'La Motif Cosmique', 23–4.

114. Lisman, *Cosmogony, Theogony, and Anthropogeny*, 180.

115. Nikita Artemov, review of *Cosmogony, Theogony and Anthropogeny in Sumerian Texts*, by Jan J. W. Lisman, *Orientalistische Literaturzeitung* 112 (2017): 213–218. Possible support for *emersio* also exists in the texts *Rulers of Lagash* 5 (Jeremy A. Black et al., eds, '2.1.2 Rulers of Lagash', *ETCSL*) and *Gilgamesh, Enkidu and the Netherworld* 1–11 (Jeremy A. Black et al., eds, '1.8.1.4 Gilgamesh, Enkidu and the Netherworld', *ETCSL*).

116. For an example of a scholar who appeals to this text in relation to anthropogenesis, see van Dijk, 'La Motif Cosmique', 30. A different view is put forward by Lisman who sees this text as describing a re-formation rather than creation of humankind; see Lisman, *Cosmogony, Theogony, and Anthropogeny*, 57.

does state: 'After An, Enlil, Enki, (and) Ninhursag had fashioned the blackheads' (*SFM* i.47–8). The OB text of *SFM* from Ur also begins with the statement: 'They (the chief deities) created humanity' (1').[117] While the occasion of humankind's creation is still only briefly described in *SFM*, the text is important as it also documents the creation of animals.[118] The following verses of the Ur manuscript state that 'the [animals/vermin?] were proliferating below/from the earth in unison. They made livestock and quadrupeds as fitting things in the steppe' (2'–3'). The version from the Nippur tablet, which differs only slightly, also states: 'they made small animals crawl out of the earth, they made goats, donkeys (and) all kinds of quadrupeds that are appropriate in the plain be there' (*SFM* ii.49–50).[119] This creation of animal life seems to somewhat reflect an *emersio* method of genesis. Just as humans in *Enki's Journey to Nibru* appear to be created out of the earth, so in *SFM* animals also seem to arise from the same origin. The *emersio* method of creation is thus evidenced in different Sumerian texts as the means by which both humans and animals were made.

4.3.1.1.5 Other texts about the creation of animals

There is a general scarcity of other references to the creation of animals in ancient Near Eastern material, however a further description of animal creation is provided in the Old Babylonian period Sumerian composition *Ninurta and the Turtle*.[120] This text about the god Ninurta relates how he defeats the mythical Anzu bird only to then be caught by a turtle. This turtle has been deliberately created by the god Enki and set as a trap for Ninurta: 'Enki fashioned a turtle from Abzu clay. He positioned the turtle at the entrance, at the Abzu gate' (*Ninurta and the Turtle* 36–7).[121] The creation of this specific animal is accomplished by Enki through the moulding or shaping of Abzu clay. Another example of this method for the creation of an animal is described within tablet 15289 from the eighteenth-century BCE

---

117. Translations from the Ur manuscript are taken from Peterson, 'The Divine Appointment', 43.

118. It is described by Peeter Espak as 'the most significant account of creation mentioning both the man and the animals'; see Peeter Espak, 'Creation of Animals in Sumerian Mythology', in *Animals and their Relation to Gods, Humans and Things in the Ancient World*, ed. Raija Mattila, Sanae Ito and Sebastian Fink, Studies in Universal and Cultural History (Wiesbaden: Springer VS, 2019), 303–312 (307).

119. This translation is taken from Lisman, *Cosmogony, Theogony, and Anthropogeny*, 318. He numbers this passage as ii.13–14.

120. For a list of manuscript sources for this text, see Bendt Alster, 'Ninurta and the Turtle: On Parodia Sacra in Sumerian Literature', in *Approaches to Sumerian Literature: Studies in Honour of Stip (H. L. I. Vanstiphout)*, ed. Piotr Michalowski and Niek Veldhuis, CM 35 (Leiden: Brill, 2006), 13–36 (14).

121. The translation is taken from Alster, 'Ninurta and the Turtle'.

Old Babylonian library at Mari.[122] One of the incantations present here is specifically directed at a scorpion and describes how it was created: 'his clay is pinched off in the Apsû; the foundation of the wall bore him' (obv.5–6).[123] While this is an Akkadian text, it is early in date and clearly reflects the same ideas about how animals were generated. This formation of a creature using the base material of Abzu/ Apsû clay quite closely reflects the *formatio* creation of humankind in *Enki and Ninmah*.

4.3.1.1.6 Summary
While there is a paucity of early Mesopotamian material about the creation of either humans or animals, the evidence presented here suggests that they were believed to have been created in the same ways. Some texts appear to describe both humans and animals as arising out of the earth itself, while others narrate how they are fashioned and shaped out of clay of the Abzu. It is therefore reasonable to agree with Peeter Espak who suggests that in such texts there is 'no difference in the process of creating the animals or humans. They both either grew or came out from the earth Ki; or were fashioned (or summoned) into existence by the gods.'[124]

4.3.1.2 Descriptions of Primordial Humans
This basic affiliation and likeness between newly-created humans and animals is corroborated by other Sumerian literature that describes how similarly these two sets of creatures behaved. The nature and behaviour displayed by primordial humans in Sumerian texts has often been considered by scholars to closely resemble that of animals.[125]

4.3.1.2.1 The Debate between Sheep and Grain
One form of this tradition appears in the Old Babylonian Sumerian composition *The Debate between Sheep and Grain,* sometimes called *Lahar and Ashnan,* which was composed in the third millennium BCE.[126] This text opens by stating that

---

122. This was published in Antoine Cavigneaux, 'Magica Mariana', *RA* 88 (1994): 155–161.

123. The translation is taken from Nathan Wasserman, 'Offspring of Silence, Spawn of a Fish, Son of a Gazelle …: Enkidu's Different Origins in the Epic of Gilgameš', in *'An Experienced Scribe Who Neglects Nothing': Ancient Near Eastern Studies in Honor of Jacob Klein,* ed. Yitzhak Sefati et al. (Bethesda, MD: CDL, 2005), 593–599 (598).

124. Espak, 'Creation of Animals', 310.

125. For example: Bernard F. Batto, 'Creation Theology in Genesis', in *Creation in the Biblical Traditions,* ed. Richard J. Clifford and John J. Collins, CBQMS 24 (Washington, DC: Catholic Biblical Association of America, 1992), 16–38 (18–19).

126. The text and translation cited here is taken from Jeremy A. Black et al., eds, '5.3.2 The Debate between Sheep and Grain', *ETCSL.* See also: Bendt Alster and Herman Vanstiphout, 'Lahar and Ashnan: Presentation and Analysis of a Sumerian Disputation', *ASJ* 9 (1987): 1–43.

neither grain nor sheep had appeared on the land, and there was also no evidence of civilization (*Sheep and Grain* 1–19). This was thus an early period before the building of cities, and before even the whole created world had been finished. The humans who lived at this time are described as living like animals:

> The people of those days did not know about eating bread. They did not know about wearing clothes; they went about with naked limbs in the Land. Like sheep they ate grass with their mouths and drank water from ditches. (*Sheep and Grain* 20–25)

These people had no clothes and thus wandered about naked. They had no bread, so they ate grass.

4.3.1.2.2 How Grain Came to Sumer

This idea is also reflected in another Sumerian composition from the third millennium BCE called *How Grain Came to Sumer*:

> Men used to eat grass with their mouths like sheep. In those times, they did not know grain, barley or flax. (*How Grain Came to Sumer* 1–2)[127]

While it provides less information than *Sheep and Grain*, this text similarly describes an ancient time when humans resembled animals in their behaviour.[128]

4.3.1.2.3 The Sumerian Flood Myth

There have also been various scholarly attempts to find such material about an animal-like primordial humanity in *SFM*. Jacobsen suggested that the fragmentary text *UET* 6.61 should be considered a duplicate or variant form of *SFM* and he reconstructed it to describe primordial humanity:

> Mankind of (those) distant days, since Shakan (the god of the flocks) had not (yet) come out on the dry lands, did not know arraying themselves in prime cloth, mankind walked about naked. (*SFM UET* 6.61.i.7–10)[129]

Jacobsen's restorations of the lacunae in this fragment are largely based on his perception of a thematic connection between *UET* 6.61 and *Sheep and Grain*. This suggestion has recently been refuted by Peterson who has made new joins between

---

127. The text and translation cited here is taken from: Jeremy A. Black et al., eds, '1.7.6 How Grain came to Sumer', *ETCSL*.

128. It has also been argued that the grammatical construction here suggests the text classifies the people as animals because they are referred to in impersonal terms; see Géza Komoróczy, 'Berosos and the Mesopotamian Literature', *ActAnt* 121 (1973): 125–152 (140).

129. See Jacobsen, 'Eridu Genesis', 517 n. 7.

fragments of the text, and is not as ambitious in his reconstruction of *UET* 6.61.[130] His translation of the same fragmentary lines is much more conservative: 'Humanity ... their eyes/faces ... Šakkan/Sumuqan [did not go out] in the desert ... Weaving the cap/headcloth ... Humanity ...'.[131] Nevertheless, despite his more conservative reconstruction, Peterson also argues that this version of *SFM* probably contained the idea of primordial humanity living like animals.[132] Therefore, while not as clear cut as Jacobsen's original suggestion, it is possible that *SFM* also provides evidence of an animal-like primordial humanity.

4.3.1.2.4 *Berossus*' Babyloniaca

This tradition seems to be absent from later Akkadian texts,[133] though its influence was long lasting as shown by the comparatively late witness in the text of Berossus' *Babyloniaca*.[134] Probably composed during the early third century BCE, the *Babyloniaca* was essentially a history of Babylon written for the Hellenized world.[135] The text as a whole is not extant and thus scholars must rely on third- or fourth-hand quotations of the text by ancient writers. It has survived in two versions: a Greek extract written by the Byzantine monk Syncellus (*ca.* 800 CE) from Eusebius' *Chronicon* (*ca.* 310 CE) who himself is quoting Alexander Polyhistor's (*ca.* 110–140 CE) version of Berossus; and a twelfth-century CE Armenian text which is a translated form of a similar version of Eusebius' *Chronicon*.[136] The *Babyloniaca* seems to be divided into three books, the first of which explains how the world was created. After giving some geographical details about the area, the text describes the people who were residing in the primordial uncivilised land in the region of Babylon: 'In Babylon there was a great crowd of men of different races, who had settled in Chaldea. They lived without order like wild animals' (Berossus, *Babyloniaca* 1b.3). Here Berossus' text describes a group of early humans as living like animals which may reflect a similar idea to the earlier tradition outlined above.

130. Peterson, 'The Divine Appointment'.

131. Peterson, 'The Divine Appointment', 43.

132. Peterson, 'The Divine Appointment', 39.

133. See Komoróczy, 'Berosos and the Mesopotamian Literature', 141.

134. Unless otherwise specified, the text, translation and numbering are from Geert de Breucker, 'Berossos of Babylon (680)', in *Brill's New Jacoby*, ed. Ian Worthington (Leiden: Brill, 2016). Consulted online on 24 June 2020 http://dx.doi.org/10.1163/1873-5363_bnj_a680.

135. For dating, see Burstein, *Babyloniaca of Berossus*, 4 n. 2.

136. For an overview of the textual situation, see Johannes Haubold, 'The World of Berossos: Introduction', in *The World of Berossos: Proceedings of the 4th International Colloquium on 'The Ancient Near East between Classical and Ancient Oriental Traditions', Hatfield College, Durham 7th–9th July 2010*, ed. Johannes Haubold et al., Classica et Orientalia 5 (Wiesbaden: Harrassowitz Verlag, 2013), 3–14 (4).

4.3.1.2.5 Summary

These varied descriptions in Mesopotamian literature show how early, primordial humanity was commonly spoken about as resembling animals. Just as they were created in the same manner as other animals, so they resembled them in their behaviour: living in the wild, eating grass, and drinking from watering holes. This similarity between primordial humans and animals has often been noted by scholars of Mesopotamian literature, however it has not usually been combined with the observation that both humans and animals were created the same way.[137] If we observe that humans were both created like animals and continued to behave like animals afterwards, it is therefore reasonable to state that within this early Mesopotamian understanding early humans were essentially indistinguishable from animals. There was thus, at the point of creation at least, no clear divide between the two.

4.3.1.3 Acquisition of Wisdom/Reason Distinguishes Humans and Animals

Within this early Mesopotamian conception of creation, the distinction or boundary between the human and animal is only instituted secondarily. While humans are not created as distinct from animals, something occurs which causes them to be distinguished from the rest of the animal world.[138]

4.3.1.3.1 The Debate between Sheep and Grain

This can be seen firstly in *Sheep and Grain*. After the description of animal-like humankind, the origins of both sheep and grain are narrated (*Sheep and Grain* 26–35). The gods then decide to give both of them to the people: 'For their own well-being in the holy sheepfold, they gave them to mankind as sustenance [*zi-ša ǧál*]' (*Sheep and Grain* 36). While some have attempted to understand this *zi-ša ǧál* as referring to the creation of humans, it actually denotes the introduction of agriculture to the people by which they can produce food.[139] This effect of the gift of sheep and grain to humans is stated later:

> They brought wealth to the assembly. They brought sustenance to the Land. They fulfilled the ordinances [*me*] of the gods. They filled the store-rooms of the Land with stock. The barns of the Land were heavy with them. (*Sheep and Grain* 54–8)

---

137. For example, Jeffrey Tigay notices the tradition of an animal-like primordial humanity but does not look at conceptions of creation; see Tigay, *Evolution of Gilgamesh*, 202–203.

138. For example, see Batto, 'Creation Theology in Genesis', 22.

139. For the idea that *zi-ša ǧál* denotes the moment of creation, see the translation in Jean Bottéro and Samuel N. Kramer, *Lorsque les Dieux Faisaient l'Homme, Mythologie Mésopotamienne* (Paris: Gallimard, 1993), 511–514. This was refuted in Pettinato, *Das altorientalische Menschenbild*, 57. See also: Lisman, *Cosmogony, Theogony, and Anthropogeny*, 280.

The people are now able to work the land and produce food. As this unfolds, it is stated that the *mes* of the gods are fulfilled (*Sheep and Grain* 56). These *mes* seem to denote the regulations of specific cultural norms, practices and institutions which are ordained by the relevant deity who governs them.[140] It is through these *mes* that civilization was mediated to people.[141] Therefore, through this gift of sheep and grain from the gods, people fulfil these *mes* (*Sheep and Grain* 56) and become civilized. It is this civilising process which is commonly seen as the way by which humans are distinguished from animals in this text, as after the gifts of sheep and grain the people no longer seem to live in an animal-like state.[142] Interestingly, when the *mes* themselves are extensively listed in the Sumerian text *Inana and Enki*, one of those specifically mentioned is wisdom.[143] If wisdom is one of these institutions of civilization, this text may provide the first hint that wisdom has a role in distinguishing humans from animals. From *Sheep and Grain*, we can therefore see that civilization, including wisdom, is transmitted to the people by the gods and appears to distinguish them from animals.

4.3.1.3.2 Berossus' *Babyloniaca*

An alternative process by which humans are distinguished from animals is recounted in the text of Berossus' *Babyloniaca*. After the animal-like description of humans who lack reason (1b.3), he describes how Oannes appeared and then began to teach the people:

> It gave men the knowledge of letters and sciences and crafts of all types. It also taught the founding of cities, the establishment of temples, and the introduction of laws and land-measurement, and showed them seeds and the gathering of fruits. In general, it taught men everything that is connected with a civilised life. (Berossus, *Babyloniaca* 1b.4)

This seems to reflect a similar narrative of the civilization of humankind through the giving or teaching of certain cultural norms or practices. However, unlike in

---

140. For discussion of the meaning of *me*, see Samuel N. Kramer, *The Sumerians: Their History, Culture, and Character* (London: University of Chicago Press, 1963), 115–116; Thorkild Jacobsen, 'Sumerian Mythology: A Review Article', *JNES* 5 (1946): 128–152 (139 n. 20); Yvonne Rosengarten, *Sumer et le sacré: Le jeu des Prescriptions (me), des dieux, et des destins* (Paris: E. de Boccard, 1977), 1–23.

141. Tigay, *Evolution of Gilgamesh*, 204–205.

142. For the idea that civilisation can distinguish human from animal, see Alster and Vanstiphout, 'Lahar and Ashnan', 2. This can also be seen in how the Sumerians refer to other cultures, whom they considered to be uncivilized, in animalising terms; see Jeremy A. Black et al., eds, '1.7.1 The Marriage of Martu', *ETCSL*, lines 127–141; Jeremy A. Black et al., eds, '2.1.5 The Cursing of Agade', *ETCSL*, lines 153–157.

143. The composite text and translation of *Inana and Enki* is available in Jeremy A. Black et al., eds, '1.3.1 Inana and Enki', *ETCSL*. For a comprehensive list of the different *mes*, see Kramer, *The Sumerians*, 116.

Sheep and Grain, this civilizing process is not initiated by the gods, but by the sages or *apkallu*.[144] Oannes is commonly linked with the first of the *apkallu* called Uanna in the Neo-Assyrian (*ca.* 900–600 BCE) Akkadian text *Bīt Mēseri*.[145] The role of the *apkallu* in the text of *Bīt Mēseri* is to ensure 'the correct functioning [*ú-ṣu-rat*] of the plans of heaven and earth' (*Bīt Mēseri* 7–9).[146] This correct functioning, or *ú-ṣu-rat*, can be plausibly equated with the *mes* which the gods govern in *Sheep and Grain*.[147] Thus, Berossus provides evidence that humankind was also thought to have been civilised and de-animalised through the teaching of the *apkallu*.[148]

However, the character of Adapa has also been commonly linked with the sage Uanna/Oannes, and thus derives from these same mythological concepts.[149] Looking again at the *Adapa* myth may therefore help us to understand what takes place during this instruction and civilization by Oannes. In the myth, Adapa is described as being perfected:

> with great intelligence, to give instruction about the ordinance [*ú-ṣu-rat*] of the earth. To him he gave wisdom, he did not give him eternal life. (*Adapa* A i.3–4)

Here Adapa also appears to take on this role of instructing in the *ú-ṣu-rat* or ways of civilization, however this civilising role is explicitly linked to wisdom. The implication of this passage is explained by Izre'el: 'Adapa's broad wisdom enabled him to instruct humanity about the ordinances of the earth.'[150] It is by his wisdom that other humans can receive civilisation and be distinguished from animals. Therefore, wisdom again plays a crucial role in creating this boundary between humans and animals.

---

144. These seem to be a type of semi-divine being. For a general discussion of the traditions of the *apkallu*, see Kvanvig, *Primeval History*, 107–158. For the distinction between these two types of civilizing of humankind, see Tigay, *Evolution of Gilgamesh*, 204–206.

145. For the text, see Erica Reiner, 'The Etiological Myth of the "Seven Sages"', *Orientalia* 30 (1961): 1–11; and Rykle Borger, 'Die Beschwörungsserie Bīt Mēseri und die Himmelfahrt Henochs', *JNES* 33 (1974): 183–196. For the link between Oannes and Uanna, see Komoróczy, 'Berosos and the Mesopotamian Literature', 143–144.

146. Reiner, 'Etiological Myth', 2–4.

147. Tigay, *Evolution of Gilgamesh*, 205–206.

148. These beliefs about the *apkallu* were possibly adapted by later Jewish writers into the 'Watchers' found in 1 Enoch. See section §5.1.6 below.

149. See Sara Denning-Bolle, *Wisdom in Akkadian Literature: Expression, Instruction, Dialogue*, Mededelingen en Verhandelingen van het Vooraziatisch-Egyptisch Genootschap 'Ex Oriente Lux' 28 (Leiden: Ex Oriente Lux, 1992), 45; and Kvanvig, *Primeval History*, 117–29. It has also been suggested that Adapa be equated with the seventh *apkallu* called Utu-Abzu; see Hallo, 'Adapa Reconsidered', 272; Komoróczy, 'Berosos and the Mesopotamian Literature', 144.

150. Izre'el, *Adapa and the South Wind*, 116.

4.3.1.3.3 The Gilgamesh Epic
Arguably the principal Mesopotamian text which reflects on humankind and its relationship to animals is *The Gilgamesh Epic*. Simonetta Ponchia calls it Mesopotamia's 'most extensive reflection on human nature and mankind's position in the cosmos, where it appears to occupy an intermediate stage between the divine and the natural'.[151] It has already been shown how the latter half of *Gilgamesh* is concerned with the human pursuit of immortality and its role in bounding and demarcating the human and divine realms. However, the earlier part has a rather different focus.[152] One of the chief characters is Gilgamesh's companion, Enkidu. Enkidu is created by the goddess Aruru (*Gilgamesh* I), befriends Gilgamesh (*Gilgamesh* II), and they proceed to overcome a number of challenges (*Gilgamesh* III–VI). The character eventually drops out of the epic upon his death (*Gilgamesh* VII) and Gilgamesh subsequently expresses his great grief at Enkidu's passing (*Gilgamesh* VIII).

Through the description and depiction of his character, Enkidu plays a crucial role in expressing how humankind is differentiated from animals in *Gilgamesh*. First, it is clear that Enkidu is formed in the same way as both animals and primordial humans. Once the gods have decided they need an equal to Gilgamesh, 'Aruru washed her hands, she took a pinch of clay, she threw it down in the wild. In the wild she created Enkidu, the hero, an offspring of silence, knit strong by Ninurta' (*Gilgamesh* I.101–104).[153] Enkidu is thus formed out of clay which is reminiscent of the method the gods use to create both animals and primordial humans within this tradition of creation.[154]

---

151. Simonetta Ponchia, 'Gilgameš and Enkidu: The Two-thirds-god and the Two-thirds-animal?' in *Animals and their Relation to Gods, Humans and Things in the Ancient World,* ed. Raija Mattila, Sanae Ito, and Sebastian Fink, Studies in Universal and Cultural History (Wiesbaden: Springer VS, 2019), 187–210 (187).

152. Patrick Barron suggests the separation of Enkidu from his animal nature is at the heart of the whole narrative; see Patrick Barron, 'The Separation of Wild Animal Nature and Human Nature in *Gilgamesh*: Roots of a Contemporary Theme', *Papers on Language and Literature* 38 (2002): 377–394 (380).

153. The description and depiction of Enkidu will be based on the SB of *Gilgamesh* from George, *BGE*. For a note on how he is depicted differently in other fragments, see Ponchia, 'Gilgameš and Enkidu', 187–190.

154. Jeffrey Tigay notes similarities between Enkidu's creation and the text of *Atrahasis*; see Tigay, *Evolution of Gilgamesh*, 192–197. While admittedly there are some parallels, crucially they differ in the material that is used to create the human. *Atrahasis* involves divine blood in the process of human's creation, however Enkidu is not made of any divine matter as there is no suggestion that anything other than clay was used. Nathan Wasserman has recently proposed another explanation for Enkidu's creation. He suggests that Enkidu may have been created through spontaneous generation, a concept he thinks is evidenced in a number of Old Babylonian texts as the method by which certain animals reproduced. However, the evidence he cites for this is fairly thin and Wasserman himself admits the argument is fairly speculative; see Wasserman, 'Offspring of Silence', 593–599.

Secondly, after he is created, Enkidu is initially described in exactly the same animalising terminology as other primordial humans:

> All his body is matted with hair, he is adorned with tresses like a woman: the locks of his hair grow thickly as Nissaba's, he knows not at all a people nor even a country. He was clad in a garment like Šakkan's, feeding on grass with the very gazelles. *Jostling at* the water-hole with the herd, he enjoyed the water with the animals. (*Gilgamesh* I.105–112)

Enkidu lives the life of an animal: he is intensely hairy, he has no ties to other cultures or civilizations, he eats grass and he drinks from watering holes. The reference to the garment of Šakkan, the god of domestic animals, probably means Enkidu wore only that which nature intended and wore no clothes.[155] In all these aspects, Enkidu exactly parallels the description of primordial humanity in texts such as *Sheep and Grain*, and this connection has a long history within scholarship.[156] It is therefore probable that Enkidu is being intentionally depicted as a primordial man. Later, in very similar words, the text provides a glimpse at how Enkidu lived with the animals in the wild:

> The animals arrived, they enjoyed the water, and also Enkidu himself, whose birthplace was the hills. Feeding on grass with the very gazelles, *jostling at* the water-hole with the herd, he enjoyed the water with the animals. (*Gilgamesh* I.173–177)

This depiction of Enkidu is remarkably similar in terminology to how other animals are described in Mesopotamian literature. A close parallel is the Neo-Assyrian (*ca.* 900–600 BCE) Akkadian text called *The Sacrificial Gazelle*:

> A pure, tawny sacrificial animal, offspring of a gazelle, whose mother bore him in the steppe, and the steppe sets its kind protection over him. The steppe raised him like a father, and the pasture like a mother. . . . He would eat grass in the steppe; never would he want for water to drink at pure pools. He would feed on the . . .-plants and then return (to his haunts). He who never knew a herdsman [   ] in the steppe. (*The Sacrificial Gazelle* III.52.d)[157]

Here a young gazelle is described as being born amongst the steppe, eating grass and drinking at pools. This understanding of the life of a gazelle seems to closely

---

155. George, *BGE*, 790 n. 109.

156. The connection between Enkidu and primordial humans was first suggested by Morris Jastrow, 'Adam and Eve in Babylonian Literature', *AJSL* 15 (1899): 193–214 (199–201). More recent examples are Tigay, *Evolution of Gilgamesh*, 202–204; Batto, *Slaying the Dragon*, 55.

157. The translation is taken from: Benjamin R. Foster, *Before the Muses: An Anthology of Akkadian Literature*, 3rd ed. (Bethesda, MD: CDL, 2005), 755–756.

parallel the depiction of Enkidu, whose birthplace is the hills and is himself described as drinking at a waterhole and feeding 'with the very gazelles' (*Gilgamesh* I.175). Such a connection is supported by Gilgamesh's word about Enkidu when mourning his death: 'O Enkidu, your mother, a gazelle, and your father, a wild donkey' (*Gilgamesh* VIII.3–4). Enkidu therefore seems to be specifically portrayed as living like a gazelle or other animal of the hills, and this wild-life seems to be symbolic of purity.[158] His similarity with the wild animals is perhaps further emphasised by how he moves. At several points it is stated that Enkidu was able to keep pace with the four-legged animals in the hills (*Gilgamesh* I.126–127, 153–154) and this may suggest Enkidu also adopted a quadrupedal method of transportation.[159] From these descriptions, it is clear that Enkidu is depicted as a human who very closely resembles the other animals in behaviour and appearance.[160] He is therefore a prime example of a primordial human, created in the same manner as the animals, and living the same way.

However, after Enkidu's early existence is narrated, he undergoes a period of profound transformation as he enters into the human community. This change in Enkidu has been seen as another way in which animal-like primordial humanity ascends to full human status.[161] A hunter encounters the wild Enkidu at the waterhole (*Gilgamesh* I.113–121) and, after consulting his father, beseeches Gilgamesh to send the prostitute Shamhat to meet Enkidu (*Gilgamesh* I.122–160). Gilgamesh agrees and Shamhat departs with the hunter (*Gilgamesh* I.161–168). The plan seems to be that 'when the herd comes down to the waterhole, she should strip off her clothing to reveal her charms. He [Enkidu] will see her and will go up to her, his herd will be estranged from him' (*Gilgamesh* I.165–167).[162] When Enkidu eventually encounters Shamhat, they have sexual intercourse for six days and seven nights (*Gilgamesh* I.188–194). Enkidu then attempts to return to his life amongst the animals, but something has changed:

---

158. Indeed, Foster suggests his life is symbolic of ritual purity; see Foster, *Before the Muses*, 29.

159. Gregory Mobley, *Samson and the Liminal Hero in the Ancient Near East*, LHBOTS 453 (London: T&T Clark, 2006), 48.

160. Aage Westenholz and Ulla Koch-Westenholz argue that while Enkidu is like an animal 'he *is* human'. See Aage Westenholz and Ulla Koch-Westenholz, 'Enkidu – the Noble Savage? in *Wisdom, Gods and Literature: Studies in Assyriology in Honour of W. G. Lambert*, ed. Andrew R. George and Irving L. Finkel (Winona Lake, IN: Eisenbrauns, 2000), 437–451 (443). Nevertheless, while Enkidu is clearly a human, he lives in an animal state virtually indistinguishable from the other animals. He can thus be considered merely another type of animal alongside the gazelles and wild asses, etc.

161. Tigay, *Evolution of Gilgamesh*, 206.

162. This plan is initially suggested by the hunter's father who describes it in almost exactly the same terms in I.142–145.

After he was sated with her delights, he turned his face toward his herd. The gazelles saw Enkidu and they started running, the animals of the wild moved away from his person. Enkidu had defiled his body so pure, his legs stood still, though his herd was on the move. Enkidu was diminished, his running was not as before, but he had *reason* [*ṭéma*], he [was] wide of understanding [*ra-pa-áš ḥa-si-sa*]. He came back and sat down at the feet of the harlot, watching the harlot, (observing) her features. Then his ears heard what the [harlot] was speaking, [as the harlot] said to him, to Enkidu: 'You are handsome, Enkidu, you are just like a god, Why do you roam the wild with the animals?' (*Gilgamesh* I.195–208)

The hunter's plan has worked and, through his sexual encounter with Shamhat, Enkidu is rejected by the animal world. Enkidu is no longer able to keep pace with the animals; his pure life has been defiled and he is decisively changed. The act of sexual intercourse clearly has a role in causing Enkidu's estrangement, though exactly how this takes place has not been resolved.[163] Nevertheless, this encounter with Shamhat is the moment which instigates Enkidu's categorical switch from animal to human. From now on he will no longer be united with the animals in the wild, but he will participate in the human world.

Many scholars also note that the transformation of Enkidu involves a second stage. First, Shamhat and Enkidu have intercourse, but then Shamhat adopts an almost maternal role in instructing Enkidu in the ways of humankind and leading him to the city of Uruk.[164] Shamhat gives Enkidu human clothes (*Gilgamesh* II.34–36) and takes him to a camp of shepherds where he is given human food and drink (*Gilgamesh* II.44–51). Unfortunately, the SB of *Gilgamesh* breaks off here, though the lacuna can seemingly be filled by the OB version which tells how he eats and drinks, has his hair cut and is anointed (*Gilgamesh* OB II.99–101). Finally, after all these activities, the humanization of Enkidu is concluded as it is stated that he 'became a man [*a-wi-li-iš i-we*]' (*Gilgamesh* OB II.108).

163. For the debate over this, see Westenholz and Koch-Westenholz, 'Enkidu – the Noble Savage?' 442 n. 13; Tigay, *Evolution of Gilgamesh,* 207; John A. Bailey, 'Male, Female and the Pursuit of Immortality in the Gilgamesh Epic', *La Parola Del Passato Rivista Di Studi Antichi* 31 (1976): 431–457 (437).

164. For this two stage process of humanisation and Shamhat's role in it, see Erica Reiner, 'City Bread and Bread Baked in Ashes', in *Languages and Areas: Studies Presented to George V. Bobrinskoy,* ed. Howard I. Aronson (Chicago: University of Chicago, 1967), 116–120 (118); Rivkah Harris, 'Images of Women in the Gilgamesh Epic', in *Lingering Over Words: Studies in Ancient Near Eastern Literature in Honor of William L. Moran,* ed. Tzvi Abusch, John Huehnergard and Piotr Steinkeller, HSS 37 (Atlanta: Scholars Press, 1990), 220–230 (223–224); Mobley, 'Wild Man in the Bible', 221; Tigay, *Evolution of Gilgamesh,* 206–207.

This whole humanizing transformation seems to be signalled at its outset by Enkidu's acquisition of wisdom. Immediately after we are told of Enkidu's rejection by the other animals, he is described both as having 'reason'/'wisdom' (*ṭéma*), and as being 'wide of understanding' (*ra-pa-áš ḫa-si-sa*) (*Gilgamesh* I.202).[165] This is important as the text explicitly connects the enhancement of his own mental abilities here with his sudden detachment and estrangement from the animal world in the previous lines (*Gilgamesh* I.197–201). Wisdom thus seems to function as the decisive feature which differentiates and divorces Enkidu from the animals. The boundary between the animal and the human thus begins with the concept of wisdom. After Enkidu is stated as possessing wisdom, Shamhat describes him as being 'just like a god' (*Gilgamesh* I.207), suggesting that the acquisition of reason or intelligence gives him some resemblance to the divine too.[166] This connects with our previous identification of wisdom and immortality as divine attributes, of which humans only share in wisdom. It can thus be argued that, by acquiring wisdom, Enkidu is set apart from the animals and possesses a divine characteristic.

Simultaneously with acquiring wisdom, Enkidu also begins to engage with human language. His previous inability to communicate or understand language may be supposed from his earlier epithet as 'an offspring of silence' (*Gilgamesh* I.104).[167] However, just after the narrator tells us about Enkidu's newly attained wisdom, he returns to sit with Shamhat and 'his ears heard what the [harlot] was speaking' (*Gilgamesh* I.205). This immediate response by Enkidu suggests that by gaining wisdom he has also gained the ability to understand words. Furthermore, it is only after Shamhat has spoken to him that Enkidu can then utter his own first words in the epic (*Gilgamesh* I.215–223). The ability to use language can be thought of as the primary signifier of wisdom in Mesopotamia[168] and this would explain why Enkidu only begins speaking after he has received wisdom. The link between his newfound reason/wisdom and language is explicitly emphasized in that, immediately before Enkidu speaks for the first time, the narrator states: 'his heart (now) wise was seeking a friend' (*Gilgamesh* I.214).

While wisdom is crucial in causing Enkidu to cross the human–animal boundary, it also plays a key role elsewhere in defining humankind in *Gilgamesh*. This can be seen by examining the other chief character in this epic: Gilgamesh himself. The text of the SB of *Gilgamesh* opens with a unique introductory section

---

165. George translates *ṭéma* here as 'reason' (George, *BGE*, 551). An example of a translation that renders it 'wisdom' is 'The Epic of Gilgamesh', trans. Ephraim A. Speiser, *ANET*, 75, tablet I, col. iv, line 29.

166. Line 207 has often been reconstructed as 'Thou art [wi]se, Enkidu, art become like a god!' to reflect this same understanding of the passage; see 'The Epic of Gilgamesh', trans. Ephraim A. Speiser, *ANET*, 75, tablet I, col. i, line 34.

167. Wasserman, 'Offspring of Silence', 595.

168. Izre'el, *Adapa and the South Wind*, 130–135.

(*Gilgamesh* I.1–28),[169] which seems to emphasize Gilgamesh's own acquisition of wisdom. Gilgamesh is introduced as:

> [He who saw the Deep, the] foundation of the country, [who knew . . .,] was wise [*ḫa-as-su*] in everything! [Gilgameš, who] saw the Deep, the foundation of the country, [who] knew [. . .,] was wise [*ḫa-as-su*] in everything! [. . .] equally [. . .,] He [*learnt*] the totality of wisdom [*né-me-qí*] about everything. He saw the secret and uncovered the hidden, He brought back a message [*ṭè-e-ma*] from the antediluvian age. (*Gilgamesh* I.1–8)

He is described as possessing vast knowledge and wisdom which originates somehow from 'the Deep'. This seems to be associated with the deep, cosmic water Apsû[170] which was the domain of Ea, the god of wisdom.[171] Confirmation of this divine source for Gilgamesh's wisdom is explicitly described later as he is said to 'become wise with Ea *of* the Apsû' (*Gilgamesh* III.104). Gilgamesh's wisdom here seems to be somewhat exceptional. He is not only described as being wise, but he has 'the totality of wisdom' (*Gilgamesh* I.6). Furthermore, he is depicted as being singularly responsible for recovering forgotten wisdom and information from an antediluvian time (*Gilgamesh* I.7–8).[172] However, to some extent, Gilgamesh represents the human condition more generally.[173] If this is the case, then it may suggest that the text of *Gilgamesh* presents wisdom as a characteristic common to humankind. While it would be imprudent to suggest all humans have Gilgamesh's level of wisdom, if this character is somewhat paradigmatic of the human condition then he may function as a signifier that a key characteristic of humankind is wisdom, as indeed witnessed elsewhere in the Mesopotamian literature.[174]

---

169. For the argument that this is a new introduction for this version, see Aaron Shaffer *apud* Donald J. Wiseman, 'A Gilgamesh Epic Fragment from Nimrud', *Iraq* 37 (1975): 157–163 (158 n. 22).

170. For an understanding of the Akkadian *naqbu* or 'deep', see Jorge Silva Castillo, 'Naqbu: Totality or Abyss in the First Verse of Gilgamesh', *Iraq* 60 (1998): 219–221; and George, *BGE*, 444–445.

171. For Ea/Enki as the god of wisdom, see Hannes D. Galter, *Der Gott Ea/Enki in der Akkadischen Überlieferung. Eine Bestandsaufnahme des vorhanden Materials*, Dissertationen der Karl-Franzens-Universität Graz 58 (Graz: Verlag für die Technische Universität Graz, 1983), 95–103; and Jean Bottéro, *Mesopotamia: Writing, Reasoning, and the Gods*, trans. Zainab Bahrani and Marc Van De Mieroop (London: University of Chicago Press, 1992), 232–250.

172. George, *BGE*, 445.

173. Mettinger, *Eden Narrative*, 120–122.

174. E.g., *Adapa* A.i.3–4.

4.3.1.3.4 Summary

A number of different traditions have been examined that describe the process by which primordial animal-like humankind was changed and effectively humanized. In all of them we have detected the key role which wisdom or reason plays in defining humankind, however it is most evident in the humanising of Enkidu in *Gilgamesh*. Through his encounter with Shamhat and other people, he receives wisdom/reason which draws him out of the animal world. In this early Mesopotamian tradition of humankind's creation and subsequent complete humanization, wisdom is thus the key distinguisher between human and animal.

4.3.2 Humankind is Created with Wisdom

The second Mesopotamian account of humankind's creation is found primarily in texts written in Akkadian. According to Lisman's findings, this Akkadian form of anthropogenesis is categorised by the motif of divine violence which occurred before humans were actually formed.[175] The slaughter of one or more gods is essential as their divine blood provides one of the ingredients to make humankind. Thus, rather than being made simply out of clay or from the earth, humans are formed, at least partly, by the use of a divine element. This is a key difference from animals, as there is no suggestion in any Mesopotamian text that animals were thought of as being created with a divine element. The only evidence available suggests animals were formed purely out of clay.[176] However, these Akkadian texts contain no reference to a pre-civilized animal humanity; instead humans seem to be different from the animals from the beginning.[177] This form of anthropogenesis in Akkadian texts therefore introduces a unique new aspect to the human creature, which marks them as both inherently and intrinsically different from the animals, and there is good reason to again associate this divine ingredient in humankind with wisdom.

4.3.2.1 The Atrahasis Epic

Chronologically, the first Akkadian text which introduces a divine ingredient into humankind's creation is *Atrahasis (ca.* 1600 BCE). In this epic, the gods decide to create humans to toil and work for them (*Atrahasis* I.189–197), however these humans cannot simply be created out of clay (*Atrahasis* I.200–203). Therefore, the god Enki declares:

> Let one god be slaughtered so that all the gods may be cleansed in a dipping. From his flesh and blood let Nintu mix clay, that god and man may be thoroughly

---

175. Lisman, *Cosmogony, Theogony, and Anthropogeny*, 201.
176. See Espak, 'Creation of Animals', 308.
177. Komoróczy, 'Berosos and the Mesopotamian Literature', 141.

mixed in the clay, so that we may hear the drum for the rest of time let there be a spirit from the god's flesh. (*Atrahasis* I.208–215).

This is then carried out later:

Wê-ila, who had personality [*ṭe-e-ma*], they slaughtered in their assembly. From his flesh and blood Nintu mixed clay. For the rest [of time they heard the drum], from the flesh of the god [there was] a spirit [*e-ṭe-em-mu*]. (*Atrahasis* I.223–228)

Humankind is thus here initially created out of both clay and the flesh and blood of a god. These divine ingredients have often been seen as giving rise to specific elements of the human being. Many scholars note that this passage from *Atrahasis* appears to be describing the origin of the human spirit [*eṭemmu*] which transcends death.[178] The text suggests that the flesh of the god Wê-ila is the basis from which the human spirit was created (*Atrahasis* I.228). The use of divine flesh is thus commonly explained as the means by which humans receive the spirit that allows for post-mortem existence in the netherworld.

However, these lines in *Atrahasis* may provide further information about the origins of humankind. The god Wê-ila, who is subsequently used as a material to create humans, is specifically described as having *ṭēmu* (I.223). Though translated by Lambert and Millard as 'personality',[179] *ṭēmu* has been understood variously, often in reference to 'intelligence',[180] and has linguistic links with wisdom.[181] The use of this wise or intelligent god as the basis for creating humans may suggest the transference of this divine wisdom to humankind. This idea may receive some support from Tzvi Abusch who has looked at wordplays in this text.[182] He has suggested the existence of a wordplay between *ṭēmu* and *damu* (or 'blood'; *Atrahasis* I.225) which have a similarity in sound. He proposes that this wordplay demonstrates how 'intelligence has been imparted to mankind through the god's

178. Lambert and Millard, *Atra-ḫasīs*, 22; Lisman, *Cosmogony, Theogony, and Anthropogeny*, 193–194; Dina Katz, '"Death They Dispensed to Mankind": The Funerary World of Ancient Mesopotamia', *Historiae* 2 (2005): 55–90 (57–59).

179. Lambert and Millard, *Atra-ḫasīs*, 153.

180. For example: Izre'el, *Adapa and the South Wind*, 121; Bottéro, *Mesopotamia*, 241; Ulrike Steinert, *Aspekte des Menschseins im Alten Mesopotamien: Eine Studie zu Person und Identität im 2. und 1. Jt. v. Chr.*, CM 44 (Leiden: Brill, 2012), 385–404.

181. See *CDA*, s.v. 'ṭēmānu', 'ṭēmītum'.

182. Wordplays have often been noticed in this text; for example, see Jean Bottéro, 'La creation de l'homme et son nature dans le poème d'*Atraḫasīs*', in *Societes and Languages of the Ancient Near East: Studies in Honour of I.M. Diakonoff*, ed. Muhammad A. Dandamayev et al. (Warminster, UK: Aris & Phillips, 1982), 24–32.

blood'.[183] If these connections are right, *Atrahasis* reveals how the divine attribute of wisdom (intelligence) is shared with humankind. Rather than receiving it secondarily (as in e.g., *Gilgamesh*), humankind is instead created with this divine characteristic of wisdom or reason.

4.3.2.2 KAR 4

This idea that humankind was made out of divine blood is also evidenced in other Near Eastern texts. Towards the end of the second millennium BCE, later texts about anthropogenesis cease referring to clay or flesh as ingredients in the creation of humankind; instead the sole requirement for anthropogenesis is divine blood.[184] The first of these texts is bilingual, being written in both Akkadian and Sumerian arranged in parallel columns.[185] It has received a variety of names (such as *Creation of Humankind*,[186] and *Another Account of the Creation of Man*[187]) though will simply be referred to here as *KAR* 4 after the numbering of the first published (and most relevant for this study) tablet of the text dated around 1200 BCE.[188] This text describes how, after the world has been created, the Annunaki gods suggest that they create humankind. They reply to Enlil's questions: 'Let us slaughter the Alla deities and make mankind from their blood' (*KAR* 4 obv.25–26). While similar to *Atrahasis*, *KAR* 4 displays some significant differences. First, multiple gods are killed rather than Wê-ila alone.[189] However, more crucially, humankind is created

---

183. Tzvi Abusch, 'Ghost and God: Some Observations on a Babylonian Understanding of Human Nature', in *Self, Soul and Body in Religious Experience*, ed. Albert I. Baumgarten, Jan Assmann and Gary G. Stroumsa, SHR 78 (Leiden: Brill, 1998), 363–383 (368).

184. Lisman, *Cosmogony, Theogony, and Anthropogeny*, 205–206.

185. A monolingual Sumerian text was announced but never published by Dietz O. Edzard and Claus Wilcke, 'Vorläufiger Bericht über die Inschriftenfunde Frühjahr 1973, Frühjahr 1974, Herbst 1974', in *Isin-Išān Baḥrīyāt I. Die Ergebnisse der Ausgrabungen 1973–1974*, ed. Barthel Hrouda, ABAW Philosophisch-Historische Klasse Neue Folge 79 (Münster: Verlag der Bayerischen Akadaemie der Wissenschaften, 1977), 83–92 (86). A fragmentary edition and brief discussion is provided in: Lambert, *Babylonian Creation Myths*, 350–352, 360.

186. Foster, *Before the Muses*, 491–493.

187. Alexander Heidel, *The Babylonian Genesis: The Story of Creation*, 2nd ed. (London: University of Chicago Press, 1951), 68–71.

188. This tablet was first published in: Erich Ebeling, ed., *Keilschrifttexte aus Assur religiösen Inhalts*, 2 vols. (Leipzig: Hinrichs, 1919–1923), 1:8 (Nr. 4). For a thorough account of the available manuscripts, editions, and translations, along with the text and translation that will be followed here, see Lambert, *Babylonian Creation Myths*, 350–60. See also Lisman, *Cosmogony, Theogony, and Anthropogeny*, 330–346.

189. It is commonly suggested that two gods were killed, to accord with the two humans named later in *KAR* 4 rev. 11–12. See Heidel, *Babylonian Genesis*, 69; Manfred Krebernik, 'Geschlachtete Gottheiten und ihre Nahmen', in *Ex Mesopotamia et Syria Lux: Festschrift für Manfried Dietrich zu seinem 65 Geburtstag*, ed. Oswald Loretz, Kai A. Metzler and Hanspeter Schaudig, AOAT 281 (Münster: Ugarit-Verlag, 2002), 289–98 (292–294).

purely out of divine blood – there is no mention of either the gods' flesh or clay being used at all.[190]

4.3.2.3 Enuma Elish

The same method of human creation is described in the Akkadian text *Enuma Elish* (composed *ca.* 1894–1595 BCE though extant tablets date to *ca.* 1300–1100 BCE).[191] After a period of divine conflict, the god Marduk approaches Ea and unveils his idea:

> I will bring together blood and form bone, I will bring into being Lullû, whose name shall be 'man', I will create Lullû-man. (*Enuma Elish* VI.5–7)

Ea agrees to this and suggests the rebel god called Qingu be sacrificed to supply the blood. The other gods then follow this plan:

> They bound him, holding him before Ea, they inflicted the penalty on him and severed his blood-vessels. From his blood he created mankind. (*Enuma Elish* VI.31–33)

Here again, though only one god is killed, divine blood is the only element used to construct humankind. This is confirmed by Marduk's original plan to 'bring together blood and form bone'. No clay is needed as the blood of Qingu is used to construct the physical matter of humans. In both *KAR* 4 and *Enuma Elish* blood is the sole element used to create humans. Thus, as with *Atrahasis*, from their very creation humans are portrayed as sharing something of the divine.

4.3.2.4 Berossus' Babyloniaca

A text which supports this interpretation of the significance of divine blood for human creation is Berossus' *Babyloniaca* (third century BCE). After narrating the creation of the world, Berossus describes the origins of humankind:

> When everything was moist and creatures had come into being in it, this god [Belos] took off his own head and the other gods mixed the blood that flowed out with earth and formed men. For this reason they are intelligent and share in divine wisdom. (Berossus, *Babyloniaca* 1b.7)

Unlike *Enuma Elish* and *KAR* 4, anthropogenesis here requires two components: blood and earth. In this regard Berossus' account seems to depend on the tradition

---

190. Some scholars have suggested that some later lines hint at the idea that humankind grew out from the earth (rev. 20); see Pettinato, *Das altorientalische Menschenbild*, 74–81. This is doubtful however (Lisman, *Cosmogony, Theogony, and Anthropogeny*, 345).

191. For date of composition, see Heidel, *Babylonian Genesis*, 14. The text, translation and tablet dating is taken from Lambert, *Babylonian Creation Myths.*

in *Atrahasis* whereby divine elements (especially blood) must be combined with a substance (clay or earth) to create human beings.[192] The importance of this divine blood in Berossus' account of anthropogenesis is also abundantly clear, as he credits it as the source for both human intelligence and their share in the divine characteristic of wisdom. This purpose for the divine blood again echoes its role in *Atrahasis* where it seems to pass on Wê-ila's intelligence to humankind. Once again, the introduction of divine blood into the process of anthropogenesis appears to serve as an originating point for how humankind received wisdom or intelligence.

Nevertheless, the account of anthropogenesis in the *Babyloniaca* is not so simple. Berossus actually includes two versions of the creation of humankind with no easy way to make sense of how they relate to one another. Both the Armenian translation and Syncellus' Greek text of the *Babyloniaca* contain this second account of anthropogenesis:

> When Belos saw the land empty and barren, he ordered one of the gods to cut off his own head and to mix the blood that flowed out with earth and to form men and wild animals that were capable of enduring the air. (Berossus, *Babyloniaca* 1b.8)

In this version both humans and animals seem to be made from divine blood. This second account seems to run counter to Berossus' earlier claim that divine blood passed on wisdom or intelligence to humans and made them distinct from the animals. Certainly there have been many attempts to create some semblance of harmony between these two divergent accounts and explain the inclusion of them alongside one another in the text.[193] However, most commonly scholars have cast doubt over the authenticity or originality of this second explanation of anthropogenesis.[194] Felix Jacoby argued that this account was an interpolation of a Jewish adaptation of Berossus' creation narrative,[195] and more recently de Breucker has confirmed the influence of Jewish or Christian readings of Genesis on this text.[196] He specifically notes that the statement of the animals' ability to endure air has no basis within the Mesopotamian tradition and is probably a later

---

192. Geert de Breucker has even argued that Berossus is here explicitly elaborating on the earlier account of human creation in *Atrahasis*; see De Breucker, 'Berossos', 1b.7.

193. See the combined text and translation in: Heidel, *Babylonian Genesis*, 78; and Johannes Haubold, 'The Wisdom of the Chaldeans: Reading Berossus, *Babyloniaca* Book 1', in *The World of Berossos: Proceedings of the 4th International Colloquium on 'The Ancient Near East between Classical and Ancient Oriental Traditions', Hatfield College, Durham 7th–9th July 2010*, ed. Johannes Haubold et al., Classica et Orientalia 5 (Wiesbaden: Harrassowitz Verlag, 2013), 31–45 (40–41).

194. For example: Heidel, *Babylonian Genesis*, 80–81.

195. Felix Jacoby, *Die Fragmente der griechischen Historiker* III C1 (Leiden: Brill, 1958), 373.

196. De Breucker, 'Berossos', 1b.7. See also the fuller treatment in de Breucker's unpublished thesis: Geert De Breucker, 'De Babyloniaca van Berossos van Babylon: Inleiding, editie en commentaar' (PhD diss., University of Groningen, 2012), 335.

interpolation.[197] Furthermore, while the creation of animals *is* described in some Mesopotamian texts, there are no other witnesses to the idea that divine blood was ever used to create animals. This is elsewhere reserved solely for creating humans. It therefore seems reasonable to conclude that Berossus' second account of the creation of humankind alongside animals (further evidencing both apparent duplication and contradiction) is likely a later interpolation.

Another potential issue with Berossus' depiction of creation with divine blood is that we have already noted that the *Babyloniaca* also evidences the first type of anthropogenesis whereby humans attained wisdom secondarily (Berossus, *Babyloniaca* 1b.3). However, in addition to receiving later interpolations from Jewish or Christian commentators, it is also apparent that the *Babyloniaca* incorporates a variety of different Babylonian sources. In addition to using cuneiform sources, Berossus also drew upon other historical traditions which he then reworked into Greek narrative form.[198] Berossus' account of the flood is a prime example of how different traditions have been manipulated into one narrative (he seems to draw upon *Gilgamesh* and *SFM*, as well as the mid-seventh-century BCE Akkadian *Epic of Erra*).[199] This means the *Babyloniaca* is to some extent a composite text which joins together various divergent traditions. It is therefore likely that Berossus has incorporated both traditions of anthropogenesis into his overall work in order to create a complete account of Babylonian history. Despite these difficulties with Berossus' text, however, it does still appear to provide clear evidence that the purpose of divine blood in human creation was to impart the wisdom/intelligence of the gods to humankind.

This range of texts all evidence a second type of Mesopotamian anthropogenesis which is characterised by the death of a god and the use of some divine components in the creation of humankind. Divine blood is a key element used in the creation of humankind and, in these accounts, this appears to have been understood as the means by which humans received wisdom from the gods. This divine wisdom is therefore imparted to humankind at the point of their creation through the use of divine blood. As there are no reliable ancient witnesses to divine blood being used

197. De Breucker, 'De Babyloniaca van Berossos', 337.

198. Geert De Breucker, 'Berossos between Tradition and Innovation', in *The Oxford Handbook of Cuneiform Culture*, ed. Karen Radner and Eleanor Robson (Oxford: Oxford University Press, 2011), 637–657. See also Paul-Alain Beaulieu, 'Berossus on Late Babylonian History', in *Special Issue of Oriental Studies: A Collection of Papers on Ancient Civilizations of Western Asia, Asia Minor and North Africa*, ed. Yushu Gong and Yiyi Chen (Beijing: University of Beijing, 2007), 116–149 (143); Geert De Breucker, 'Berossos and the Construction of a Near Eastern Cultural History in Response to the Greeks', in *Constructions of Greek Past: Identity and Historical Consciousness from Antiquity to the Present*, ed. Hero Hokwerda (Groningen: Brill, 2003), 25–34 (31–32).

199. De Breucker, 'Berossos between Tradition and Innovation', 644. For background to *Epic of Erra*, see Andrew R. George, 'The Poem of Erra and Ishum: A Babylonian Poet's View of War', in *Warfare and Poetry in the Middle East*, ed. Hugh Kennedy (London: I. B. Tauris, 2013), 39–72 (47).

to create other animals (with the exception of the disputed *Babyloniaca* 1b.8, which itself contradicts 1b.7), we can conclude that this form of anthropogenesis depicts humankind as being created distinct from animals. The human–animal boundary is here instituted at the moment of creation, as humankind uniquely is made from divine blood and receives the divine characteristic of wisdom.

4.3.2.5 Summary

From this general survey of ancient Near Eastern literature, there seem to be two different attempts to describe the creation of humankind. The first depicts humans as created solely out of clay or earth; in the second, humans are created primarily out of a dead god's blood. Each of these traditions recount humankind's creation differently, however in each case it is clear that through this formational process humans receive wisdom, thus separating them from the rest of the animal world. In the first tradition of anthropogenesis, primordial humanity must *acquire* wisdom. The second type of anthropogenesis describes humankind as being *created with* wisdom. In both traditions, wisdom is therefore presented as giving humans a higher status than the animals and makes them resemble the gods.[200] Thus, if we are to speak of a human–animal boundary in this Mesopotamian textual evidence, the principal concept which helps to form this boundary is the presence or absence of wisdom.

4.4 Conclusion

While earlier scholars have noted the roles of wisdom and immortality in distinguishing between different types of creatures in ancient Mesopotamia, this chapter has significantly bolstered these previous conclusions and confirmed that such statements broadly reflect the evidence in the sources themselves. Through a more expansive survey of ancient Near Eastern textual material, two key divine attributes have been noted in these ancient Mesopotamian texts: wisdom and immortality. Both of these are significant qualities which are identified with the gods. The first half of the chapter focused primarily on immortality and noted that humans are ultimately denied access to this and have a mortal life. Immortality thus functions as a key boundary marker between deity and human. In the second half of the chapter the concept of wisdom was assessed. It was concluded that humans are granted the divine characteristic of wisdom, and it is this attribute which most significantly distinguishes them from animals. While other Mesopotamian texts may describes further differences between humans, animals

---

200. This observation is supported by several other scholars of ancient Mesopotamia who have noticed that wisdom/intelligence seems to indicate a clear demarcation between humans and animals in Mesopotamia; see Chikako E. Watanabe, *Animal Symbolism in Mesopotamia: A Contextual Approach*, WOO 1 (Vienna: Institut für Orientalistik der Universität Wien, 2002), 156; Steinert, *Aspekte des Menschseins*, 25.

and the divine, from the survey conducted here the twin divine concepts of wisdom and immortality play the key role in such distinctions.

Equipped with these insights, it is possible to now sketch a general impression of a three-tiered structure of beings within the Mesopotamian literature distinguishing between gods, humans and animals.[201] Gods possess wisdom and immortality; humans possess wisdom but remain mortal; and animals acquire neither of these divine characteristics. Humans are therefore situated in an intermediate position between the two, and only partially participate in the divine, or as Ulricke Steinert concludes 'der Mensch eine Zwischenposition einnimmt: Er teilt Eigenschaften mit den Tieren und den Göttern, andererseits unterscheidet er sich von beiden.'[202] It is therefore reasonable to state that in this ancient Mesopotamian worldview the conceptual boundaries between gods, humans and animals could be identified by the markers of immortality and wisdom. Thus, to transform into a different category of being, and to transgress such conceptual divine–human–animal boundaries, would involve the acquisition or loss of one of these divine characteristics.[203] In particular, and crucially for the purposes of this study, the human–animal boundary itself has little, if anything, to do with appearance; rather the critical identifier is the presence or lack of wisdom.

201. The overall categorisation of beings within Mesopotamia would clearly be more complex than this. Other heavenly being, such as demons or angels, would complicate, though not invalidate, the boundary markers identified here.

202. She also notes the role of 'Sterblichkeit' and 'Verstand' in distinguishing humans from animals and gods. Steinert, *Aspekte des Menschseins,* 512. Espak similarly refers to humans as higher than animals due to their 'way of thinking', but lower than the gods because they have 'eternal life', Espak, 'Creation of Animals', 306.

203. Physical metamorphoses *are* possible in ancient Mesopotamian texts, and Karen Sonik has recently conducted an assessment of what she calls a 'radical *physical* transformation from one category of being into another' in such material; see Karen Sonik, 'Breaking the Boundaries of Being: Metamorphoses in the Mesopotamian Literary Texts', *JAOS* 132 (2012): 385–393 (386). However she observes that the only reversible metamorphoses are conducted by deities upon themselves. Other types of metamorphoses, including the change of a human into a theriomorphic figure, are evidenced very infrequently and are permanent, paired with death, and result in 'the complete effacement of what had previously existed' (Sonik, 'Breaking the Boundaries', 391–392).

Chapter 5

REASSESSING THE HUMAN–ANIMAL BOUNDARY IN DANIEL 4

In light of the ancient Mesopotamian conceptual boundaries between gods, humans and animals which have now been recognized, this chapter will build a case that such boundaries are also detectable within the narrative of Dan. 4. This tradition may therefore provide a useful context by which Nebuchadnezzar's own affliction could be understood. In order to assess the possibility of their influence, the first section of this chapter will argue that these same boundaries evidenced in Mesopotamian traditions can also be more generally identified within the Hebrew Bible and other early Jewish material. This will provide a context for the second section of the chapter which will specifically examine Dan. 4, arguing that these Mesopotamian divine–human–animal boundaries serve to better explain the perceived (and contested) 'metamorphosis' of Nebuchadnezzar. Crucially, despite the apparent absence of a *physical* transformation (as demonstrated in chapter 3), it is argued that the concept of wisdom/reason, and the human–animal boundary which it governs, are nevertheless specifically used to depict Nebuchadnezzar's animalising experience as an altogether more significant categorical change from human to animal.

5.1 Boundaries between Gods, Humans and Animals in the Hebrew Bible and Second Temple Texts

This section will initially search for a similar understanding of divine–human–animal boundaries within the Hebrew Bible and other Second Temple period texts. Scholars have frequently and habitually proposed that ancient Near Eastern traditions have influenced the Hebrew Bible, although the specific way in which these texts relate can vary markedly.[1] Some biblical texts appear to be borrowing specific material from a Near Eastern source (e.g., the apparent use of the ancient

---

1. Some of the various ways ancient Near Eastern texts may have influenced the Hebrew Bible are described in Christopher B. Hays, *Hidden Riches: A Sourcebook for the Comparative Study of the Hebrew Bible and Ancient Near East* (Louisville, KY: Westminster John Knox, 2014), 7.

Egyptian text *The Wisdom of Amenemope* in Prov. 22:17–24:22)[2] while others seem to deliberately rework earlier Near Eastern traditions (e.g., the apparent rewriting of *Gilgamesh* XI in Gen 6:5–9:17).[3] In a similar way, echoes of the same divine–human–animal boundaries which were perceived in Mesopotamian texts (associated with the concepts of wisdom and immortality) can also be traced in both the Hebrew Bible and other Second Temple period Jewish texts. This is not to say that the Hebrew Bible only reflects one specific type of boundary between divine, human and animal, but the similarity between this Mesopotamian understanding of boundaries and such early Jewish texts is seemingly indicative of a shared worldview, one which may help shed light upon the significance of Nebuchadnezzar's affliction in Dan. 4.[4]

5.1.1 Genesis 2–3

The prime example of a biblical text that appears to deal with the boundaries between humans, animals and deities is Genesis 2–3.[5] The Eden narrative contained in these

---

2. Adolf Erman, 'Eine ägyptische Quelle der "Spüche Salomos"', *SPAW* 15 (1924): 86–93. For a recent assessment of their relationship, see Michael V. Fox, 'The Formation of Proverbs 22:17–23:11', *WO* 38 (2008): 22–37.

3. See for example Amanda Norsker, 'Genesis 6,5–9,17: A Rewritten Babylonian Flood Myth', *SJOT* 29 (2015): 55–62.

4. The situation is complex and it is unlikely that there was one unified view; see Ken Stone, 'The Dogs of Exodus and the Question of the Animal', in *Divinanimality: Animal Theory, Creaturely Theology*, ed. Stephen D. Moore, Transdisciplinary Theological Colloquia (New York: Fordham University Press, 2014), 36–50 (49). For a problematization of the idea of definite boundaries between the divine, human and animal in biblical texts, see Hannah M. Strømmen, *Biblical Animality after Jacques Derrida*, Semeia Studies 91 (Atlanta: SBL Press, 2018).

5. There is an alternative creation account in Gen. 1–2:4a but, while Gen. 2–3 seems to be primarily concerned with the creation of the particular (humankind, their status in relation to the rest of creation, and 'the Fall'), Gen. 1 is better understood as a universal creation account (outlining how each part of the entire world came to be). For this classification of creation accounts, see Claus Westermann, *Genesis 1–11: A Continental Commentary*, trans. John J. Scullion (Minneapolis: Fortress Press, 1994), 22–25. Gen. 1–2:4a is commonly thought to be part of the later Priestly (P) source (*ca.* sixth–fifth century BCE), whereas Gen. 2:4b–3:24 is traditionally ascribed to the Yahwist (J) source (and traditionally dated *ca.* tenth–ninth century BCE). See Gordon J. Wenham, *Genesis 1–15*, WBC 1 (Waco, TX: Word Books, 1987), xxv–xxxii. These sources and their respective dates have more recently been contested: see T. Desmond Alexander, *From Paradise to the Promised Land: An Introduction to the Pentateuch*, 3rd ed. (Grand Rapids: Baker Academic, 2012), 43–63; and Thomas B. Doseman and Konrad Schmid, eds, *A Farewell to the Yahwist? The Composition of the Pentateuch in Recent European Interpretation* (Atlanta: SBL Press, 2006). Recently, Ken Stone has problematized the simple distinction between human and animal that has been read in both these creation texts; see Ken Stone, *Reading the Hebrew*

two chapters has often been read by scholars as an attempt to explain the position of humankind in relation to the divine.[6] Significantly for the purposes of this study, this human position is directly associated with the two concepts of wisdom and immortality. The presence of these two key characteristics in the narrative seems to be indicated by the existence of two trees, 'the tree of life [עץ החיים]' and 'the tree of the knowledge of good and evil [עץ הדעת טוב ורע]' (cf. Gen. 2:9).

The first of these trees, the tree of life, seems to function somewhat as a symbol of divine immortality.[7] Eating the fruit of this tree seems to confer eternal life on the consumer, and in Gen. 3:22 Yahweh is concerned that the humans may 'take also from the tree of life, and eat, and live forever [ולקח גם מעץ החיים ואכל וחי לעלם]'. While this connection between the tree and immortality is fairly uncontroversial, there is some scholarly disagreement about whether humankind, prior to their expulsion from Eden (Gen. 3:23–24), initially had access to the tree of life and thus immortality. Some scholars argue that humans were always mortal, though initially they had the *potential* to acquire immortality.[8] This is suggested by Yahweh's fear that humans may subsequently eat from the tree in Gen. 3:22 and is also supported by ancient Near Eastern parallels such as Adapa's failed chance to get immortality himself (*Adapa* B.67–68).[9] Others argue that humans were originally able to eat from this tree and thus had access to eternal life.[10] This would seem to correlate with Yahweh's command that humans could eat from any tree except the tree of knowledge (Gen. 2:16–17), thus at least implying they could eat from the tree of life.[11] Nevertheless, whichever interpretation is followed it is clear by the end of the

Bible with Animal Studies (Stanford: Stanford University Press, 2018), 36–9. However, while a watertight division between human and animal in Gen. 1–3 may be problematic, I nevertheless argue there is compelling evidence that the Eden narrative uses these specific conceptual divine–human–animal boundaries I have previously outlined.

6. Theodore Hiebert, *The Yahwist's Landscape: Nature and Religion in Early Israel* (Oxford: Oxford University Press, 1996), 64–65; Mettinger, *Eden Narrative*, 60; John Day, *From Creation to Babel: Studies in Genesis 1–11* (London: Bloomsbury, 2013), 41–44; John Day, 'Wisdom and the Garden of Eden', in *Perspectives on Israelite Wisdom: Proceedings of the Oxford Old Testament Seminar*, ed. John Jarick, LHBOTS 618 (London: T&T Clark, 2016), 336–352.

7. Mettinger, *The Eden Narrative*, 60; Day, 'Wisdom and the Garden of Eden', 336.

8. E.g., Mettinger, *The Eden Narrative*, 47–9.

9. For a discussion of connections between *Adapa* and Gen. 2–3, see Dexter E. Callender Jr., *Adam in Myth and History: Ancient Israelite Perspectives on the Primal Human*, HSS 48 (Winona Lake, IN: Eisenbrauns, 2000), 79.

10. E.g., Clifford, *Creation Accounts*, 147–148.

11. The notion of original immortality also has a potential parallel in *The Atrahasis Epic*, however this is contested; see above: §4.2.2. For a historical overview of both interpretations, see Paul Humbert, *Etudes sur le récit du Paradis et de la chute dans la Genèse* (Neuchâtel: Secrétariat de l'université, 1940), 125–127.

narrative that the remaining boundary between human and deity is based around the concept of immortality. After Yahweh has expressed fear that the humans may eat the tree's fruit and gain eternal life (Gen. 3:22), they are decisively cast out of the garden with both cherubim and a flaming sword positioned to stop them accessing the tree of life (Gen. 3:24). This creates a crucial division between humankind and divine immortality, one that seems to echo Mesopotamian tradition.

The second tree, the tree of the knowledge of good and evil (ורע עץ הדעת טוב), seems to function similarly though as a symbol of the other divine attribute: wisdom. The fruit of this tree appears to confer wisdom to the individual, a fact recognized by the woman who saw 'that the tree was to be desired to make one wise [להשכיל]' (Gen. 3:6). The serpent further clarifies that after eating the fruit 'your eyes will be opened, and you will be like God [/gods], knowing good and evil [ונפקחו עיניכם והייתם כאלהים ידעי טוב ורע]' (Gen. 3:5).[12] Wisdom here is clearly considered a divine attribute; by gaining this new knowledge the humans 'will be like God' or 'will be like gods' (כאלהים). This is latterly confirmed by Yahweh himself who states, after the humans have eaten the fruit, that 'the man has become like one of us [i.e., one of the *elohim*], knowing good and evil' (Gen. 3:22). Wisdom was therefore part of the original distinction between divine and human. After humans acquire wisdom, immortality must be categorically denied to them in order to prevent them becoming fully divine (cf. Gen. 3:22–24). It is striking that this parallels so closely the acquisition of wisdom but failure to acquire immortality found across wider ancient Near Eastern mythology.[13]

The significance or meaning of this wisdom/knowledge imparted by the tree's fruit has been much debated. Many interpretations have been offered,[14] but one in particular seems to be most pertinent in the context of comparative Mesopotamian material. Jeffrey Tigay proposed that the wisdom conferred by the tree of knowledge should be understood as 'the mental capacity which distinguishes man from beast' which he named as 'civilizing human rationality'.[15] He noted a parallel with the figure of Enkidu in *The Gilgamesh Epic*, whose acquisition of wisdom/reason in *Gilgamesh* I.202 begins the process of his civilization and humanization. Tigay specifically points out how this wisdom is said to make Enkidu 'like a god' (*ki-i ili ta-ba-aš-ši*) (*Gilgamesh* I.207) which is echoed in the serpent's claim that 'you will be like God/gods' (Gen. 3:5) and Yahweh's statement that humans have become 'like one of us' (Gen. 3:22). This divine-like

---

12. The link between 'knowledge of good and evil' and 'wisdom' is supported by 2 Sam. 14:17–20; see Callender, *Adam in Myth and History*, 69–70.

13. For example: *Adapa* A.i.3–4; *Gilgamesh* I.1–8; *Gilgamesh* OB VA+BM iii.2–5.

14. For a survey of these different interpretative options, see Westermann, *Genesis 1–11*, 242–5; and Day, 'Wisdom and the Garden of Eden', 337–339.

15. Tigay, 'Paradise', 625.

wisdom therefore initiates humankind's civilization and ultimate distinction from the animal world.[16]

In fact, there are several further ways in which Gen. 2–3 parallels the Mesopotamian tradition of humankind's acquisition of wisdom. Before receiving wisdom, the newly-created humans in Eden are initially naked (Gen. 2:25) and ate directly from trees (Gen. 2:16–17) rather than grow crops or make bread. This is strikingly reminiscent of the primordial humans in *Sheep and Grain* 20–25 who were naked, ate grass like sheep and did not know how to make bread. This may indicate the absence of any clear boundary between animals and humans at this stage.[17] Even the communication between the woman and the serpent in Gen. 3:1–5 perhaps suggests an original closeness between humans and animals.[18] There does seem to be some difference between humans and animals in Gen. 2–3 as animals are not satisfactory partners for the man and, having been created first, he names the rest (Gen. 2:18–20). However, this does not necessitate the existence of a categorical boundary or hierarchy between them – rather, this simply suggests the lack of close physical kinship.[19] By contrast, after receiving wisdom through consumption of the fruit of the tree of knowledge, the humans become aware of their nakedness and put on garments (Gen. 3:7), they get food through the agricultural working of the ground (Gen. 3:17–19), and they are cast out of the company of the animals (Gen. 3:23–24). These are all typical markers of civilization seen in other Mesopotamian texts. For example, after gaining wisdom/reason, Enkidu both acquires human clothing (*Gilgamesh* II.34–36) and becomes disconnected from the animal world (*Gilgamesh* I.195–202), whilst the introduction of agriculture is the defining characteristic of civilization (and thus separation from the animals) in *Sheep and Grain* 54–58.

Therefore, by the end of the Eden narrative in Gen. 2–3, the divine–human boundary has been established through the denial of the tree of life (and thus immortality) to humankind. Furthermore, through their consumption of fruit from the tree of the knowledge of good and evil, humankind has acquired wisdom,

---

16. See further David P. Melvin, 'Divine Mediation and the Rise of Civilization in Mesopotamian Literature and in Genesis 1–11', *JHebS* 10.17 (2010): 1–15 (14); and Newsom with Breed, *Daniel: A Commentary*, 141.

17. Batto, *Slaying the Dragon*, 56. For the idea that clothing functions as a marker of the human–animal boundary in Gen. 2–3, see Isaac Alderman, *The Animal at Unease with Itself: Death Anxiety and the Animal-Human Boundary in Genesis 2–3* (London: Lexington Books/ Fortress Academic, 2020).

18. Interestingly, the book of Jubilees initially depicts greater solidarity between humans and animals until Adam is subsequently distinguished from the animals by retaining his ability to speak (which the other animals lose); see A. Rahel Wells, '"One Language and One Tongue": Animal Speech in *Jubilees* 3:27–31', *JSP* 28 (2019): 319–337.

19. See Joseph Blenkinsopp, *Creation, Un-creation, Re-creation: A Discursive Commentary on Genesis 1–11* (London: T&T Clark, 2011), 70.

separating them from the animals and thereby also establishing the human–animal boundary too. The use of both wisdom and immortality in this narrative to construct and maintain divine–human–animal boundaries echoes the influence and adaptation of the same Mesopotamian worldview identified in chapter 4. Here too the divine has both wisdom and immortality, humans are characterized by their acquisition of the former but failure to acquire the latter, and animals have neither. Humankind is thus defined over and against the other animals by their divine-like wisdom and rationality.

5.1.2 Ezekiel 28:1–10

While Gen. 2–3 is the prime example, there are further biblical passages which appear to allude to this same ancient Near Eastern worldview regarding divine–human–animal boundaries. Within Ezek. 28:13–16 there are many parallels with the Genesis Eden narrative (e.g., a garden in Eden, a cherub guardian, the casting out of the man), and interestingly in this immediate context there is another reiteration of such boundaries.[20] Ezek. 28:1–10 contains an oracle against a ruler of Tyre who is described as claiming divine status:

[28:2]Mortal [בן־אדם], say to the prince of Tyre, Thus says the Lord God: Because your heart is proud and you have said, 'I am a god [אל אני]; I sit in the seat of the gods, in the heart of the seas,' yet you are but a mortal [אדם], and no god, though you compare your mind with the mind of a god [לבך כלב אלהים]. [3]You are indeed wiser [חכם] than Daniel; no secret is hidden from you; [4]by your wisdom [בחכמתך] and your understanding [ובתבונתך] you have amassed wealth for yourself, and have gathered gold and silver into your treasuries. [5]By your great wisdom [חכמתך] in trade you have increased your wealth, and your heart has become proud in your wealth. (Ezek 28:2–5)[21]

20. For a discussion of parallels and differences between Ezek. 28:11–19 and Gen. 1–3, see John L. McKenzie, 'Mythological Allusions in Ezek 28:12–18', *JBL* 75 (1956): 322–327 (326–327); Callender, *Adam in Myth and History*, 87–135; Mettinger, *Eden Narrative*, 87–90. It is worth noting that expressions of the concept of the *imago dei* in Ezekiel and Genesis differ significantly; see Casey A. Strine, 'Ezekiel's Image Problem: The Mesopotamian Cult Statue Induction Ritual and the *Imago Dei* Anthropology in the Book of Ezekiel', *CBQ* 76 (2014): 252–272; Casey A. Strine, 'Theological Anthropology and Anthropological Theology in the Book of Ezekiel', in *Das Buch Ezechiel: Komposition, Redaktion und Rezeption*, ed. Jan Christian Gertz, Corinna Körting, and Markus Witte, BZAW 516 (Berlin: De Gruyter, 2019), 233–254.

21. The apparent reference to Daniel (or Danel) in this section (Ezek. 28:3) is particularly intriguing; however, any identification of this figure with the eponymous character in the book of Daniel is difficult to maintain. Nevertheless, John Day argues it is possible that 'features of the Daniel alluded to by Ezekiel have contributed to the depiction of the hero of the book of Daniel'. See John Day, 'The Daniel of Ugarit and Ezekiel and the Hero of the Book of Daniel', *VT* 30 (1980): 174–184 (174).

The Tyrian prince sets himself up as divine and this is communicated by likening his mind (לב) to a god's (Ezek. 28:2, 6). The Hebrew word for mind or heart (לב) is often associated with mental or intellectual faculties (e.g., Job 11:12; Hos. 4:11) and suggests that to become god-like requires particular rational characteristics.[22] Moreover, the mind or heart is also often associated with being wise (e.g., Exod. 31:6 and Prov. 23:15) and the ruler of Tyre's attempted self-deification is explicitly linked with his great wisdom (חכם).[23]

While the ruler of Tyre is god-like in his wisdom, his claim to divinity ultimately seems to fail due to his own mortality. This is not explicitly laid out within the Tyrian prince's assertions (Ezek. 28:2–5), however in the following verses Yahweh states that strangers will be brought against Tyre:[24]

> [28:8]They shall thrust you down to the Pit, and you shall die a violent death in the heart of the seas. [9]Will you still say, 'I am a god' [אלהים אני], in the presence of those who kill you, though you are but a mortal [אדם], and no god [ולא אל], in the hands of those who wound you? (Ezek. 28:8–9)

This section clearly outlines the method by which Yahweh can defeat claims to divinity. When faced with the prospect of death, embodied in 'those who kill' and 'those who wound' (Ezek. 28:9), the Tyrian prince's claims to be a god will come to nothing and he will realize his essentially human status. Thus, mortality functions as the distinguishing feature which disproves the divinity of the human ruler.[25] Therefore, by comparing himself to gods through his wisdom (which is seemingly an attempted self-deification), the prince of Tyre is threatened with death which makes his humanity apparent to him. This text seems to similarly use the divine characteristics of wisdom and immortality as indicators of the divine–human boundary.

---

22. Nancy R. Bowen, *Ezekiel*, AOTC (Nashville: Abingdon, 2010), 170; Mettinger, *Eden Narrative*, 91–92.

23. Some scholars argue that the references to wisdom in Ezek. 28:3–5 are a later insertion; see Robert R. Wilson, 'The Death of the King of Tyre: The Editorial History of Ezekiel 28', in *Love and Death in the Ancient Near East: Essays in Honor of Marvin H. Pope*, ed. John H. Marks and Robert M. Good (Guildford, CT: Four Quarters, 1987), 211–218 (212). However, the wisdom theme occurs elsewhere in this section where it is reiterated as the reason for the king's punishment (Ezek. 28:6). Nevertheless, even if 28:3–5 was a subsequent addition to the passage it still demonstrates an essential association between wisdom and divine status albeit expressed on the part of a later editor. For similar arguments, see Mettinger, *Eden Narrative*, 90–92; Peter T. Lanfer, 'Solomon in the Garden of Eden: Autonomous Wisdom and the Danger of Discernment', in *Sibyls, Scriptures, and Scrolls: John Collins at Seventy*, ed. Joel Baden, Hindy Najman, and Eibert Tigchelaar (Leiden: Brill, 2016), 714–725 (722 n. 18).

24. While mortality is not mentioned in these opening verses, note the NRSV translation of אדם at 28:2 as 'mortal'.

25. For a similar interpretation, see Mettinger, *Eden Narrative*, 93.

5.1.3 Psalm 8

Another such case is Psalm 8 which seems to describe a similar tripartite division of humans, animals and the divine. The chief concern of the psalm is to assert the majesty and glory of Yahweh, illustrated by the opening and closing remarks of the poem (Ps. 8:1, 9). However, a secondary interest is to describe the place of humankind within the world. After extolling Yahweh, the psalmist then asks:

> [8:4]What are human beings [אֱנוֹשׁ] that you are mindful of them, mortals [בֶּן־אָדָם] that you care for them? [5]Yet you have made them a little lower than God [וַתְּחַסְּרֵהוּ מְעַט מֵאֱלֹהִים], and crowned them with glory and honour. [6]You have given them dominion over the works of your hands; you have put all things under their feet, [7]all sheep and oxen, and also the beasts of the field, [8]the birds of the air, and the fish of the sea, whatever passes along the paths of the seas. (Ps. 8:4–8)

Humans are here situated within a strict hierarchy of beings: they are lower than gods (Ps. 8:5), but other animals are in turn beneath humans (Ps. 8:6–8).[26] While precise details about these distinctions are thin, many commentators note that the psalm appears to describe humankind as being granted divine-like qualities which somehow divide them from the animals.[27] Thus Ps 8, while not referring to wisdom or immortality directly,[28] appears to nevertheless envisage a similar tripartite distinction between humans, animals, and the divine.

5.1.4 Proverbs 30:2–3, Job 18:3 and Psalm 73:22

Other biblical texts do seemingly refer to wisdom as a distinctly human characteristic, differentiating humankind from the animals. The words of Agur in Proverbs 30 begin with the statement:

> [30:2]Surely I am too stupid to be human; I do not have human understanding. [3]I have not learned wisdom, nor have I knowledge of the holy ones.
> כי בער אנכי מאיש ולא־בינת אדם לי: ולא־למדתי חכמה ודעת קדשים אדע: (Prov. 30:2–3)

---

26. This tripartite hierarchy is represented pictorially in Keith Carley, 'Psalm 8: An Apology for Domination', in *Readings from the Perspective of Earth*, ed. Norman C. Habel, The Earth Bible 1 (Sheffield: Sheffield Academic Press, 2000), 111–124 (114).

27. For example: Nahum M. Sarna, *On the Book of Psalms: Exploring the Prayers of Ancient Israel* (New York: Schocken Books, 1993), 66; and Marvin E. Tate, 'An Exposition of Psalm 8', *Perspectives in Religious Studies* 28 (2001): 343–359 (355).

28. Note, however, the NRSV translation of בֶּן־אָדָם (lit. 'son of Adam/man') at 8:4 as 'mortals'.

The author is clearly being self-deprecating, but the language used here reveals a functional distinction between human and animal. Agur distances himself from humans by describing himself as lacking both human understanding (בינת אדם) and wisdom (חכמה), and further affirms that he is too stupid (בער) to be human. The declared lack of these mental capacities forces him to surrender his identity as a human. Simultaneous with Agur's confession about his lack of wisdom and understanding is his re-identification with an animal status. He describes himself as בער which is derived from the word for beast or livestock (בעיר), suggesting that Agur sees himself as animal-like rather than human.[29] In fact, בער can be specifically described as a lack of 'the rationality that differentiates men from animals'.[30] Thus, without the capacity for wisdom/reason associated with humans, Agur equates himself with an animal. Other wisdom texts make the same rhetorical point:

> Why are we counted as cattle [כבהמה]? Why are we stupid [נטמינו] in your sight? (Job 18:3)

> I was senseless [בער] and ignorant [אדע]; I was a brute beast [בהמות] before you. (Ps. 73:22)

These statements do not literally indicate the authors' complete lack of reason nor a new adopted status as animals, as the reference to being like an animal is an established wisdom metaphor about the foolish.[31] However, while this assertion is evidently rhetorical, such language nevertheless provides evidence of wisdom/reason functioning as a marker of humanity and the defining feature of the human–animal boundary, without which an individual is rendered animal-like.

5.1.5 Ecclesiastes 3:18–21 and Psalm 49:12, 20

The shared mortal nature of humans and animals (as distinct from that of the gods) is also evidenced in the Hebrew Bible. While the divine characteristic of wisdom/reason seems to be uniquely human, Eccl. 3:18–21 nevertheless recognizes their mortality along with other animals:

> [3:18]I said in my heart with regard to human beings [בני האדם] that God is testing them to show that they are but animals [בהמה]. [19]For the fate of humans [בני־האדם] and the fate of animals [הבהמה] is the same; as one dies, so dies the other [כמות זה כן מות זה]. They all have the same breath, and humans have no

---

29. Crawford H. Toy, *A Critical and Exegetical Commentary on the Book of Proverbs*, ICC (Edinburgh: T&T Clark, 1899), 521; Tremper Longman III, *Proverbs*, BCOTWP (Grand Rapids: Baker Academic, 2006), 521

30. Chou-Wee Pan, 'בער' *NIDOTTE*, 1:691.

31. Frank-Lothar Hossfeld and Erich Zenger, *Psalms 2: A Commentary on Psalms 51–100*, trans. Linda M. Maloney, Hermeneia (Minneapolis: Fortress, 2005), 233.

advantage over the animals [ומותר האדם מן־הבהמה אין]; for all is vanity. [20]All go to one place; all are from the dust, and all turn to dust again. [21]Who knows whether the human spirit [רוח בני האדם] goes upward and the spirit of animals [רוח הבהמה] goes downward to the earth? (Eccl. 3:18–21)

This statement is reminiscent of Qoheleth's earlier statement that both the wise (החכם) and the foolish (הכסיל) must die (Eccl. 2:12–16). In each case, despite one group possessing more advanced wisdom/reason which seemingly elevates them above the other, both groups are ultimately united in death.[32] To emphasize the shared mortality of human and animal, Qoheleth recalls their common origin as creatures made from the dust (Eccl. 3:20). This not only recalls their creation in Eden (Gen. 2:7, 19; 3:19), but seems to echo the description of the shared origins of humans and animals in the Mesopotamian tradition (see above: §4.3.1.1). This emphasis on the mortality of humankind also highlights their distinction from the divine who does have eternal life. Marie Turner argues that the 'testing' (לברם; Eccl. 3:18) is to help humankind learn that immortality is an exclusively divine characteristic.[33] Not only does mortality unite humankind with animals, it also categorically divides them from the divine. This again seems to correlate with the principle within Mesopotamian tradition that only the divine have immortality (e.g., *Gilgamesh* OB VA+BM iii.2–5; etc.).

Similar sentiments are found in Psalm 49, which also focuses on mortality and wisdom.[34] Ps 49:20 affirms that:

> Man in his pomp, yet without understanding, is like the beasts that perish. [ESV]
> (Ps 49:20) אדם ביקר ולא יבין נמשל כבהמות נדמו

In their mortality, humans are equal to animals. However, it is also possible to deduce from this text that a human's capacity for understanding or discernment could make them distinct from animals. This same sentiment was probably also at one time expressed in Ps. 49:12.[35] These two verses appear to not only emphasize

---

32. Despite these comments, Qoheleth does not view humans and animals as categorically equal. See Choon-Leong Seow, *Ecclesiastes: A New Translation with Introduction and Commentary*, AB 18c (London: Doubleday, 1997), 175.

33. Marie Turner, *Ecclesiastes: An Earth Bible Commentary: Qoheleth's Eternal Earth*, Earth Bible Commentary (London: Bloomsbury T&T Clark, 2017), 65–66.

34. For its relationship to Ecclesiastes 3, see Pierre Casetti, *Gibt es ein Leben vor dem Tod?: Eine Auslegung von Psalm 49*, OBO 44 (Göttingen: Vandenhoeck & Ruprecht, 1982), 285.

35. The extant texts of the MT of v. 12 actually have ילין ('to lodge') rather than יבין ('to understand') although the Qumran evidence suggests v. 12 should be reconstructed identically to v. 20. See Patrick W. Skehan, Eugene Ulrich and Peter W. Flint, '85. 4QPsᶜ', in *Qumran Cave 4.XI: Psalms to Chronicles*, ed. Eugene Ulrich et al., DJD 16 (Oxford: Clarendon, 2000), 49–61 (56–57). This is also why the ESV translation cited (so too the KJV, etc.) is preferable to the NRSV here.

their shared mortality but also indicate the role of wisdom/reason in nevertheless distinguishing between human and animal.

5.1.6 1 Enoch 7–9 and 69

An example of later Second Temple period material that appears to inherit Mesopotamian traditions about the divine-human-animal boundary is 1 Enoch. The first part of 1 Enoch, known as the Book of the Watchers (1 En. 1–36), describes how rebel angels (the Watchers) took human wives who engendered giant offspring. These angels also began to teach their human wives about 'magical medicine, incantations, the cutting of roots, and taught them (about) plants' (1 En. 7:1).[36] Further detail about this is provided in 1 En. 8:1–4, before the Watchers are later described as having 'taught all (forms of) oppression upon the earth. And they revealed eternal secrets which are performed in heaven (and which) man learned' (1 En. 9:6). Furthermore, this same tradition about angelic instruction is revised and recounted in the second section of 1 En. known as the Book of Parables or the Similitudes of Enoch (1 En. 37–71).[37] Amongst the various activity of the angels, the work of one called Pineme is described:

> [69:8]This one demonstrated to the children of the people the bitter and the sweet and revealed to them all the secrets of their wisdom [ኩሎ ጎቡአተ ጥበቦሙ | *kʷulo ḫəbuʾata ṭababomu*]. [9]Furthermore he caused the people to penetrate (the secret of) writing and (the use of) ink and paper; on account of this matter, there are many who have erred from eternity to eternity, until this very day. [10]For human beings are not created for such purposes to take up their beliefs with pen and ink. [11]For indeed human beings were not created but to be like angels, permanently to maintain pure and righteous lives. Death, which destroys everything, would have not touched them, had it not been through their knowledge [አእምሮቶሙ | *ʾaʾəmarotomu*] by which they shall perish; death is (now) eating us by means of this power. (1 En. 69:8–11)

---

36. Translated by Ephraim Isaac, *OTP* 1:5–90. Some Aramaic fragments of these relevant sections of 1 En. have been found at Qumran; see Jozef T. Milik, ed., *The Books of Enoch: Aramaic Fragments of Qumran Cave 4* (Oxford: Clarendon, 1976). The Ethiopic is quoted from the critical text in: Michael A. Knibb, *The Ethiopic Book of Enoch: A New Edition in the Light of the Aramaic Dead Sea Fragments*, 2 vols (Oxford: Clarendon, 1978).

37. For the relationship between these two traditions in 1 En., see George W. E. Nickelsburg and James C. Vanderkam, *1 Enoch 2: A Commentary on the Book of 1 Enoch Chapters 37–82*, Hermeneia (Minneapolis: Fortress, 2012), 55–7. The Book of the Watchers has been dated *ca.* 250 BCE, and the Book of Parables *ca.* 75 CE; see Philip S. Alexander, 'The Enochic Literature and the Bible', in *The Bible as Book: The Hebrew Bible and the Judaean Desert Discoveries*, ed. Edward D. Herbert and Emanuel Tov (London: British Library & Oak Knoll Press in association with The Scriptorium Center for Christian Antiquities, 2002), 57–69 (69). Cf. Isaac, '1 (Ethiopic Apocalypse of) Enoch', 6–7.

In all of these passages, the angelic instruction is depicted as the revelation to humankind of a knowledge or wisdom which was otherwise concealed from them. Through the acquisition of this secret divine knowledge, humankind is changed. This revelation of 'the secrets of their wisdom' (1 En. 69:8) is described by George Nickelsburg as a transgression of the divine–human boundary which provides 'a means for earthlings to play God by (attempting to) learn of a future that was rightly hidden from them'.[38] As well as granting humans divine wisdom, this angelic revelation also affirms the distinctly mortal nature of humans. Death is explicitly related to humankind's acquisition of new knowledge and has a crucial role in differentiating them from heavenly creatures (1 En. 69:11). This Enochic tradition thus seems once again to use notions of wisdom and immortality to define humankind and its boundaries with other creatures.

Moreover, while there is a clear similarity between the Enochic tradition and the previously described Mesopotamian tradition with regard to the role played by wisdom and immortality, both also provide similar roles for divine intermediaries. The dissemination of divine knowledge by the Watchers in 1 En. closely resembles the role of the *apkallu* who (as previously seen) provide civilizing knowledge to humans in the Mesopotamian tradition (e.g., Berossus, *Babyloniaca* 1b.4; *Bīt Mēseri* 7–9; see §4.3.1.3.2). Such is the degree of similarity that the Watchers appear to be a deliberate and distinctly Jewish reinterpretation of the *apkallu*.[39] Through this adaptation, the *apkallu* have become wicked rebels who corrupted humankind.[40]

The presentation of the Watchers outlined here indicates that Mesopotamian traditions about both wisdom and immortality, and the boundaries they govern, were being adopted and adapted within the Enochic tradition. This itself suggests that, during the Second Temple period, Jewish texts were still to some extent shaped and influenced by such divine–human–animal boundaries found in ancient Mesopotamia.

5.1.7 Sirach 17:1-10, 4QWords of the Luminaries, and 4QMeditation on Creation

A final selection of Second Temple period texts also seem to refer to humankind's relationship with immortality and knowledge/wisdom and their significance

---

38. George W. E. Nickelsburg, *1 Enoch 1: A Commentary on the Book of 1 Enoch Chapters 1–36; 81–108*, Hermeneia (Minneapolis: Fortress, 2001), 46 and 40–41.

39. For example, see Amar Annus, 'On the Origin of the Watchers: A Comparative Study of the Antediluvian Wisdom in Mesopotamian and Jewish Traditions', *JSP* 19 (2010): 277–320; Kvanvig, *Primeval History*, 523–526.

40. Annus, 'On the Origin of the Watchers', 280.

for divine–human–animal boundaries. This is evidenced, for instance, in Sirach 17:[41]

> ¹The Lord created human beings out of earth, and makes them return to it again. ²He gave them a fixed number of days, but granted them authority over everything on the earth. ³He endowed them with strength like his own, and made them in his own image. ⁴He put the fear of them in all living beings, and gave them dominion over beasts and birds. ⁶Discretion and tongue and eyes, ears and a mind for thinking he gave them [καρδιαν ἔδωκεν διανοεισθαι αὐτοις]. ⁷He filled them with knowledge and understanding [ἐπιστημην συνεσεως ἐνεπλησεν αὐτους], and showed them good and evil [και ἀγαθα και κακα ὑπεδειξεν αὐτοις]. ⁸He put the fear of him into their hearts to show them the majesty of his works. ¹⁰And they will praise his holy name, ⁹to proclaim the grandeur of his works. (Sir. 17:1–10)[42]

Firstly, the text reiterates the mortality of humankind by describing their eventual return to the earth and the limitation of their days. This mortality appears to be presented as the intended nature of humans from their creation, as opposed to immortality which is elsewhere pronounced as belonging to the divine (Sir. 18:1; 36:22). Yet, after stressing the transience of humankind, Sirach then enumerates the variety of other gifts that Yahweh has given to humans. For example, they have authority (Sir. 17:2), strength (17:3), and dominion (17:4). While the statement of their mortality likens humans to all other living creatures (cf. Sir. 16:30), these other gifts represent the attributes which make humankind unique.[43] Such gifts

---

41. The original Hebrew version of Ben Sira was probably composed *ca.* 190 BCE; see Friedrich Vinzenez Reiterer, 'Review of Recent Research on the Book of Ben Sira (1980–1996)', in *The Book of Ben Sira in Modern Research: Proceedings of the First International Ben Sira Conference 28–31 July 1996 Sosterberg, Netherlands*, ed. Pancratius C. Beentjes, BZAW 255 (Berlin: De Gruyter, 1997), 23–60 (37).

42. Sadly, there is no extant Hebrew text for this section of Sirach. Verse 5 (attested only in the Lucianic recension manuscripts: 248, 493, 637; plus 404 and 795) is probably a Greek gloss reflecting Stoic ideas so is not included above, however it is worth quoting here: 'They obtained the use of the five faculties of the Lord; as sixth he distributed to them the gift of mind [νουν], and as seventh, reason [λογον], the interpreter of one's faculties.' There are further complications with the Greek text between verses 8–10, reflected in the non-linear verse numberings. For a discussion of this, see Patrick W. Skehan and Alexander Di Lella, *The Wisdom of Ben Sira: A New Translation with Notes*, AB 39 (London: Yale University Press, 1987), 279 n. 8b–10. The Greek text is taken from: Joseph Ziegler, ed., *Sapientia Iesu Filii Sirach*, Septuaginta: Vetus Testamentum Graecum 12.2, 2nd ed. (Göttingen: Vandenhoeck & Ruprecht, 1980).

43. For a treatment of humankind's unique attributes in Sir. 17, see Hilary Marlow, '"What Am I in a Boundless Creation?" An Ecological Reading of Sirach 16 & 17', *Biblical Interpretation* 22 (2014): 34–50 (44–46).

appear to liken them to the divine (Sir. 17:3), and divorce them from other creatures (17:4). These uniquely human characteristics specifically include intellectual abilities such as 'a mind for thinking [καρδιαν ... διανοεισθαι]'[44] (Sir. 17:6), 'knowledge and understanding [ἐπιστημην συνεσεως]' (17:7), and knowledge of 'good and evil [ἀγαθα και κακα]' (17:7). Scholars have noted how this passage of Sir. 17 seems to be a perceptible revision of the Eden narrative.[45] Unlike Gen. 2–3, where knowledge of good and evil (wisdom) is initially off limits to humans, Sirach proposes that humans were deliberately given this intellectual faculty. Wisdom and knowledge are not forbidden but specifically bestowed by Yahweh upon humankind at their creation.[46] This understanding of humankind's original access to divine wisdom provokes possible parallels with another previously seen Mesopotamian tradition that, rather than having to acquire wisdom, humans were created with it (e.g., *Atrahasis* I.223–9; Berossus, *Babyloniaca* 1b.7). So too in Sir 17, wisdom/knowledge is not acquired secondarily by humankind but nevertheless remains the key attribute which distinguishes humans from animals.

A comparable view of humankind's initial inherent association with wisdom and knowledge is found in a number of Qumran texts. The text of 4QWords of the Luminaries (4Q504–506)[47] seems to reinterpret Gen. 2–3 to propose that humans were originally invested with wisdom:

> [4][... Adam,] our [fa]ther, you fashioned in the image of [your] glory [...] [5][...
> the breath of life] you [b]lew into his nostril, and intelligence and knowledge
> [ובינה ודעת]. (4Q504 8.4–5)[48]

44. Literally: 'a heart for thinking'.

45. For the idea that Sir. 17 is alluding to the tree of the knowledge of good and evil (Gen. 2:7), see John R. Levison, *Portraits of Adam in Early Judaism: From Sirach to 2 Baruch*, JSPSup 1 (Sheffield: Sheffield Academic Press, 1988), 37. The specific meaning of the 'knowledge' has also probably shifted between Genesis and Sirach; see Shane Berg, 'Ben Sira, the Genesis Creation Accounts, and the Knowledge of God's Will', *JBL* 132 (2013): 139–157 (149–151).

46. It could be speculated that, for Ben Sira as a sage and proponent of wisdom, it may have seemed unthinkable that Yahweh might have intended to withhold wisdom from humankind; Skehan and Di Lella, *Wisdom of Ben Sira*, 282.

47. It is also known as 4QDibHam[a-c]. For a discussion of the relationship between 4Q504 and Sir. 17, see Esther G. Chazon, 'The Creation and Fall of Adam in the Dead Sea Scrolls', in *The Book of Genesis in Jewish and Oriental Christian Interpretation: A Collection of Essays*, ed. Judith Frishman and Lucas Van Rompay, Traditio Exegetica Græca 5 (Leuven: Peeters, 1997), 13–23, esp. 19–20.

48. The translation is taken from: Florentino García Martínez and Eibert J. C. Tigchelaar, eds, *The Dead Sea Scrolls Study Edition*, 2 vols. (Leiden: Brill, 1997–1998), 2:1008–1009. See also Maurice Baillet, '504. Paroles des Luminaires (Premier Exemplaire: DibHam[a])', in *Qumran Grotte 4 III (4Q482–4Q520)*, ed. Maurice Baillet, DJD VII (Oxford: Clarendon, 1982), 137–75.

Here, the originating point of humankind's wisdom is not when they eat of the tree of the knowledge of good and evil (Gen. 3:6–7), but instead is identified as the moment when the breath of life is blown into the human's nostrils (Gen. 2:7).[49] Equally, 4QMeditation on Creation (4Q303–4Q305) seemingly refers to humankind receiving knowledge of good and evil before the creation of the woman (Gen. 2:20–22), and thus before their encounter with the tree of knowledge (4Q303 line 8; 4Q305 II.2–3).[50] Thus, in both instances, humankind appears to be given wisdom either around or at the point of their creation, and it is this which separates them from the animals.

5.1.8 Summary

This brief survey has demonstrated that the previously observed Mesopotamian traditions relating to the formation and definition of divine–human–animal boundaries through the twin concepts of wisdom and immortality are also reflected in biblical and early Jewish material. There is evidence within the Hebrew Bible for a similar tripartite hierarchical division of divine, human and animal creatures (e.g., Ps. 8). Immortality seems to be a uniquely divine feature which distinguishes the divine from both humans and animals, who are specifically identified as mortal.[51] Equally, the divine characteristic of wisdom/reason is referred to as the identifying human trait which differentiates them from the animals. It is this which makes them human. The Eden narrative of Gen. 2–3 seemingly uses both these concepts in tandem to describe the origins of humankind's condition, in a manner strikingly similar to that found in other ancient Near Eastern texts (e.g., *Adapa* A.i.3–4, etc.). This section has therefore provided compelling evidence that the general Mesopotamian worldview regarding divine–human–animal boundaries is shared by, and can be found within, early Jewish and Hebrew Bible material, even through the Second Temple period (e.g., 1 Enoch, Sirach, etc.). Having established this relationship, focus can now return to Dan. 4 in order to demonstrate the influence of this worldview on

---

49. It is possible that the knowledge given at this point in 4Q504 should be understood as knowledge about just that which is 'good', and knowledge of 'good *and* evil' comes later. See Jeremy D. Lyon, *The Genesis Creation Account in the Dead Sea Scrolls* (Eugene, OR: Pickwick Publications, 2019), 66–67.

50. For the texts, see Timothy H. Lim, '303. 4QMeditation on Creation A', in *Qumran Cave 4. XXV: Sapiential Texts, Part 1*, ed. Torleif Elgvin et al., DJD 20 (Oxford: Clarendon, 1997), 151–154; Timothy H. Lim, '305. 4QMeditation on Creation C', in *Qumran Cave 4. XXV: Sapiential Texts, Part 1*, ed. Torleif Elgvin et al., DJD 20 (Oxford: Clarendon, 1997), 157–158. For a discussion of knowledge in these texts, see Lyon, *Genesis Creation Account*, 122–125.

51. Stuart Lasine argues that mortality is the basic factor of the human condition in the Hebrew Bible. See Stuart Lasine, *Jonah and the Human Condition: Life and Death in Yahweh's World*, LHBOTS 688 (London: T&T Clark, 2020), 3–20.

that narrative as well, and how it can shed light on the question of Nebuchadnezzar's animal transformation.

5.2 Boundaries in Daniel 4

This worldview that incorporates identifiable divine–human–animal boundaries through the concepts of wisdom/reason and immortality, and which has been seen in Near Eastern, Hebrew Bible and Second Temple texts, is also discernible within Dan. 4 itself. The narrative contains evidence that suggests Nebuchadnezzar interacts with both the boundary between divine and human, and that between human and animal. In this section these boundaries are addressed each in turn, to demonstrate how the king potentially threatens the divine–human boundary with claims to immortality, then secondly and crucially for my argument, how the king is varyingly positioned across the human–animal boundary through his possession or loss of wisdom/reason. This analysis will primarily assess the narrative in the MT textual tradition for evidence of these boundaries as, for the most part, Θ follows the MT in its depiction of the king's affliction and the OG's animalising portrayal of the king's affliction ultimately relies upon the MT too.[52] This study will therefore conclude that, while it was previously demonstrated that the portrayal of Nebuchadnezzar in the texts of Dan. 4 is not indicative of a *physical* metamorphosis, when the narrative is examined with this ancient worldview and these divine–human–animal boundaries in mind, the king seems to legitimately transgress the human–animal boundary. There is thus evidence for a far more significant or meaningful animal transformation than that envisaged and debated by the interpreters discussed in chapter 2, one that is conceptual rather than physical.

5.2.1 *The Divine–Human Boundary: Immortality*

The first of the two boundaries that will be focused on is the divine–human boundary and the related concept of immortality. Various evidence can be found within Dan. 4 for this conceptual boundary, particularly in relation to the figure of Nebuchadnezzar. The king appears to threaten the divine–human boundary by attempting to claim possession of divine status for himself, and this is communicated in the narrative using the concept of immortality.

The narrative of Dan. 4 portrays Nebuchadnezzar as exhibiting excessive pride or hubris which causes him to offend the divine. As the chapter closes,

---

52. For the relationship between the depiction of Nebuchadnezzar's affliction in MT and OG, see §3.3.2. The only significant discrepancies between MT and Θ have already been addressed in §3.3.3. All references to Dan. 4 will therefore be from the MT tradition unless otherwise specified.

Nebuchadnezzar concludes his narration by praising the god who 'is able to bring low those who walk in pride [גוה]' (Dan. 4:34) which functions almost as the 'moral' of the tale.[53] This focus on the king's pride is confirmed when the tale is recounted in Dan. 5:20 and Daniel explains that the reason for the royal affliction was that Nebuchadnezzar's 'heart was lifted up [רם] and his spirit grew strong with pride [להזדה]'. The primary failing of Nebuchadnezzar thus appears to be his own pride which incites divine punishment.[54]

On the surface, Nebuchadnezzar's pride might not appear to provide any evidence of the divine–human boundary in Dan. 4; nevertheless, this unfavourable personality trait probably also functions as an attempt by the human king to approach closer to the divine. Interestingly, when Nebuchadnezzar's royal hubris is described, the text uses Aramaic cognates (גוה and רם) of Hebrew verbs (גאה and רום) that are usually utilised to indicate both height and pride, sometimes simultaneously, within the Hebrew Bible.[55] Therefore, through indulging his pride, Nebuchadnezzar is also described as exalting himself, or, quite literally, lifting himself high. This proud self-exaltation necessarily brings Nebuchadnezzar into conflict with the divine who occupies the highest position in the narrative.[56] This exalted divine location is evident simply by the predominant nomenclature that is persistently used about Daniel's god in the narrative; the title: 'the Most High' (Dan. 3:32; 4:14, 21, 22, 29, 31; cf. 5:18, 21). This proper place for the divine is again apparent at the end of the narrative when the king states: 'I, Nebuchadnezzar, praise, exalt (מרומם) and glorify the king of the heavens' (Dan. 4:34).[57] Nebuchadnezzar uses a form of the same verb which previously described his pride or self-exaltation (רם) to now exalt the divine to the highest position in the proper hierarchy. Therefore, at the start of the narrative by claiming a higher position for himself, Nebuchadnezzar is, wittingly or not, appropriating this exalted position of the divine.

Furthermore, this presentation of Nebuchadnezzar's pride as a threat to the divine is perhaps even more explicit in the OG. While this textual edition seems to

53. Heaton, *Book of Daniel*, 145, 156.

54. Cf. Prov. 16:18.

55. Ari Mermelstein, 'Constructing Fear and Pride in the Book of Daniel: The Profile of a Second Temple Emotional Community', *JSJ* 46 (2015): 449–483 (461). For the use of this terminology to denote both height and pride, see Donald E. Gowan, *When Man Becomes God: Humanism and Hybris in the Old Testament*, PTMS 6 (Pittsburgh: Pickwick Publications, 1975), 19–23.

56. Mermelstein, 'Constructing Fear and Pride', 462.

57. The title 'the king of the heavens' (4:34) is the only divine title, other than 'the Most High', to appear in this narrative. Curiously, it is also the only occurrence of this title in the Hebrew Bible; John Collins suggests it is equivalent to the title 'the God of heaven' (e.g., Ezra 1:2; Jonah 1:9) while also emphasising the kingship theme; see Collins, *Daniel: A Commentary*, 232.

be focused upon events surrounding the destruction of Jerusalem's temple (see §3.3.2), it depicts this event as the specific moment of his threat to the divine–human boundary itself:

> Your heart has been exalted in pride and power towards the Holy One and his angels. Your works were seen, how you desolated the house of the living God on account of the sins of the sanctified people. (Dan. 4:19 OG)

Here, his pride and power are juxtaposed with his destructive action in Jerusalem. Through this association, the destruction of the temple is presented as the symbolic event by which Nebuchadnezzar has exalted himself, as well as symbolizing how he has approached and threatened the divine. Thus, even though the OG may have diverse interests, the focus of the narrative on the king's threat to the divine–human boundary is maintained.

Nebuchadnezzar's threatening of the divine position in the narrative, and thus the boundary between human and divine, is confirmed by how the tree, which represents the king, is described in his dream:[58]

> Behold a tree in the middle of the earth and its height [רום] was great. The tree grew great and strong, and its height [רום] reached to the heavens [ימטא לשמיא] and it was visible to the ends of the earth. (Dan. 4:7–8)

The tree's height (רום) is emphasized here (Dan. 4:7, 8; cf. 4:17), resonating with the king's own proud self-exaltation (cf. Dan. 5:20). Significantly however, the tree's height is also described as having 'reached to the heavens' (ימטא לשמיא), a claim repeated later in Dan. 4:17 and 4:19. Within the narrative, 'heaven' seems to

---

58. Interpretation of the great tree in Dan. 4 has been much disputed and a variety of ancient imagery has been proposed to provide the background to Nebuchadnezzar's tree. Most often it has been explained as a form of the Cosmic Tree, e.g.: Lacocque, *Book of Daniel*, 73–8; Gowan, *When Man Becomes God*, 103–104; John E. Goldingay, *Daniel*, WBC 30 (Dallas: Word Books, 1989), 87–8. Recent interpretations have nuanced this idea, e.g.: Newsom with Breed, *Daniel: A Commentary*, 137; Bunta, 'The *Mēsu*-Tree', 364–384; Martin Metzger, 'Zeder, Weinstock, und Weltenbaum', in *Ernten, was man sät: Festschrift für Klaus Koch zu seinem 65. Geburtstag*, ed. Dwight R. Daniels, Uwe Glessmer, and Martin Rösel (Neukirchen-Vluyn: Neukirchener Verlag, 1991), 197–229; Michaela Bauks, 'Sacred Trees in the Garden of Eden and Their Ancient Near Eastern Precursors', *Journal of Ancient Judaism* 3 (2012): 267–301 (288–92). However, it is difficult to ascertain the precise background and context for Nebuchadnezzar's tree because of the complexity of tree symbolism in the ancient Near East. For the historic difficulty of untangling the different branches of such symbolism, see Mariana Giovino, *The Assyrian Sacred Tree: A History of Interpretations*, OBO 230 (Göttingen: Vandenhoeck & Ruprecht, 2007).

represent the divine (Dan. 4:23),[59] so here Nebuchadnezzar's advance towards the divine boundary is made explicit. He has elevated himself so far as to approach the divine realm and thus implicitly claim divinity for himself. In the OG some aspects of the tree's description differ from that in the MT, which may indicate the OG is drawing upon other material,[60] but the key point that the tree is drawing near to the divine realm is evident here too. The top of the tree is said to have 'approached as far as the heaven and its trunk as far as the clouds filling that which is under the heaven, the sun and the moon dwell in it' (Dan. 4:8 OG). The image of the great tree, and thus Nebuchadnezzar, is still depicted as a threat to the boundary between heaven and earth. In fact, this idea seems to be even further elaborated during Daniel's interpretation:

> But that tree was exalted [ἀνυψωθῆναι] and approached the heaven and its trunk touched the clouds – You, O King, have been exalted [ὑψώθης] above all humans who are upon the face of all the earth, your heart has been exalted [ὑψώθη] in pride and power towards the Holy One and his angels. (Dan. 4:19 OG)

Daniel's explanation here explicitly details how Nebuchadnezzar has exalted himself above the rest of humankind and towards the divine. The threatening of the divine–human boundary is thus even more explicitly laid out in Dan. 4:19 OG than in the MT.[61]

This human effort 'to approach the heavens' is found elsewhere in the Hebrew Bible where it also seems to indicate an attempt to seize divine status. A pronounced example is Isa. 14 where the king of Babylon is accused of saying:[62]

> I will ascend to heaven [השמים אעלה]; I will raise [ארים] my throne above the stars of God; I will sit on the mount of assembly on the heights of Zaphon; I

---

59. See Danna N. Fewell, *Circle of Sovereignty: Plotting Politics in the Book of Daniel,* 2nd ed. (Nashville: Abingdon, 1991), 67.

60 The description of the tree touching the clouds may rely on Ezek. 31:10; see Collins, *Daniel: A Commentary,* 224. Various types of ancient sources have been proposed as influences for the reference to both sun and moon; see Henze, *Madness of King Nebuchadnezzar,* 81–83; Holm, *Of Courtiers and Kings,* 453–455.

61. David Satran understands this unique OG section as displaying an amplification of the king's arrogance; see Satran, 'Early Jewish and Christian Interpretation', 80. However, the OG lacks much of the spatial differentiation between divine and human found in the MT. It lacks explicit references to Nebuchadnezzar's self-exaltation which occur at 4:34 MT and 5:20 MT. The divine title of 'the Most High' is also less prominent, appearing as just one of many divine titles in the narrative. This is because the OG is specifically interested in depicting the king's sins; see §3.3.2.

62. Another example is Ezek. 28:1–10 where the prince of Tyre exalts [גבה] his heart and states he is a god (Ezek. 28:2). For further discussion, see §5.1.2.

will ascend to the tops of the clouds, I will make myself like the Most High [אדמה לעליון]. (Isa. 14:13–14)

The Babylonian king's attempt to ascend to heaven betrays an ambition to seize the position of 'the Most High' and assume a divine-like status for himself. Furthermore, apparent parallels between the Danielic depiction of the great tree and the tower of Babel in Gen. 11 support this possible threatening of the divine–human boundary in Dan. 4.[63] There are various parallels between the texts;[64] crucially, however, the tower itself is intended to be built by the people 'with its top in the heavens [וראשו בשמים]' (Gen. 11:4). The pinnacle of this huge construction will stretch beyond the earth and be within the divine realm of the heavens. It may thus be seen as a human attempt to approach the divine or become god-like.[65] This threat to the divine realm is confirmed by the divine response it inspires as Yahweh says:

> 'Come, let us go down [נרדה], and confuse their language there, so that they will not understand one another's speech.' So the LORD scattered [ויפץ] them abroad from there over the face of all the earth. (Gen. 11:7–8)

The tower is so tall that it disturbs the heavenly realm and causes a divine response. Firstly, Yahweh must descend to the people and, once there, he scatters them across the face of the earth. Both of these responses are paralleled in the dream of Dan. 4. In response to the tree's height reaching to the heavens, 'a watcher, a holy one, was descending [נחת] from the heavens' (Dan. 4:10) who then announces the sentence for the tree which will involve the tree being cut down, its branches being stripped and its fruit scattered (בדרו) (Dan. 4:11). Both texts describe a specific tall creation approaching the heavens, which in turn causes a heavenly being to descend in order to stop its growth and scatter its supporters.[66] Additionally, the shared use of cohortative language (Gen. 11:7) with Gen. 3:22 suggests that the Babel story reflects yet another threat to the divine–human boundary, one which again necessitates divine intervention. This parallel between Dan. 4 and Gen 11 therefore lends further weight to the suggestion that Nebuchadnezzar's pride likewise constitutes a threat to the divine realm. Nebuchadnezzar's attempts to reach into

---

63. Many scholars have noticed this parallel, e.g.: Jean Steinmann, *Daniel: Texte français, introduction et commentaires,* Connaître la Bible (Bruges: Desclée de Brouwer, 1961), 57–63; Hartman, 'Great Tree', 78; Coxon, 'Great Tree of Daniel 4', 92; Daewoong Kim, 'Biblical Interpretation in the Book of Daniel: Literary Allusions in Daniel to Genesis and Ezekiel' (PhD diss., Rice University, 2013), 126–166; Alexandria Frisch, *The Danielic Discourse on Empire in Second Temple Literature,* JSJSup 176 (Leiden: Brill, 2016), 112–116.

64. For a wider assessment of connections between the narratives, see Kim, 'Biblical Interpretation', 128–139.

65. Wenham, *Genesis 1–15,* 239.

66. Frisch, *Danielic Discourse on Empire,* 114.

the heavens can thus be understood as an attempt to cross the divine–human boundary and implicitly usurp the divine position.

This interpretation of Nebuchadnezzar as claiming divine status in Dan. 4 is supported by similar attestations outside the Danielic narrative too. The book of Judith (*ca.* 100 BCE)[67] describes Nebuchadnezzar by employing a variety of phrases and qualities that are normally reserved for God.[68] However, this theme is taken further when the activity of Holofernes, Nebuchadnezzar's general, is portrayed:

> He demolished all their shrines and cut down their sacred groves; for he had been commissioned to destroy all the gods of the land, so that all nations should worship [λατρευσωσι] Nebuchadnezzar alone, and that all their dialects and tribes should call upon him as a god [ἐπικαλεσωνται αὐτον εἰς θεον]. (Jdt 3:8)[69]

The Nebuchadnezzar of this story appears to have specifically outlawed all other cults with the intention of setting himself up as the object of worship. Later, in a heated conversation with the Ammonite captain Achior, Holofernes declares:

> Who are you . . . to prophesy among us as you have done today and tell us not to make war against the people of Israel because their God will defend them? *What god is there except Nebuchadnezzar?* (Jdt 6:2, emphasis mine)

In the book of Judith, the king is positioned in direct opposition to the Jewish god, whose own power Holofernes declares is no match for Nebuchadnezzar. Interestingly, the character of Nebuchadnezzar in the book of Judith never directly makes claims to divinity himself, rather they are always on the lips of Holofernes. In fact, after the first two chapters Nebuchadnezzar is absent from the narrative completely. This removal from events helps to portray Nebuchadnezzar as remote and distant, which only adds to this godlike depiction of the king.[70] How exactly this divine depiction of Nebuchadnezzar in Judith relates to Dan. 4 is unclear. Lawrence Wills argues that Judith's Nebuchadnezzar is largely based on the Danielic kings, specifically Nebuchadnezzar's requirement for worship of his golden statue (Dan. 3) and Darius' interdict to pray to any gods aside from the king (Dan. 6).[71] While the Nebuchadnezzar of Dan. 4 never asserts his divinity in such an overt way, his proud self-exaltation towards the divine would fit within this

---

67. For arguments regarding the date of Judith, see Deborah L. Gera, *Judith*, CEJL (Berlin: De Gruyter, 2014), 26–44.

68. For examples, see Gera, *Judith*, 127 and 140; Lawrence M. Wills, *Judith: A Commentary*, Hermeneia (Minneapolis: Fortress, 2019), 181.

69. The Greek text is taken from: Robert Hanhart, ed., *Iudith*, Septuaginta: Vetus Testamentum Graecum 8.4 (Göttingen: Vandenhoeck & Ruprecht, 1979).

70. Gera, *Judith*, 7.

71. Wills, *Judith: A Commentary*, 201.

wider literary context of Nebuchadnezzar's assumption of divine status. Moreover, parallels with Isa. 14, Gen. 11 and Judith, where threats to the divine–human boundary are more explicit, lend further weight to the suggestion that this is similarly implied in Dan. 4.

From the analysis thus far, the narrative of Dan. 4 seems to be concerned with the divine–human boundary. It spatially depicts the difference between divine and human: the divine is above, and the human is below. Nebuchadnezzar, through his pride, attempts to elevate himself which thus threatens the hierarchical distinction between divine and human. Despite this evident interest in the divine–human boundary, the divine attribute of immortality has not thus far been detected in the narrative. However, there is evidence that immortality and eternal life also play a significant role in the relationship between divine and human in Dan. 4.

The purpose of Nebuchadnezzar's affliction is to force him to acknowledge divine authority over his kingdom ('until when you know that the Most High has authority over the human kingdom and he will give it to those whom he desires'; Dan. 4:29). This sentiment is repeatedly asserted throughout the narrative by the Watcher (Dan. 4:14), Daniel (4:22, cf. 4:23 and 5:21), and the heavenly voice (4:29). These statements convey the message that human kings are subject to divine rule which can bring them low at any moment.[72] Nebuchadnezzar's human authority may stretch 'to the ends of the earth' (Dan. 4:19) but ultimately his rule is finite and reliant upon divine approval. On the other hand, divine rule is portrayed as eternal. This is first suggested in the introduction of Dan. 4, which is in the style of a letter, where Nebuchadnezzar provides a doxology based on the lesson he has had to learn. Here, Nebuchadnezzar specifically declares the eternity of divine rule: his 'kingdom is an eternal kingdom' (Dan. 3:33). This theme is picked up again when the narrative closes and as Nebuchadnezzar ends his letter:

> I praised and glorified the one who lives forever, for his authority is an eternal [עלם] authority and his kingdom is from generation and generation. (Dan. 4:31)

By this point Nebuchadnezzar has realized that while his human kingdom is finite, divine sovereignty is eternal, or, as Carol Newsom puts it, 'what distinguishes divine sovereignty from human sovereignty is its everlastingness'.[73] While Nebuchadnezzar seems to have *spatial* sovereignty (Dan. 4:19), 'the Most High' has an *everlasting* sovereignty (3:33; 4:31).

Moreover, these assertions about everlasting divine rule also reinforce the eternal nature of the divine in general. Amongst his claims about eternal divine

---

72. For this as the overall message of Dan. 4, see John J. Collins, *Daniel with an Introduction to Apocalyptic Literature*, FOTL 20 (Grand Rapids: Eerdmans, 1984), 65. For an examination of the contrast between human and divine rule in all the Danielic narratives, see Naama Golan, 'The Daniel Narratives (Dan. 1–6): Structure and Meaning', *JHebS* 19.3 (2019): 1–24.

73. Newsom with Breed, *Daniel: A Commentary*, 135.

authority, Nebuchadnezzar makes the further declaration that 'the Most High' is 'the one who lives for ever' (Dan. 4:31). The response which Nebuchadnezzar takes away from his affliction in the narrative is to acknowledge not only God's everlasting kingdom, but also to recognize that God is immortal – God lives forever. This statement of divine immortality seems to be a general way to refer to the deity, as evidenced in other texts from around a similar time (for example 'the one who lives forever' in Dan. 12:7; or 'he who lives forever created the whole universe' in Sir. 18:1; also cf. Dan. 6:27). Yet this way of referring to the divine runs counter to how Nebuchadnezzar has been presented thus far in the book of Daniel. When he is initially approached by his courtiers, Nebuchadnezzar is greeted with the statement 'O king, live forever!' (Dan. 2:4; 3:9) which was a common ancient Near Eastern royal address and which continues to be used of other kings in the book of Daniel (Dan. 5:10; 6:6, 21).[74] Hannah Strømmen has read this formulaic address as a 'denial of mortal life, as if human kings are nonhuman and could live ad infinitum'.[75] Like other kings in the book of Daniel, Nebuchadnezzar has thus been accustomed to being addressed as if he were immortal and thus more than simply human.[76] The lack of this royal greeting for King Nebuchadnezzar in Dan. 4 is noticeable. Despite being approached by all his magicians and diviners (Dan. 4:4), and by Daniel himself (4:5), no one in Dan. 4 utters this address. Furthermore, the omission of this statement of the king's immortality is especially noticeable as it is the only one of the Aramaic Danielic tales to omit it (cf. Dan. 2:4; 3:9; 5:10; 6:6, 21). Nebuchadnezzar's previous denial of his humanity through his royal status seems therefore to be corrected in Dan. 4 by his admission that the divine is the only one who will truly live for ever (4:31). Immortality thus seems to function as an indicator of the divine–human boundary in Dan. 4. While the king has previously declared immortality for himself and so identified himself with the divine, the effect of the events in Dan. 4 is that Nebuchadnezzar realizes only the divine is truly immortal.

Nebuchadnezzar's claim to immortality may also be seen as the direct cause of his divine affliction. Whilst walking upon his palace, Nebuchadnezzar declares:

> Is this not magnificent Babylon, which I have built as a royal capital by my mighty power and for my glorious majesty? (Dan. 4:27)[77]

74. Collins, *Daniel: A Commentary*, 156.

75. Strømmen, *Biblical Animality*, 105.

76. Daniel James Waller has recently argued that the character of Nebuchadnezzar and the dreams he sees in Dan. 1–4 reflect his anxiety about his own mortality; see Daniel James Waller, 'Sympathy for a Gentile King: Nebuchadnezzar, Exile, and Mortality in the Book of Daniel', *Biblical Interpretation* 28 (2020): 327–346.

77. The OG preserves this same pronouncement (Dan. 4:27 OG) and, at this section, the MT and OG are close enough that the OG may simply be a Greek translation from the Aramaic with only minor adjustments; see Wenthe, 'Old Greek Translation', 143–144.

He proudly asserts his own glory through the construction of his capital city Babylon, and it is this boast which directly results in a heavenly voice declaring that his affliction will come upon him (Dan. 4:28). There is undoubtedly a measure of pride in what the king claims, but his words may also reflect his own attempted pursuit of immortality. Ancient Mesopotamian texts seem to depict the completion of large and permanent construction projects as a means by which to achieve relative or indirect immortality.[78] The builder's name and reputation will be continually honoured, long after their physical death, due to the large architectural achievements they have left behind. This is demonstrated, for example, in *Gilgamesh* XI.323–326 where the king shows off the walls and foundations of his city Uruk (see §4.2.3). Moreover, further evidence for the continued existence of this understanding is found in Sir. 40:19: 'Children and the building of a city establish one's name, but better than either is the one who finds wisdom.' While Ben Sira clearly denigrates such ideas, this text demonstrates the continued existence of the link between building cities and the eternity of a person's name (cf. Eccl 2:1–11). The text of Dan. 4:27 appears to fit this same mould: a king (Nebuchadnezzar) who builds an entire city (Babylon) and proclaims his achievement. Indeed, the literary Nebuchadnezzar's statement here about Babylon is reminiscent of building inscriptions which the historical Nebuchadnezzar made and which have since been discovered.[79] If architecture functioned in this way, as giving an individual a measure of permanence and perpetuity, then by declaring the greatness of his own construction projects it is possible that we can see another trace of Nebuchadnezzar's appropriation of immortality.[80] Furthermore, it is this boast which is the direct cause of the king's affliction. By attempting to claim a form of immortality for himself, Nebuchadnezzar brings upon himself the divine affliction and his exile from the kingdom.

From this assessment of Dan. 4, it has been demonstrated that Dan. 4 is concerned with the divine–human boundary. Nebuchadnezzar presents a threat to this boundary, evidenced by his own proud self-exaltation and his attempt to reach

---

78. Tigay, *Evolution of Gilgamesh*, 7 and 144; Thorbjørnsrud, 'What can the Gilgamesh Myth Tell Us', 130.

79. For example, an inscription on Nebuchadnezzar's palace reads: 'the palace, the house for people to behold, binding bar of the land, bright dwelling place, abode of my royal power, in the land of Babylonia which is in the midst of Babylon'. The text is taken from: Stephen Langdon, *Building Inscriptions of the Neo-Babylonian Empire, Part I: Nabopolassar and Nebuchadnezzar* (Paris: Leroux, 1905), 134–135, no.15, col.7, lines 36–37.

80. It is also plausible that the great tree (Dan. 4:7–9) should be understood as a related form of the tree of life (Gen. 2:9, 3:22, 24). If this connection is made, then it provides further support for the interpretation of Nebuchadnezzar's claim to immortality. He would thus be depicted as a symbol of immortality itself, and it is then this symbol which is destined to be cut down (Dan. 4:11). Parallels between the trees in Dan. 4 and Gen. 2–3 have been noted by: Di Lella, 'Daniel 4:7–14', 255–258. The concept of the tree of life has also previously been associated with Dan. 4; see Widengren, *King and the Tree of Life*, 58.

up to the heavens. However, through the course of events, he is forced to accept his human position beneath the divine authority of 'the Most High'. The exclusively divine characteristic of immortality can also be seen to play a role in how the narrative communicates this divine-human boundary. It is only ever explicitly ascribed to the divine in the narrative, while any assertions of Nebuchadnezzar's immortality are conspicuously absent. When he does seem to claim some form of immortality, a divine affliction is unleashed upon him to remind him of his humanity. It is therefore reasonable for us to see how immortality indicates where the divide between human and divine lies, and that Nebuchadnezzar's claim to possess this attribute can be seen as an overstep of his limits.

5.2.2 The Human–Animal Boundary: Wisdom

The second, and for this study more significant, boundary is that between humans and animals which elsewhere relies upon the characteristic of wisdom/reason. While the degree with which the MT and the OG deal with wisdom varies, it will first be demonstrated how both textual editions are concerned with portraying a specific hierarchical human-animal boundary. Following this, the divine characteristic of wisdom/reason will be examined to see how its presence or absence is indicated in the narrative and how it effectively causes Nebuchadnezzar to be recategorized. Finally, further evidence for the king's loss of wisdom/reason will be assessed including the use of animalising imagery and the change of narration. This discussion will conclude that the human–animal boundary in Dan. 4 is principally indicated by this divine characteristic of wisdom/reason. As part of his divine affliction, wisdom/reason is depicted as being removed from Nebuchadnezzar which in turn is presented as a crossing of the human–animal boundary. Dan. 4 thus uses the divine characteristic of wisdom/reason as the principal indicator of the boundary between human and animal.[81]

---

81. Jared Beverly argues the animalising affliction in Dan. 4 is not a text about the descent of the king and the loss of his reason, rather it concerns the acquisition of an animal mind that he argues is just a different *type* of rationality. To argue this, he relies upon an alternate strand within Hebrew Bible texts which portrays animals as possessing knowledge; see Beverly, 'Nebuchadnezzar and the Animal Mind'. However, while I do not deny the presence of certain texts which ascribe some understanding to animals in the Hebrew Bible, I see no compelling justification for seeing this strand at work in Dan. 4. Furthermore, while Beverly argues that animals may have a different *type* of rationality to humans (rather than lack it completely), beyond admitting that animals have some knowledge of the divine that humans lack he never specifically outlines what makes animal rationality categorically different from humans (or, to use the language of Dan. 4:13, what makes an animal heart categorically different from a human heart). Instead, and for the reasons I outline in the ensuing sections, I propose that the more applicable Hebrew Bible perspective on animal rationality, when explicating Dan. 4, is that animals lack wisdom/reason.

5.2.2.1 Tripartite Hierarchy
The existence of a divide between humans and animals is initially suggested in Dan. 4 through the imagery of the great tree which represents Nebuchadnezzar. At the same time that the tree is depicted as growing up and approaching the heavens (Dan. 4:8), the text also describes how the 'animals of the field sheltered beneath it' (4:9). This description of the great tree, which represents Nebuchadnezzar, is possibly rooted in earlier prophetic material which depicts him as ruling over the animals (Jer. 27:5–6; 28:14; Dan. 2:37–38).[82] In such texts, Nebuchadnezzar is presented as having divinely ordained dominion directly over and above the animal world. However, in Dan. 4 this animal dominion places the king in a specific location. Spatially, the animals are beneath the tree/Nebuchadnezzar (Dan. 4:9), while the tree/Nebuchadnezzar is in turn still beneath the heavens (Dan. 4:8). This spatial hierarchy, already discussed in relation to the divine–human boundary (see §5.2.1), is later re-emphasized in relation to the king's affliction. It is often noted how this affliction functions as an inversion of the king's original dominion so that he becomes just like one of the animals he once ruled.[83] Instead of being the supreme ruler over all peoples and creatures, Nebuchadnezzar is reduced to a position at the bottom of the hierarchy, with the wild animals (Dan. 4:30 MT). Yet, this also seems to reveal the position which the animals themselves occupy. Compared to the height (רום) of hubris which he sought after, by becoming like an animal Nebuchadnezzar assumes a lowlier position. He states how the divine 'is able to bring low [להשפלה]' (Dan. 4:34) even the king of Babylon. The word שפל is used in opposition to רום to indicate not only pride and humility but also the narrative's hierarchical positioning of the characters.[84] Animal life, and the position of Nebuchadnezzar when he is afflicted, is described as lower than both the divine and the usual position of humans.[85] Thus, just as the narrative depicts the divine

---

82. Coxon, 'Great Tree of Daniel 4', 100. For an attempt to understand how this prophetic material relates to one another, see Johanna Erzberger, 'Nebuchadnezzar, Lord of the Wild Animals: Understanding a Difference Between LXX Jer and MT Jer in Light of Dan', in *Die Septuaginta – Orte und Intentionen 5. Internationale Fachtagung veranstaltet von Septuaginta Deutsch (LXX.D), Wuppertal 24.–27. Juli 2014*, ed. Siegfried Kreuzer et al., WUNT 361 (Tübingen: Mohr Siebeck, 2016), 678–687. There may even be explicit links between Dan. 4:7–9 and 2:37–38; see Joshua M. Scheetz, *The Concept of Canonical Intertextuality and the Book of Daniel* (Eugene, OR: Pickwick Publications, 2011), 66.

83. Di Lella, 'Daniel 4:7–14', 257; Coxon, 'Great Tree of Daniel 4', 100; Alec Basson, '"A King in the Grass": Liminality and Inversion in Daniel 4:28–37', *Journal for Semitics* 18 (2009): 1–14 (4); Lacocque, *Book of Daniel*, 80.

84. Mermelstein, 'Constructing Fear and Pride', 462.

85. While I argue that animals are in general conceived as lower than humankind in such a conceptual tripartite hierarchy, I also recognize that there is something unique about animality in Dan. 4. Nebuchadnezzar becomes an animal for a specific purpose, and this leads to his new understanding of 'the Most High'. This suggests that there is something to be learnt from being an animal which the king could not learn by remaining human. For more, see Eric Daryl Meyer, *Inner Animalities: Theology and the End of the Human*, Groundworks: Ecological Issues in Philosopher and Theology (New York: Fordham University Press, 2018), 98–103.

and the heavens as being above humans, animal life is depicted as below them. This is suggestive of some conception of a hierarchical separation between the human and the animal within the text of Dan. 4.

5.2.2.2 Loss of Wisdom/Reason

While there is evidence in the narrative for a division between human and animal, crucially there are also significant reasons to suggest the divine characteristic of wisdom/reason has a role in constructing it. Wisdom itself has a clear presence in the text; e.g., the king's wise counsellors (חכים) are called to interpret his dream (Dan. 4:3) but are ultimately unable to do this (4:4, 15).[86] However the importance of the characteristic of wisdom/reason for the human–animal boundary is only first revealed when the Watcher declares about the king:

> Let its heart [לבב] be changed from that of a human, and let the heart [לבב] of an animal be given to it. (Dan. 4:13)

This change in the king's heart is reiterated by Daniel in the following chapter when he tells Belshazzar how Nebuchadnezzar's 'heart [לבב] became like that of an animal' (Dan. 5:21). This Aramaic word לבב (heart) is related to the Hebrew cognate term that is frequently used elsewhere in the Hebrew Bible. Usage of this Hebrew term לבב is almost always in reference to the human heart,[87] and may refer to a physical aspect of the body (e.g., Exod. 28:29–31; 2 Sam. 18:24; Nah. 2:8), or may be linked to feelings like joy (e.g., 1 Chr. 16:10), sadness (e.g., Jer. 8:18), courage (e.g., Ps. 76:6) and fear (e.g., Deut. 28:65). However, principally the human heart is associated with the mind and reason/wisdom.[88] In such usage, the heart occurs in relation to knowledge (דעת e.g., Deut. 29:3; Prov. 15:14; 18:15; Isa. 47:10), understanding (בינה e.g., 1 Kgs 3:9, 12; Prov. 3:5–6; Isa. 32:4; 44:18–19) and wisdom (חכמה e.g., Exod. 31:6; Ps. 90:12; Prov. 23:15; 16:23; Job 34:34). Such links mean that other English translations often render לבב in Dan. 4:13 as 'mind', for example:

> Let his mind be changed from that of a human, and let the mind of an animal be given to him. (Dan. 4:16 NRSV)

---

86. For a discussion of wisdom in Daniel, see Meadowcroft, *Aramaic Daniel and Greek Daniel*, 42–44.

87. Hans Wolff states there are 858 occurrences of לבב and לב in both Hebrew and Aramaic within the Old Testament. Of these, 27 are associated with a divine heart, 11 with the heart of the sea, and 5 with an animal heart. The rest are exclusively about the human heart; see Hans W. Wolff, *Anthropology of the Old Testament*, trans. Margaret Kohl (London: SCM, 1974), 40. See the earlier discussion of this term in §3.3.1.

88. *DCH* 4, s.v. 'לב'. See also: Wolff, *Anthropology of the Old Testament*, 40–58 (esp. 46); Thomas Krüger, 'Das 'Herz' in der alttestamentlichen Anthropologie', in *Anthropologie Aufbrüche: Alttestamentliche und unterdisziplinäre Zugänge zur historischen Anthropologie*, ed. Andreas Wagner, Forschungen zur Religion und Literatur des Alten und Neuen Testaments 232 (Göttingen: Vandenhoeck & Ruprecht, 2009), 103–118.

While the human heart may be associated with rationality, such Hebrew Bible references to animal hearts do not make this same connection. Other than the two verses describing Nebuchadnezzar, there are only three other situations where לבב refers to animal hearts. These indicate that the animal heart is a physical feature (Job 41:24), and also associate it with feelings (2 Sam. 17:10 seems to suggest a lion's heart is courageous). However, there are no examples which intimate that animal hearts were linked with such mental faculties; indeed Hos. 7:11 seems to explicitly indicate an animal has no intelligence.[89] While the textual evidence about animal hearts in the Hebrew Bible may be limited, those texts which do describe them show that animals lack the rational faculties so commonly associated with human hearts. Thus, by suggesting Nebuchadnezzar's human heart became an animal's, the Danielic text indicates that the king lost his mind and thus wisdom/reason.

This is further strengthened by comparing Dan. 4:13 with Ezek. 28:1–10. As seen earlier (§5.1.2), the ruler of Tyre is described as claiming 'the mind of a god [כלב אלהים]' (Ezek. 28:2 NRSV) which he can do due to his great wisdom (Ezek. 28:3–5). However, as well as demonstrating a link between the heart/mind [לב] and wisdom, comparisons with Ezek 28. also demonstrate how an individual's identity is affected by receiving a different mind. The Tyrian prince compares his 'mind with the mind of a god' which allows him to say, 'I am a god' (Ezek. 28:2). He claims to transcend the divine–human boundary by asserting his possession of a god's mind due to his wisdom. Dan. 4:13 can be understood in a similar way in that the Babylonian ruler Nebuchadnezzar crosses the human–animal boundary by receiving an animal's heart and the lack of wisdom this entails.[90]

Despite varying significantly from the MT in its account about Nebuchadnezzar, the OG indicates a similar connection between his affliction and his heart. Interestingly, there are actually comparatively more references to Nebuchadnezzar's heart (καρδια) in the OG (Dan. 4:19, 25, 30b OG) and, while there is no explicit statement that his heart became like an animal's, it does still change. He states that:

> my hairs became like wings of an eagle, my nails like those of a lion. My flesh and my heart were changed [ἠλλοιώθη ἡ σαρξ μου και ἡ καρδια μου]. (Dan. 4:30b OG)

While this version of events does not explicitly refer to the king's heart being changed into an animal's (as 4:13 MT does), it can still be interpreted this way.

---

89. For a discussion of Hos 7:11, see Mayer I. Gruber, *Hosea: A Textual Commentary,* LHBOTS 653 (London: Bloomsbury, 2017), 324–325.

90. For other possible connections between Ezek 28 and Dan. 4, see Carla Sulzbach, 'Nebuchadnezzar in Eden? Daniel 4 and Ezekiel 28', in *Stimulation from Leiden: Collected Communications to the XVIIIth Congress of the International Organization for the Study of the Old Testament, Leiden 2004,* ed. Hermann M. Niemann and Matthias Augustin, BEATAJ 54 (Frankfurt: Peter Kang, 2006), 125–136.

Firstly, the Greek term καρδια suggests a reference to a mental affliction.[91] Καρδια is often employed in the LXX to translate the Hebrew and Aramaic terms לֵב and לֵבַב (e.g., 1 Sam 16:7; Job 37:1), hence its range of meanings are similar to the Aramaic term (e.g., a physical part of the body, the seat of emotions, etc.) but it is especially used to refer to the source of human rational thought.[92] An example of καρδια used in this way can be found in Sir. 17:6–7 which links it with knowledge, understanding and rational thought (see §5.1.7 above). It is thus reasonable to suggest that, if the OG text is using καρδια in its more common meaning as denoting human thought, then it may suggest that Nebuchadnezzar's human reason has been affected by his affliction. Furthermore, the animalising effect of his change of heart is likewise suggested by the context. It was noted previously that the OG appears to be reworking the affliction of Nebuchadnezzar in order to more closely relate it to the first beast described in Dan. 7:4 (see §3.3.2). Based on this proposed textual relationship, the change of Nebuchadnezzar's heart narrated in Dan. 4:30b OG must be towards an animal's in order for it to then be able to return to a 'human heart' in the corresponding passage in Dan. 7. This understanding seems to be further supported by the proximity with which the phrase 'my flesh and my heart were changed' is placed to the statement that 'my hairs became like wings of an eagle, my nails like those of a lion' (Dan. 4:30b OG). This description, while *not* constituting an actual metamorphosis as the king does not actually acquire animal features (see §3.3.2), does describe specific physical changes undergone by Nebuchadnezzar which give him a physical likeness or resemblance to the beast described in Dan. 7:4. The king's appearance is being presented as similar to an animal which, due to their connection in the text, should guide how we understand the change of the king's heart. Thus, if the change of his physical form causes the king to bear some resemblance to various animals, then the change of his heart in the second half of Dan. 4:30b OG should equally be interpreted as referring to an animalising change. Therefore, the change of the king's heart is associated with both his reason being affected and an animalising change which are both highly indicative that the text is working with similar human–animal boundaries as the ancient Mesopotamian texts.

This link between wisdom/reason and the human heart is made explicit later in the narrative of Dan. 4. After the appointed time has passed and the king's affliction is about to end, Nebuchadnezzar twice states 'my reason [מנדעי] was returned to me' (Dan. 4:31; 33). This Aramaic term מנדע can be defined as 'knowledge, power of knowing',[93] and occurs elsewhere in Dan. 2:21 associated with wisdom (חכמה) and understanding (בינה). Elsewhere in the Hebrew Bible, the corresponding Hebrew term מדע is often explicitly paired with wisdom (חכמה) including in Dan. 1:4, 17.[94]

---

91. See Meadowcroft, *Aramaic Daniel and Greek Daniel*, 41.

92. LEH, s.v. 'καρδία'; *GELS*, s.v. 'καρδία'.

93. BDB, s.v. 'מַנְדַּע'. The act of 'knowing' seems to be a central motif in the MT text of Dan. 4; see Wenthe, 'Old Greek Translation', 137.

94. Similar usage is found in, e.g., 2 Chr. 1:10–12.

Thus when the king received the heart of an animal his reason must also be absent, while the return of Nebuchadnezzar from his exile at the end of his affliction is signalled by the return of his reason. This role of reason/wisdom is strikingly reminiscent of how it is portrayed in other ancient Mesopotamian texts as signalling the change from animal to human (e.g., Enkidu's crossing of the human–animal boundary in *Gilgamesh* I.202).[95] References to Nebuchadnezzar's reason returning to him therefore provide critical evidence that Dan. 4 depicts a similar human–animal boundary to that identified earlier in wider Mesopotamian material.

While the OG lacks references to the king's 'reason' returning to him (cf. Dan. 4:31, 4:33 MT), further evidence for the presence of wisdom/reason occurs with the introduction of a new phrase: Nebuchadnezzar's 'ignorances'. After the seven years have passed, Nebuchadnezzar says:

> I prayed before the Lord God of the heaven concerning my sins [των ἁμαρτιων μου] and I petitioned the great God of gods about my ignorances [των ἀγνοιων μου]. (Dan. 4:30a OG)

Later when the time comes for his affliction to end, he declares 'my sins [αἱ ἁμαρτιαι μου] and my ignorances [αἱ ἀγνοιαι μου] were fulfilled before the God of heaven', and he then asks God 'about my ignorances [περι των ἀγνοιων]' (Dan. 4:30c OG). The term ἀγνοια is linked to the verb 'to know' (γινωσκω) but often refers to an error made through ignorance.[96] This could be the best way to understand the term in 4:30a–c OG, as it appears to be paralleled with the king's sins (ἁμαρτιες) which the Greek narrative shows significant interest in.[97] However, if these references to the king's ignorances are read amidst the context of Nebuchadnezzar's heart change then they may also plausibly be a reference to the king's loss of wisdom/reason. Literally, ἀγνοια refers to ignorance as the want of perception or knowledge, and as such it is in opposition to both γνωσις (knowledge) and σοφια (wisdom).[98] It thus could suggest a lack of knowledge or wisdom and, furthermore, was used in ancient Greek about a general sense of unknowing which denoted being 'uncivilised'.[99] This usage of ἀγνοια may also be found in the LXX; e.g., ignorance appears to result from the abandonment of reason in Wisdom 17:

---

95. The similarity between Dan. 4 and *Gilgamesh* is striking enough that some scholars have attempted to find a greater connection between them; see Ferguson, 'Nebuchadnezzar, Gilgamesh, and the "Babylonian Job"', 326–9. However, the lack of any explicit linguistic connections makes any argument for direct literary dependence between them unconvincing. This scepticism is shared by: Henze, *Madness of King Nebuchadnezzar*, 99; Stökl, 'Nebuchadnezzar', 260.

96. *GELS*, s.v. 'ἀγνοια'; LEH, s.v. 'ἀγνοια'.

97. The pairing of these two Greek terms may be a translation of a specific Hebrew word pairing; see Grelot, 'La Septante de Daniel IV', 21.

98. Eduard Schütz, 'ἀγνοέω', *NIDNTT* 2:406.

99. Rudolph Bultmann, 'ἀγνοια', *TDNT* 1:116.

> For fear is nothing but a giving up of the helps that come from reason [λογος]; and hope, defeated by this inward weakness, prefers ignorance [ἀγνοια] of what causes the torment. (Wis 17:12–13)[100]

Ignorance (ἀγνοια) therefore may denote the lack of wisdom/reason which leads to a human becoming uncivilised. In the context of Dan. 4, where the king's change of heart is described, these ignorances can plausibly be read as the result of Nebuchadnezzar's loss of wisdom/reason. The fact that these ignorances are only fulfilled once his affliction is over (4:30c OG), suggests a link between his lack of wisdom/reason and the animalising affliction he is forced to endure. This therefore may also demonstrate how the text presents the lack of wisdom/reason (ignorance) as signifying an animal change. Thus wisdom/reason, as indicated by this variety of passages from the narrative, functions as the primary indicator of where the human–animal boundary lies.

5.2.2.3 Animal Imagery

The role of wisdom/reason in demonstrating the human–animal boundary is further confirmed by how Nebuchadnezzar himself is described when he undergoes his animalising affliction. He lives out with the animals away from other humans (Dan. 4:22; 4:29; 4:30; 5:21; cf. 4:12, 22, 29 OG), he is exposed to the elements and made wet by them (Dan. 4:12; 4:20; 4:22; 4:29; 4:30; 5:21; cf. 4:12, 13, 14a, 29, 30a OG), and he must eat grass like the animals too (Dan. 4:12; 4:20; 4:22; 4:29; 4:30; 5:21; cf. 4:12, 13, 14a, 29a, 30a OG). He begins to behave like and live with the animals. These descriptions of the king are very reminiscent of how other ancient Near Eastern texts depict humankind when they lack the divine characteristic of wisdom/reason. Humans without wisdom/reason are similarly said to dwell in the wild with the animals (e.g., *Gilgamesh* I.108; 208), and eat grass like various animals (like sheep in *Sheep and Grain* 20–25 and *How Grain Came to Sumer* 1–2; or like gazelle in *Gilgamesh* I.105–112, 173–177). Thus, the use of such language to describe Nebuchadnezzar in Dan. 4 should indicate that he ought to also be considered as a human lacking wisdom/reason. Indeed, this makes plain the animalising effect of lacking wisdom/reason.

Additionally, the OG contains a piece of significant unique material that is absent from the MT. Here Nebuchadnezzar is described as being naked during his affliction. The king declares: 'I was walking about naked [γυμνος] with the animals

---

100. David Winston interprets these verses as saying that those who 'abandoned reason as a key to the understanding of their lives, find their greatest source of misery to lie in their ignorance of the causes which lead to their various troubles'; David Winston, *The Wisdom of Solomon*, AB 43 (London: Doubleday, 1981), 308. The Greek text is from Joseph Ziegler, ed., *Sapientia Salomonis*, Septuaginta: Vetus Testamentum Graecum 12.1 (Göttingen: Vandenhoeck & Ruprecht, 1962).

of the earth' (Dan. 4:30b OG).[101] Nebuchadnezzar's lack of clothes is specifically linked with his proximity with the other animals suggesting that, by walking around naked, he is behaving in an animal-like way. Moreover, as well as suggesting a link to an animal existence, nakedness is a feature often mentioned in ancient Near Eastern texts that depict humans who lack wisdom/reason (e.g., *Sheep and Grain* 20–25; *UET* 6.61.i.7–10; *Gilgamesh* I.105–110), and is also frequently used in Gen. 2–3 to describe the man and woman before they receive wisdom/reason (Gen. 2:25; 3:7, 10, 11). In fact, in each of these instances, Gen. 2–3 LXX uses γυμνός to describe the nakedness of the people in Eden. Therefore, the reference to Nebuchadnezzar's nakedness in Dan. 4:30b OG further corroborates the portrayal of king as being like the animals and also lacking wisdom.

5.2.2.4 Change in Narration

The fact that Nebuchadnezzar's human wisdom or intelligence was absent is further suggested by the change in the narration of Dan. 4.[102] Daniel 4 is mostly given in the first-person perspective as if Nebuchadnezzar himself is narrating his letter; however, in verses 19–33 it is provided in the third-person voice. This first-person narration by Nebuchadnezzar stops just before the animalising affliction comes upon him (Dan. 4:28), and he only resumes his narration upon the return of his reason (Dan. 4:34) once his affliction has concluded. This is commonly explained by scholars as a way of demonstrating the king's condition as he becomes unable to provide a rational account of events.[103] As Jennifer Koosed and Robert Seesengood explain: 'the king quite literally loses his voice. Reason and language are lost in the transformation from human to animal.'[104] The fact that he can no longer narrate events implies that the king could no longer use human language. This conclusion is supported by the fact that, while undergoing his animal affliction, Nebuchadnezzar does not make any kind of vocalization in the narrative at all. Even once his exile ends, he does not immediately respond with spoken repentance. Instead he merely lifts his eyes to heaven (Dan. 4:31), described by Carol Newsom as evidence Nebuchadnezzar 'cannot speak, but he signals as an animal might.'[105] The repentant response which the king offers is not in human language, but in the motions with which an animal may indicate something.

---

101. While the description of Nebuchadnezzar getting wet from the dew of the heavens (4:12, 20, 22, 30 MT) may suggest he is naked in the MT too, it is nowhere explicitly stated.

102. For a description of the effect of narration changes, see Fewell, *Circle of Sovereignty*, 73–5.

103. Hartman and Di Lella, *Book of Daniel*, 174; Montgomery, *Critical and Exegetical Commentary on Daniel*, 223; Fewell, *Circle of Sovereignty*, 75.

104. Jennifer L. Koosed and Robert P. Seesengood, 'Daniel's Animal Apocalypse', in *Divinanimality: Animal Theory, Creaturely Theology*, ed. Stephen D. Moore (New York: Fordham University Press, 2014), 182–195 (185).

105. Newsom with Breed, *Daniel: A Commentary*, 148.

Moreover, Dan. 4 OG also depicts Nebuchadnezzar's language as being affected during his affliction. However, unlike the MT, which ceases the king's first-person narration of the account to indicate his loss of speech, the OG noticeably switches from third-person narration (Dan. 4:25–30 OG) to relate the king's exile in the first person (Dan. 4:30a–33 OG). The OG therefore deals with the narration of Nebuchadnezzar's affliction in the opposite way to the MT.[106] Nevertheless, this does not mean the OG presents Nebuchadnezzar as maintaining his use of language throughout the period of affliction. The narration he provides is entirely in the past tense; thus Nebuchadnezzar relates his affliction only after the fact when presumably his language has been returned to him. This lack of language on the part of the king is explicitly confirmed in another unique OG section where Nebuchadnezzar is told that during his affliction 'you will never be seen nor will you ever speak with any human' (Dan. 4:29 OG). While this may be the result of the king being imprisoned as part of his punishment (i.e., being physically separated from other people),[107] the lack of Nebuchadnezzar's speech during his affliction is unambiguous. It is worth observing that, unlike in the MT, the king does pray and supplicate before God in the wilderness (Dan. 4:30a OG); however, this does not necessitate the use of human language on the part of Nebuchadnezzar. The ability of animals to praise or worship deities is attested in the Hebrew Bible and this does not require language.[108] Furthermore, Nebuchadnezzar only begins his prayers once seven years have passed so his affliction may be at an end by this point and his reason thus reinstated.[109] Therefore, the OG evidence also suggests that Nebuchadnezzar lost his human language during his period of affliction.

This loss of language on the part of Nebuchadnezzar is critical because, as Shlomo Izre'el states, 'in the mythology of ancient Mesopotamia, language symbolises intelligence', and was 'the fundamental element that contrasts humans with animals'.[110] A range of other Mesopotamian texts (e.g., *Gilgamesh* I.104, 195–208; and *Adapa* A.i.2–7) portray this link between wisdom/reason and language.[111] In a similar way, by depicting King Nebuchadnezzar as losing the

---

106. The change of narration in the OG has been explained as the result of editorial activity; see Meadowcroft, *Aramaic Daniel and Greek Daniel*, 36–37.

107. For a discussion of how the OG depicts Nebuchadnezzar as being imprisoned, see §3.3.2.

108. Peter J. Atkins, 'Praise by Animals in the Hebrew Bible', *JSOT* 44 (2020): 500–513.

109. Dean Wenthe suggests that the return of the king's reason is part of the common core of the narrative and the OG has simply joined this motif with the animalising affliction in 4:30; see Wenthe, 'Old Greek Translation', 120, 146.

110. Izre'el, *Adapa and the South Wind*, 132 and 135.

111. For previous discussion of language and wisdom in these examples, see §4.2.4 and §4.3.1.3.3.

Further Mesopotamian texts which display this link are provided in: Izre'el, *Adapa and the South Wind*, 130–135.

ability to speak, Dan. 4 depicts the king as losing his intelligence or wisdom and thus losing his distinctive human capacity.

5.2.2.5 Summary

From this analysis, it is clear that the narrative of Nebuchadnezzar's affliction in Dan. 4 appears to rely upon a particular construction of the human–animal boundary. The presence of a distinct hierarchy between divine, human and animal within the narrative was initially noted, before focus shifted to examine the relationship of the divine characteristic of wisdom/reason to the human–animal boundary in Dan. 4. Considering the effect upon the king's heart, reason and knowledge in turn revealed that, just as with other Mesopotamian and biblical texts, wisdom/reason is used in Dan. 4 as a key indicator of the conceptual location of the human–animal boundary. Additionally, the narrative's animalising imagery and the change of narration in the text also indicated that the king in the narrative has lost this wisdom/reason and thus behaves like an animal.

The characteristic of wisdom/reason which was identified in ancient Mesopotamian, biblical and early Jewish texts to be a divine-human characteristic (see §4.2 and §5.1) can thus be seen to play a pivotal role in how the king is situated in relation to the human–animal boundary in both Aramaic and Greek narratives of Dan. 4. The possession or loss of this attribute signals whether Nebuchadnezzar is identified with the human or animal side of the boundary. Therefore, within the wider context of these ancient Near Eastern human–animal boundaries, Nebuchadnezzar's affliction results in the loss of his wisdom/reason which causes him to cross the human–animal divide and become categorically identified as an animal. Thus, although the narrative lacks any real evidence for an intended physical metamorphosis (see chapter 3), there is evidence of a far more significant *categorical* animal transformation present within Dan. 4.

5.3 Conclusion

This chapter has first demonstrated a shared worldview about divine–human–animal boundaries between the Mesopotamian material surveyed in chapter 4 and a range of Hebrew Bible and Second Temple period texts. These examples showed how such texts appear to share a common understanding which divides up gods, humans and animals using characteristics like immortality and wisdom/reason. In a similar way to Mesopotamian texts, this range of biblical and early Jewish material appears to construct a divine–human boundary through the presence or absence of the attribute of immortality, and a human–animal boundary through the presence or absence of the attribute of wisdom.

Based on this context and apparent shared worldview, the presence of such categories or boundaries within the narrative of Dan. 4 was examined. Through this assessment, it was made clear that the two key concepts of immortality and wisdom/reason, and the boundaries between beings which they govern, can both be found within the narrative of Dan. 4. First, the divine–human boundary, when viewed through the lens of immortality, helps us understand the transgressive pride of Nebuchadnezzar. By claiming eternal life for himself, he overreaches and effectively attempts to claim divine status (cf. Jdt. 3:8; etc.), for which he is punished. Nevertheless, much more perceptible and critical for interpreting the narrative is the characteristic of wisdom/reason. In response to the king's pride, 'the Most High' causes the king to lose his wisdom/reason. Read against a backdrop of this wider ancient Near Eastern worldview, this causes him to cross the human–animal boundary and thus (in a categorical rather than merely superficial manner) truly become an animal. Through his appropriation of divine immortality, Nebuchadnezzar loses human wisdom and reason. Therefore, by claiming to cross the divine–human boundary and make himself like a god, Nebuchadnezzar is instead forced to cross the human–animal boundary and is made an animal.

Having established these various connections between Dan. 4 and the widespread evidence for ancient Near Eastern conceptual boundaries formed through wisdom and immortality, the debate about whether the character of Nebuchadnezzar undergoes an animal transformation can be returned to. While it has been established that there is no evidence in the primary edition of Nebuchadnezzar's animalising affliction for an intended physical metamorphosis as it is commonly understood (§3), there is clear evidence for an animal transformation of a different type, and thus it is equally inadequate to claim that no such transformation takes place (§2). The narrative of Dan. 4 has been shown to correlate with the same worldview and conceptual boundaries as the Mesopotamian, biblical and early Jewish texts which likewise depict wisdom and immortality as bounding off classes of beings. Therefore crucially, despite the apparent absence of a *physical* transformation here (the focus of so much of the text's later interpretation and reception; see, e.g., chapter 2), Nebuchadnezzar loses his wisdom/reason and in so doing is forced to cross the human–animal boundary which this characteristic governs. Thus, within this shared ancient Near Eastern worldview and literary context, Nebuchadnezzar's animalising experience depicts an altogether more significant transformation of the king than has been previously recognized, from *categorically* human to *categorically* animal.

Chapter 6

CONCLUSION

This study has tackled the interpretative struggle surrounding how to understand the remarkable imagery used to describe Nebuchadnezzar's animalising affliction in Dan. 4. Typically, interpreters have either affirmed a physical metamorphosis in the narrative, or they have instead read the narrative in an alternative way that precludes or denies any animal transformation in Dan. 4. This study contended that neither of these traditional lines of interpretations is satisfactory. The primary edition of Nebuchadnezzar's animalising affliction in Dan. 4 MT provides little support for a supposed physical metamorphosis of the king, and this interpretation seems to be reliant instead on later developments within the textual tradition. On the other hand, it has also been demonstrated that this should not be taken to mean that the narrative contains no animal transformation whatsoever. Examining this animalising affliction within a wider ancient Near Eastern context, this study maintains that there *is* a more subtle, yet far more profound transformation of the king as he clearly transgresses the conceptual boundary between human and animal. This animal transformation cannot be classified as a *physical* metamorphosis, but it is rather predicated upon the possession or loss of wisdom/reason.

6.1 Summary of Findings

Following the Introduction (chapter 1), the second chapter surveyed the different interpretations of Nebuchadnezzar's animalising affliction focusing on those concerned with the question of a physical metamorphosis within the Danielic narrative. This constituted the first comprehensive scholarly attempt to trace the course of such explanations from early post-biblical interpretations through to their representation within contemporary scholarship. It was argued that the question of animal metamorphosis in Dan. 4 is a significant and contentious issue detectable throughout the history of this narrative's interpretation, and interpretative responses can largely be grouped into two loose categories. On the one hand, there are those interpreters who contend that a type of physical metamorphosis best explains the animalising affliction of Nebuchadnezzar in the text. Equally, however, there are interpreters who propose other alternative explanations in order to provide less fantastical or 'magical' accounts and obviate the need for any actual animal transformation within the narrative. Thus traditionally the contention has been that either Nebuchadnezzar should be considered to have *physically* metamorphosed into an animal in Dan. 4, or that no animal transformation takes place.

The third chapter began investigating these differing claims about the narrative by assessing the textual material relating to Dan. 4 for evidence that a physical metamorphosis was being described. By looking at potentially underlying sources for the narrative (e.g., evidence for Nabonidus' sojourn in Teima, and the Abydenus fragment), any pre-Danielic origin for the specifically *animalising* portrayal of Nebuchadnezzar's affliction or for any perceived metamorphic element to the tale were discounted. Instead, contrary to the previous conclusions of Haag and Wills, it was argued that the king's animalising affliction may be seen as innovative to Dan. 4 and speculated that it may have arisen due to the particular combination of these various sources, rather than originating in any one pre-Danielic strand.

It was further demonstrated that it is equally difficult to find evidence for a physical metamorphosis in the textual evidence for Dan. 4 itself. There are three main editions of Nebuchadnezzar's affliction: an Aramaic edition (MT), the Old Greek edition (OG) and the Theodotion edition (Θ). The MT and OG are best considered double literary editions of the same narrative which have undergone separate secondary expansion, whereas the Θ is likely a fresh translation of a text similar to the MT which shows evidence of adjustment (in some cases towards the OG). An independent redactional layer in both the MT and the OG editions was identified which, in both cases, seems to be occasioned by the specific chapter sequence of each edition of Daniel. Daniel 4 MT seems to have influenced subsequent redaction of Dan. 5 MT due to the repetition of the king's affliction in Dan. 5:18–22 MT that is absent in Dan. 5 OG. Likewise, it was argued that Dan. 4 OG has been redacted towards Dan. 7:4 as it appears to be influenced by the physical animal imagery in the later chapter. Due to this influence of Dan. 7:4 upon Dan. 4 OG, while the MT and OG can generally be considered double literary editions, it has been argued that Dan. 4 MT is the primary edition and origin for the depiction of the king's exile as an animalising affliction.

It was subsequently demonstrated how each of these editions portray Nebuchadnezzar's affliction differently, though none of them contain compelling evidence that the author/editor(s) seem to envisage it as a physical metamorphosis. The MT describes only superficial physical changes of the king (all of which are characterized as mere similes) but does contain significant changes to both his behaviour and location which are linked with a loss of reason. The OG has a more physical description of the affliction, but still does not go so far as to unequivocally suggest that this is supposed to be a metamorphosis. In fact, it seems more focused on depicting Nebuchadnezzar's exile as a punishment for the desolation of Jerusalem's temple, rather than an animalisation. The Θ edition is largely similar to the MT but, through minor variations, does perhaps come closest to a depiction of a physical animal metamorphosis, although there is little evidence that such a transformation was actually intended by the editor/translator(s). A detailed assessment of the editions of Dan. 4 suggests that it is the reworked portrayals of the king's affliction in these two Greek editions which seem to have been the main influence for subsequent metamorphic readings of Dan. 4 in, for example, the *Vita Danielis* or the writings of Cyril of Jerusalem. Thus, the metamorphic line of interpretation of Dan. 4 seems to be primarily reliant upon later changes to the textual tradition found within the OG and Θ editions which depict the king's affliction in more physical terms. Nevertheless, the primary edition of Nebuchadnezzar's animalising affliction in Dan. 4 MT, which both Greek versions to differing extents rely upon, crucially lacks evidence for a physical metamorphosis and seems rather to be predominantly characterized instead by a loss of reason. Though clearly a significant and influential strand of *later* interpretation (one which can furthermore now be explained), a physical metamorphosis does not therefore appear to be an authentic part of the king's affliction as envisioned in Dan. 4.

However, while the various editions of Dan. 4 seem to contain no explicit evidence that a metamorphosis was ever intended, the fourth and fifth chapters went on to demonstrate that it is equally inadequate to claim that the king does not undergo an animal transformation at all. Building upon the prior work of Pedersen, Mettinger and Izre'el, an expansive survey of a variety of ancient Mesopotamian material was conducted in the fourth chapter in order to outline one of the ways in which the human-animal boundary appears to have been both conceived and constructed in the wider ancient Near East. It was argued that these conceptual ontological boundaries in ancient Mesopotamia tend to be based around the possession of the divine characteristics of wisdom and immortality which leads to a tripartite division between beings. Gods possess both of these characteristics, humans have only wisdom, and animals possess neither. These characteristics, and the divine–human– animal boundaries they govern, recur frequently throughout a diverse array of ancient Near Eastern literature, revealing that in ancient Mesopotamia this conception of the human–animal boundary had little, if anything, to do with an individual's appearance. A being's characterization (and categorization) as 'human' or 'animal' would thus be dictated not by physical appearance but, crucially, by the presence or absence of wisdom/reason.

In the fifth chapter, the focus returned to the biblical text where compelling evidence was found that numerous Hebrew Bible and Second Temple texts appear to reflect the same conceptual ancient Near Eastern worldview of divine–human– animal boundaries based around the characteristics of wisdom and immortality. Immortality is portrayed as a uniquely divine feature, whereas wisdom appears to differentiate humans from animals. Together, both of these characteristics appear to establish a similar tripartite hierarchical division between gods, humans and animals to that found elsewhere in the ancient Near East. This conception is perhaps most clearly evident in the Eden Narrative in Gen. 2–3, which contains an account of the origin of humankind's condition (possessing wisdom but lacking immortality) and the origin of such boundaries, one which seems to closely resemble ancient Near Eastern accounts. Significantly, this examination demonstrated that both Gen. 2–3 and a range of other Hebrew Bible and Second Temple texts appear to share this general Mesopotamian worldview regarding divine–human–animal boundaries and the role of wisdom and immortality in constructing them.

Finally, this study turned back to focus once again upon Dan. 4, arguing that the narrative of Nebuchadnezzar's affliction ultimately relies upon this same conception of divine–human–animal boundaries which was identified in ancient Mesopotamian, biblical and early Jewish texts. The evidence for immortality's role in signifying the divine–human boundary within the narrative was demonstrated, and this revealed how Nebuchadnezzar's desire for immortality could effectively constitute an attempt to claim divine status. More importantly, I argued that the characteristic of wisdom/ reason plays a pivotal role in discerning how to understand the king's animalising affliction. As a signifier of the human–animal boundary, possession or loss of wisdom/reason is critical for determining Nebuchadnezzar's conceptual ontological status and, as Dan. 4 appears to portray the king as losing this divine–human characteristic, the narrative can best be understood as describing how Nebuchadnezzar crosses this human–animal boundary and becomes identified as categorically animal. In light of these ancient Near Eastern conceptual boundaries, it would appear that Dan. 4 should therefore be read as a narrative revolving around Nebuchadnezzar's claim to transgress the divine–human boundary (through his *purported* possession of immortality), and his subsequent and enforced crossing of the human–animal boundary (through his loss of wisdom).

The conclusions of this study therefore mean that, by working with these conceptual boundaries, the narrative of Dan. 4 describes how the loss of the king's wisdom/reason causes him to essentially shift categories from human to animal (and ultimately back again). Nebuchadnezzar's animalising affliction is thus essentially a reclassification or recategorization of the king based on the characteristic of wisdom/reason. He does not become an animal in his physical appearance or form, but Nebuchadnezzar *does* become an animal in category. Therefore, though Dan. 4 does not contain a physical metamorphosis (contrary to one popular and persistent strand of interpretative tradition), it is equally inadequate to claim that the king does not undergo an animal transformation at all (as reflected in the other dominant interpretative tradition). Rather the king's loss of reason in fact represents a far more significant categorical change from human to animal than has hitherto been recognized. Read in the context of a wider ancient Near Eastern worldview concerning divine–human–animal boundaries, the animalising affliction of Nebuchadnezzar should be situated between these two extremes as a categorical, not physical, animal transformation. This represents a more subtle yet far more profound crossing of the human–animal boundary, one which further constitutes an essential undoing and reversal of Gen. 3. Only once Nebuchadnezzar acknowledges his place in the world and has his reason restored to him is he once again human.

6.2 Further Implications

Beyond the specific implications for how to understand Nebuchadnezzar's animalising affliction in Dan. 4, the findings of this study can perhaps help to illuminate a key distinction between divine, human and animal in the Hebrew

Bible more generally. As noted earlier, this study does not contend that all biblical texts share the same understanding of such boundaries; however, it has been demonstrated in a variety of instances that the divine–human–animal boundaries which were identified in wider ancient Mesopotamian material are prevalent in early Jewish and Hebrew Bible texts as well. It is therefore plausible that immortality or wisdom/reason might constitute key signifiers of conceptual divine–human or human–animal boundaries in other such texts. For example, an understanding of the role immortality plays in delineating the divine–human boundary might help assist interpretations of the idol polemics in Isa. 40, 44 or Jer. 10. Perhaps one of the reasons idols are so forcefully denigrated in these passages is that they are demonstrably not immortal. Equally, the narrative about Balaam and his donkey in Num. 22:21–35 might be illumined by consideration of how wisdom/reason plays a role in situating the human apart from animal. Future studies on the Hebrew Bible, and the boundaries between divine, human and animal therein, may thus find it fruitful to examine the role that the characteristic of wisdom/reason has in conceptually distinguishing humans from other animals, along with the role that immortality has in forming the divine–human boundary.

Furthermore, as noted above, this recognition of the role such boundaries play in Nebuchadnezzar's animalising affliction suggests that the narrative of Dan. 4 might arguably be read and understood as an unravelling of the outcome of the Eden narrative.[1] While Gen. 2–3 describes the establishment of the human–animal boundary (as well as the enforcement of the divine-human boundary) and thus the process of delineating humankind's position (§5.1.1), Dan. 4 effectively reverses this process of definition. Just as Adam's acquisition of knowledge caused him to be bound off from the animals (Gen. 3:23–24), so Nebuchadnezzar's *loss* of knowledge and reason causes him to become an animal. In Nebuchadnezzar's animalising affliction we may then see a reestablishment of the Edenic state where human and animal are not so clearly distinguished. An additional potential point of comparison could be with humankind's instruction in 1 En. 7–9 and 69 where humans receive divine wisdom and knowledge through the mediation of the angelic Watchers (§5.1.6). Dan. 4 might also be read as a specific reversal or removal of this previous instruction. The similarity of the role played by the divine watchers in both texts might further evidence this link. Watchers initiate the revelation of wisdom and knowledge to humankind in 1 En. 69:8–11 and it is again a Watcher who announces Nebuchadnezzar's loss of reason in Dan. 4:13–14. We could then speculate that Nebuchadnezzar's animalising affliction functions as a deliberate undoing of the divine education that humans receive in 1 En.

While this study has demonstrated the presence and function of this scheme of conceptual divine–human–animal boundaries in Dan. 4 (one seemingly shared

---

1. Similar suggestions have been made on other grounds, for example by Eric W. Heaton and André Lacocque, but without providing any detailed understanding of how the human–animal boundary is constructed in such narratives; see Heaton, *Book of Daniel*, 149; Lacocque, *Book of Daniel*, 80.

with and drawing upon a much wider ancient Near Eastern context), it is also clear that these boundaries are not impenetrable. As the narrative considers the categories of human and animal, the king's affliction in Dan. 4 is useful as a means to determine how the human–animal boundary was conceived, but the nature of the narrative is such that it also blurs and transgresses these same distinctions. Nebuchadnezzar does not stay on the human side of the boundary but, through the intervention of 'the Most High', he is repositioned and reclassified depending on his possession or loss of wisdom/reason. The human–animal boundary therefore seems to be permeable and porous, and it is possible for an individual to both interact with it and be repositioned in relation to it. Indeed, if the human–animal boundary is based principally around wisdom, reason or rationality, the *loss* of such characteristics whether through divine intervention or not, would result in an individual being recategorized as an animal. An example of this kind of repositioning may be demonstrated for example in texts such as Psalm 73:22 (see §5.1.4) where the Psalmist can legitimately refer to themselves as an animal due to their loss of knowledge. Clearly such a conceptual worldview has other far-reaching (and possibly undesirable) implications in relation to issues of mental health or cognitive impairment, as well as animal cognition and welfare. Indeed, while unequivocally at odds with our modern sensibilities, among other things it seems to imply a non-human status for anyone exhibiting cognitive impairment. Given the frequency with which perceived loss of reason or rationality might be considered to occur, one further implication of such a worldview in Dan. 4 is that an animal transformation and transgression of the human–animal boundary along these lines is in fact arguably a far more common occurrence and familiar event (certainly more so than any physical metamorphosis!), rendering the human–animal boundary within an ancient context ever more permeable.

Finally, this discussion can fruitfully relate to contemporary attitudes towards animals. Humans have tried for centuries to identify characteristics that make them distinct from animals, but more recent advances in knowledge have led to a radical shift in how we think of a human–animal boundary.[2] Claims that humans exclusively possess characteristics or behaviours (such as language, consciousness, tool-use, culture) are continually proving untenable as further research into animals is conducted, and similar conclusions are beginning to be reached in biblical studies.[3] While this book has demonstrated one of the ways in which biblical texts, and the humans who composed them, have adopted a specific concept of a human–animal boundary that creates a unique position for humankind, this work can also help us to reflect on the great similarity between humans and animals. The loss of Nebuchadnezzar's wisdom reveals that, apart from this divine characteristic, he is

---

2. Matthew Calarco states that 'one of the defining characteristics of our age is the radical breakdown of the human/animal distinction'. See Matthew Calarco, *Thinking Through Animals: Identity, Difference, Indistinction* (Stanford: Stanford University Press, 2015).

3. For example, see Stone, *Reading the Hebrew Bible with Animal Studies*, 140–163; and Atkins, 'Praise by Animals'.

already effectively an animal. For example, his physical form or flesh aligns him with the animals and allows him (sans reason) to become categorized as such. As David Cunningham argues, flesh 'helpfully blurs the boundaries of human beings and other animals'.[4] Although this study has demonstrated that, in biblical texts, differences clearly exist, it also hopefully highlights the benefit of reflecting on those features which are shared by humans and animals. By undertaking such reflection, we might find that there are far more points of overlap between humans and animals in the Hebrew Bible than we might anticipate.

Overall, this study has demonstrated the inadequacy of both traditional readings of Nebuchadnezzar's animalising affliction and proposed that, in its ancient context, the narrative describes a more subtle, yet much more significant animal transformation. While this transformation may not be termed a physical metamorphosis, within the conceptual worldview of the ancient Near East outlined here the king's animalising affliction in Dan. 4 cuts deeper to affect the heart of his nature and cause a transformation, not in how the king appears, but in how he is classified. By focusing on his loss of reason, the narrative of Dan. 4 in fact provides a far more meaningful account of Nebuchadnezzar's full and categorical transformation into an animal, one that has far-reaching implications and which is fully contextualized within the wider ancient Near Eastern worldview to which it belongs.

---

4. David S. Cunningham, 'The Way of All Flesh: Rethinking the *Imago Dei*', in *Creaturely Theology: On God, Humans and Other Animals*, ed. Celia Deane-Drummond and David Clough (London: SCM Press, 2009), 100–117 (101). For some further useful reflections on how Dan. 4 might be seen to make the human–animal distinction blurrier, see Strømmen, *Biblical Animality*, 102–107.

Appendix A

TABLE OF PRIMARY DANIEL MANUSCRIPTS

Manuscript	Approx. Date	Language	Chapter Sequence																
				1	2	3		4	5	6	7	8	9	10	11	12			
Qumran Fragments[1]	150 BCE–70 CE[2]	Hebrew/Aramaic		1	2	3		4	5	6	7	8	9	10	11	12			
Papyrus 967	100–200 CE	Greek		1	2	3	Prayer and Song	4	7	8	5	6	9	10	11	12	Bel and the Dragon		Susanna
Codex Vaticanus	300–325 CE	Greek	Susanna	1	2	3	Prayer and Song	4	5	6	7	8	9	10	11	12	Bel and the Dragon[3]		
Codex Alexandrinus	400–440 CE	Greek	Susanna	1	2	3	Prayer and Song[4]	4	5	6	7	8	9	10	11	12	Bel and the Dragon		
Codex Marchalianus	500–600 CE	Greek	Susanna	1	2	3	Prayer and Song	4	5	6	7	8	9	10	11	12	Bel and the Dragon[5]		
Codex Ambrosianus	800–900 CE	Syriac		1	2	3	Prayer and Song	4	5	6	7	8	9	10	11	12	Bel and the Dragon	Ruth[6]	Susanna
Codex Chisianus 88	800–1000 CE	Greek		1	2	3	Prayer and Song	4	5	6	7	8	9	10	11	12	Susanna	Bel and the Dragon	
Codex Leningradensis B 19A	1008–1009 CE	Hebrew/Aramaic		1	2	3		4	5	6	7	8	9	10	11	12			

[1] Due to the fragmentary nature of the material from Qumran, the order is speculative and based upon the reconstructed arrangement of fragments in DJD. While this assumes there was only one version of Daniel present at Qumran, it is entirely possible that multiple texts with differing chapter orders were present within the community at Qumran.

[2] For the dating of the Qumran material, see Collins, *Daniel: A Commentary*, 2.

[3] Codex Vaticanus and Alexandrinus both treat this as part of 'Vision 12'.

[4] These are also included in the 'Odes' section after Psalm 151.

[5] See note 3.

[6] The Codex Ambrosianus created what has been termed 'the Book of Women' by collecting together Ruth, Susanna, Esther and Judith. Thus Ruth interrupts the Danielic material.

Appendix B

SYNOPSIS OF EDITIONS OF DANIEL 4

NRSV[1]	Qumran Fragments	Masoretic Text (MT)		Theodotion (Θ)		Old Greek (OG)	
4:1	[...]	3:31	King Nebuchadnezzar, to all the peoples, nations, and languages that live in all the earth. May your prosperity be increased.	3:98	King Nabouchodonosor to all the peoples, tribes, languages that live in all the earth. May peace be increased to you.	[4:34c]	[King Nabouchodonosor to all the nations and to all the lands and to all inhabitants of them: May peace be increased to you all times.]
4:2	[...]	3:32	It has seemed good to me to make known the signs and wonders which the Most High god did with me.	3:99	I am pleased to recount to you all the signs and the wonders which the Most High god did with me.	[4:34c cont.]	[And now I will make known to you the deeds that the great god has done with me. It seemed good to me to proclaim to you and your wise men that god is one]
4:3	[...]	3:33	How great are his signs and how mighty are his wonders, his kingdom is an eternal kingdom and his authority is from generations and generations.	3:100	How great and mighty they are; his kingdom is an eternal kingdom, and his authority is from generations and generations.	[4:34c cont.]	[and his wonderful deeds are great, his palace is eternal, his authority is from generations to generations.]
4:4	---	4:1	I, Nebuchadnezzar, was at ease in my house and flourishing in my palace.	4:1	I, Nabouchodonosor, was prospering in my house and flourishing.	4:1	In the eighteenth year of his reign Nabouchodonosor said, "I was at peace in my house and flourishing on my throne.
4:5	---	4:2	I saw a dream, and it terrified me, the fantasies upon my bed and the visions of my head were disturbing me.	4:2	I saw a dream, and it terrified me, and I was disturbed upon my bed, and the visions of my head confused me.	4:2	I saw a dream, and I was frightened, and terror fell upon me upon my bed.
4:6	---	4:3	And by me was made a decree to bring all the wise men of Babylon before me that they would make known to me the interpretation of the dream.	4:3	And by me was made a decree to bring all the wise men of Babylon before me that they would make known to me the interpretation of the dream.	---	

[1] The left-hand anchor column provides the verse-numbering from the NRSV English translation. I then include the corresponding verse-numbering from each edition of Daniel. All translations of the different editions are my own.

NRSV[1]	Qumran Fragments	Masoretic Text (MT)		Theodotion (Θ)		Old Greek (OG)	
4:7	---	[...]	4:4	Then the magicians, the conjurers, the Chaldeans and the diviners came in, and I told the dream before them, and its interpretation they could not make known to me.	4:4	And the enchanters, magicians, diviners, Chaldeans came in, and I told the dream before them, and its interpretation they could not make known to me.	---
4:8	4QDan^d 3.1–2	[... name is Bel] teshazzar [... and in whom is the spirit of the holy gods, and I told the dream to him.]	4:5	Until at last before me came Daniel, whose name is Belteshazzar like the name of my god, and in whom is a spirit of the holy gods, and I told the dream to him.	4:5	Until when Daniel came, whose name is Baltasar according to the name of my god, who has a holy spirit of God in himself, to whom I said:	---
4:9	4QDan^d 3.2–3	"Belteshazza[r...] [... and ev]ery[mys]tery for you is no trouble [...]	4:6	"Belteshazzar chief of the magicians, I know that the spirit of the holy gods is in you and every mystery is no trouble for you. See my dream that I saw and tell its interpretation.	4:6	"Baltasar, chief of the enchanters, I know that the holy spirit of God is in you and every mystery is no trouble for you. Listen to the vision of the dream that I saw and tell me its interpretation.	---
4:10	---	[...]	4:7	I was seeing visions of my head upon my bed and behold a tree in the middle of the earth and its height was great.	4:7	I was looking upon my bed and behold a tree in the middle of the earth, and its height was great.	4:7	I was sleeping and behold a tall tree was growing upon the earth and its appearance was great, and there was no other like it.
4:11	4QDan^d 3.5	[The] tree grew gr[eat ...]	4:8	The tree grew great and strong, and its height reached to the heavens and it was visible to the ends of the earth.	4:8	The tree grew great and strong, and its height reached up to the heaven and its trunk to the ends of the whole earth.	4:9	Its branches were about thirty stadia long, and all the animals of the earth found shade beneath it, and the birds of the heaven were hatching their brood in it. Its fruit was plentiful and good, and it supplied all the living creatures.

NRSV¹	Qumran Fragments		Masoretic Text (MT)		Theodotion (Θ)		Old Greek (OG)	
4:12	4QDan^d 3.6–8	[Its leaves] were beautiful, and [its] fruits [...]	4:9	Its leaves were beautiful, and its fruit was plentiful, and in it was food for all. Animals of the field sheltered beneath it, and birds of the heavens lived in its branches, and from it all flesh fed was fed.	4:9	Its leaves were beautiful, and its fruit was plentiful, and in it was food for all. And the animals of the field sheltered beneath it, and the birds of the heaven lived in its branches, and from it all flesh was fed.	4:8	And its appearance was great. Its top approached as far as the heaven and its trunk as far as the clouds filling that which is under the heaven, the sun and the moon dwelt in it and illuminated all the earth.
4:13	---		4:10	I was looking, in the visions of my head upon my bed, and behold a watcher, a holy one, was descending the heavens.	4:10	I was looking in the vision of the night upon my bed, and behold an Ir and a holy one descended from the heaven.	4:10	I was looking in my sleep, behold an angel was sent in power out of the heaven.
4:14	---		4:11	He called out in power and thus he said 'Cut down the tree and cut off its branches, strip off its leaves and scatter its fruit. Let the animals flee from beneath it and the birds from its branches.	4:11	And he called out in power and thus he said 'Cut down the tree and pluck off its branches and strip off its leaves and scatter its fruit. Let the animals be shaken beneath it and the birds from its branches.	4:11	And he called out and said 'Cut it down and destroy it, for it has been decreed by the Most High to uproot and to render it useless.'
4:15	4QDan^d 4–6.11–12	[...] leave the stump of its roots in [the] ea[r]th, and in an iron and copper band [...of the field.] Let it be wet with the dew of the heavens and, with the animals, let its portion be the grass of the earth.	4:12	Only leave the stump of its roots in the earth, and in an iron and copper band in the grass of the field. Let it be wet with the dew of the heavens and, with the animals, let its portion be in the grass of the earth.	4:12	Only leave the growth of its roots in the earth and in an iron and copper band and in the tender grass outside. And it will lie down in the dew of the heaven and, with the animals, its portion will be in the grass of the earth.	4:12	And thus he said 'Leave one root for it in the earth that, with the animals of the earth in the mountains, it may feed on grass like an ox.

NRSV[1]	Qumran Fragments		Masoretic Text (MT)		Theodotion (Θ)		Old Greek (OG)	
4:16	4QDan^d 4–6.12–14	Let [its] heart be [c]hanged [from that of a human], and let the heart of the animals be given to it. And let se[v]en tim[es] pa[ss over it.]	4:13	Let its heart be changed from that of a human, and let the heart of an animal be given to it And let seven times pass over it.	4:13	Its heart will be changed from that of humans, and a heart of an animal will be given to it And seven times will be changed over it.	4:13	And its body may be changed from the dew of the heaven, and he may graze with them seven years,
4:17	4QDan^d 4–6. 14–16	The command is [by decree] of the watchers and the decis[ion] is by the word of the holy ones, [until the living may know th]at the Mo[st] High has authority over [the human] king[dom and he will give it to those whom he desires, and over it he will set the lowliest human being.']	4:14	The command is by decree of the watchers and the decision is by the word of the holy ones, until the living may know that the Most High has authority over the human kingdom and he will give it to those whom he desires, and over it he will set the lowliest human being,'	4:14	The word is by decree of Ir, and the decision by the command of the holy ones, in order that the living may know that the Most High is Lord over the human kingdom and he will give it to whom he desires and over it he will set what is contemptible of humans.'	4:14	until he acknowledges that the Lord of the heaven has authority over everything which is in the heaven and which is upon the earth, and he does whatever he wishes to them.'
							4:14a	It was cut down before me in one day, and its destruction in one hour of the day; and its branches were given to every wind, and it was dragged and it was put down. It ate the grass with the animals of the earth, and it was delivered into prison, it was bound in copper manacles and shackles by them. I was greatly amazed at all these things, and my sleep left my eyes.

NRSV[1]	Qumran Fragments	Masoretic Text (MT)	Theodotion (Θ)	Old Greek (OG)
4:18	4QDan^d 4–6. 16–18: [This is the dream I, King Nebuchadnezzar], saw. And you, Belteshazzar], say the [in]terpretation, as [all the wise men of my kingdom were unable to make the interpretation known to me. But you are] able for the spirit of the ho[ly] gods [is in you."]	4:15 This is the dream I, King Nebuchadnezzar, saw. And you, Belteshazzar, say the interpretation, as all the wise men of my kingdom were unable to make the interpretation known to me. But you are able for the spirit of the holy gods is in you."	4:15 This is the dream I, King Nabouchodonosor, saw. And you, Baltasar, say the interpretation, as all the wise men of my kingdom were unable to explain the interpretation to me. But you, Daniel, are able for a holy spirit of God is in you."	4:15 And when I rose early from my bed I called to Daniel, the chief of the wise men and the leader of the interpreters of dreams, and I described the dream to him, and he showed me its entire interpretation
4:19	4QDan^d 4–6.18–19: [Then Daniel, whose name was Belte]shazzar, was devastated [...]	4:16 Then Daniel, whose name was Belteshazzar, was devastated for one moment and his thoughts troubled him. The king responded and said "Belteshazzar, do not let the dream and the interpretation trouble you." Belteshazzar responded and said "My lord, may the dream be for those who hate you, and may the interpretation be for your enemies."	4:16 Then Daniel, whose name was Baltasar, was mute for one hour and his thoughts troubled him. And the king responded and said "Baltasar, do not let the dream and the interpretation agitate you." And Baltasar responded and said "Lord, may the dream be for those who hate you, and may its interpretation for your enemies."	4:16 But Daniel was greatly amazed. Foreboding pressed him and he was afraid, trembling seized him and his appearance changed, shaking his head, marvelling for one hour he responded to me with a soft voice 'O King, may this dream be for those who hate you and may its interpretation come upon your enemies.
4:20	[...]	4:17 The tree that you saw, which grew great and strong, whose height reached to the heavens and was visible to all the earth;	4:17 The tree that you saw, which grew great and strong, whose height reached to the heaven and its trunk to all the earth;	4:17 The tree that was planted in the earth, whose appearance was great, it is you, O King.

[2] This is where the fragment of 4QDan^a breaks off, the rest of 5:19 is taken from 4QDan^b.

NRSV¹	Qumran Fragments	Masoretic Text (MT)		Theodotion (Θ)		Old Greek (OG)	
4:21 ---	[...]	4:18	and its leaves were beautiful, and its fruit was plentiful, and in it was food for all; beneath it the animals of the field lived, and birds of the heavens dwelt in its branches.	4:18	and its leaves were flourishing, and its fruit was plentiful, and in it was food for all; beneath it the animals of the field lived, and the birds of the heaven sheltered in its branches.	4:18	And all the birds of the heaven are nesting in it. The power of the earth and the nations and all the languages unto the ends of the earth, and all the countries serve you.
4:22 ---	[...]	4:19	It is you, O King, who has grown great and strong, your greatness grew greater and it reached to the heavens and your authority to the ends of the earth.	4:19	It is you, O King, because you have grown great and strong. And your greatness grew greater and reached to the heaven and your authority to the ends of the earth.	4:19	But that tree was exalted and approached the heaven and its trunk touched the clouds – You, O King, have been exalted above all humans who are upon the face of all the earth, your heart has been exalted in pride and power towards the Holy One and his angels. Your works were seen, how you desolated the house of the living God on account of the sins of the sanctified people.
4:23 ---	[...]	4:20	And that the king saw a watcher and a holy one descending from the heavens and saying 'Cut down the tree and destroy it. Only leave the stump of its roots in the earth, and in an iron and copper band in the grass of the field. Let it be wet with the dew of the heavens and, with the animals of the field, let his portion be until seven times have passed over him.'	4:20	And that the king saw an Ir and a holy one descending from the heaven, and he said 'Pluck off the tree and destroy it. Only leave the growth of its roots in the earth and in an iron and copper band and in the tender grass outside, and it will lodge in the dew of the heaven and, with the animals of the field, its portion will be until seven times change over him.'	4:20	And the vision, which you saw, that an angel was sent in power from the Lord and that he said to cut down the tree. The judgement of the great God will come upon you

NRSV[1]	Qumran Fragments		Masoretic Text (MT)		Theodotion (Θ)		Old Greek (OG)	
4:24	---	[...]	4:21	This is the interpretation, O King and it is a decree of the Most High that has come upon my lord the king:	4:21	This is its interpretation, O King, and it is a decree of the Most High that has come upon my lord the king:	4:21	and the Most High and his angels will pursue you.
4:25	---	[...]	4:22	And you will be driven out from humanity, and with the animals of the field will be your dwelling, and they will feed you grass like oxen, and you will be wet from the dew of the heavens, and seven times will pass over you until when you know that the Most High has authority over the human kingdom and he will give it to whom he desires.	4:22	And they will drive you out from humanity, and with animals of the field will be your dwelling, and they will feed you grass like an ox, and you will be lodged from the dew of the heaven, and seven times will be changed over you until when you know that the Most High has authority over the human kingdom, and he will give it to whom he desires.	4:22	They will lead you away to prison and they will send you out into a deserted place.
4:26	---	[...]	4:23	And as they said to leave the stump of the roots of the tree, your kingdom will endure for you from when you acknowledge the authority of the heavens.	4:23	And as they said, 'Leave the growth of the roots of the tree', your kingdom remains for you, from when you acknowledge the authority of the heaven."	4:23	And the root of the tree that was left since it was not uprooted: the place of your throne will be preserved for you for a time and hour. Behold, they are preparing against you and they will whip you and they will bring judgements against you. The Lord lives in heaven, and his authority is upon the whole earth.

NRSV[1]	Qumran Fragments		Masoretic Text (MT)		Theodotion (Θ)		Old Greek (OG)	
4:27	---	[. . .]	4:24	Therefore, O King, let my counsel be appealing to you. Break off your sins with almsgiving and your iniquity by having mercy on the poor. Perhaps then your prosperity will be lengthened."	4:24	On account of this, O King, may my counsel be appealing to you, and atone for your sins with almsgiving and for your iniquity with compassion to the poor; perhaps god will be patient with your transgressions.	4:24	Implore him concerning the sins and atone for all your iniquity with almsgiving, so that mercy may be given to you and you may be upon the throne of your kingdom for many days, and not be destroyed. Love these words; for my words are accurate and your time is complete."
4:28	---	[. . .]	4:25	All this came upon King Nebuchadnezzar.	4:25	All these things came upon King Nabouchodonosor.	4:25	And at the completion of the words, Nabouchodonosor, as he heard the judgement of the vision, preserved the words in his heart.
4:29	---	[. . .]	4:26	At the end of twelve months as he was walking upon the palace of the kingdom of Babylon	4:26	After a year, as he was walking upon the temple shrine of the kingdom in Babylon	4:26	And after twelve months, the king was walking upon the walls of the city in all his glory and he was going through its towers
4:30	---	[. . .]	4:27	and responding the king said "Is this not the great Babylon which I built as the house of the kingdom by the power of my might for the glory of my majesty?"	4:27	the king responded and said "Is this not the great Babylon which I built into the house of the kingdom in the power of my might for the honour of my glory?"	4:27	and responding he said "This is the great Babylon, which I built in the might of my power and it will be called the house of my kingdom."

NRSV¹	Qumran Fragments		Masoretic Text (MT)		Theodotion (Θ)		Old Greek (OG)	
4:31	---	[. . .]	4:28	While the word was still in the king's mouth, a voice fell from the heavens, "O King Nebuchadnezzar, it is said to you: the kingdom has passed from you!	4:28	While the word was still in the king's mouth, a voice came from the heaven, "O King Nabouchodonosor, they say to you: The kingdom has passed from you!	4:28	And at the completion of his word, he heard a voice from the heaven, "O King Nabouchodonosor, it is said to you: The kingdom of Babylon has been taken away from you and is being given to another, to a human who was despised in your house. Behold I am appointing him over your kingdom, and he will receive your authority and your glory and your luxury, so that you may know that God of the heaven has authority in the human kingdom, and he will give it to those whom he desires. But at the rising of the sun another king will rejoice in your house and will take hold of your glory and your power and your authority.

NRSV[1]	Qumran Fragments		Masoretic Text (MT)		Theodotion (Θ)		Old Greek (OG)	
4:32	4QDanª 8.17	[. . .] the [human . . .] and [. . .] to those whom [. . .]	4:29	And from humanity you will be driven out, and with the animals of the field is your dwelling, they will feed you grass like oxen, and seven times will pass over you until when you know that the Most High has authority over the human kingdom and he will give it to those whom he desires."	4:29	And from humanity they will drive you out, and with animals of the field will be your dwelling, and they will feed you grass like an ox, and seven times will be changed over you until when you know that the Most High has authority over the human kingdom and he will give it to those whom he desires."	4:29	And the angels will drive you for seven years, and you will never be seen nor will you ever speak with any human. They will feed you grass like an ox, and your pasture will be the tender grass of the earth. Behold, instead of your glory they will bind you, and another will have your luxurious house and the kingdom.
4:33	4QDanª 8.18	[. . .] grass [. . .]	4:30	In that moment the word was fulfilled upon Nebuchadnezzar, and from humanity he was driven out and he was eating grass like oxen and his body was wet from the dew of the heavens, until when his hair grew long like that of eagles and his nails were like those of birds.	4:30	That same hour the word was fulfilled upon Nabouchodonosor, and he was driven away from humans and he was eating grass like a cow, and from the dew of the heaven his body was bathed, until when his hair lengthened like that of lions and his nails were those of birds.	4:30	By early morning everything concerning you will be completed, O Nabouchodonosor King of Babylon, and not one of all these things will be lacking."
							4:30a	"I, Nabouchodonosor King of Babylon, was bound seven years. They fed me grass like an ox, and from the green shoots of the earth I was eating. And after seven years I gave my soul to supplication, and I prayed before the Lord God of the heaven concerning my sins and I petitioned the great God of gods about my ignorances.

NRSV[1]	Qumran Fragments	Masoretic Text (MT)	Theodotion (Θ)	Old Greek (OG)
				4:30b And my hairs became like wings of an eagle, my nails like those of a lion. My flesh and my heart were changed, I was walking about naked with the animals of the earth. I saw a dream, and forebodings took hold of me, and after a time a great sleep took me and drowsiness fell upon me.
				4:30c And at the completion of seven years my time of redemption came, and my sins and my ignorances were fulfilled before the God of the heaven. And I asked the great God of the gods about my ignorances, and behold one angel called me from heaven: 'Nabouchodonosor, serve the holy God of the heaven and give glory to the Most High. The palace of your nation is being given back to you.'

NRSV[1]	Qumran Fragments	Masoretic Text (MT)		Theodotion (Θ)		Old Greek (OG)	
4:34	-	[...]	4:31	And at the end of the days, I, Nebuchadnezzar, lifted up my eyes to the heavens and my reason was returned to me, and I blessed the Most High and I praised and glorified the one who lives forever, for his authority is an eternal authority and his kingdom is from generation and generation.	4:31	And after the end of the days, I, Nabouchodonosor, lifted my eyes to the heaven, and my reason was returned to me, and I blessed the Most High and I praised and glorified the one who lives forever, for his authority is an eternal authority and his kingdom is from generation and generation.	---	
4:35	---	[...]	4:32	And all the inhabitants of the earth are counted as nothing, and he does what he desires with the army of the heavens and the inhabitants of the earth, and there is none who will stay his hand and say to him "What have you done?"	4:32	And all the inhabitants of the earth are counted as nothing, and he acts according to his will with the army of the heaven and the settlements of the earth, and there is no one who will stay his hand or say to him "What have you done?"	---	
4:36	---	[...]	4:33	At that time my reason was returned to me, and for the honour of my kingdom my glory and my splendour returned to me, and my counsellors and lords sought me, and I was established in my kingdom and even more greatness was added to me.	4:33	At the same time my reason was returned to me, and I came into the honour of my kingdom, and my form returned to me, and my tyrants and my nobles sought me, and I was made strong over my kingdom, and even more greatness was added to me.	4:33	On that day my kingdom was restored to me, and my glory was given back to me.

NRSV[1]	Qumran Fragments	Masoretic Text (MT)	Theodotion (Θ)	Old Greek (OG)
4:37	---	4:34 Now I, Nebuchadnezzar, praise, exalt and glorify the king of the heavens for all his works are true and his ways are justice and he is able to bring low those who walk in pride.	4:34 Now, therefore, I, Nabouchodonosor, praise and exalt and glorify the kingdom of the heaven for all his works are true and his ways and all those who walk in pride he is able to bring low.	4:34 I give thanks to the Most High and I praise the creator of the heaven and the earth and the seas and the rivers and everything in them. I confess and I praise, that He is the God of gods and Lord of lords and Lord of kings, that he does signs and wonders and changed times and seasons removing a kingdom from kings and appointing others in place of them.
	[...]			4:34a From now on I will serve him, and from the fear of him trembling took, and I praise all his holy ones. For the gods of the nations do not have power in themselves to turn over a kingdom of a king to another and to kill and to make alive and to make signs and great and terrible wonders and to change immensely great events just as the God of the heaven did in me and he changed great events with me. I will offer a sacrifice to the Most High as a

NRSV[1]	Qumran Fragments	Masoretic Text (MT)	Theodotion (Θ)	Old Greek (OG)
				sweet fragrance to the Lord for my soul all the days of my kingdom and I will do that which is pleasing before him, I and my people [my nation] and my lands that are under my authority. And as many as have spoken against the God of the heaven, and whoever might be caught speaking anything, I will condemn these to death."
				4:34b Then the King Nabouchodonosor wrote a circular letter to all the nations in each place and to lands and languages who live in all the lands to generations and generations: "Praise the Lord the God of the heaven, offer a sacrifice and an offering to him gloriously. I, king of kings, give thanks to him gloriously, that he did thus with me. On the same day he sat me upon my throne, and I took hold of my authority and my kingdom

NRSV[1]	Qumran Fragments	Masoretic Text (MT)	Theodotion (Θ)	Old Greek (OG)
				4:34c among my people, and my majesty was restored to me." King Nabouchodonosor to all the nations and to all the lands and to all inhabitants of them: May peace be increased to you all times. And now I will show you the deeds that the great God has done with me. It seemed good to me to proclaim to you and your wise men that God is one, and his wonders are great, his palace is eternal, his authority is from generation to generations. And he sent letters about all that happened to him in his kingdom to every nation which were under his rule.
…	…	…	…	…
5:17	4QDan[a] 12.2–3 Then Da[n]iel [res]ponded and he said before the king: "Let [your] g[i]fts [be for yourself] and give your rewards to another. Nevertheless [I will re]ad [the] writing to the king and make kno[wn] its interpretation for him.	5:17 Then Daniel responded and he said before the king: "Let your gifts be for yourself and give your rewards to another. Nevertheless I will read the writing to the king and make known the interpretation for him.	5:17 And Daniel said before the king: "Let your gifts be for yourself and give your rewards to another. Nevertheless I will read the writing and make known its interpretation.	5:17 Then Daniel stood before the writing and read it and thus he answered to the king: "This is the writing; it has been numbered, it has been reckoned, it has been taken away. And the writing hand stopped, and this is their interpretation.

NRSV[1]	Qumran Fragments	Masoretic Text (MT)		Theodotion (Θ)		Old Greek (OG)
5:18	4QDan[a] 12.3–4	5:18	You, O King, the Most High god gave your father Nebuchadnezzar the kingdom, greatness, honour and glory.	5:18	You, O King, the Most High god gave your father Nabouchodonosor the kingdom, greatness, honour and glory.	---
	[You, O King,] the [Mo] st High god [. . .] [. . . the] kingdom, [greatness,] glory and honou[r.]					
5:19	4QDan[a] 12.4–6 and 4QDan[b] 5.1–2.	5:19	And because of the greatness which he gave him, all peoples, nations, and languages were trembling and fearful before him. He killed those he wanted to kill and he kept alive those he wanted to keep alive, he exalted those he wanted to exalt and he humbled those he wanted to humble.	5:19	And because of the greatness which he gave him, all peoples, tribes, languages were trembling and fearful before him. He would kill those he wanted, and he would beat those he wanted, and he would exalt those he wanted, and he would humble those he wanted.	---
	[And because of the] greatness [. . .] [. . . and] lan[guages . . .] [. . .] those [. . .][2] [. . .] those he want[ed . . .] [. . . h]e exalt[ed . . .]					
5:20	4QDan[b] 5.3	5:20	And when his heart was lifted up and his spirit grew strong with pride, he was deposed from the throne of his kingdom and they took his honour from him.	5:20	And when his heart was lifted up and his spirit was strengthened so that he behaved arrogantly, he was deposed from the throne of the kingdom, the honour was stripped from him.	---
	[. . . gr]ew strong with [. . .]					

NRSV[1]	Qumran Fragments		Masoretic Text (MT)		Theodotion (Θ)		Old Greek (OG)
5:21	4QDan[b] 6.6	[...]the Most High god [...] [...] over the [...] kingdom [...]	5:21	From the sons of humanity he was driven out and his heart became like that of an animal, and with the wild asses was his dwelling, they fed him grass like oxen and his body was wet from the dew of the heavens until he knew that the Most High god has authority over the human kingdom and over it he will set those whom he desires.	5:21	And from humans he was driven out and his heart was given with the animals, and with wild asses was his dwelling, and they would feed him grass like an ox, and from the dew of the heaven his body was bathed until he knew that the Most High god is lord over the human kingdom, and he will give it to whom he desires.	---
5:22	4QDan[b] 6.7	[... Be]l[shazzar, have] n[ot ...]	5:22	And you, his son Belshazzar, have not humbled your heart even though you knew all these things.	5:22	And you, his son Baltasar, have not humbled your heart before all these things you knew.	---

BIBLIOGRAPHY

Abusch, Tzvi. "Ghost and God: Some Observations on a Babylonian Understanding of Human Nature." Pages 363–383 in *Self, Soul and Body in Religious Experience*. Edited by Albert I. Baumgarten, Jan Assmann, and Gary G. Stroumsa. SHR 78. Leiden: Brill, 1998.

Albertz, Rainer. *Der Gott des Daniel: Untersuchungen zu Daniel 4–6 in der Septuagintafassung sowie zur Komposition und Theologie des aramäischen Danielbuches*. SBS 131. Stuttgart: Katholisches Bibelwerk, 1988.

Albertz, Rainer. "The Social Setting of the Aramaic and Hebrew Book of Daniel." Pages 171–204 in *The Book of Daniel: Composition and Reception*. Edited by John J. Collins and Peter W. Flint. VTSup 83. Leiden: Brill, 2001.

Aldama, José A. de. *Repertorium Pseudochrysostomicum*. Documents, Études et Répertoires publiés par l'Institut de Recherche et d'Histoire des Texts 10. Paris: Éditions du Centre National de la Recherche Scientifique, 1965.

Alderman, Isaac. *The Animal at Unease with Itself: Death Anxiety and the Animal–Human Boundary in Genesis 2–3*. London: Lexington Books/Fortress Academic, 2020.

Alexander, Philip S. "The Enochic Literature and the Bible." Pages 57–69 in *The Bible as Book: The Hebrew Bible and the Judaean Desert Discoveries*. Edited by Edward D. Herbert and Emanuel Tov. London: British Library & Oak Knoll Press in association with The Scriptorium Center for Christian Antiquities, 2002.

Alexander, T. Desmond. *From Paradise to the Promised Land: An Introduction to the Pentateuch*. 3rd ed. Grand Rapids: Baker Academic, 2012.

Almond, Philip C. *England's First Demonologist: Reginald Scot and 'The Discoverie of Witchcraft'*. London: I. B. Tauris, 2011.

Alobaidi, Joseph, ed. and trans. *The Book of Daniel: The Commentary of R. Saadia Gaon: Edition and Translation*. Bible in History 6. Oxford: Peter Lang, 2006.

Alster, Bendt. "Ninurta and the Turtle: On Parodia Sacra in Sumerian Literature." Pages 13–36 in *Approaches to Sumerian Literature: Studies in Honour of Stip (H.L.I. Vanstiphout)*. Edited by Piotr Michalowski and Niek Veldhuis. CM 35. Leiden: Brill, 2006).

Alster, Bendt, and Herman Vanstiphout. "Lahar and Ashnan: Presentation and Analysis of a Sumerian Disputation." *ASJ* 9 (1987): 1–43.

Amara, Dalia. "18.3.2. Daniel: Primary Translations: Septuagint." *THB* 1c:542–554.

Amara, Dalia. "The Old Greek Version of Daniel: The Translation, the *Vorlage* and the Redaction" [Hebrew]. PhD diss., Ben Gurion University of the Negev, 2006.

Andreasen, Niels-Erik. "Adam and Adapa: Two Anthropological Characters." *AUSS* 19 (1981): 179–194.

Angel, Joseph L. "The Humbling of the Arrogant and the 'Wild Man' and 'Tree Stump' Traditions in the *Book of Giants* and Daniel 4." Pages 61–80 in *Ancient Tales of Giants from Qumran and Turfan: Contexts, Traditions, and Influences*. Edited by Matthew Goff, Loren T. Stuckenbruck, and Enrico Morano. WUNT 360. Tübingen: Mohr Siebeck, 2016.

Annus, Amar. "On the Origin of the Watchers: A Comparative Study of the Antediluvian Wisdom in Mesopotamian and Jewish Traditions." *JSP* 19 (2010): 277–320.

Arbesmann, Rudolph, Emily Joseph Daly, and Edwin A. Quain, eds and trans. *Tertullian, Apologetical Works and Minucius Felix, Octavius.* Repr. FC 10. Washington, DC: Catholic University of America Press, 1985.

Archer, Gleason L., ed. and trans. *Jerome's Commentary on Daniel.* Eugene, OR: Wipf and Stock, 2009.

Artemov, Nikita. Review of *Cosmogony, Theogony and Anthropogeny in Sumerian Texts,* by Jan J.W. Lisman. *Orientalistische Literaturzeitung* 112 (2017): 213–218.

Ashley, Timothy R. "The Book of Daniel Chapters I–VI: Text, Versions and the Problems of Exegesis." PhD diss., University of St. Andrews, 1975.

Atkins, Peter J. "Mythology or Zoology: A Study on the Impact of Translation History in Isaiah 13:21." *Biblical Interpretation* 24 (2016): 48–59.

Atkins, Peter J. "Praise by Animals in the Hebrew Bible." *JSOT* 44 (2020): 500–513.

Avalos, Hector. "Nebuchadnezzar's Affliction: New Mesopotamian Parallels for Daniel 4." *JBL* 133 (2014): 497–507.

Bailey, John A. "Male, Female and the Pursuit of Immortality in the Gilgamesh Epic." *La Parola Del Passato Rivista Di Studi Antichi* 31 (1976): 431–457.

Baillet, Maurice. "504. Paroles des Luminaires (Premier Exemplaire: DibHamᵃ)." Pages 137–175 in *Qumran Grotte 4 III (4Q482–4Q520).* Edited by Maurice Baillet. DJD VII. Oxford: Clarendon, 1982.

Baldwin, Joyce. *Daniel: An Introduction and Commentary.* TOTC. Leicester: Inter-Varsity, 1978.

Banks, S. E., and J. W. Binns, eds and trans. *Gervase of Tilbury: Otia Imperialia: Recreation for an Emperor.* Oxford: Clarendon, 2002.

Bardenhewer, Otto. *Geschichte der altkirchlichen Literatur.* 5 vols. Freiburg: Herder, 1913–1932.

Barnes, Albert. *Notes, Critical, Illustrative, and Practical on the Book of Daniel.* New York: Leavitt & Allen, 1853.

Barnes, Timothy D. "Constantine and the Christians of Persia." *Journal of Roman Studies* 75 (1985): 126–136.

Barnes, Timothy D. *Tertullian: A Historical and Literary Study.* Oxford: Clarendon, 1971.

Barron, Patrick. "The Separation of Wild Animal Nature and Human Nature in *Gilgamesh*: Roots of a Contemporary Theme." *Papers on Language and Literature* 38 (2002): 377–394.

Barthélemy, Dominique. *Critique textuelle de l'Ancien Testament: Tome 3. Ézéchiel, Daniel et les 12 Prophètes.* OBO 50/3. Göttingen: Vandenhoeck & Ruprecht, 1992.

Barthélemy, Dominique. *Les Devaniers d'Aquila: Première publication intégrale du texte des fragments du Dodécaprophéton.* VTSup 10. Leiden: Brill, 1963.

Bartholin, Thomas. *De Morbis Biblicis Miscellanea Medica.* Frankfurt: Danielis Paulli, 1672.

Barton, George A. "The Story of Aḥiḳar and the Book of Daniel." *AJSL* 16 (1900): 242–247.

Bartra, Roger. *Wild Men in the Looking Glass: The Mythic Origins of European Otherness.* Ann Arbor, MI: University of Michigan Press, 1994.

Basson, Alec. "'A King in the Grass': Liminality and Inversion in Daniel 4:28–37." *Journal for Semitics* 18 (2009): 1–14.

Batto, Bernard F. "Creation Theology in Genesis." Pages 16–38 in *Creation in the Biblical Traditions.* Edited by Richard J. Clifford and John J. Collins. CBQMS 24. Washington, DC: Catholic Biblical Association of America, 1992.

Batto, Bernard F. *Slaying the Dragon: Mythmaking in the Biblical Tradition.* Louisville, KY: Westminster John Knox, 1992.

Bauks, Michaela. "Sacred Trees in the Garden of Eden and Their Ancient Near Eastern Precursors." *Journal of Ancient Judaism* 3 (2012): 267–301.

Baum, Guilielmus, Eduardus Cunitz, and Eduardus Reuss, ed. *Ioannes Calvini, Opera Quae Supersunt Omnia.* 59 vols. Vols 29–87 of *Corpus Reformatorum.* Brunswick: C.A. Schwetschke and Son, 1863–1900.

Beaulieu, Paul-Alain. "Berossus on Late Babylonian History." Pages 116–149 in *Special Issue of Oriental Studies: A Collection of Papers on Ancient Civilizations of Western Asia, Asia Minor and North Africa.* Edited by Yushu Gong and Yiyi Chen. Beijing: University of Beijing, 2007.

Beaulieu, Paul-Alain. "Nabonidus the Mad King: A Reconsideration of His Steles from Harran and Babylon." Pages 137–166 in *Representations of Political Power: Case Histories from Times of Change and Dissolving Order in the Ancient Near East.* Edited by Marlies Heinz and Marian H. Feldman. Winona Lake, IN: Eisenbrauns, 2007.

Beaulieu, Paul-Alain. *The Reign of Nabonidus King of Babylon 556–539 B.C.* YNER 10. New Haven: Yale University Press, 1989.

Berg, Shane. "Ben Sira, the Genesis Creation Accounts, and the Knowledge of God's Will." *JBL* 132 (2013): 139–157.

Bevan, Anthony A. *A Short Commentary on the Book of Daniel.* Cambridge: Cambridge University Press, 1892.

Beverly, Jared. "Nebuchadnezzar and the Animal Mind (Daniel 4)." *JSOT* 45 (2020): 145–157.

Beyer, Klaus. "זיז." *TDOT* 16:235–236.

Bing, John D. "Adapa and Humanity: Mortal or Evil?" *JANES* 18 (1986): 1–2.

Bing, John D. "Adapa and Immortality." *UF* 16 (1984): 53–56.

Binsfeld, Peter. *Tractatus De Confessionibus Maleficarum et Sagarum.* Trier: Heinrich Bock, 1596.

Black, Jeremy A., Graham Cunningham, Jarle Ebeling, Esther Flückiger-Hawker, Eleanor Robson, Jon Taylor, and Gábor Zólyomi. *The Electronic Text Corpus of Sumerian Literature.* Oxford 1998–2006 (http://etcsl.orinst.ox.ac.uk/).

Bledsoe, Amanda M. Davis. "The Identity of the 'Mad King' of Daniel 4 in Light of Ancient Near Eastern Sources." *Christianesimo nella storia* 33 (2012): 743–758.

Bledsoe, Amanda M. Davis. "The Relationship of the Different Editions of Daniel: A History of Scholarship." *CurBR* 13 (2015): 175–190.

Bledsoe, Amanda M. Davis. *See also* Davis, Amanda M.

Blenkinsopp, Joseph. *Creation, Un-creation, Re-creation: A Discursive Commentary on Genesis 1–11.* London: T&T Clark, 2011.

Bludau, August. *Die alexandrinische Übersetzung des Buches Daniels und ihr Verhältniss zum massorethischen Text.* BibS(F) 2.2.3. Freiburg: Herder, 1897.

Bodin, Jean. *De la Démonomanie des Sorciers.* Paris: Jacques Du Puys, 1580.

Bodin, Jean. *Universae naturae theatrum.* Frankfurt: Wechel, 1597.

Boguet, Henri. *Discours exécrable des Sorciers.* 2nd ed. Lyon: Pierre Rigaud, 1608.

Böhl, Franz Marius Theodor de Liagre. "Die Mythe vom weisen Adapa." *WO* 2 (1959): 416–431.

Borger, Rykle. "Die Beschwörungsserie *Bīt Mēseri* und die Himmelfahrt Henochs." *JNES* 33 (1974): 183–196.

Borgnet, Augustus, ed. *B. Alberti Magni Opera Omnia.* 38 vols. Paris: Vivè, 1890–1899.

Bottéro, Jean. "La creation de l'homme et son nature dans le poème d'*Atraḫasīs.*" Pages 24–32 in *Societes and Languages of the Ancient Near East: Studies in Honour of I.M. Diakonoff.* Edited by Muhammad A. Dandamayev et al. Warminster, UK: Aris & Phillips, 1982.

Bottéro, Jean. *L'épopée de Gilgameš: Le grand homme qui ne voulait pas mourir*. Paris: Galimard, 1992.

Bottéro, Jean. *Mesopotamia: Writing, Reasoning, and the Gods*. Translated by Zainab Bahrani and Marc Van De Mieroop. London: University of Chicago Press, 1992.

Bottéro, Jean, and Samuel N. Kramer. *Lorsque les Dieux Faisaient l'Homme, Mythologie Mésopotamienne*. Paris: Gallimard, 1993.

Bowen, Nancy R. *Ezekiel*. AOTC. Nashville: Abingdon, 2010.

Braasch, Birte. *Die LXX-Übersetzung des Danielbuches: Eine Orientierungschilfe für das religiöse und politisch-gesellschaftliche Leben in der ptolemäischen Diaspora: Eine rezeptionsgeschichtliche Untersuchung von Daniel 1–7*. PhD diss., Fachbereich Evangelische Theologie der Universität Hamburg, 2004.

Bregman, Marc. *The Tanhuma-Yelammedenu Literature: Studies in the Evolution of the Versions*. Piscataway, NJ: Gorgias, 2003.

Bregman, Marc. "Textual Witnesses of the Tanhuma-Yelamdenu Midrashim" [Hebrew]. Pages 49–56 in *Proceedings of the Ninth World Congress of Jewish Studies, Division C: Jewish Thought and Literature*. Edited by David Assaf. Jerusalem: Magnes, 1986.

Bromiley, Geoffrey W., ed. *International Standard Bible Encyclopedia*. Rev. ed. 4 vols. Grand Rapids: Eerdmans, 1979–1988.

Brown, Dennis. *Vir Trilinguis: A Study in the Biblical Exegesis of Saint Jerome*. Kampen: Kok Pharos, 1992.

Brown, Francis, S. R. Driver, and Charles A. Briggs, *A Hebrew and English Lexicon of the Old Testament*. Oxford: Clarendon, 1907.

Bruns, Peter. "Polychronius von Apamea: Der Exeget und Theologie." *Studia Patristica* 37 (2001): 404–412.

Buccellati, Giorgio. "Adapa, Genesis, and the Notion of Faith." *UF* 5 (1973): 61–70.

Bultmann, Rudolph. "ἄγνοια." *TDNT* 1:116–119.

Bunta, Silviu N. "The *Mēsu*-Tree and the Animal Inside: Theomorphism and Theriomorphism in Daniel 4." Pages 364–384 in *The Theophaneia School: Jewish Roots of Eastern Christian Mysticism*. Edited by Basil Lourié and Andrei Orlov. Scrinium 3. St Petersburg: Byzantinorossica, 2007.

Burstein, Stanley M. *The Babyloniaca of Berossus*. Sources from the Ancient Near East 1.5. Malibu, CA: Udena, 1978.

Bynum, Caroline Walker. *Metamorphosis and Identity*. New York: Zone Books, 2001.

Bynum, Caroline Walker. "Metamorphosis, or Gerald and the Werewolf." *Speculum* 73 (1998): 987–1013.

Calarco, Matthew. *Thinking Through Animals: Identity, Difference, Indistinction*. Stanford: Stanford University Press, 2015.

Callender, Dexter E., Jr. *Adam in Myth and History: Ancient Israelite Perspectives on the Primal Human*. HSS 48. Winona Lake, IN: Eisenbrauns, 2000.

Calmet, Augustin. *Commentaire Litteral sur Tous les Livres de L'Ancien et du Nouveau Testament: Ezechiel, et Daniel*. Paris: Pierre Emery, 1715.

Calov, Abraham. *Biblia Veteris et Novi Testament Illustrata*. 4 vols. Frankfurt: Wustius, 1672–1676.

Carley, Keith. "Psalm 8: An Apology for Domination." Pages 111–124 in *Readings from the Perspective of Earth*. Edited by Norman C. Habel. The Earth Bible 1. Sheffield: Sheffield Academic Press, 2000.

Casetti, Pierre. *Gibt es ein Leben vor dem Tod?: Eine Auslegung von Psalm 49.* OBO 44.
Göttingen: Vandenhoeck & Ruprecht, 1982.

Cason, Thomas S. "Confessions of an Impotent Potentate: Reading Daniel 4 through the
Lens of Ritual Punishment Theory." *JSOT* 39 (2014): 79–100.

Cavigneaux, Antoine. "Magica Mariana." *RA* 88 (1994): 155–161.

Cavigneaux, Antoine. "Shulgi, Nabonide, et les Grecs." Pages 63–72 in *An Experienced
Scribe Who Neglects Nothing: Ancient Near Eastern Studies in Honor of Jacob Klein.*
Edited by Yitschak Sefati et al. Bethesda, MD: CDL, 2005.

Cavigneaux, Antoine. "Une versions sumérienne de la légende d'Adapa. Textes de Tell
Haddad X." *ZA* 104 (2014): 1–41.

Cavigneaux, Antoine, and Farouk N. H. Al-Rawi. *Gilgameš et la Mort. Textes de Tell
Haddad VI.* CM 19. Groningen: Styx, 2000.

Ceccarelli, Manuel. *Enki und Ninmah: Eine mythische Erzählung in sumerischer Sprache.*
Orientalische Religionen in der Antike 16. Tübingen: Mohr Siebeck, 2016.

Ceriani, Antonio M. *Codex syro-hexaplaris Ambrosianus photolithographice editus.*
Monumenta sacra et profana 7. Milan: Pogliani, 1874.

Charles, Robert H. *A Critical and Exegetical Commentary on the Book of Daniel.* Oxford:
Clarendon, 1929.

Châtelet, Émilie du. *Examens de la Bible.* ed. Betram Eugene Schwarzbach. 3 vols. Paris:
Honoré Champion, 2011.

Chazan, Robert. "Daniel 9:24–27: Exegesis and Polemics." Pages 144–159 in *Contra
Iudaeos: Ancient and Medieval Polemics between Christians and Jews.* Edited by Ora
Limor and Guy G. Stroumsa. Tübingen: Mohr Siebeck, 1996.

Chazon, Esther G. "The Creation and Fall of Adam in the Dead Sea Scrolls." Pages 13–23
in *The Book of Genesis in Jewish and Oriental Christian Interpretation: A Collection of
Essays.* Edited by Judith Frishman and Lucas Van Rompay. Traditio Exegetica Græca 5.
Leuven: Peeters, 1997.

Chen, Yi S. *The Primeval Flood Catastrophe: Origins and Early Development in
Mesopotamian Traditions.* Oxford: Oxford University Press, 2013.

Civil, Miguel. "Sumerian Flood Story." Pages 138–145 in *Atra-ḫasīs: The Babylonian Story
of the Flood.* Edited by Wilfred G. Lambert and Alan R. Millard. Winona Lake, IN:
Eisenbrauns, 1999.

Clarke, Samuel. *The Life and Death of Nebuchadnezzar the Great.* London: William Miller,
1665.

Clifford, Richard J. *Creation Accounts in the Ancient Near East and in the Bible.* CBQMS
26. Washington, DC: Catholic Biblical Association of America, 1994.

Clines, David J.A., ed. *Dictionary of Classical Hebrew.* 9 vols. Sheffield: Sheffield Phoenix,
1993–2016.

Collins, John J. "4QPrayer of Nabonidus ar." Pages 83–94 in *Qumran Cave 4.XVII:
Parabiblical Texts, Part 3.* Edited by George J. Brooke et al. DJD 22. Oxford: Clarendon,
1996.

Collins, John J. "The Court-Tales in Daniel and the Development of Apocalyptic." *JBL* 94
(1975): 218–234.

Collins, John J. *Daniel: A Commentary on the Book of Daniel.* Hermeneia. Minneapolis:
Fortress, 1993.

Collins, John J. *Daniel with an Introduction to Apocalyptic Literature.* FOTL 20. Grand
Rapids: Eerdmans, 1984.

Collins, John J. "New Light on the Book of Daniel From the Dead Sea Scrolls." Pages
180–196 in *Perspectives in the Study of the Old Testament and Early Judaism: A*

Symposium in Honour of Adam S. van der Woude on the Occasion of His 70th Birthday. Edited by Florentino García Martínez and Ed Noort. Leiden: Brill, 1998.

Collins, Matthew A. "An Ongoing Tradition: Aronofsky's *Noah* as 21st-Century Rewritten Scripture." Pages 8–33 in *Noah as Antihero: Darren Aronofsky's Cinematic Deluge.* Edited by Rhonda Burnette-Bletsch and Jon Morgan. Routledge Studies in Religion and Film 9. London: Routledge, 2017.

Conybeare, Frederick C., James R. Harris, and Agnes S. Lewis. *The Story of Ahikar from the Aramaic, Syriac, Arabic, Armenian, Ethiopic, Old Turkish, Greek and Slavonic Versions.* 2nd ed. Cambridge: Cambridge University Press, 1913.

Courtray, Régis. *Prophète des temps derniers: Jérôme commente Daniel.* ThH 119. Paris: Beauchesne, 2009.

Coxon, Peter W. "Another Look at Nebuchadnezzar's Madness." Pages 211–222 in *The Book of Daniel in the Light of New Findings.* Edited by Adam S. van der Woude. BETL 106. Leuven: Leuven University Press and Peeters, 1993.

Coxon, Peter W. "The Great Tree of Daniel 4." Pages 91–112 in *A Word in Season: Essays in Honour of William McKane.* Edited by James D. Martin and Philip R. Davies. JSOTSup 42. Sheffield: JSOT Press, 1986.

Cross, Frank M. *The Ancient Library of Qumran.* 3rd ed. Sheffield: Sheffield Academic Press, 1995.

Cross, Frank M. "Fragments of the Prayer of Nabonidus." *IEJ* 34 (1984): 260–264.

Cunningham, David S. "The Way of All Flesh: Rethinking the *Imago Dei.*" Pages 100–117 in *Creaturely Theology: On God, Humans and Other Animals.* Edited by Celia Deane-Drummond and David Clough. London: SCM Press, 2009.

Dalley, Stephanie. *Myths from Mesopotamia: Creation, the Flood, Gilgamesh, and Others.* Oxford: Oxford University Press, 1989.

David, Pablo S. "The Composition and Structure of the Book of Daniel: A Synchronic and Diachronic Reading." PhD diss., Katholieke Universiteit, 1991.

Davis, Amanda M. "A Reconsideration of the MT and OG Editions of Daniel 4." MA diss., Emory University, 2012.

Davis, Amanda M. *See also* Bledsoe, Amanda M. Davis.

Davis, Kipp, and Torleif Elgvin. "1QDan[b] (1Q72) with MS 1926/4b (Dan 3.26–27)." Pages 257–270 in *Gleanings from the Caves: Dead Sea Scrolls and Artefacts from the Schøyen Collection.* Edited by Torleif Elgvin, Kipp Davis and Michael Langlois. LSTS 71. London: T&T Clark, 2016.

Day, John. "The Daniel of Ugarit and Ezekiel and the Hero of the Book of Daniel." *VT* 30 (1980): 174–184.

Day, John. *From Creation to Babel: Studies in Genesis 1–11.* London: Bloomsbury, 2013.

Day, John. "Wisdom and the Garden of Eden." Pages 336–352 in *Perspectives on Israelite Wisdom: Proceedings of the Oxford Old Testament Seminar.* Edited by John Jarick. LHBOTS 618. London: Bloomsbury T&T Clark, 2016.

De Breucker, Geert. "De Babyloniaca van Berossos van Babylon: Inleiding, editie en commentaar." PhD diss., University of Groningen, 2012.

De Breucker, Geert. "Berossos and the Construction of a Near Eastern Cultural History in Response to the Greeks." Pages 25–34 in *Constructions of Greek Past: Identity and Historical Consciousness from Antiquity to the Present.* Edited by Hero Hokwerda. Groningen: Brill, 2003.

De Breucker, Geert. "Berossos between Tradition and Innovation." Pages 637–657 in *The Oxford Handbook of Cuneiform Culture.* Edited by Karen Radner and Eleanor Robson. Oxford: Oxford University Press, 2011.

De Breucker, Geert. "Berossos of Babylon (680)." *Brill's New Jacoby*. Edited by Ian Worthington. Leiden: Brill, 2016. Consulted online on 24 June 2020 http://dx.doi.org/10.1163/1873-5363_bnj_a680.

Debel, Hans. "Retracing Authoritative Traditions behind the Scriptural Texts: The Book of Daniel as a Case in Point." Pages 117–138 in *The Process of Authority: The Dynamics in Transmission and Reception of Canonical Texts*. Edited by Jan Dušek and Jan Roskovec. DCLS 27. Berlin: De Gruyter, 2016.

Decker, E., et al. *Tertullianus Opera I. Opera Catholica. Adversus Marcionem*. Corpus Christianorum: Series Latina 1. Turnhout: Brepols, 1954.

Denis, Albert-Marie. *Introduction aux pseudépigraphes grecs d'Ancien Testament*. STVP 1. Leiden: Brill, 1970.

Denning-Bolle, Sara. *Wisdom in Akkadian Literature: Expression, Instruction, Dialogue*. Mededelingen en Verhandelingen van het Vooraziatisch-Egyptisch Genootschap "Ex Oriente Lux" 28. Leiden: Ex Oriente Lux, 1992.

Deusing, Anton. *Fasciculus Dissertationum Selectarum*. Groningen: Johannis Colleni, 1660

Di Lella, Alexander A. "Daniel 4:7–14: Poetic Analysis and Biblical Background." Pages 247–258 in *Mélanges bibliques et orientaux en l'honneur de M. Henri Cazelles*. Edited by André Caquot and Mathias Delcor. AOAT 212. Neukirchen-Vluyn: Neukirchener Verlag, 1981.

Di Lella, Alexander A. "The Textual History of Septuagint-Daniel and Theodotion-Daniel." Pages 586–607 in *The Book of Daniel: Composition and Reception*. Edited by John J. Collins and Peter W. Flint. VTSup 83. Leiden: Brill, 2001.

Dickson, Keith. "Enki and Ninhursag: The Trickster in Paradise." *JNES* 66 (2007): 1–32.

Dietz O. Edzard, "Eas doppelzüngiger Rat an Adapa: ein Lösungsvorschlag," *Orientalia* 71 (2002): 415–416.

Dijk, Jan J. A. van. "La Motif Cosmique dans la Pensée Sumérienne." *AcOr* 28 (1964): 1–59.

Dijk, Jan J. A. van. "Sumerische Religion." Pages 431–496 in *Handbuch der Religionsgeschichte* I. Edited by Jes P. Assmussen and Jorgen Læssøe. Göttingen: Vandenhoeck & Ruprecht, 1971.

Dillinger, Johannes. "'Species', 'Phantasia', 'Raison': Werewolves and Shape-Shifters in Demonological Literature." Pages 142–158 in *Werewolf Histories*. Edited by Willem de Blécourt. Palgrave Historical Studies in Witchcraft and Magic. Basingstoke: Palgrave Macmillan, 2015.

Diodati, Giovanni. *Pious Annotations upon the Holy Bible*. Translated by Robert Gentili. 3rd edition. London: James Flesher, 1651.

DiPalma, Brian Charles. "The Animalistic Nebuchadnezzar and the Heroic Encounter: Daniel 4:30 Iconographically Revisited." *JBL* 139 (2020): 499–520.

DiTomasso, Lorenzo. *The Book of Daniel and the Apocryphal Daniel Literature*. STVP 20. Leiden: Brill, 2005.

Dommershausen, Werner. *Nabonid im Buche Daniel*. Mainz: Grünewald, 1964.

Doob, Penelope B. R. *Nebuchadnezzar's Children: Conventions of Madness in Middle English Literature*. London: Yale University Press, 1974.

Doseman, Thomas B., and Konrad Schmid, eds. *A Farewell to the Yahwist? The Composition of the Pentateuch in Recent European Interpretation*. Atlanta: SBL Press, 2006.

Dougherty, Raymond P. *Nabonidus and Belshazzar: A Study of the Closing Events of the Neo-Babylonian Empire*. YOSR 15. New Haven: Yale University Press, 1929.

Driver, Samuel R. *The Book of Daniel*. The Cambridge Bible for Schools and Colleges. Cambridge: Cambridge University Press, 1900.

Ebeling, Erich, ed., *Keilschrifttexte aus Assur religiösen Inhalts.* 2 vols. Leipzig: Hinrichs, 1919–1923.

Edzard Dietz O., and Claus Wilcke. "Vorläufiger Bericht über die Inschriftenfunde Frühjahr 1973, Frühjahr 1974, Herbst 1974." Pages 83–92 in *Isin-Išān Baḥrīyāt I. Die Ergebnisse der Ausgrabungen 1973–1974.* Edited by Barthel Hrouda. ABAW Philosophisch-Historische Klasse Neue Folge 79. Münster: Verlag der Bayerischen Akadaemie der Wissenschaften, 1977.

Eggler, Jürg. *Influences and Traditions Underlying the Vision of Daniel 7:2–14.* OBO 177. Göttingen: Vandenhoeck & Ruprecht, 2000.

Elliger, Karl, and Wilhelm Rudolph, eds. *Biblia Hebraica Stuttgartensia.* 5th ed. Stuttgart: Deutsche Bibelstiftung, 1977.

Ellis, Richard S. *Foundation Deposits in Ancient Mesopotamia.* YNER 2. New Haven: Yale University Press, 1968.

Erman, Adolf. "Eine ägyptische Quelle der 'Spüche Salomos.'" *SPAW* 15 (1924): 86–93.

Erzberger, Johanna. "Nebuchadnezzar, Lord of the Wild Animals: Understanding a Difference Between LXX Jer and MT Jer in Light of Dan." Pages 678–687 in *Die Septuaginta – Orte und Intentionen 5. Internationale Fachtagung veranstaltet von Septuaginta Deutsch (LXX.D), Wuppertal 24.–27. Juli 2014.* Edited by Siegfried Kreuzer et al. WUNT 361. Tübingen: Mohr Siebeck, 2016.

Eshel, Esther. "Possible Sources of the Book of Daniel." Pages 387–394 in *The Book of Daniel: Composition and Reception.* Edited by John J. Collins and Peter W. Flint. VTSup 83. Leiden: Brill, 2001.

Espak, Peeter. "Creation of Animals in Sumerian Mythology." Pages 303–312 in *Animals and their Relation to Gods, Humans and Things in the Ancient World.* Edited by Raija Mattila, Sanae Ito, and Sebastian Fink. Studies in Universal and Cultural History. Wiesbaden: Springer VS, 2019.

Faulhaber, Michael. *Die Propheten-Catenen nach römischen Handschriften.* BibS(F) 4.2.3. Freiburg: Herder, 1899.

Faust, Manfred. "Metaphorische Schimpfwörter." *Indogermanische Forschungen* 74 (1969): 54–125.

Ferguson, Paul. "Nebuchadnezzar, Gilgamesh, and the 'Babylonian Job.'" *JETS* 37 (1994): 321–331.

Fewell, Danna N. *Circle of Sovereignty: Plotting Politics in the Book of Daniel.* 2nd ed. Nashville: Abingdon, 1991.

Flint, Peter W. "The Daniel Tradition at Qumran." Pages 41–60 in *Eschatology, Messianism, and the Dead Sea Scrolls.* Edited by Craig A. Evans and Peter W. Flint. Grand Rapids: Eerdmans, 1997.

Foster, Benjamin R. *Before the Muses: An Anthology of Akkadian Literature.* 3rd ed. Bethesda, MD: CDL, 2005.

Foster, Benjamin R. "Wisdom and the Gods in Ancient Mesopotamia." *Orientalia* 43 (1974): 345–354.

Fox, Michael V. "The Formation of Proverbs 22:17–23:11." *WO* 38 (2008): 22–37.

Freedman, David N. "The Prayer of Nabonidus." *BASOR* 145 (1957): 31–32.

Fretté, Stanislai E., and Pauli Maré, eds. *Doctoris Angelici Divi Thomae Aquinatis Sacria Ordinis F. F. Praedicatorum Opera Omnia.* 34 vols. Paris: Vivès, 1871–1880.

Friedrich, Johannes B. *Analekten zu Natur-und Heilkunde.* 3 vols. 2nd edition. Ansbach: Carl Brügel, 1846.

Frisch, Alexandria. *The Danielic Discourse on Empire in Second Temple Literature.* JSJSup 176. Leiden: Brill, 2016.

Gadd, Cyril J. "The Harran Inscriptions of Nabonidus." *AnSt* 8 (1958): 35–92.

Gadd, Cyril J. *History and Monuments of Ur.* London: Chatto & Windus, 1929.

Galter, Hannes D. *Der Gott Ea/Enki in der Akkadischen Überlieferung. Eine Bestandsaufnahme des vorhanden Materials.* Dissertationen der Karl-Franzens-Universität Graz 58. Graz: Verlag für die Technische Universität Graz, 1983.

García Martínez, Florentino. *Qumran and Apocalyptic: Studies on the Aramaic Texts from Qumran.* STDJ 9. Leiden: Brill, 1992.

García Martínez, Florentino, and Eibert J. C. Tigchelaar, eds. *The Dead Sea Scrolls Study Edition.* 2 vols. Leiden: Brill, 1997–8.

Gardner, Anne E. "Decoding Daniel: The Case of Dan 7,5." *Bib* 88 (2007): 222–233.

Garlipp, Petra, et al. "Lycanthropy — psychopathological and psychodynamical aspects." *Acta Psychiatrica Scandinavica* 109 (2004): 19–22.

Gaster, Moses. *The Chronicles of Jerahmeel or, The Hebrew Bible Historiale.* London: Royal Asiatic Society, 1899.

Geier, Martin. *Praelectiones Academicae in Danielem Prophetam Habitae Antehac Lipsiae.* Leipzig: Lanckisch, 1667.

Geissen, Angelo. *Der Septuaginta-Text des Buches Daniel, Kap. 5–12, zusammen mit Susanna, Bel et Draco, nach dem Kölner Teil des Papyrus 967.* Papyrologische Texte und Abhandlungen 5. Bonn: R. Habelt, 1968.

Geller, Markham J. *Healing Magic and Evil Demons: Canonical Udug-hul Incantations.* Berlin: De Gruyter, 2016.

George, Andrew R. *The Babylonian Gilgamesh Epic: Introduction, Critical Edition and Cuneiform Texts.* 2 vols. Oxford: Oxford University Press, 2003.

George, Andrew R. "The Poem of Erra and Ishum: A Babylonian Poet's View of War." Pages 39–72 in *Warfare and Poetry in the Middle East.* Edited by Hugh Kennedy. London: I.B. Tauris, 2013.

George, Andrew R., and Farouk N.H. Al-Rawi. "Tablets from the Sippar Library VI. Atrahasis." *Iraq* 58 (1996): 147–190.

Gera, Deborah L. *Judith.* CEJL. Berlin: De Gruyter, 2014.

Gesner, Salomon. *Daniel Propheta Disputationibus XII. Et Praefatione Chronologica Breviter Explicatus.* Wittenberg: Martin Henckel, 1606.

Gevaryahu, Haim M. Y. "The Prayer of Nabonidus of the Scrolls of the Judean Desert" [Hebrew]. Pages 12–23 in *Studies on the Scrolls of the Judean Desert.* Edited by Jacob Liver. Jerusalem: Israel Society for Biblical Research, 1957.

Giovino, Mariana. *The Assyrian Sacred Tree: A History of Interpretations.* OBO 230. Göttingen: Vandenhoeck & Ruprecht, 2007.

Goclenius, Rudolph. *Scholae seu Disputations Physicae, More Academic Fere Propositae et Haitae Plaeraeque Omnes in Schola Illustri Cattorum.* Marburg: Paul Egenolphus, 1591.

Golan, Naama. "The Daniel Narratives (Dan 1–6): Structure and Meaning." *JHebS* 19.3 (2019): 1–24.

Goldingay, John E. *Daniel.* WBC 30. Dallas: Word, 1988.

Gowan, Donald E. *When Man Becomes God: Humanism and Hybris in the Old Testament.* PTMS 6. Pittsburgh: Pickwick Publications, 1975.

Graves, Michael. "18.3.6 Daniel: Primary Translations: Vulgate." *THB* 1c:568–570.

Grayson, Albert K. *Assyrian and Babylonian Chronicles.* TCS 5. Winona Lake, IN: Eisenbrauns, 1975.

Grayson, Albert K. *Babylonian Historical-Literary Texts.* Toronto Semitic Texts and Studies 3. Toronto: University of Toronto Press, 1975.

Grelot, Pierre. "Nabuchodonosor changé en bête." *VT* 44 (1994): 10–17.

Grelot, Pierre. "La Septante de Daniel IV et son substrat sémitique." *RB* 81 (1974): 5–23.

Grelot, Pierre. "Les versions grecques de Daniel." *Bib* 47 (1966): 381–402.

Gruber, Mayer I. *Hosea: A Textual Commentary*. LHBOTS 653. London: Bloomsbury, 2017.

Guinot, Jean-Noël. *L'Exégèse de Théodoret de Cyr*. ThH 100. Paris: Beauchesne, 1995.

Gwynn, John. "Theodotion." *DCB* 4:970–979.

Gzella, Holger. "לבב." *TDOT* 16:384–388.

Haag, Ernst. *Die Errettung Daniels aus der Löwengrube: Untersuchungen zum Ursprung der biblischen Danieltradition*. SBS 110. Stuttgart: Katholisches Bibelwerk, 1983.

Hallo, William W. "Adapa Reconsidered: Life and Death in Contextual Perspective." *Scriptura* 87 (2004): 267–277.

Hamm, Winfried. *Der Septuaginta-Text des Buches Daniel, Kap. 1–2, nach dem Kölner Teil des Papyrus 967*. Papyrologische Texte und Abhandlungen 21. Bonn: R. Habelt, 1969.

Hanhart, Robert, ed. *Iudith*. Septuaginta: Vetus Testamentum Graecum 8.4. Göttingen: Vandenhoeck & Ruprecht, 1979.

Hare, Douglas R. A. "The Lives of the Prophets." Pages 379–400 in vol. 2 of *OTP*.

Harle, Jonathan. *An Historical Essay on the State of Physick in the Old and New Testament and the Apocryphal Interval*. London: Richard Ford, 1729.

Harris, Jay M. "Midrash Halachah." Pages 336–368 in *The Late Roman-Rabbinic Period*. Edited by Steven T. Katz. *CHJ* 4. Cambridge: Cambridge University Press, 2006.

Harris, Rivkah. "Images of Women in the Gilgamesh Epic." Pages 220–230 in *Lingering Over Words: Studies in Ancient Near Eastern Literature in Honor of William L. Moran*. Edited by Tzvi Abusch, John Huehnergard, and Piotr Steinkeller. HSS 37. Atlanta: Scholars Press, 1990.

Harrison, Roland K. *Introduction to the Old Testament*. Grand Rapids: Eerdmans, 1969.

Hartman, Louis F. "The Great Tree and Nabuchodonosor's Madness." Pages 75–82 in *The Bible in Current Catholic Thought*. Edited by John L. McKenzie. New York: Herder & Herder, 1962.

Hartman, Louis F., and Alexander A. Di Lella. *The Book of Daniel*. AB 23. Garden City, NY: Doubleday, 1978.

Hasel, Gerhard F. "The Book of Daniel: Evidences Relating to Persons and Chronology." *AUSS* 19 (1981): 37–49.

Haubold, Johannes. "The Wisdom of the Chaldeans: Reading Berossus, *Babyloniaca* Book 1." Pages 31–45 in *The World of Berossos: Proceedings of the 4th International Colloquium on "The Ancient Near East between Classical and Ancient Oriental Traditions", Hatfield College, Durham 7th–9th July 2010*. Edited by Johannes Haubold et al. Classica et Orientalia 5. Wiesbaden: Harrassowitz Verlag, 2013.

Haubold, Johannes. "The World of Berossos: Introduction." Pages 3–14 in *The World of Berossos: Proceedings of the 4th International Colloquium on "The Ancient Near East between Classical and Ancient Oriental Traditions", Hatfield College, Durham 7th–9th July 2010*. Edited by Johannes Haubold et al., Classica et Orientalia 5. Wiesbaden: Harrassowitz Verlag, 2013.

Hays, Christopher B. "Chirps from the Dust: The Affliction of Nebuchadnezzar in Daniel 4:30 in Its Ancient Near Eastern Context." *JBL* 126 (2007): 305–325.

Hays, Christopher B. *Hidden Riches: A Sourcebook for the Comparative Study of the Hebrew Bible and Ancient Near East*. Louisville, KY: Westminster John Knox, 2014.

Heaton, Eric W. *The Book of Daniel: Introduction and Commentary*. TBC. London: SCM Press, 1956.

Heidel, Alexander. *The Babylonian Genesis: The Story of Creation.* 2nd ed. London: University of Chicago Press, 1951.

Heinemann, Joseph. "Profile of a Midrash: The Art of Composition in Leviticus Rabba." *Journal of the American Academy of Religion* 39 (1971): 141–150.

Henze, Matthias. *The Madness of King Nebuchadnezzar: The Ancient Near Eastern Origins and Early History of Interpretation of Daniel 4.* JSJSup 61. Leiden: Brill, 1999.

Henze, Matthias. "Nebuchadnezzar's Madness (Daniel 4) in Syriac Literature." Pages 550–571 in *The Book of Daniel: Composition and Reception.* Edited by John J. Collins and Peter W. Flint. VTSup 83. Leiden: Brill, 2001.

Hiebert, Theodore. *The Yahwist's Landscape: Nature and Religion in Early Israel.* Oxford: Oxford University Press, 1996.

Hill, Robert C. *Reading the Old Testament in Antioch.* The Bible in Ancient Christianity 5. Leiden: Brill, 2005.

Hill, Robert C. *Theodoret of Cyrus: Commentary on Daniel.* Writings from the Greco-Roman World 7. Atlanta: SBL Press, 2006.

Hjälm, Miriam Lindgren. "18.3.7 Daniel: Primary Translations: Arabic Translations." *THB* 1c:571–574.

Holm, Tawny L. *Of Courtiers and Kings: The Biblical Daniel Narratives and Ancient Story Collections.* EANEC 1. Winona Lake, IN: Eisenbrauns, 2013.

Hommel, Fritz, "Die Abfassungszeit des Buches Daniel und der Wahnsinn Nabonids." *Theologisches Literaturblatt* 23 (1902): 145–150.

Hossfeld, Frank-Lothar, and Erich Zenger. *Psalms 2: A Commentary on Psalms 51–100.* Translated by Linda M. Maloney. Hermeneia. Minneapolis: Fortress, 2005.

House, Paul R. *Daniel: An Introduction and Commentary.* TOTC. London: Inter-Varsity, 2018.

Humbert, Paul. *Etudes sur le récit du Paradis et de la chute dans la Genèse.* Neuchâtel: Secrétariat de l'université, 1940.

Isaac, Ephraim. "1 (Ethiopic Apocalypse of) Enoch: A New Translation and Introduction." Pages 5–90 in vol. 1 of *OTP.*

Izre'el, Shlomo. *Adapa and the South Wind: Language Has the Power of Life and Death.* MC 10. Winona Lake, IN: Eisenbrauns, 2001.

Jackson, Pamela. "Cyril of Jerusalem's Use of Scripture in Catechesis." *TS* 52 (1991): 431–450.

Jacobsen, Thorkild. "The Eridu Genesis." *JBL* 100 (1981): 513–529.

Jacobsen, Thorkild. "The Investiture and Anointing of Adapa in Heaven." *AJSL* 46 (1930): 201–203.

Jacobsen, Thorkild. "Sumerian Mythology: A Review Article." *JNES* 5 (1946): 128–152.

Jacoby, Felix. *Die Fragmente der griechischen Historiker* III C1. Leiden: Brill, 1958.

Jahn, Gustav. *Das Buch Daniel nach dem Septuaginta hergestellt.* Leipzig: Pfeiffer, 1904.

Jastrow, Morris. "Adam and Eve in Babylonian Literature." *AJSL* 15 (1899): 193–214.

Jeansonne, Sharon Pace. *The Old Greek Translation of Daniel 7–12.* CBQMS 19. Washington, DC: Catholic Biblical Association, 1988.

Jeansonne, Sharon Pace. "The Stratigraphy of the Text of Daniel and the Question of Theological *Tendenz* in the Old Greek." *BIOSCS* 17 (1984): 15–35.

Jellicoe, Sidney. *The Septuagint and Modern Study.* Oxford: Clarendon, 1968.

Jobes, Karen H. "A Comparative Syntactic Analysis of the Greek Versions of Daniel: A Test Case for New Methodology." *BIOSCS* 28 (1995): 18–41.

Katz, Dina. "'Death They Dispensed to Mankind': The Funerary World of Ancient Mesopotamia." *Historiae* 2 (2005): 55–90.

Keil, Carl F. *Biblischer Kommentar über den Propheten Daniel.* Leipzig: Dörffling und Franke, 1869.

Kelly, John N.D. *Jerome: His Life, Writings, and Controversies.* London: Duckworth, 1975.

Kenyon, Frederic G. *The Chester Beatty Biblical Papyri: Descriptions and Texts of Twelve Manuscripts on Papyrus of the Greek Bible.* London: Walker, 1937.

Kilmer, Anne. "Verse Translation of Adapa (Amarna Version)." Pages 111–114 in *Mesopotamian Poetic Language: Sumerian and Akkadian.* Edited by Marianna E. Vogelzang and Herman L. J. Vanstiphout. CM 6. Proceedings of the Groningen Group for the Study of Mesopotamian Literature 2. Groningen: Styx, 1996.

Kim, Daewoong. "Biblical Interpretation in the Book of Daniel: Literary Allusions in Daniel to Genesis and Ezekiel." PhD diss., Rice University, 2013.

Klein, Jacob, ed. "Enki and Ninmah," Pages 516–522 in *The Context of Scripture I: Canonical Compositions from the Biblical World.* Edited by William W. Hallo. Leiden: Brill, 1997.

Knibb, Michael A. "The Book of Daniel in Its Context." Pages 16–36 in *The Book of Daniel: Composition and Reception.* Edited by John J. Collins and Peter W. Flint. VTSup 83. Leiden: Brill, 2001.

Knibb, Michael A. *The Ethiopic Book of Enoch: A New Edition in the Light of the Aramaic Dead Sea Fragments.* 2 vols. Oxford: Clarendon, 1978.

Koch, Klaus. *Daniel: Kapitel 1,1–4,34.* BKAT 22.1. Neukirchen-Vluyn: Neukirchener Verlag, 2005.

Koch, Klaus. "Gottes Herrschaft über das Reich des Menschen: Daniel 4 im Licht neuer Funde." Pages 77–120 in *The Book of Daniel in the Light of New Findings.* Edited by Adam S. van der Woude. BETL 106. Leuven: Leuven University Press and Peeters, 1993.

Komorócy, Géza. "Berosos and the Mesopotamian Literature." *ActAnt* 121 (1973): 125–152.

Kooij, Arie van der. "Compositions and Editions in Early Judaism: The Case of Daniel." Pages 428–448 in *The Text of the Hebrew Bible and Its Editions: Studies in Celebration of the Fifth Centennial of the Complutensian Polyglot.* Edited by Andrés P. Otero and Pablo T. Morales. Supplements to the Textual History of the Bible 1. Leiden: Brill, 2017.

Koosed, Jennifer L., and Robert P. Seesengood. "Daniel's Animal Apocalypse." Pages 182–195 in *Divinanimality: Animal Theory, Creaturely Theology.* Edited by Stephen D. Moore. New York: Fordham University Press, 2014.

Kraft, Robert A. "Septuagint." *IDBSup,* 807–815.

Kramer, Samuel N. "Dilmun: Quest for Paradise." *Antiquity* 37 (1963): 111–115.

Kramer, Samuel N. "The Sumerian Deluge Myth: Reviewed and Revised." *AnSt* 33 (1983): 115–121.

Kramer, Samuel N. *The Sumerians: Their History, Culture, and Character.* London: University of Chicago Press, 1963.

Kratz, Dennis M. "Fictus Lupus: The Werewolf in Christian Thought." *Classical Folia* 30 (1976): 57–78.

Kratz, Reinhard G. "Nabonid in Qumran," Pages 253–270 in *Babylon: Wissenskultur in Orient und Okzident.* Edited by Eva Cancik-Kirschbaum, Margarete van Ess, and Joachim Marzahn. Topoi 1. Berlin: De Gruyter, 2011.

Kratz, Reinhard G. "The Visions of Daniel." Pages 91–113 in *The Book of Daniel: Composition and Reception.* Edited by John J. Collins and Peter W. Flint. VTSup 83. Leiden: Brill, 2001.

Kraus, Fritz R. "Altmesopotamisches Lebensgefühl." *JNES* 19 (1960): 117–132.

Krebernik, Manfred. "Geschlachtete Gottheiten und ihre Nahmen." Pages 289–298 in *Ex Mesopotamia et Syria Lux: Festschrift für Manfried Dietrich zu seinem 65 Geburtstag.* Edited by Oswald Loretz, Kai A. Metzler, and Hanspeter Schaudig. AOAT 281. Münster: Ugarit-Verlag, 2002.

Krüger, Thomas. "Das 'Herz' in der alttestamentlichen Anthropologie." Pages 103–118 in *Anthropologie Aufbrüche: Alttestamentliche und unterdisziplinäre Zugänge zur historischen Anthropologie.* Edited by Andreas Wagner. Forschungen zur Religion und Literatur des Alten und Neuen Testaments 232. Göttingen: Vandenhoeck & Ruprecht, 2009.

Kvanvig, Helge S. *Primeval History: Babylonian, Biblical, and Enochic: An Intertextual Reading.* JSJSup 149. Leiden: Brill, 2011.

Lacocque, André. *The Book of Daniel.* Translated by David Pellauer. London: SPCK, 1979.

Lamberg-Karlovsky, Clifford C. "Dilmun: Gateway to Immortality." *JNES* 41 (1982): 45–50.

Lambert, Wilfred G. *Babylonian Creation Myths.* MC 16. Winona Lake, IN: Eisenbrauns, 2013.

Lambert, Wilfred G. *Cuneiform Texts from Babylonian Tablets in the British Museum Part XLVI: Babylonian Literary Texts.* London: Trustees of the British Museum, 1965.

Lambert, Wilfred G. "dingir.šà.dib.ba Incantations." *JNES* 33 (1974): 267–322.

Lambert, Wilfred G. "The Relationship of Sumerian and Babylonian Myth as Seen in Accounts of Creation." Pages 129–135 in *La Circulation des Biens, des Personnes et des Idées dans le Proche-Orient Ancien. Actes de la XXXVIIIe Rencontre Assyriologique Internationale (Paris, 8–10 juillet 1991).* Edited by Dominique Charpin and Francis Joannès. Paris: Éditions Recherche sur les Civilisations, 1992.

Lambert, Wilfred G. Review of *Das altorientalische Menschenbild und die sumerischen und akkadischen Schöpfungsmythen,* by Giovanni Pettinato. *BSOAS* 35 (1972): 134–135.

Lambert, Wilfred G. "The Theology of Death." Pages 53–66 in *Death in Mesopotamia: Papers Read at the XXVIe Rencontre Assryiologique Internationale.* Edited by Bendt Alster. Mesopotamia. Copenhagen Studies in Assyriology 8. Copenhagen: Akademisk Forlag, 1980.

Lambert, Wilfred G., and Alan R. Millard, eds. *Atra-ḫasīs: The Babylonian Story of the Flood.* Winona Lake, IN: Eisenbrauns, 1999.

Lancre, Pierre de. *Tableau de L'Inconstance des Mauvaius Anges et Démons.* Paris: Nicholas Buon, 1612.

Lanfer, Peter T. "Solomon in the Garden of Eden: Autonomous Wisdom and the Danger of Discernment." Pages 714–725 in *Sibyls, Scriptures, and Scrolls: John Collins at Seventy.* Edited by Joel Baden, Hindy Najman, and Eibert Tigchelaar. Leiden: Brill, 2016.

Langdon, Stephen. *Building Inscriptions of the Neo-Babylonian Empire, Part I: Nabopolassar and Nebuchadnezzar.* Paris: Leroux, 1905.

Lange, Armin. "18.2.1 Daniel: Ancient Hebrew-Aramaic Texts: Ancient Manuscript Evidence." *THB* 1c:528–532.

Lange, Isaac S., and Samuel Schwartz, eds and trans. *Midrash Daniel and Midrash Ezra Rabbi Samuel Ben Rabbi Nissim Masnut* [Hebrew]. Jerusalem: Mekize Nirdamim Society, 1968.

Lapide, Cornelius. *Commentaria in Quattor Prophetas Maiores.* Antwerp: Iacobum Meursium, 1675.

Larsen, Mogens T. "The Mesopotamian Lukewarm Mind: Reflections on Science, Divination and Literacy." Pages 202–225 in *Language, Literature, and History: Philological and Historical Studies Presented to Erica Reiner.* Edited by Francesca Rochberg-Halton. AOS 67. New Haven: American Oriental Society, 1987.

Lasine, Stuart. *Jonah and the Human Condition: Life and Death in Yahweh's World.* LHBOTS 688. London: T&T Clark, 2020.

Lasker, Daniel J. "Saadya Gaon on Christianity and Islam." Pages 165–77 in *The Jews of Medieval Islam: Community, Society, and Identity*. Edited by Daniel Frank. Leiden: Brill, 1995.

Lauterbach, Jacob Z., ed. and trans. *Mekhilta de-Rabbi Ishmael: A Critical Edition on the Basis of the Manuscripts and Early Editions with an English Translation, Introduction, and Notes*. 3 vols. Philadelphia: Jewish Publication Society, 1933-35.

Le Saint, William P., trans. *Tertullian: Treatises on Penance*. ACW 28. London: Longmans, 1959.

Lea, Henry Charles. *Materials toward a History of Witchcraft*. Edited by Arthur C. Howland. 3 vols. Philadelphia: University of Pennsylvania Press, 1939.

Levison, John R. *Portraits of Adam in Early Judaism: From Sirach to 2 Baruch*. JSPSup 1. Sheffield: Sheffield Academic Press, 1988.

Levy, Alfred L. "Soul." *EncJud* 19:33–35.

Lim, Timothy H. "303. 4QMeditation on Creation A." Pages 151–154 in *Qumran Cave 4. XXV: Sapiential Texts, Part 1*. Edited by Torleif Elgvin et al. DJD 20. Oxford: Clarendon, 1997.

Lim, Timothy H. "305. 4QMeditation on Creation C." Pages 157–158 in *Qumran Cave 4. XXV: Sapiential Texts, Part 1*. Edited by Torleif Elgvin et al. DJD 20. Oxford: Clarendon, 1997.

Lindenberger, James M. "Ahiqar." Pages 279–293 in vol. 2 of *OTP*.

Lisman, Jan J. W. *Cosmogony, Theogony and Anthropogeny in Sumerian Texts*. AOAT 409. Münster: Ugarit-Verlag, 2013.

Liverani, Mario. "Adapa, guest of the gods." Pages 3–26 in *Myth and Politics in Ancient Near Eastern Historiography*. Edited by Zainab Bahrani and Marc Van De Mieroop. London: Cornell University Press, 2004.

Livingstone, Alasdair. "'Taimā' and Nabonidus: It's a Small World." Pages 29–39 in *Writing and Ancient Near East Society: Papers in Honour of Alan R. Millard*. Edited by Piotr Bienkowski, Christopher Mee, and Elizabeth Slater. LHBOTS 426. London: T&T Clark, 2005.

Locke, John. *The Reasonableness of Christianity as Delivered in the Scriptures*. London: Awnsham and John Churchill, 1695.

Longman, Tremper, III. *Proverbs*. BCOTWP. Grand Rapids: Baker Academic, 2006.

Lucas, Ernest C. *Daniel*. Apollos Old Testament Commentary. Leicester: Inter-Varsity, 2002.

Luginbühl, Marianne. *Menschenschöpfungsmythen. Ein Vergleich zwischen Griechenland und dem Alten Orient*. Paris: Peter Lang, 1992.

Lust, Johan. "The Septuagint Version of Daniel 4–5." Pages 39–53 in *The Book of Daniel in the Light of New Findings*. Edited by Adam S. van der Woude. BETL 56. Leuven: Leuven University Press and Peeters, 1993.

Lyon, Jeremy D. *The Genesis Creation Account in the Dead Sea Scrolls*. Eugene, OR: Pickwick Publications, 2019.

MacKay, Christopher S., ed. and trans. *The Hammer of Witches: A Complete Translation of the Malleus Maleficarum*. Cambridge: Cambridge University Press, 2009.

Magistris, Simon D. *Daniel secundum Septuaginta ex tetraplis Origenis nunc primum editus e singulari Chisiano códice*. Rome: Typis Propagandae Fidei, 1772.

Mai, Angelo, ed. *Scriptorum Veterum Nova Collectio e Vaticanis Codicibus Edita*. 10 vols. Rome: Typis Vaticanis, 1825–1838.

Maldonado, Juan. *Commentaria in Prophetas Quattor: Ieremiam, Baruch, Ezechielem et Danielem*. Tournon: Horace Cardon, 1611.

Margoliouth, David S., ed. and trans. *A Commentary on the Book of Daniel by Jephet ibn Ali the Karaite*. Oxford: Clarendon, 1889.

Margulies, Mordechai, ed. and trans. *Midrash Vayyikra Rabba*. 5 vols. New York: Jewish Theological Seminary of America, 1953–1960.

Marlow, Hilary. "'What Am I in a Boundless Creation?' An Ecological Reading of Sirach 16 & 17." *Biblical Interpretation* 22 (2014): 34–50.

Massey, Jeffrey A. "*Corpus Lupi*: The Medieval Werewolf and Popular Theology." PhD diss., Emory University, 2003.

Mayer, John. *A Commentary upon all the Prophets Both Great and Small*. London: Abraham Miller and Ellen Cotes, 1652.

Mazzolini, Silvestro. *De Strigimagarum Daemonumque Mirandis Libri Tres*. Rome: In Aedibus Populil Romani, 1575.

McCrystall, Arthur. "Studies in the Old Greek Translation of Daniel." PhD diss., University of Oxford, 1980.

McKenzie, John L. "Mythological Allusions in Ezek 28:12–18." *JBL* 75 (1956): 322–327.

McLay, R. Timothy. "The Greek Translations of Daniel 4–6." Pages 211–238 in *The Temple in Text and Tradition: A Festschrift in Honour of Robert Hayward*. Edited by R. Timothy McLay. LSTS 83. London: Bloomsbury T&T Clark, 2015.

McLay, R. Timothy. "It's a Question of Influence: The Theodotion and the Old Greek Texts of Daniel." Pages 231–254 in *Origen's Hexapla and Fragments: Papers Presented at the Rich Seminar on the Hexapla*. Edited by Alison Salvesen. TSAJ 58. Tübingen: Mohr Siebeck, 1998.

McLay, R. Timothy. *The OG and Th Versions of Daniel*. SCS 43. Atlanta: Scholars Press, 1996.

McLay, R. Timothy. "The Old Greek Translation of Daniel Chapters IV–VI and the Formation of the Book of Daniel." *VT* 55 (2005): 304–323.

McLay, R. Timothy. "The Relationship between the Greek Translations of Daniel 1–3." *BIOSCS* 37 (2004): 29–54.

Mead, Richard. *Medica Sacra; or, A Commentary on the Most Remarkable Diseases Mentioned in the Holy Scriptures*. Translated by Thomas Stack. London: J. Brindley, 1755.

Meadowcroft, Timothy J. *Aramaic Daniel and Greek Daniel: A Literary Comparison*. JSOTSup 198. Sheffield: Sheffield Academic Press, 1995.

Medina, Miguel de. *Christianae paraenesis sive de recta in deum fide libri septem*. Venice: Jordani Zileti, 1564.

Melvin, David P. "Divine Mediation and the Rise of Civilization in Mesopotamian Literature and in Genesis 1–11." *JHebS* 10.17 (2010): 1–15.

Mercuriale, Girolamo. *Variarum Lectionum in Medicinae Scriptoribus et Alijs Libri VI*. Venice: Apud Iuntas, 1598.

Mermelstein, Ari. "Constructing Fear and Pride in the Book of Daniel: The Profile of a Second Temple Emotional Community." *JSJ* 46 (2015): 449–483.

Mettinger, Tryggve. *The Eden Narrative: A Literary and Religio-Historical Study of Genesis 2–3*. Winona Lake, IN: Eisenbrauns, 2007.

Metzger, Martin. "Zeder, Weinstock, und Weltenbaum." Pages 197–229 in *Ernten, was man sät: Festschrift für Klaus Koch zu seinem 65. Geburtstag*. Edited by Dwight R. Daniels, Uwe Glessmer, and Martin Rösel. Neukirchen-Vluyn: Neukirchener Verlag, 1991.

Metzger, Nadine. "Battling Demons with Medical Authority: Werewolves, Physicians and Rationalization." *History of Psychiatry* 24 (2013): 341–355.

Meyer, Eric Daryl. *Inner Animalities: Theology and the End of the Human*. Groundworks: Ecological Issues in Philosopher and Theology. New York: Fordham University Press, 2018.

Meyer, Rudolf. *Das Gebet des Nabonid: Eine in den Qumran-Handschriften wiederentdeckte Weisheitserzählung*. Sitzungsberichte der Säcsischen Akademie der Wissenschaften zu Leipzig, Philologisch-historische Klasse 107.3. Berlin: Akademie, 1962.

Meyer, Rudolf. *Zur Geschichte und Theologie des Judentums in hellenistisch-römischer Zeit*. Berlin: Evangelische Verlagsanstalt, 1989.

Michaelis, Johann David. *Deutsche Übersetzung des Alten Testaments mit Anmerkungen für Ungelehrte. Der Zehnte Theil welcher Ezechiel und Daniel enthalt*. Göttingen: Vandenhoeck, 1781.

Migne, Jacques-Paul, ed. Patrologia Graeca [= Patrologiae Cursus Completus: Series Graeca]. 162 vols. Paris, 1857–1886.

Migne, Jacques-Paul, ed. Patrologia Latina [= Patrologiae Cursus Completus: Series Latina]. 217 vols. Paris, 1844–1864.

Milik, Jozef T., ed. *The Books of Enoch: Aramaic Fragments of Qumran Cave 4*. Oxford: Clarendon, 1976.

Milik, Jozef T., ed. "'Prière de Nabonide' et autres écrits d'un cycle de Daniel." *RB* 63 (1956): 407–415.

Milstein, Sara J. "The Origins of Adapa." *ZA* 105 (2015): 30–41.

Mobley, Gregory. *Samson and the Liminal Hero in the Ancient Near East*. LHBOTS 453. London: T&T Clark, 2006.

Mobley, Gregory. "The Wild Man in the Bible and the Ancient Near East." *JBL* 116 (1997): 217–233.

Molés, Vicente. *De Morbis in Sacris Litteris Pathologia*. Madrid: Juan Sanchez, 1642.

Molitor, Ulrich. *De Lamiis et Pithonicis Mulieribus*. Strasbourg: Johann Prüss, 1489.

Montgomery, James A. *A Critical and Exegetical Commentary on the Book of Daniel*. ICC. Edinburgh: T&T Clark, 1927.

Montgomery, James A. "The Hexaplaric Strata in the Greek Texts of Daniel." *JBL* 44 (1925): 289–302.

Moore, Carey A. *Daniel, Esther, and Jeremiah: The Additions*. AB 44. Garden City, NY: Doubleday, 1977.

Moran, William L. "Atrahasis: The Babylonian Story of the Flood." *Biblica* 52 (1971): 51–61.

Morey, James H. "Peter Comestor, Biblical Paraphrase, and the Medieval Popular Bible." *Speculum* 68 (1993): 6–35.

Morrison, Craig E. "The Reception of the Book of Daniel in Aphrahat's Fifth Demonstration, 'On Wars'." *Hugoye: Journal of Syriac Studies* 7 (2017): 55–82.

Moukarzel, Kabalan. "The Religious Reform of Nabonidus: A Sceptical View." Pages 129–189 in *Melammu: The Ancient World in an Age of Globalization*. Edited by Markham J. Geller. Max Planck Research Library for the History and Development of Knowledge Proceedings 7. Berlin: Edition Open Access, 2014.

Munnich, Olivier. "The Masoretic Rewriting of Daniel 4–6: The Septuagint Version as Witness." Pages 149–172 in *From Author to Copyist: Essays on the Composition, Redaction, and Transmission of the Hebrew Bible in Honor of Zipi Talshir*. Edited by Cana Werman. Winona Lake, IN: Eisenbauns, 2015.

Munnich, Olivier. "Les nomina sacra dans les versions grecques de Daniel et leurs suppléments deuterocanoniques," Pages 93–120 in κατα τους ό: *Selons les Septante: Trente études sur la Bible Grecque des Septante*. Edited by Gilles Dorival and Olivier Munnich. Paris: Cerf, 1995.

Munnich, Olivier. "Texte Massorétique et Septant dans la Livre de Daniel." Pages 93–120 in *The Earliest Text of the Hebrew Bible: The Relationship between the Masoretic Text and the Hebrew Base of the Septuagint Reconsidered.* Edited by Adrian Schenker. SCS 52. Atlanta: SBL Press, 2003.

Munnich, Olivier. "Les versions grecques de Daniel et leur substrats sémitiques." Pages 291–308 in *VIII Congress of the International Organization for Septuagint and Cognate Studies.* Edited by Leonard Greenspoon and Olivier Munnich. SCS 41. Atlanta: Scholars Press, 1995.

Murray, Robert. *Symbols of Church and Kingdom: A Study in Early Syriac Tradition.* London: Cambridge University Press, 1975.

Neef, Heinz-Dieter. "Menschliche Hybris und göttliche Macht. Dan 4 LXX und Dan 4 Th im Vergleich." *JNSL* 31 (2005): 59–89.

Nelson, William B. *Daniel.* Understanding the Bible Commentary Series. Grand Rapids: Baker Books, 2013.

Neusner, Jacob. *Aphrahat and Judaism: The Christian-Jewish Argument in Fourth-Century Iran.* Studia Post-Biblica 19. Leiden: Brill, 1971.

Neusner, Jacob. *Judaism and Scripture: The Evidence of Leviticus Rabbah.* Chicago: University of Chicago Press, 1986.

Newsom, Carol A. "Now You See Him, Now You Don't: Nabonidus in Jewish Memory." Pages 270–282 in *Remembering Biblical Figures in the Late Persian and Early Hellenistic Periods: Social Memory and Imagination.* Edited by Diana V. Edelman and Ehud Ben Zvi. Oxford: Oxford University Press, 2013.

Newsom, Carol A. "Why Nabonidus? Excavating Traditions from Qumran, the Hebrew Bible, and Neo-Babylonian Sources." Pages 57–79 in *The Dead Sea Scrolls: Transmission of Traditions and Production of Texts.* Edited by Sarianna Metso, Hindy Najman, and Eileen Schuller. STDJ 92. Leiden: Brill, 2010.

Newsom, Carol A., with Brennan W. Breed. *Daniel: A Commentary.* OTL. Louisville, KY: Westminster John Knox, 2014.

Nickelsburg, George W. E. *1 Enoch 1: A Commentary on the Book of 1 Enoch Chapters 1–36; 81–108.* Hermeneia. Minneapolis: Fortress, 2001.

Nickelsburg, George W. E., and James C. Vanderkam. *1 Enoch 2: A Commentary on the Book of 1 Enoch Chapters 37–82.* Hermeneia. Minneapolis: Fortress, 2012.

Niditch, Susan, and Robert Doran. "The Success Story of the Wise Courtier: A Formal Approach." *JBL* 96 (1977): 179–193.

Noort, Ed. "The Stories of the Great Flood: Notes on Gen 6:5–9:17 in its Context of the Ancient Near East." Pages 1–38 in *Interpretations of the Flood.* Edited by Florentino G. Martínez and Gerard P. Luttikhuizen. TBN 1. Leiden: Brill, 1998.

Norsker, Amanda. "Genesis 6,5–9,17: A Rewritten Babylonian Flood Myth." *SJOT* 29 (2015): 55–62.

Nougayrol Jean, et al. *Ugaritica V: nouveaux textes accadiens, hourrites et ugaritiques des archives et bibliothèques privies d'Ugarit. Commentaires des textes historiques (première partie).* Mission de Ras Shamra XVI. Paris: Librairie Orientaliste Paul Geuthner, 1968.

Obiajunwa, Chukwudi J. "Semitic Interference in Theodotion-Daniel." PhD diss., The Catholic University of America, 1999.

Oden, Robert A. "Divine Aspirations in Atrahasis and in Genesis 1–11." *ZAW* 93 (1981): 197–216.

Oecolampadius, Johannes. *Commentarium In Danielem Prophetam Libri Duo.* Basel: Ioannem Bebel, 1530.

Olariu, Daniel. "Criteria for Determining the Common Basis of the Greek Versions of Daniel." *Textus* 28 (2019): 105–124.

Olivares, Carlos. "El Léon con Alas de Águila en Daniel 7:4: Un Resumen de la Locura y Restauración de Nabucodonosor (Dn 4)." *DavarLogos* 4 (2002): 149–158.

Oppenheim, Adolf L. *Ancient Mesopotamia: Portrait of a Dead Civilisation.* Edited by Erica Reiner. Rev. ed. Chicago: University of Chicago Press, 1977.

Osborn, Eric. *Tertullian, First Theologian of the West.* Cambridge: Cambridge University Press, 1997.

Oshima, Takayoshi M. "Nebuchadnezzar's Madness (Daniel 4:30): Reminiscence of a Historical Event or Legend?" Pages 645–676 in *"Now It Happened in Those Days": Studies in Biblical, Assyrian, and Other Ancient Near Eastern Historiography Presented to Mordechai Cogan on His 75th Birthday.* Edited by Amitai Baruchi-Unna et al. Winona Lake, IN: Eisenbrauns, 2017.

Pan, Chou-Wee. "בער." *NIDOTTE*, 1:691.

Parker, N. "On Lycanthropy or Wolf-madness, a Variety of Insania Zoanthropica." *The Asylum Journal* 1.4 (1854): 52–53.

Parker, T. H. L., trans. *Daniel I: Chapters 1–6.* Calvin's Old Testament Commentaries 20. Carlisle: Paternoster, 1993.

Parry, Jason T. "18.3.2 Daniel: Primary Translations: Other Greek Versions Prior to the Hexapla." *THB* 1c:554–558.

Pedersen, Johannes. "The Fall of Man." Pages 162–172 in *Interpretationes ad Vetus Testamentum pertinentes SIgmundo Mowinckel septuagenario missae.* Edited by Nils A. Dahl and Arvid S. Kapelrud. Oslo: Forlaget Land og Kirke, 1955.

Pedersen, Johannes. "Wisdom and Immortality." Pages 238–246 in *Wisdom in Israel and in the Ancient Near East: Presented to Professor Harold Henry Rowley.* Edited by Martin Noth and David W. Thomas. VTSup 3. Leiden: Brill, 1955.

Pemble, William. *The Period of the Persian Monarchie.* London: Richard Capel, 1631.

Pereira, Benedict. *Commentariorum in Danielem Prophetam Libri Sexdecim.* Antwerp: Aedibus Petri Belleri, 1594.

Perhai, Richard J. *Antiochene Theōria in the Writings of Theodore of Mopsuestia and Theodoret of Cyrus.* Minneapolis: Fortress, 2005.

Perrin, Andrew B. *The Dynamics of Dream-Vision Revelation in the Aramaic Dead Sea Scrolls.* JAJSup 19. Göttingen: Vandenhoeck & Ruprecht, 2015.

Peterson, Jeremiah. "The Divine Appointment of the First Antediluvian King: Newly Recovered Content from the Ur Version of the Sumerian Flood Story." *JCS* 70 (2018): 37–51.

Peterson, Jeremiah. "A Middle Babylonian Sumerian Fragment of the Adapa Myth and an Overview of the Middle Babylonian Sumerian Literary Corpus at Nippur." Pages 255–276 in *The First Ninety Years: A Sumerian Celebration in Honor of Miguel Civil.* Edited by Lluís Feliu, Fumi Karahashi, and Gonzalo Rubio. Studies in Ancient Near Eastern Records 12. Berlin: De Gruyter, 2017.

Pettinato, Giovanni. *Das altorientalische Menschenbild und die sumerischen und akkadischen Schöpfungsmythen.* Heidelberg: Carl Winter, Universitätsverlag, 1971.

Pfann, Stephen. "The Aramaic Text and Language of Daniel and Ezra in the Light of Some Manuscripts from Qumran." *Textus* 16 (1991): 127–137.

Pinches, Theophilus G. "On a Cuneiform Inscription Relating to the Capture of Babylon by Cyrus and the Events which Preceded and Led Up to It." *Transactions of the Society of Biblical Archaeology* 7 (1882): 139–176.

Pleins, John D. *When the Great Abyss Opened: Classic and Contemporary Readings of Noah's Flood*. Oxford: Oxford University Press, 2003.

Plöger, Otto. *Das Buch Daniel*. Kommentar zu Alten Testamentum 18. Gütersloh: G. Mohn, 1965.

Ponchia, Simonetta. "Gilgameš and Enkidu: The Two-thirds-god and the Two-thirds-animal?" Pages 187–210 in *Animals and their Relation to Gods, Humans and Things in the Ancient World*. Edited by Raija Mattila, Sanae Ito, and Sebastian Fink. Studies in Universal and Cultural History. Wiesbaden: Springer VS, 2019.

Popper, Nicholas. *Walter Ralegh's "History of the World" and the Historical Culture of the Late Renaissance*. London: University of Chicago Press, 2012.

Porten, Bezalel, and Ada Yardeni. *Textbook of Aramaic Documents from Ancient Egypt, vol. 3: Literature, Accounts, Lists*. Jerusalem: Hebrew University Press, 1993.

Porteous, Norman W. *Daniel: A Commentary*. OTL. London: SCM, 1965.

Portier-Young, Anathea. "Three Books of Daniel: Plurality and Fluidity among the Ancient Versions." *Interpretation* 71 (2017): 143–153.

Pott, Sandra. *Medizin, Medizinethik und schöne Literatur: Studien zu Säkularisierungsvorgängen vom frühen 17. bis zum frühen 19. Jahrhundert*. Säkularisierung in den Wissenschaften seit der Frühen Neuzeit 1. Berlin: De Gruyter, 2002.

Poulakou-Rebelakou, E., et al. "Lycanthropy in Byzantine times (AD 330–1453)." *History of Psychiatry* 20 (2009): 468–479.

Prince, John Dynely. *A Critical Commentary on the Book of Daniel*. New York: Lemcke & Buechner, 1899.

Pritchard, James B., ed. *Ancient Near Eastern Texts Relating to the Old Testament*. 3rd ed. Princeton: Princeton University Press, 1969.

Pusey, Edward B. *Daniel the Prophet: Nine Lectures, Delivered in the Divinity School of the University of Oxford*. Oxford: John Henry and James Parker, 1864.

Putthoff, Tyson L. *Gods and Humans in the Ancient Near East*. Cambridge: Cambridge University Press, 2020.

Quasten, Johannes. *Patrology*. 4 vols. Utrecht: Spectrum, 1950–1986.

Raleigh, Walter. *The History of the World in Five Books*. London: William Stansby, 1614.

Reiner, Erica. "City Bread and Bread Baked in Ashes." Pages 116–120 in *Languages and Areas: Studies Presented to George V. Bobrinskoy*. Edited by Howard I. Aronson. Chicago: University of Chicago, 1967.

Reiner, Erica. "The Etiological Myth of the 'Seven Sages.'" *Orientalia* 30 (1961): 1–11.

Reinhard, Christian Tobias Ephraim. *Bibelkrankheiten welche im alten Testamente vorkommen*. 2 vols. Frankfurt-Leipzig: Günther, 1767.

Reiterer, Friedrich Vinzenez. "Review of Recent Research on the Book of Ben Sira (1980–1996)." Pages 23–60 in *The Book of Ben Sira in Modern Research: Proceedings of the First International Ben Sira Conference 28–31 July 1996 Sosterberg, Netherlands*. Edited by Pancratius C. Beentjes. BZAW 255. Berlin: De Gruyter, 1997.

Riessler, Paul. *Das Buch Daniel: Textkritische Untersuchung*. Kurzgefasster wissenschaftlicher Kommentar zu den Heiligen Schriften des Alten Testaments 3.3.2. Stuttgart: Roth, 1899.

Roling, Bernd. *Physica Sacra: Wunder, Naturwissenschaft und historischer Schriftsinn zwischen Mittelalter und Früher Neuzeit*. Mittellateinische Studien und Texte 45. Leiden: Brill, 2013.

Rosengarten, Yvonne. *Sumer et le sacré: Le jeu des Prescriptions (me), des dieux, et des destins*. Paris: E. de Boccard, 1977.

Rowley, H. H. "The Unity of the Book of Daniel." *HUCA* 23 (1950–1951): 233–273.

Sack, Ronald H. *Images of Nebuchadnezzar: The Emergence of a Legend.* 2nd rev. and exp. ed. London: Associated University Presses, 2004.

Sanctius, Caspar. *In Danielem Prophetam Commentarii cum Paraphrasi.* Lyon: Horatii Cardon, 1619.

Sarna, Nahum M. *On the Book of Psalms: Exploring the Prayers of Ancient Israel.* New York: Schocken Books, 1993.

Sasson, Jack M. "Another Wrinkle on Old Adapa." Pages 1–10 in *Studies in Ancient Near Eastern World View and Society presented to Marten Stol on the occasion of his 65th birthday.* Edited by Robartus V. van der Spek et al. Bethesda, MD: CDL, 2008.

Satran, David. *Biblical Prophets in Byzantine Palestine: Reassessing the Lives of the Prophets.* Studia in Veteris Testament Pseudepigrapha 11. Leiden: Brill, 1995.

Satran, David. "Daniel: Seer, Philosopher, Holy Man." Pages 33–48 in *Ideal Figures in Ancient Judaism: Profiles and Paradigms* Edited by John J. Collins and George W. E. Nickelsburg. SCS 12. Chico, CA: Scholars Press, 1980.

Satran, David. "Early Jewish and Christian Interpretation of the Fourth Chapter of the Book of Daniel." PhD diss., Hebrew University, 1985.

Satran, David. Fingernails and Hair: Anatomy and Exegesis in Tertullian." *JTS* 40 (1989): 116–120.

Schaudig, Hanspeter. *Die Inschriften Nabonids von Babylon und Kyros' des Großen samt den in ihrem Umfeld entstandenen Tendenzschriften. Textausgabe und Grammtik.* AOAT 256. Münster: Ugarit-Verlag, 2001.

Scheetz, Joshua M. *The Concept of Canonical Intertextuality and the Book of Daniel.* Eugene, OR: Pickwick Publications, 2011.

Schermann, Theodor, ed. *Prophetarum vitae fabulosae indices apostolorum discipulorumque Domini Dorotheo, Epiphanio, Hippolyto aliisque vindicate.* Bibliotheca Scriptorum Graecorum et Romanorum Teubneriana. Leipzig: Teubner, 1907.

Schermann, Theodor, ed. *Propheten- und Apostellegenden nebst Jüngerkatalogen des Dorotheus und verwandter Texte.* TUGAL 31.3. Leipzig: Hinrichs, 1907.

Scheuchzer, Johann Jacob. *Physica Sacra Iconibus Aeneis Illustrata.* 4 vols. Augsburg: Johannes Andreas Pfeffel, 1731–1735.

Schlossberg, Eliezer. "Concepts and Methods in the Commentary on Daniel by R. Saadia Gaon" [Hebrew]. PhD diss., Bar Ilan Unversity, 1988.

Schmitt, Armin. "Die griechischen Danieltexte und das Theodotionsproblem." *BZ* 36 (1992): 1–29.

Schmitt, Armin. *Stammt der sogenannte 'Th' Text bei Daniel wirklich von Theodotion?.* MSU 9. Göttingen: Vandenhoeck & Ruprecht, 1966.

Schnyder, André, ed. *Malleus Maleficarum von Heinrich Institoris (alias Kramer) unter Mithilfe Jakob Sprengers aufgrund der dämonologischen Tradition zusammengestellt: Widergabe des Erstdrucks von 1487 (Hain 9238).* Göppingen: Kümmerle Verlag, 1993.

Schor, Adam M. "Theodoret on the 'School of Antioch': A Network Approach." *Journal of Early Christian Studies* 15 (2007): 517–562.

Schrader, Eberhard. "Die Sage vom Wahnsinn Nebuchadnezzar's." *Jahrbücher für protestantische Theologie* 4 (1881): 618–629.

Schütz, Eduard. "ἀγνοέω." *NIDNTT* 2:406–409.

Schwarzbach, Bertram Eugene. "Reason and the Bible in the So-Called Age of Reason." *Huntington Library Quarterly* 74 (2011): 437–470.

Scot, Reginald. *The Discoverie of Witchcraft.* London: William Brome, 1584.

Segal, Michael. "18.2.2 Daniel: Ancient Hebrew-Aramaic Texts: Masoretic Texts and Ancient Texts Close to MT." *THB* 1c:532–537.

Segal, Michael. "18.2.3 Daniel: Ancient Hebrew-Aramaic Texts: Other Texts." *THB* 1c:537–542.

Segal, Michael. *Dreams, Riddles, and Visions: Textual, Contextual, and Intertextual Approaches to the Book of Daniel.* BZAW 455. Berlin: De Gruyter, 2016.

Selz, Gebhard J. "Who is a God? A Note on the Evolution of the Divine Classifiers in a Multilingual Environment." Pages 605–614 in *Libiamo ne' lieti calici: Ancient Near Eastern Studies Presented to Lucio Milano on the Occasion of his 65th Birthday by Pupils, Colleagues and Friends.* Edited by Paola Corò et al. AOAT 436. Münster: Ugarit-Verlag, 2016.

Seow, Choon-Leong. *Ecclesiastes: A New Translation with Introduction and Commentary.* AB 18c. London: Doubleday, 1997.

Shyovtiz, David I. "Christians and Jews in the Twelfth-Century Werewolf Renaissance." *Journal of the History of Ideas* 75 (2014): 521–543.

Shyovtiz, David I. *A Rememberance of His Wonders: Nature and the Supernatural in Medieval Ashkenaz.* Philadelphia: University of Pennsylvania Press, 2017.

Silva Castillo, Jorge. "*Naqbu*: Totality or Abyss in the First Verse of Gilgamesh." *Iraq* 60 (1998): 219–221.

Simoons-Vermeer, Ruth E. "The Mesopotamian Floodstories: A Comparison and Interpretation." *Numen* 21 (1974): 17–34.

Skehan, Patrick W., and Alexander Di Lella. *The Wisdom of Ben Sira: A New Translation with Notes.* AB 39. London: Yale University Press, 1987.

Skehan, Patrick W., Eugene Ulrich, and Peter W. Flint. "85. 4QPs^c." Pages 49–61 in *Qumran Cave 4.XI: Psalms to Chronicles.* Edited by Eugene Ulrich et al. DJD 16. Oxford: Clarendon, 2000.

Slotki, Judah J. *Daniel, Ezra, Nehemiah: Hebrew Text and English Translation with Introductions and Commentary.* Soncino Books of the Bible. London: Soncino, 1951.

Smith, Sidney. *Babylonian Historical Texts Relating to the Capture and Downfall of Babylon.* London: Methuen, 1924.

Soden, Wolfram von. "Eine babylonische Volksüberlieferung von Nabonid in den Danielerzählungen." *ZAW* 53 (1935): 81–89.

Soden, Wolfram von. "Konflikte und ihre Bewältigung in babylonischen Schöpfungs- und Fluterzählungen. Mit einer Teil-Übersetzung des Atramḫasīs-Mythos." *MDOG* 111 (1979): 1–33.

Soden, Wolfram von. "Der Mensch bescheidet sich nicht: Überlegungen zu Schöpfungserzählungen in Babylonien und Israel." Pages 349–358 in *Symbolae Biblicae et Mesopotamicae Francisco Mario Theodoro de Liagre Böhl dedicatae.* Edited by Martinus A. Beek et al. Leiden: Brill, 1973.

Sonik, Karen. "Breaking the Boundaries of Being: Metamorphoses in the Mesopotamian Literary Texts." *JAOS* 132 (2012): 385–393.

Stackhouse, Thomas. *A New History of the Holy Bible: From the Beginning of the World to the Establishment of Christianity.* 6 vols. Edinburgh: Alexander Donaldson, John Wood and James Meuros, 1767.

Steinert, Ulrike. *Aspekte des Menschseins im Alten Mesopotamien: Eine Studie zu Person und Identität im 2. und 1. Jt. v. Chr.* CM 44. Leiden: Brill, 2012.

Steinmann, Andrew. "The Chicken and the Egg: A New Proposal for the Relationship Between the *Prayer of Nabonidus* and the *Book of Daniel.*" *RevQ* 20 (2002): 557–570.

Steinmann, Jean. *Daniel: Texte français, introduction et commentaires*. Connaître la Bible. Bruges: Desclée de Brouwer, 1961.

Stökl, Jonathan. "Nebuchadnezzar: History, Memory and Myth-Making in the Persian Period." Pages 257–269 in *Remembering Biblical Figures in the Late Persian and Early Hellenistic Periods: Social Memory and Imagination*. Edited by Diana V. Edelman and Ehud Ben Zvi. Oxford: Oxford University Press, 2013.

Stone, Ken. "The Dogs of Exodus and the Question of the Animal." Pages 36–50 in *Divinanimality: Animal Theory, Creaturely Theology*. Edited by Stephen D. Moore. Transdisciplinary Theological Colloquia. New York: Fordham University Press, 2014.

Stone, Ken. *Reading the Hebrew Bible with Animal Studies*. Stanford: Stanford University Press, 2018.

Strine, Casey A. "Ezekiel's Image Problem: The Mesopotamian Cult Statue Induction Ritual and the *Imago Dei* Anthropology in the Book of Ezekiel." *CBQ* 76 (2014): 252–272.

Strine, Casey A. "Theological Anthropology and Anthropological Theology in the Book of Ezekiel." Pages 233–254 in *Das Buch Ezechiel: Komposition, Redaktion und Rezeption*. Edited by Jan Christian Gertz, Corinna Körting, and Markus Witte. BZAW 516. Berlin: De Gruyter, 2019.

Strømmen, Hannah M. *Biblical Animality after Jacques Derrida*. Semeia Studies 91. Atlanta: SBL Press, 2018.

Strong, Anise K. "Mules in Herodotus: The Destiny of Half-Breeds." *The Classical World* 103 (2010): 455–464.

Stuart, Moses. *A Commentary on the Book of Daniel*. Boston: Crocker and Brewster, 1850.

Stuckenbruck, Loren T. "The Formation and Re-formation of Daniel in the Dead Sea Scrolls." Pages 101–130 in *The Bible and the Dead Sea Scrolls: Volume One: Scripture and Scrolls*. Edited by James H. Charlesworth. Waco, TX: Baylor University Press, 2006.

Sulzbach, Carla. "Nebuchadnezzar in Eden? Daniel 4 and Ezekiel 28." Pages 125–136 in *Stimulation from Leiden: Collected Communications to the XVIIIth Congress of the International Organization for the Study of the Old Testament, Leiden 2004*. Edited by Hermann M. Niemann and Matthias Augustin. BEATAJ 54. Frankfurt: Peter Kang, 2006.

Swart, Gerhard J. "Divergences between the OG and Th Versions of Daniel 3: Evidence of Early Hellenistic Interpretation of the Narrative of the Three Young Men in the Furnace?" *Acta Patristica et Byzantina* 16 (2005): 106–120.

Swete, Henry B. *An Introduction to the Old Testament in Greek*. Cambridge: Cambridge University Press, 1902.

Ta-Shma, Israel M. "Masnut, Samuel Ben Nissim." *EncJud* 11:1097–1098.

Tate, Marvin E. "An Exposition of Psalm 8." *Perspectives in Religious Studies* 28 (2001): 343–359.

Taylor, Richard A. "18.3.3 Daniel: Primary Translations: Peshitta." *THB* 1c:558–560.

Tcherikover, Anat. "The Fall of Nebuchadnezzar in Romanesque Sculpture (Airvault, Moissac, Bourg-Argental, Foussais)." *Zeitschrift für Kunstgeschichte* 49 (1986): 288–300.

Thomasius, Jacobus and Fredericus Tobius Moebius. *De Transformatione Hominum in Bruta Dissertationem Philosophicam*. Leipzig: Hahnius, 1667.

Thorbjørnsrud, Berit. "What can the Gilgamesh Myth Tell Us about Religion and the View of Humanity in Mesopotamia?" *Temenos* 19 (1983): 112–137.

Tigay, Jeffrey. *The Evolution of the Gilgamesh Epic*. Wauconda, IL: Bolchazy-Carducci, 2002.

Tigay, Jeffrey. "Paradise." *EncJud* 15:623–629.

Tinney, Steve. "On the Curricular Setting of Sumerian Literature." *Iraq* 61 (1999): 159–172.

Toorn, Karel van der. *Scribal Culture and the Making of the Hebrew Bible*. Cambridge, MA: Harvard University, 2007.

Torrey, Charles C. *The Lives of the Prophets: Greek Text and Translation*. Journal of Biblical Literature Monograph Series 1. Philadelphia: SBL Press, 1946.

Torrey, Charles C. "Notes on the Aramaic Part of Daniel." *Transactions of the Connecticut Academy of Arts and Sciences* 15 (1909): 239–282.

Tov, Emanuel. "Three Strange Books of the LXX: 1 Kings, Esther, and Daniel Compared with Similar Rewritten Compositions from Qumran and Elsewhere." Pages 369–393 in *Die Septuaginta: Texte, Kontexte, Lebenswelten*. Edited by Martin Karrer et al. WUNT 219. Tübingen: Mohr Siebeck, 2008.

Toy, Crawford H. *A Critical and Exegetical Commentary on the Book of Proverbs*. ICC. Edinburgh: T&T Clark, 1899.

Trapp, John. *Annotations upon the Old and New Testament*. 5 vols. London: Robert White, 1662.

Trusen, Johann P. *Die Sitten, Gebräuche und Krankheiten der alten Hebräer*. 2nd edition. Breslau: W.G. Korn. 1853.

Turner, Marie. *Ecclesiastes: An Earth Bible Commentary: Qoheleth's Eternal Earth*. Earth Bible Commentary. London: Bloomsbury T&T Clark, 2017.

Ulrich, Eugene C. "114. 4QDan^c." Pages 269–278 in *Qumran Cave 4.XI Psalms to Chronicles*. Edited by Eugene Ulrich et al. DJD 16. Oxford: Clarendon, 2000.

Ulrich, Eugene C. "The Canonical Process, Textual Criticism, and Latter Stages in the Composition of the Bible." Pages 51–78 in *The Dead Sea Scrolls and the Origins of the Bible*. Studies in the Dead Sea Scrolls and Related Literature. Grand Rapids: Eerdmans, 1999.

Ulrich, Eugene C. "Double Literary Editions of Biblical Narratives and Reflections on Determining the Form to be Translated." Pages 101–116 in *Perspectives on the Hebrew Bible: Essays in Honor of Walter J. Harrelson*. Edited by James L. Crenshaw. Macon, GA: Mercer University, 1988.

Ulrich, Eugene C. "Origen's Old Testament Text: The Transmission History of the Septuagint to the Third Century C.E." Pages 3–33 in *Origen of Alexandria: His World and His Legacy*. Edited by Charles Kannengiesser and William L. Peterson. Christianity and Judaism in Antiquity 1. Notre Dame: University of Notre Dame, 1988.

Ulrich, Eugene C. "Orthography and Text in 4QDan^a and 4QDan^b and in the Received Masoretic Text." Pages 29–42 in *Of Scribes and Scrolls: Studies on the Hebrew Bible, Intertestamental Judaism, and Christian Origins Presented to John Strugnell on the Occasion of his Sixtieth Birthday*. Edited by Harold W. Attridge, John J. Collins, and Thomas H. Tobin. College Theological Society Resources in Religion 5. Lanham, MD: University Press of America, 1990.

Ulrich, Eugene C. "Pluriformity in the Biblical Text, Text Groups, and Questions of Canon." Pages 23–41 in vol. 1 of *The Madrid Qumran Congress: Proceedings of the International Congress on the Dead Sea Scrolls - Madrid, 18–21 March, 1991*. Edited by Julio Trebolle Barrera and Luis Vegas Montaner. STDJ 11. Leiden: Brill, 1992.

Ulrich, Eugene C. "The Text of Daniel in the Qumran Scrolls." Pages 573–585 in *The Book of Daniel: Composition and Reception*. Edited by John J. Collins and Peter W. Flint. VTSup 83. Leiden: Brill, 2001.

Vallés, Francisco. *De Iis Quae Scripta sunt Physice in Libris Sacris*. Turin: Nicola Beuilaquae, 1587.

Van den Eynde, Ceslas, ed. *Commentaire d'Išo'dad de Merv sur l'Ancien Testament: V. Jérémie, Ézéchiel, Daniel*. 2 vols. CSCO 328–329. Scriptores Syri 146–147. Leuven: Peeters, 1972.

Van Ee, Joshua John. "Death and the Garden: An Examination of Original Immortality, Vegetarianism, and Animal Peace in the Hebrew Bible and Mesopotamia." PhD diss., University of California, 2013.

Vanstiphout, Herman L. J. "The Craftmanship of *Sîn-leqi-unninnī*." *OLP* 21 (1990): 45–79.

Villalpando, Francesco Torreblanca. *Daemonologia Sive de Magia Naturali, Daemoniaca, Licita et Illicita, Deque Aperta et Occulta.* Mainz: Schoenwetterus, 1623.

Vogler, Valentin Heinrich. *De Rebus Naturalibus ac Medicis, Quarum in Scripturis Sacris fit Mentio Commentarius.* Helmstedt: George Wolfgang Hamm, 1682.

Volk, Konrad, and Jana Matuszak. *Sumerische literarische Texte in der Martin Schøyen Collection.* Bethesda, MD: CDL, forthcoming.

Voltaire. *Philosophie de L'Histoire.* Amsterdam: Changuion, 1765.

Waerzeggers, Caroline. "Facts, Propaganda, or History? Shaping Political Memory in the Nabonidus Chronicle." Pages 95–124 in *Political Memory in and after the Persian Empire.* Edited by Jason M. Silverman and Caroline Waerzeggers. ANEM 13. Atlanta: SBL Press, 2015.

Wallace-Hadrill, David S. *Christian Antioch: A Study of Early Christian Thought in the East.* Cambridge: Cambridge University Press, 1982.

Waller, Daniel James. "Sympathy for a Gentile King: Nebuchadnezzar, Exile, and Mortality in the Book of Daniel." *Biblical Interpretation* 28 (2020): 327–346.

Walsh, P. G., trans. *Letters of St. Paulinus of Nola.* 2 vols. ACW 35–36. New York: Paulist, 1966.

Wasserman, Nathan. "Offspring of Silence, Spawn of a Fish, Son of a Gazelle...: Enkidu's Different Origins in the Epic of Gilgameš." Pages 593–599 in *"An Experienced Scribe Who Neglects Nothing": Ancient Near Eastern Studies in Honor of Jacob Klein.* Edited by Yitzhak Sefati et al. Bethesda, MD: CDL, 2005.

Watanabe, Chikako E. *Animal Symbolism in Mesopotamia: A Contextual Approach.* WOO 1. Vienna: Institut für Orientalistik der Universität Wien, 2002.

Watanabe, Kazuko. "Die literarische Überlieferung eines babylonisch-assyrischen Fluchthemas mit Anrufung des Mongottes Sîn." *ASJ* 6 (1984): 99–119.

Weber, Robert, ed. *Biblia Sacra iuxta vulgatam versionem.* 2nd ed. 6 vols. Stuttgart: Würtembergische Bibelanstalt, 1975.

Wells, A. Rahel. "'One Language and One Tongue': Animal Speech in *Jubilees* 3:27–31." *JSP* 28 (2019): 319–337.

Wells, David A. "The Medieval Nebuchadnezzar: The Exegetical Tradition of Daniel IV and Its Significance for the Ywain Romances and for German Vernacular Literature." *Frühmittelalterliche Studien* 16 (1982): 380–432.

Wells, David A. *The Wild Man from the Epic of Gilgamesh to Hartmann von Aue's Iwein: Reflections on the Development of a Theme in World Literature.* New Lecture Series 78. Belfast: Queen's University Press, 1975.

Wenham, Gordon J. *Genesis 1–15.* WBC 1. Waco, TX: Word Books, 1987.

Wenthe, Dean O. "The Old Greek Translation of Daniel 1–6." PhD diss., University of Notre Dame, 1991.

Westenholz, Aage, and Ulla Koch-Westenholz. "Enkidu – the Noble Savage?" Pages 437–451 in *Wisdom, Gods and Literature: Studies in Assyriology in Honour of W.G. Lambert.* Edited by Andrew R. George and Irving L. Finkel. Winona Lake, IN: Eisenbrauns, 2000.

Westermann, Claus. *Genesis 1–11: A Continental Commentary.* Translated by John J. Scullion. Minneapolis: Fortress, 1994.

Weyer, Johann. *De Praestigiis Daemonum et Incantationibus ac Venificiis.* Basel: Oporinus, 1563.

Widengren, Geo. *The King and the Tree of Life in Ancient Near Eastern Religion (King and Saviour IV)*. UUA 1951:4. Uppsala: Lundequist, 1951.

Wigand, Johann. *Danielis Prophetae Explicatio Brevis: Tradita in Academia Ienensi*. Jena: Hüttlich, 1571.

Wiggermann, Frans A.M. "Nammu." *RIA* 9:135–140.

Willet, Andrew. *Hexapla in Danielem*. Cambridge: Cambridge University Press, 1610.

Willis, James, ed. and trans. *On Diseases in the Bible: A Medical Miscellany, 1672*. Edited by Johan Schioldann-Nielsen and Kurt Sorensen. Acta Historica Scientiarum Naturalium et Medicinalium 41. Copenhagen: Danish National Library of Science and Medicine, 1994.

Wills, Lawrence M. *The Jew in the Court of the Foreign King*. HDR 26. Minneapolis: Fortress, 1990.

Wills, Lawrence M. *The Jewish Novel in the Ancient World*. Myth and Poetics Series. Ithaca, NY: Cornell University Press, 1995.

Wills, Lawrence M. *Judith: A Commentary*. Hermeneia. Minneapolis: Fortress, 2019.

Wilson, Robert R. "The Death of the King of Tyre: The Editorial History of Ezekiel 28." Pages 211–218 in *Love and Death in the Ancient Near East: Essays in Honor of Marvin H. Pope*. Edited by John H. Marks and Robert M. Good. Guildford, CT: Four Quarters, 1987.

Winckler, Hugo. *Altorientalische Forschungen*, 3 vols. Leipzig: Eduard Pfeiffer, 1893–1905.

Winston, David. *The Wisdom of Solomon*. AB 43. London: Doubleday, 1981.

Wiseman, Donald J. "A Gilgamesh Epic Fragment from Nimrud." *Iraq* 37 (1975): 157–163.

Wiseman, Donald J. "The Vassal-Treaties of Esarhaddon," *Iraq* 20 (1958): 1–99.

Wolff, Hans W. *Anthropology of the Old Testament*. Translated by Margaret Kohl. London: SCM Press, 1974.

Woude, Adam S. van der. "Bemerkungen zum Gebet des Nabonid." Pages 120–129 in *Qumrân: Sa Piété, Sa Théologie et Son Milieu*. Edited by Mathias Delcor. Leuven: Leuven University Press, 1978.

Würthwein, Ernst. *The Text of the Old Testament: An Introduction to the Biblia Hebraica*. Translated by Errol F. Rhodes. 2nd ed. Grand Rapids: Eerdmans, 1995.

Xella, Paolo. "L'inganno di Ea nel mito di Adapa." *OrAnt* 12 (1973): 257–266.

Xeravits, Géza. "Poetic Passages in the Aramaic Part of the Book of Daniel." *BN* 124 (2005): 29–40.

Yamauchi, Edwin M. "Nabonidus." *ISBE* 3:468–470.

Yardeni, Ada. "Maritime Trade and Royal Accountancy in an Erased Customs Account from 475 B.C.E. on the Aḥiqar Scroll from Elephantine." *BASOR* 293 (1994): 67–78.

Ziegler, Joseph, ed. *Sapientia Iesu Filii Sirach*. Septuaginta: Vetus Testamentum Graecum 12.2. 2nd ed. Göttingen: Vandenhoeck & Ruprecht, 1980.

Ziegler, Joseph, ed. *Sapientia Salomonis*. Septuaginta: Vetus Testamentum Graecum 12.1. Göttingen: Vandenhoeck & Ruprecht, 1962.

Ziegler, Joseph, and Olivier Munnich. eds. *Susanna, Daniel, Bel et Draco*. 2nd ed. Septuaginta: Vetus Testamentum Graecum 16.2. Göttingen: Vandenhoeck & Ruprecht, 1999.

Zier, Mark A. "The Medieval Latin Interpretation of Daniel: Antecedents to Andrew of St Victor." *Recherches de théologie ancienne et médiévale* 58 (1991): 43–78.

INDEX OF REFERENCES

INDEX OF AUTHORS